NPL|F

Nashville Public Library | FOUNDATION

HOUSEHOLD GODS

HOUSEHOLD GODS

The Religious Lives of
the Adams Family

SARA GEORGINI

OXFORD
UNIVERSITY PRESS

OXFORD
UNIVERSITY PRESS

Oxford University Press is a department of the University of Oxford. It furthers
the University's objective of excellence in research, scholarship, and education
by publishing worldwide. Oxford is a registered trade mark of Oxford University
Press in the UK and certain other countries.

Published in the United States of America by Oxford University Press
198 Madison Avenue, New York, NY 10016, United States of America.

Library of Congress Cataloging-in-Publication Data
Names: Georgini, Sara, author.
Title: Household gods : the religious lives of the Adams family / Sara Georgini.
Description: New York, NY : Oxford University Press, [2019] |
Includes bibliographical references and index.
Identifiers: LCCN 2018027755 (print) | LCCN 2018048436 (ebook) |
ISBN 9780190882594 (updf) | ISBN 9780190882600 (epub) |
ISBN 9780190882587 (hardback : alk. paper)
Subjects: LCSH: Adams, John, 1735–1826—Family. | Adams, John,
1735–1826—Religion. | Adams family. | Massachusetts—Biography. |
Presidents—Religious life—United States—History. |
Christianity—United States—History. | Massachusetts—Religious life and customs. |
United States—Religious life and customs.
Classification: LCC E322.1 (ebook) | LCC E322.1 .G46 2019 (print) |
DDC 973.4/4092—dc23
LC record available at https://lccn.loc.gov/2018027755

1 3 5 7 9 8 6 4 2

Printed by Sheridan Books, Inc., United States of America

This book is dedicated to Philip and Susan Georgini,
wise guides on the journey.

CONTENTS

ACKNOWLEDGMENTS

―――――――

"GREAT NECESSITIES CALL OUT GREAT VIRTUES," Abigail Adams wrote to her son John Quincy in early 1780. Across oceans and over years, I am deeply grateful to family, friends, and colleagues for their unwavering support of my research adventure with the Adams clan. Recently I unearthed an early graduate school relic, a computer file composed of a single line: "history of one American family's religion." As that project wraps up a decade later, I have many people and communities to thank for its progress. Within the family circle, Philip and Susan Georgini, Jenevra Georgini and Steve Macy, and Dorothy Korchinsky were mainstays of moral strength who provided delicious care packages and indulged my long-distance chats about fresh discoveries. As the proud daughter of a social worker and an art historian, I appreciate their knowledge in ways to look at the religious and aesthetic journeys of an American family. At a key moment in this project's early stages, my late grandmother refined my analysis with Abigail-like acuity. Enduring my whirlwind monologue on archival treasure, she smiled gently and said, "Yes, but what's it all about?" To her credit, I have asked that on every project since, remembering that archival work plus synthesis can equal good history.

At Boston University, Jon H. Roberts and Brooke L. Blower reviewed chapter drafts and shepherded me through the intellectual and cultural byways of American history. Their patience, expertise, and good humor eased the challenge of a three-century subject. Jon, especially, served as an invaluable mentor throughout my tenure as a graduate student, introducing me to new platforms and professional networks that honed my intellectual focus on this project and others. I deeply appreciate his steady support of my choice to explore public history as a full-time career while working through the doctoral process. May you all have advisers who encourage you to pick a project that you are passionate about; tell you to sin boldly; and take the time to scrutinize your drafts with great care (even during Red Sox season). I am very grateful for his guidance, as a single line grew into this story.

Brooke's rigorous review enhanced my thinking on the connections between religion and culture, pushing me to replace academic jargon with a clear narrative. Her seminar assignments, which blended analysis of historiography and material culture, also led me to reconsider the evidence of how Americans interpreted modernity. Telling a story that begins with the Puritans and ends with the Progressives meant investigating the long shadows of early America. Louis A. Ferleger and Bruce J. Schulman renewed my interest in twentieth-century life, clarifying my understanding of the period's cultural and intellectual contributions. At Harvard Divinity School, David F. Holland sharpened my approach to showing the theological nuances of providentialism, prophecy, and Protestantism.

I owe a great debt to the Massachusetts Historical Society, which has served as a second home for scholars and a public forum for the past since 1791. To thank all of the wise scholars and colleagues who nurtured my research, I would need to list the entire staff directories from 2006 to present. Adams Papers editors then and now—especially C. James Taylor, Sara Martin, Gregg L. Lint, Margaret A. Hogan, Hobson P. Woodward, and Judith S. Graham—have shared resources, read manuscript drafts, attended talks, and good-naturedly endured my ramblings over much-needed coffee breaks. Catherine Allgor, a scholarly champion of the Adams women as political agents, has been a beacon of support. Peter Drummey, Elaine Heavey, and Katherine H. Griffin pointed me to collections that placed the Adamses' experience of religion in better context. Conrad Edick Wright asked key questions that I needed to hear along the research journey. Many thanks to the entire Massachusetts Historical Society Library staff, who pulled materials on busy days; to Sabina Beauchard and Laura Wulf for illustrating the Adamses' story; and to the terrific facilities staff, who always gave me five more minutes to write, and alerted me to free cookies on the premises. I am grateful to the interns, volunteers, teachers, and researchers we have hosted over the past decade. You make us think, every day, about how we can make the archive more accessible.

The society has preserved the family papers with diligence, but nothing beats seeing how the Adamses really lived, in Quincy and around the world. Marianne Peak, Caroline Keinath, Kelly Cobble, and the Adams National Historical Park team kindly opened doors. Their scholarly understanding of how to connect the family's letters with their home is exceptional and engaging. Visit! At United First Parish Church in Quincy, Pastor Emeritus Sheldon Bennett aided with records access and helped with the mindset of the colonial clergy. Reverend Rebecca Froom provided me with unique opportunities to share my work. Staffs at the National Archives, Library of Congress, British Library, and Harvard Libraries shared expertise. At the Congregational Library, Margaret Bendroth walked me through a vast sea of material, improving my portrait of a faith in transition.

Scholarly dialogue and conversations in an array of communities have refined this work. I thank James Schmidt, Karin Wulf, Natalie Mears, and Chris Beneke for their ongoing support. I am also indebted to the many members of the American Society of Church History, the Organization of American Historians, the Association for Documentary Editing, and the North American Religion Colloquium at Harvard Divinity School and to my peers at *The Junto* and the Society for U.S. Intellectual History blogs. I am grateful for the extraordinary generosity of the "BookSquad" crew—Liz Covart, Heather Cox Richardson, Megan Kate Nelson, Kevin M. Levin, and Nina Silber—who improved my prose and fed me enough mint chip ice cream to finish the manuscript. Christine Axen and David Mislin offered cheerful support and expert insights on medieval history and liberal Protestantism, respectively, that crystallized Victorian encounters with both fields of thought. Finally, I thank Nancy Toff of Oxford University Press, an extraordinary editor and friend to scholars at all stages, and also Elizabeth Vaziri, for her patient aid in bringing the story of the Adamses' faith to life.

Thanks, all, for the great virtue of your support.

Introduction

JOHN QUINCY ADAMS, BUSY PACKING up Bibles and letterbooks for his new mission as American minister to Britain, rushed through Napoleon's Paris on last-minute errands. By May 10, 1815, the forty-seven-year-old diplomat and his wife, Louisa, longed for a fresh start in London and for a happy family reunion with their three sons after nearly six years apart.[1] Ducking down a side street, John Quincy paused at the studio of Antoine-André Ravrio, bronze-worker to the newly reinstated emperor.[2] There, Adams purchased six small busts of Cicero, Homer, Plato, Virgil, Socrates, and Demosthenes. They traveled to his White House mantel; then to the east study and writing chamber of the family's ancestral home in Quincy, Massachusetts; and, finally, through the colonial garden where his mother Abigail's pink-white roses bloomed, to the family's Stone Library of books and manuscripts in Quincy. The statues passed from him to son Charles, and to grandson Henry. John Quincy and his well-traveled heirs always referred to the set as the "household gods," republican talismans that they could carry away with them, at a moment's notice, just as Virgil's Aeneas carried mementos of tradition on his flight.[3] Brooks Adams hurried Jazz Age tourists right up to that mantel; a century on, he believed that the household gods handpicked by John Quincy—always guarding the Adamses' cache of Bibles and letterbooks—were the best symbols of the family's Christian service and civic sacrifice.[4]

A closer look at the Adams family's multigenerational archive demonstrates how pivotal Christianity—as the different generations understood it—was in shaping their decisions great and small about the course of the American republic that they served for three centuries. Christianity was the cultural language that Abigail Adams used to interpret her husband John's political setbacks. Scripture armed their son John Quincy to act as parent, statesman, and antislavery advocate. Unitarianism gave Abigail's Victorian grandson Charles Francis the "religious confidence," as he called it, to persevere in political battles on the Civil War home front. By contrast, his son Henry found religion hollow and repellent when he compared it to the purity of modern science. Finally, Christianity was the missing link that explained world economic ruin to Abigail's great-grandson Brooks, a Gilded Age critic of capitalism and the lay prophet of two world wars. Constant globetrotters who documented their religious travels in words and images that total nearly three hundred thousand manuscript pages in the Adams Family Papers alone, over time the Adamses created a cosmopolitan Christianity that blended discovery and criticism, faith and doubt.

In tackling such a sprawl of chronology and subject, I focus on the Adamses who left behind the greatest archival evidence for religious biography. The story begins with the first Henry Adams's departure from the religious chaos of late Stuart-era Somerset, England, to the new world of Puritan Massachusetts Bay, and it ends with Brooks Adams's early twentieth-century critique of that same Christian civilization. This arc covers the Adams family's experience of English persecution, early Congregationalism and town governance, Enlightenment-era education of men and women, biblical poetry and Christian patriotism, Victorian fascination with the visual religion of churches, the cosmopolitan Christianity of Gilded Age culture, and the use of faith and the "household gods" to assess modernity. I draw this story mainly from the diaries, letters, miscellany books, photographs, and related resources of the Adams Family Papers at the Massachusetts Historical Society and the Adams National Historical Park in Quincy. The comprehensive nature of this archive, which features the public and private papers of more than ten generations, provides a unique opportunity to offer a new history of how and why Americans experiment with religion in a democracy.

The Adamses emerge as key interpreters and innovators of religious culture within a rapidly changing American republic facing denominational turf wars, anti-Catholic violence, a burgeoning market economy, the Civil War, and shifting gender roles. Over the course of the long nineteenth century, personal and public Christianity changed dramatically, leaving lasting imprints on how families lived, worked, played, and prayed. For most American families, Christianity was the cultural framework that they used to explore notions of a special destiny for the new nation, as promised by an omniscient Providence, and of their share in realizing that prophecy. This multigenerational history of the Adams family's religion provides a unique window into that evolving project.

Asked for their religious affiliation, many Americans now begin their reply with "Well, I was *raised* . . . ," but individual family stories of religious life in American history are curiously rare.[5] Yet, as the Adamses knew it for three hundred years, at the center of American life lay the Christian family, constructed as a microcosm of national peace, stability, and godliness.[6] By using religious biography to frame one influential family's conversations on faith and doubt, we can capture changes in family worship over time and thereby illuminate greater structural changes in the development of American religion during a turbulent period of revolution, urbanization, and industrialization. We can personalize the working narrative of religious history in America stretching back to the first stages of settlement, by harvesting the private records of individual religious experience as fresh evidence of large-scale social change. And we can linger over a much larger question: What did it mean for the Adamses of Massachusetts to be "raised" Christian in America?

The American family offers a valuable path to comprehending the nation's major transformations in religious culture.[7] In describing American religious change and identifying major intellectual networks, scholars have looked to main-line denominations, iconic preachers, and voluntary associations. Yet the family remains a surprisingly understudied sphere for the development of faith. American religion mirrored major changes in family and politics, and vice versa.[8] Given the numerous sermons preached to guide family life since the nation's founding, it is worth investigating how one American family actually received, interpreted, and challenged those instructions.

Family history is a vital primary source for intellectual and cultural historians, since the home is a place where religious ideas are inherited, debated, discarded, reinvented, or renewed.[9] Families archive signs of faith and pass along religious memories in a way that even churches and clergy cannot record or control. From the colonial period to the early twentieth century, the home was still the primary site for cultivating the education and devotion of religious sentiment. An interior subject as sacred and sensitive as religion was an open topic in Adams family letters, something that parents and siblings frequently used to signal personal or political growth.

Finally, it is high time to reintroduce some very well-known historical actors through the genre of religious biography.[10] For the

Affectionately known in the Adams family as the "household gods," these small bronze busts have stood watch over a vast cache of private papers in Quincy for more than two centuries. En route between high-profile diplomatic appointments, John Quincy Adams purchased the set of six orators (Cicero, Homer, Plato, Virgil, Socrates, and Demosthenes) in Paris in 1815. *Antoine-André Ravrio, 1815; Adams National Historical Park*

nineteenth century's prolific first family, the distinguished Adamses of Massachusetts, the ways they "lived religion" were particularly dynamic and well documented.[11] As cosmopolitan men and women operating at the heart of American political and cultural power, the Adamses knew that prevailing notions of Christian citizenship laid out duties for them to fulfill, and they repeatedly sought out God for help. Theology supplied an intellectual framework, but the Adamses were far more interested in the practical application of religion to daily life. What could they do with it? Overall, religion served as a kind of moral shorthand or social technology, informing their intellectual and cultural contributions. At critical moments in American history, when they served at the forefront of social change—colonial settlement, the Revolution, the Civil War, the dawn of modern mass culture—the Adamses turned to religion to make sense of new social norms, to guide diplomacy, and to adapt Christian ethics for civic duty.

Less sure-footed in their understanding of non-Western religion and long fascinated by foreign rites, the Adamses were eager to interact with new faiths. Whether traveling for pleasure or to negotiate treaties, they were sensitive to the view that they represented a Protestant nation. Suddenly shipwrecked in northwestern Spain for Christmas 1779, young John Quincy jotted down his confusion at Catholic observance: "They dress up and go to mass but after that's over all is. So if they call this religion I wonder what is not it; after Mass, almost all the Shops in town are open'd." Then the budding diplomat hauled himself up short. "But stop. I must not say any thing against their religion while I am in their country but must change the subject."[12]

For three centuries, the Adamses chose Protestant Christianity as their main spiritual path. Later and more liberal descendants also explored Catholicism, atheism, and non-Western religion by visiting foreign religious sites, recording rituals in their diaries, trying out new languages of belief in their letters, and bringing home artifacts of religion. But from John Adams through his grandson Charles Francis, the Adams family creed was conventionally Unitarian. They believed in a guiding Providence. They trusted that human will empowered them to freely accept or reject God's grace. They turned away from miracles and revelation, preferring biblical criticism and lay inquiry to broaden the mind beyond the passive reception of dogma. Acknowledging Jesus as a "master workman" and gifted moral teacher, they grew fuzzy about his divinity, opting instead to scrutinize his teachings and doctrines as they related to contemporary culture. In line with their Protestant peers, most Adamses mistrusted the sensory emphasis and hierarchical nature of "Romish" Catholicism, but they revered Judaism as a source of lawmaking and ethics.

The Adamses were Christian, cosmopolitan, curious—and famous for it. In popular memory, stories circulated widely about what they believed (and did not) in terms of church and state. Edith Forbes Perkins, a New Englander transplanted to Iowa in the 1870s, noted that the Adamses even found their way into bedtime Bible tales for her six-year-old son. "Don't you remember about the people whom I read to you about in the Bible, and who lived in that beautiful garden, and whom God created first of their kind?" Perkins asked. " 'Oh! yes,' he replied, with innocent satire, 'you mean the Adams family!' And such, no doubt, is the theology of that remarkable New England tribe.' "[13] At home and abroad, the Adamses' religion evolved as the new nation grew. This is their story.

I

The Providence of John and Abigail Adams

IN THE EARLY WINTER OF 1823, the elderly former president John Adams came out to honor the family's dead. Emerging from years of rural semiretirement in Quincy, Massachusetts, Adams proudly marked the completion of his last great family project, to commission and place new granite headstones on his ancestors' graves in Hancock Cemetery. Many of his forebears were buried there, directly across from the First Parish Congregational Church where John prayed twice each Sunday, just as much of his family had done since the community regathered as an independent church in 1639.[1] The largest monument he created was for Henry Adams, the English emigrant who arrived in 1638, fleeing the "Dragon persecution in Devonshire" with his wife "and eight sons." John Adams drafted the text to carve into the native stone, "placed in this yard, by a great-great grandson, from a veneration of the Piety, humility, simplicity, prudence, patience, temperance, frugality, industry and perseverance, of his Ancestors, in hopes of Recommending an imitation of their virtues to their posterity."[2] Some of the history recorded on the plaque later proved to be a bit hazy—scholars have never found a "Dragon persecution"; Henry Adams came from Somerset, and the eight sons who first emigrated were really seven, plus a daughter—but far more indelible was John's articulation, etched for the public and posterity, of the Adams family values that he was charged to maintain.[3]

The monument's inscription and placement echoed an intellectual ideal that Americans before and after the second president struggled with throughout their lives, in both public and private matters: Christianity as *the* key to implementing duty and reform. To know how they got that way, it is important to see the first Adamses within their native religious ecosystems, and to understand their guiding ideology of Christian providentialism, the belief that God spoke through historical events and intervened in individual lives to fulfill a predestined plan.[4] Like many colonists, the Anglo-American Adamses fought to thrive within the cultural and intellectual boundaries of a "double scope, mans good, and Gods honour," as the English preacher John White put it.[5] Identifying and tracking "providences," or signs of divine will, filled their days.[6] That idea carried the Adamses out of England, and the congregations they founded in America led them through the Revolution and, fitfully, into the early republic. The men and women of John's generation honed their political arguments for independence by invoking the Congregationalist tradition of claiming liberty and articulating dissent.[7] They were less successful, however, in mustering that same providentialist rhetoric to address the needs of the new nation. The ways in which John and Abigail Adams used New England Christianity to navigate the world—then returned to Quincy as cosmopolitan critics of that same faith—derived from the family's earliest roots in American religion. What kind of faith made the Adamses cross the Atlantic and, later on, take up the argument for liberty?

In family memory, the figure of Henry Adams remained forever in flight. Even within the nineteenth-century family circle, no one agreed on the finer points of the English emigrant's tale. The two Adams presidents, father and son, sparred over Henry's origin story. John asserted that Henry came from Bristol in 1640, whereas John Quincy upheld an Adams attachment to Reverend Thomas Hooker's Braintree contingent from Essex County in 1650.[8] Both of the amateur genealogists tried—and failed—to pinpoint the number of Henry's children (nine) who ended up in New England pews. Paying his respects at the Adams cemetery monument in 1824, the Harvard senior Charles Francis reckoned that he marked "the seventh generation since we have been in the new world. In the old we have no traces."[9] As late as 1853, many Adamses claimed a vague link to the Welsh baronial clan of ap-Adams in County Devon.[10] They filled out intricate genealogy wheels, circling round and round different points of English origin. So murky were Henry's Puritan roots that his heirs considered hiring a private detective to scour the Anglican parish churches of Bath and Wells for manuscript clues. His Victorian namesake, who labeled the Puritans an admirable but "intolerant" class of newcomers to New England, shrugged off the family's storied past: "I know nothing about the genealogy, and do not invest in it."[11]

One reason for the family's constant myth-making was that Henry Adams made for a difficult research topic. Like other elusive Puritan progenitors who were remodeled by their elite Unitarian heirs, the first Henry Adams left no clear paper trail explaining his abrupt decision, at age fifty-five, to replant the family in Quincy (then called Braintree).[12] Little historical residue of the Puritan progenitor remained, beyond his signature on a few wills, deeds, and church records. It was far easier, as time went on, for Adams family members to paint Henry's portrait in broad strokes of good Protestant virtue. Exhibiting a vaguely Anglo-American dissenter's pedigree helped three generations of Adams statesmen and their wives to blend in at foreign courts. En route to the Paris peace talks with England in 1779, John Adams gently refuted the claim of one Spanish official who hoped that the American minister might be of Catalan descent: "I thought these questions very whimsical and ridiculous, but I determined to keep my Spanish gravity and answered them civilly and candidly that I was born in America, and so was my Father and Grandfather, but my Great Grandfather and Great Great Grandfather came from England, where their Ancestors had lived for any Thing I knew, from the Days of the first Adam."[13]

A malt-maker by trade, Henry Adams brewed good beer, read widely, and married well.[14] The Puritan-era Henry's daily experience revolved around the three institutional markers of town life that his American descendant John Adams most prized: the meetinghouse, the militia field, and the schoolroom.[15] Growing up in the southeastern portion of Somerset, Henry worshipped at the cramped church in Barton St. David; the population has hovered around five hundred since his time. The fifteenth-century church cemetery, oriented around a weather-beaten statue of St. David collecting alms, held no Adams gravestones, but the family's Protestant affiliation there was multigenerational, even in

Henry's day. He attended Sunday service in a sixty-three-by-seventeen-foot chapel with Saxon arches. A set of four church bells pealed out on the holy days of the Anglican calendar or to summon his father, a parish tax gatherer and constable, to muster drills with the local militia. As American descendants claimed, Henry and his Somerset friends were "persons in humble but respectable Stations of Life. Not illiterate or uneducated, nor yet of learned professions."[16] Henry's signature on his father's 1604 will and, five years later, on his marriage bond, shows the round, Italian-style penmanship of a well-educated Elizabethan youth. Over time, Henry acquired a core library of "ould books" that he willed to his daughter and sons.[17]

Between duties as a copyhold (tenant) farmer, Henry evidently found time to read, write, and master the math needed to trade goods in England's developing market towns. The nearest city was Glastonbury, six miles away. Yet Henry would have understood that his ancient church functioned as the true cultural and economic heart of the region. Frequently, Henry and his fellow tradesmen pooled their profits to hire popular traveling preachers for lectures on Sunday afternoons and market mornings. Adams and his neighbors regularly tithed to raise the ten-pound annual salary needed for a permanent pastor.[18] The steady presence of a vicar in Barton St. David linked it to hamlets such as Charlton Mackrell, Keinton Mandeville, Charlton Adam, and Kingweston. It was likely through that church connection that Henry met Edith Rosamund Squire, a blacksmith's daughter and the granddaughter of William Squire, rector of Charlton Mackrell. When he married Edith in October 1609, Henry acquired a generous share of her family's glebe (church) lands, which he used to set up a brewing business spread over forty-seven acres.[19] Between Sundays, Henry and Edith spent their time farming and following the seasonal tasks of a seventeenth-century rural distillery: harvesting barley or oats to dry on a kill floor for malting, then soaking grains in a wooden mash tub with sugar, adding hops to the liquid in a copper keeler as it boiled, and, finally, transferring the English ale to barrels for sale.[20] The Adams family's fortune—and likely their prayers—varied from harvest to harvest.

At first, Henry's native landscape was relatively untroubled by waves of religious dissent. Aside from some clerical redistricting, the Protestant

Reformation took root easily in Somerset. Henry's village followed the standard liturgy and devotional practice of the Church of England.[21] His evolution into Puritan émigré, therefore, largely happened due to the storm of episcopal reforms that swept through English religious life in the 1630s. In 1633, the Church disciplinarian and radical reformer William Laud was named archbishop of Canterbury. Within months, the look and feel of Anglican religion changed dramatically. The anti-Calvinist Laud's overarching vision of the Church relied on a more dominant clergy and a weaker laity.[22] He centered power in the bishops. He required churchwardens to submit annual conduct reports on the behavior of parishioners like Edith and Henry.

Tightening his surveillance one notch more, Laud mandated that churchwardens, ministers, and schoolmasters must report on each other. Laud's dreaded "interrogatories" meant that Henry could be accosted at any time with an impromptu quiz: Did he remember to bow at Jesus's name, and to kneel when receiving the sacrament of Holy Communion? Did a mother of nine like Edith Adams don a modest veil each time she returned to the Church after childbirth?[23] To the sizable number of clergy and laity who flouted his crusade for conformity, the archbishop meted out excommunication, imprisonment, and deprivation of land. For Henry and Edith, a new symbol of religion took shape on Somerset roads: the white-robed penitent newly released from thirty days of jail, bearing a white wand and heading toward Barton St. David to pay a hefty fine.[24]

Laud's economic reforms—standardizing tithe rates in London and improving the professional salaries of rural preachers—reshaped how the Somerset laity lived their religion.[25] Adams family profits, for example, changed after Laud reinstituted church support for Sunday sports and ale feasts. Despite the extra income, the marketplace of religious ideas for the Adamses contracted, once Laud terminated the townsmen's privilege to select and employ itinerant pulpit talent. Acting on Laud's orders, ministers and churchwardens could rifle the contents of Henry's private library whenever they chose, reporting him for punishment if they deemed his reading material immoral. Laud's next move—to transform the Reformation-era "communion tables" into fenced, railed altars suitable for genuflection—met with widespread resistance.

Before crossing over to America, the English Adamses worshipped at the ancient church of Barton St. David in rural Somerset. *Photography by Geoff Pick / CC BY-SA 2.0*

To Henry's generation, re-enshrining "God's residence on earth" was not only expensive but also a treacherous omen that Protestants now favored the same idolatrous adoration as did the Catholic Church. In Somerset, they balked at moving the altar. Henry's Puritan peers struck back with a few reforms of their own, banning post-church revels and ale feasts. Laud retaliated with royal force. Though he lacked firm reasoning for initiating such severe reforms, the archbishop denounced Henry Adams's dissenting neighbors as unchristian Englishmen. In Laud's view, the men and women who grew bold in turning against the Church's laws might revolt next against their monarch. The Adams family was caught in Laud's tide.

Given Henry's need to sell ale and his background as a longtime Anglican, it is hard to know how "Puritan" he really was. Many parishioners encountered Puritanism through their existing webs of kinship. Rather than functioning as a monolithic structure, Puritanism was able to spread largely because worshippers could seize on different messages and themes.[26] Family history reveals that Henry mixed easily with Puritan clergy and their ideas, especially those of the Reverend John White, an influential advocate of American colonization. The Adams children's schoolmaster and uncle was Aquila Purchase, a prominent parishioner at White's Holy Trinity Church in neighboring Dorset.[27] Henry and Edith likely attended a few services there; certainly, they heard White's emigration sermons repeated and debated at home. White, a moderate Puritan and the "patriarch" of the Dorchester Company's efforts to land colonists at Gloucester, Massachusetts, dabbled in joint-stock ventures. In 1629 he helped to obtain the £3,000 capital from London merchants that funded the Massachusetts Bay Colony's royal charter.[28]

He never left England, but White's zeal led the Adamses to join the estimated twenty-one thousand colonists who made the Great Migration to America between 1629 and 1640.[29] Fueling entire families with the godly goals that constituted Puritanism, White leveraged two themes in his lectures: the power of Providence to induce emigration and the mission of Anglo-American colonization as a way to salvage Western Christianity from the meddling attacks of both Archbishop Laud and a host of insurgent Catholics.[30] White's words—amplifying the idea that God wanted them to go, in order to do good—helped to set the Adamses on course for America.

John White's widely circulated pamphlet of 1630, *The Planter's Plea*, furnished Henry's peers with a providentialist schematic for rationalizing Protestant emigration to the New World. According to White, English families like the Adamses formed the "pettie Colonies" needed to restore and replant Christianity in the new Jerusalem of New England. The act of settling "new States requireth justice and affection to the common good," White preached, stressing the power of colonization to refine faith through trial.[31] He enumerated the mission's well-publicized perils (snow, serpents, famine) and acknowledged its related costs. He needled his readers, noting that French and Dutch émigrés had managed to flourish there. Then, White warned that it would be worse for a Christian to stay and root in England's rotten moral climate, growing nearer to the native sins of "cou[v]etousnesse, fraud, and violence" and, thus, farther from heaven.[32] John White's America held new paths to spiritual and temporal profits, along with a native "heathen" populace ripe for conversion.[33] White used historical providentialism to drive home his final point. Providence had appointed England for the task, White argued, since it boasted the *only* surplus of "reformed" believers capable of such a quasi-biblical, millennialist undertaking. "It seems, this end, in plantation, hath beene specially reserved for this later end of the world," he wrote.[34] Henry's brother-in-law Aquila was one of the first to agree. In 1633, he and wife, Ann, sailed for Massachusetts on the *Mary & John.*[35]

Over the next five years, religious and economic conditions darkened in the Adams household, and, as with many other Puritans, kinship networks tugged them toward America.[36] Letters from the Purchases to the Adamses probably carried conflicting accounts of New England's climate, resources, and landscape.[37] In Somerset, by contrast, Laud's decrees meant extra scrutiny and restriction; the archbishop condemned Puritanism as "a wolf held by the ears" that would lunge to kill the "divinely appointed" Charles I.[38] Between 1634 and 1640, the king took the unusual and urgent step of collecting the ship-money tax in peacetime, which fell heavily on inland communities like Barton St. David. Charles's decision to levy the tax, without Parliamentary support—issuing three writs in the first two years alone—imposed heavy debt on rural laborers like the Adamses and invigorated the popular mistrust of the monarchy resulting in Charles's execution in 1649.[39] A wave of poor harvests caused the Adams family brewery to fail, and Henry's license was revoked in 1637.[40] Anxious to leave Laud's persecution and seek out profitable farmland, the Adamses followed their Providence to New England. They arrived in Braintree in the fall of 1638. Like many Puritan family reunions, their welcome to the new "Zion" was bittersweet.[41] Aquila Purchase had died at sea in 1633, and Edith's sister Ann had remarried, to the surgeon Thomas Oliver, a founding elder of Boston's First Parish Church.[42]

For the first Adamses of early America, bits of John White's vision held true.[43] To Puritan émigrés like Henry and Edith, a Calvinist form of Christianity functioned to regulate town government and to inculcate a communal ethos of what constituted "good" behavior.[44] Operating beneath a watchful Providence, they nourished a colonial life of profit in the New England wilderness. In February 1639, Henry was granted forty acres of land "at the Mount," near Mount Wollaston, a property cache that the family owned and farmed well into the nineteenth century.[45] Henry Adams built a malthouse on the northern tip of Quincy's present-day Elm Street and re-established his brewing business. On Sabbath days, Henry and his family headed along unfinished trails to reach the center of town. There, a two-tiered wooden structure sealed with mud corners served as their new Puritan meetinghouse, municipal hall, and emergency fort.[46]

Once again, the Adamses experienced a seismic shift in their modes of religious practice. This Puritan meetinghouse, later known as the First (Parish) Church, became the Adamses' home church for the next three centuries. It sat at a key fording point between two brooks. When local residents constructed a "country highway" in 1648, they built it around the "chapell of ease," so that parishioners traveling from opposite corners of Dorchester and Weymouth converged in the house of prayer to address the sacred and secular duties that Providence prescribed for them to share.[47] In this way, Henry's Anglo-American neighbors reified the Puritan tenet that a church was the social embodiment of a spiritual covenant.[48]

Henry and Edith Adams now saw and heard a different call to service. They knew it was time for prayer from the flutter of a red silk flag hung over the meetinghouse door, or the somber echo of a solo drummer at the town's center. Few descriptions of the First Church's predecessor survive, but most Puritan meetinghouses of early New England looked like large schoolrooms.[49] The unheated interior was plainer and grittier than that of Barton St. David. Henry and Edith may have added chairs from home to line their pew. They received Holy Communion from a small, hinged table that dropped down from the deacon's pew. The meetinghouse was more than a quiet place for prayer. With regular maintenance paid for by precinct taxes, the meetinghouse doubled as a site for trials, elections, medical surgery, concerts, and gunpowder storage. Outside the meetinghouse doors stood a stark reminder of those who shunned the lessons of Providence: the pillories and stocks.[50] Inside, as Charles Francis Adams Jr. described it in his 1892 church history, prayed a "devout and expectant" laity whose Puritan pastors did very little to "restore theological tranquillity" for newcomers like Henry and Edith.[51] Unwittingly, Henry Adams had traded one scene of religious turmoil for another.

The Braintree meetinghouse was the fifteenth congregation founded in Massachusetts Bay, and Puritans were already familiar with the price of dissenting from the main-line tradition. As the first generation of American Adamses soon realized, the religious ideas that they carried over—notably, the disciplinary doctrine of spiritual preparation for salvation, and an abiding belief in an omnipotent Providence—faced new challengers from within the fragile community.[52] When Henry arrived in late 1638, the fledgling Puritan municipality was rebuilding in the wake of the Antinomian Controversy.[53] Swirling around the teachings of radical prophet Anne Hutchinson, the debates splintered the covenanted community over questions of whether she and others had gone "against the law" in contesting notions of the "right" path to heaven.

For Hutchinson, sanctification (and thus salvation) emanated from direct, inner contact with God, not through the outward show of good works, nor via any adherence to the social constructs and institutions of moral law. Her ideas were a startling departure from orthodox Puritan thought. Hutchinson and a small but loud band of followers, including her brother-in-law John Wheelwright, were brought to trial. She was convicted, banished, and subsequently excommunicated. Wheelwright, whose fast-day sermon of January 16, 1636, had particularly riled up the local magistrates, found himself cast out of Boston.[54] In a series of widely publicized twists and turns, the inaugural controversy exposed a significant reason for transatlantic Protestantism's jagged growth in early America: replanting nonconformists abroad did not mean they could cohere as a community.

Like Wheelwright, several of Anne Hutchinson's supporters fled Boston. They found new havens where they sustained dissenting views. Shortly after the Massachusetts General Court found Wheelwright guilty of sedition, the Adamses' First Church briefly welcomed the controversial clergyman as pastor. On his arrival in Braintree, the fiery sermon-giver continued to teach that a covenant of grace—rather than a covenant of works—empowered individuals to secure their own salvation. Wheelwright told worshippers that the real "children of God" looked beyond the "gifts of his Spiritt" to find godly strength. "They doe not seeke only to know the Lord by fruits & effects, but looke upon the Lord wth a direct eye of faith they seeke his face, and this is the generation of seekers spoken of" in scripture, Wheelwright preached.[55] Braintree worshippers tolerated Wheelwright's sermons, but the Massachusetts Bay magistrates were not ready to welcome his brand of theology, and Wheelwright was banished in late 1637. He went on to found settlements near Exeter, New Hampshire, and in Wells, Maine.[56]

When Henry and Edith Adams arrived in Braintree in late 1638, then, the local Puritan community was emerging from a period of crisis and attempting to forge ahead without a pastor. They needed to find a new, public way to recommit to piety. They hoped to reassure God they had not forgotten what faith could build in the New World. To do so, the émigré congregants renewed their joint pledge with a new First Church covenant. Its language reflected the vulnerabilities that came with following Providence's hazy road map to the colonies. Under the direction of pastor Henry Flynt, they signed a new promise to God on September 16, 1639. Henry's peers professed to be "poor unworthy creatures, who have sometime lived without Christ and without God in the world . . . being called of God out of this world to the fellowship of Christ by the Ministry of the Gospel."[57] In this way, the First Church parishioners began grafting their Anglo-American odyssey onto notions of what Providence planned next. They speculated as to how piety might help to meet those goals. Henry Adams endured eight winters in the wilderness of the New England fellowship and died in 1646. Edith married a neighbor, and the young Adams siblings set up a string of farms across Massachusetts Bay.[58]

From Somerset persecution to Massachusetts Puritanism, the Adamses' saga of migration and resettlement reinforces the importance of the local church as a key actor in religious history. It explains why they left behind Barton St. David, and what Henry and Edith lived for in Braintree. At every level, from architecture to theology, the contrast between English and American faith must have been apparent to that first generation. Imagine entering a roomful of refugees and dissenters in rural Braintree, seats shoved together to accommodate strangers, friends, or criminals—however the community commanded the needs of the day. This was the chaotic First Church experience that Henry and Edith shared with their fellow colonists. For the early Adamses, the echo of John White's glowing reiteration of "the gift of the earth to the sonnes of man" likely faded a bit after battling New England famines and frosts. Christianity helped Henry, Edith, and their children to cope with waves of colonial hardship. Once the seventeenth-century Adamses had established a toehold in the new country, they pivoted to please God through bouts of service to the Braintree congregation, always a short ride away.

After the founding generation of Henry and Edith, the following decades marked an era of steady, rapid growth in the regathered First Church, which transitioned to a fairly liberal Congregationalism in the early part of the eighteenth century along with the rest of the region.[59] Pastor Flynt held the pulpit for nearly thirty years, and he counted 204 adult members in the pews. His successor, Moses Fiske, was equally successful.[60] In 1666, the meetinghouse was rebuilt in stone and enlarged, then capped with a steeple bell.[61] Within the next quarter-century, the church bureaucracy formalized and began to produce the first sacramental records.[62] By 1732, the congregation was able to fund another expansion and upgrade, this time under the stewardship of the Reverend John Hancock.

Among Hancock's 558 parishioners were two future signers of the Declaration of Independence—his own son and John Adams, baptized months apart.[63] The Adamses were one of eleven families who installed a private pew, although they remained land-rich and cash-poor. The second president's father, John, was a shoemaker who served as a deacon, town selectman, and militia captain. On his father's will, John Adams scribbled that he had been ever "a Man of Strict Piety and great Integrity: much esteemed and beloved, wherever he was known, which was not far, his Sphere of Life being not extensive."[64] Deacon Adams, through his covenanted service to God and God's Braintree version of "a city upon a hill," taught his son that Christianity illuminated a family path of duty and dissent. At the same time, it inspired the younger Adams's quest to expand his religious horizons beyond the Braintree town limits.

What did the Puritan experience of Henry and Edith Adams teach their descendants of religion and rebellion? For the Anglo-American Adamses, Christianity was both a means of attaining the grace of salvation and an interpretive tool to mold New England to suit God's plan. In history and literature, illustrating lessons drawn from the Puritans' ordeal thus became vital to crafting American destiny as revolutionary sentiments grew throughout the eighteenth century. The men and women of John Adams's generation nurtured a culture that obsessed over the various providentialist ideas that the Puritans had sacrificed—or fumbled—by challenging major ecclesiastical policies and dissenting from royal restraints.[65] Looking at history and at themselves, New Englanders played around with regional identities that meshed together Puritanism and progress.[66] The religious inheritances of the Old World were particularly tricky for them to square with New World ideas of liberty and justice. John Adams's attempt to embed his ancestral backstory in the broader sweep of American history, issued in a Revolutionary-era series of popular newspaper essays, offers one example of this effort.

When John Adams drafted his "Dissertation on the Canon and the Feudal Law" in the summer of 1765, it was the idealized memory of Puritans like his great-great-grandfather that guided his pen. He had only a vague guess at where Henry hailed from, but John was confident that his Puritan ancestor exemplified what any good colonist could dare when acting in concert with God's will. By mapping the outer contours of the Puritan trial—especially the suppression of religious and political liberties at the corrosive hands of the Church—John embraced the providentialist rhetoric that served the revolutionaries whom he later met in America and Europe. God had helped American history along, and would do so again. Providence, as John thought, had blessed Henry Adams to live in an era when access to "general knowledge" generated opportunities for education and dissent. God then "raised up the champions, who began and conducted the reformation," John wrote, and from this intellectual wellspring came men like Henry. Sensible that religious persecution was a moral wrong, Puritans seized on emigration as a way to dissent from the established Church and secure new revenue.

For John, the Puritan ordeal held valuable lessons in legal precedent, too. Henry's evasion of Charles I's ship-money tax resonated with John's contemporary Boston readers, then groaning under the Intolerable Acts of George III. It was Henry and Edith whom John Adams pictured when he wrote that the "desperate" and "vexed" Puritans, a "people tortured by the powers of those days, for no other crime than their knowledge, and their freedom of enquiry and examination . . . at last resolved to fly to the *wilderness* for refuge, from the temporal and spiritual principalities and powers, and plagues, and scourges of their *native* country."[67]

Twenty years later, Abigail Adams reiterated the importance of binding together the Puritan past and the American future. "She was not planted like most other Countries with a Lawless Banditti, or an Ignorant savage Race who cannot even trace their origon, but by an enlightned a Religious and polished people," Abigail wrote of early America. "The Numerous improvement which they have made during a Century and half, in what was then but a howling Wilderness, proves their state of civilisation. Let me recommend to you my dear Girl to make yourself perfect mistress of the History of your own Country if you are not so allready; no one can be sufficiently thankfull for the Blessings they enjoy, unless they know the value of them."[68] Be thankful for the venerable (if rigid) Puritans, the Adamses lectured their kin, or the lessons of their history might be lost.

It was best, his descendants agreed, that Henry Adams evoked an automatic mention when they retold the heroic American past—to children, to voters, to scholars. Why did Henry Adams and his Puritan faith persist in their political brand as it evolved? First, the family's continual reinvention of their Puritan roots conditioned their historical understanding of Christianity's movement into colonial America. The Adams family saga, quite simply, started with the colonies' origins story. The chance to claim a foundational part in a larger, providentialist narrative endowed Adams statesmen with a glossy "status" history worth advertising in the political arena. Puritan genealogy underlined the family's long-standing commitment to religious nonconformity. Henry Adams's extreme expression of liberty, in John's mind, was what religion meant to the first Adamses who left England: he took the chance to choose *American* Christianity. Providence had led Protestants to seed New England, as John's generation believed, and would therefore also guide the colonies to independence and prosperity. While they ratified and amended Protestantism for the new nation, many, like the Adamses, wrestled with a fractious political scene and kept up the practice of dissent. Increasingly, they explored faiths that lay beyond the bounds of small-town life. But, as John and his wife, Abigail, learned, applying New England providentialism to American goals would prove difficult—even dangerous—in the stormy era of party politics that followed revolution.

John Adams was, in his own words, "a notorious . . . church-going animal."[69] Although scholars harbor an ongoing interest in linking the founders and popular ideas of God's "special" design for America, surprisingly few have focused on John Adams's religious journey.[70] Yet the cultivation of a Christian conscience, to be used in the service of American interests, shaped the lives of John and Abigail Smith Adams. In July 1812, tracking through nearly two centuries of settlement and pondering his legacy, John Adams pored over the family archive and identified Christianity as his family's intellectual constant in weathering periods of change. Despite the political turbulence that he faced, Adams believed that cementing Protestant Christianity as a social institution laid the best route to achieving individual and national success. "What has preserved this race of Adams's in all their ramifications, in Such Numbers, health peace Comfort and Mediocrity?" he wrote to his old friend Benjamin Rush. "I believe it is Religion. Without which they would have been Rakes Fops Sots Gamblers, Starved with hunger, frozen with Cold, Scalped by Indians &c &c &c been melted away and disappeared."[71] Far from disappearing, the Adams family contributed significantly to the intellectual ventures and cultural opportunities of the new nation.

John Adams's first real brush with Providence came in 1753, when God called him *away* from pulpit service and prodded him *toward* learning law—or so he recalled in his diary.[72] Like most Harvard students, John investigated the traditional New England career paths of medicine, ministry, and law. The shoemaker's son, conscious of the family's strain to fund his college education, veered away from seeking out a trade apprenticeship.[73] He weighed and rejected the "infinite toil" of a physician's life.[74] Again in step with his peers, John Adams spun next to preparing for life in the Congregationalist ministry. Between 1751 and 1753, John oriented his spare reading time at Harvard to theological debates and divinity studies. And, by his account, this was the moment when Providence intervened and assigned him new purpose. A simmering crisis at his home church in Braintree, now led by the Reverend Lemuel Briant, altered John Adams's choice of profession and solidified his belief in Providence. Briant and Adams were close in age and theological perspective. More than evangelical awakenings or wider religious changes, it was this small-town controversy that impacted young Adams's sense of faith.

Lemuel Briant, a twenty-four-year-old rookie preacher from Scituate, was, when he came to the Adamses' First Church in 1745, off to a promising start with a congregation still basking in its centennial glow. Briant had been the unanimous choice for pastor, in no large part because he agreed to a lower salary (fifty pounds a year on credit, plus firewood) than his predecessors were paid.[75] John characterized him as "a jocular and liberal scholar and divine."[76] Briant ably led the flourishing and prosperous congregation. John Adams's teenage memories of his sermons capture the first traces of the radical theology that Briant brought to publication in 1749.[77] In his sermon on moral virtue, printed that year, Briant made some divisive claims about the erosion of good New England preaching. He derided Calvinist ideals in favor of an Arminian approach to salvation.[78] By Briant's account, Providence made available a path to grace. In turn, pious congregants like the young John Adams could exercise the free will to accept or reject it. For example, Briant preached that scripture demonstrated a "gracious Influence that the Spirit of God has upon every well disposed Mind in forming it to the same Image; so the Effects of Operations which we sometimes call the Graces, and sometimes the Fruits of the Spirit are nothing else . . . than moral Virtues."[79]

Overturning several generations of Puritan tenets with his preaching, Briant surged ahead with an even bolder set of ideas. Practicing a Christian life, Briant advised, was more vital to salvation than adhering to the old, threadbare Calvinist dogma about predestination. In his stab at articulating these new themes, Briant came close to anticipating the Unitarian and universalist notions that William Ellery Channing and his circle would champion roughly a century on—or so an elderly John Adams later observed. For some, Lemuel Briant was *too* far ahead of his time. His wounded peers fired back in print. At the height of the debate, Briant's wife suddenly left him, charging him with "several scandalous sins" and thereby fueling the complaint that young Briant lacked Christian morality.[80] Briant battled on. "He was young, it was true," one of his biographers recalled, "but his church was with him, and he had a vigorous pen."[81]

Not all of Briant's church was behind him, and soon theological rancor spilled over into the heart of the Adams household. The evangelical revivals of the early eighteenth century, along with local main-line scandals like Briant's, exposed many different (and clashing) stripes of "Protestant temperament" in New England's religious palette.[82] Those changes left lasting marks within the household, too. "I may say I was born & bred in the centre of Theological & Ecclesiastical controversy," John Adams observed of the Briant affair. "It broke out like the eruption of a volcano and blazed with portentious aspect for many years."[83] It was a troubled time for the faithful in the Adamses' hometown, with the local Anglican clergy squaring off as well in a separate theological arena. Between 1749 and 1753, as the religious pamphlet wars raged on, one of Briant's more passionate supporters, John Adams, left to begin his studies at Harvard. There, the young divinity student kept close tabs on the "hot controversy," mainly through family letters and frequent trips home.

Local families like the Adamses fractured along lines for or against Briant. These signs of how theological dissent encroached on private life radically changed John Adams's future plans. His father, Deacon John, backed Briant, but his uncle Ebenezer did not. A series of ecclesiastical councils, held in the Adamses' cramped saltbox cottage throughout 1753, led to a congregational vote of support for Briant. John Quincy, the grandfather of Abigail Smith Adams, presided over the meetings and authored the final report largely exonerating Briant in April 1753.[84] Briant's health failed, and he retired before suffering an early death a year later. Aside from Briant's frenetic effort to introduce proto-Unitarian ideas to the sons and grandsons of Puritans, the controversy had a singular impact on John Adams's decision to pursue a law career. For the tone of the debates that he overheard at the family hearth—brimming with an ugly "Spirit of Dogmatism and Bigotry"—persuaded him that a career in the pulpit meant signing on to a life of thwarted intellectualism. Studying theology, Adams decided, would "involve me in endless Altercations and make my Life miserable, without any prospect of doing any good to my fellow Men."[85]

Overall, John Adams believed that Providence had intervened in Braintree to show that liberal-minded Protestants must weather strong criticism and challenge long-standing cultural views, especially if they wanted to better their odds of salvation. Adams graduated from Harvard in 1755. After an unhappy stint teaching at a boys' school in Worcester, he moved on to study law. By 1762, when he began courting the clergyman's daughter in the next town over, John was sure that institutional religion perpetuated a quagmire of theological debates that stagnated inquiry and progress. High theology, even for the good Christian citizen, was a speed bump best avoided.

The provincial lawyer married Abigail Smith in the late autumn of 1764. Abigail, the middle daughter of a prominent Weymouth pastor, served as a second mother to her two sisters, an alcoholic brother, and her parents' slaves.[86] The Reverend William Smith ran a blossoming suburban parish, performing roughly twenty to thirty marriages a year and hundreds of baptisms during his long tenure, which lasted from 1734 to 1783.[87] Like John, Abigail's appreciation for Christian sentiment was colored by her experience of growing up in a home that doubled as the venue for settling major church-town disputes. As a teenager, she watched her father wrangle successfully with the town over church property rights. She helped to rebuild the Weymouth religious community after a catastrophic fire. When farm tasks allowed, young Abigail, too, indulged widely in modes of Protestant self-education. Equipped with a smattering of self-taught French and her brother's Harvard reading lists, Abigail Adams gathered her knowledge of Christian precepts from a rich and innovative blend of Sunday sermons and literary classics.[88]

Abigail's sense of Providence was highly attuned to the act of interpreting the linked social worlds—daughter, sister, wife, mother, eventually First Lady—that she moved through. From her earliest days of Christian life, Abigail Smith Adams trained a providentialist lens on events within the family circle, giving a precise emphasis when literature supplemented or explained happenings that scripture did not. Like other elite women of the Revolutionary era, Abigail read whichever tracts and literary offerings were left at home; her father loaned out his books daily.[89] Free to enjoy his well-stocked library of Anglo-American radicals, Abigail chose works by the gamut of nonconformists: Pierre Bayle's *Historical and Critical Dictionary* (1697), John Tillotson's twelve volumes' worth of sermons (1742); Philip Doddridge's *Course of Lectures on Pneumatology, Ethics and Divinity* (1763); Jonathan Edwards's *A History of the Work of Redemption* (1774); and Gilbert Burnet's *The*

History of the Reformation of the Church of England (1697).[90] Abigail quoted the ribald verse of Laurence Sterne in letters, and she, too, proved to be a "church-going animal" once John's diplomatic career sent the family to Europe. In contrast to John, Abigail's religious world was one where Providence focused the finer brushstrokes of the arts. Her perception of Providence was omnipresent. She saw God in history, literature, and art in a way that John Adams did not always mirror.

There was little religion in the courtship notes that "Portia" and her "Lysander" had first exchanged in 1762. Steadily, Abigail and John's correspondence grew to nearly twelve hundred letters over the course of their marriage, peaking during his difficult stint in the Continental Congress from 1774 to 1777. When war separated the family—John heading off to persuade fractured representatives of the need for independence and Abigail left with four small children to endure a city besieged by the British and by smallpox—they relied on Christianity to make sense of events.[91] New Englanders like the Adamses were certain that Providence still held them in favor; every affliction signaled a divine lesson or a future reward. The Revolutionary generation that (initially) favored John's political rise drew on historical, national, and private forms of providentialism to interpret the war's episodes of crisis and change. Seen in family letters, the Adamses' joint construction of Providence reveals how this intellectual project really worked.

For John and Abigail, Providence was a close and powerful force. So, too, was the experience of detecting "providences," or signs of God's will at work in the world. God hovered over the pages of history, pushing their Puritan forebears to emigrate and to establish American Christianity. The Adamses believed that God governed the family's fate and guided the mismatched neighbors who now united in a defiant bid for liberty from Great Britain.[92] "Certainly, There is a Providence—certainly, We must depend upon Providence or We fail," John Adams wrote home in the chaotic late spring of 1775. "Certainly the sincere Prayers of good Men, avail much. But Resignation is our Duty in all Events."[93] When Abigail replied, listing American losses at the Battle of Bunker Hill in June 1775, she offset the worst news with the reassuring warmth of scripture: "God is a refuge for us.—Charlstown is laid in ashes."[94]

As the British burned and looted Boston, John Adams tried to replenish his Christianity. On the road between Braintree and Philadelphia for congressional duties throughout the 1770s, Adams searched for signs of faith. He believed that an omniscient (if distant) Providence carved out the landscape where he walked and generated any reasons to journey past it. Encountering new American iterations of Christianity, then, intrigued him. The "church-going animal" craved religious experience, foreign or familiar. A man of sensation who embodied eighteenth-century curiosity about the world, Adams set down his eclectic trips with candor.[95] This was especially true of John Adams's sensory travels along new roads of faith. When he experimented, it was with the tacit acknowledgment that religion had a taste, a touch, and a feel that he *must* record and share. Like other eighteenth-century Americans and Europeans, a special mixture of wonder, history, sense, and sensation informed his course of Christian self-education.

As a New Englander, John Adams inherited a distinctive set of religious memories. His local reference points for understanding Christianity's impact included a range of actors: Puritans who waged war on Native Americans and prosecuted possible heretics, Anglicans who vied with Congregationalists for social power and fought off the "popery" of Catholic newcomers, and migratory evangelicals who amplified the religious voices of women and blacks.[96] As he traveled through the colonies, physical markers and cultural echoes of New England Christianity permeated John's daily landscape. The sight of swaying locust trees, planted as a memorial at Salem's "Witchcraft Hill," reminded him of "that memorable Victory over the Prince of the Power of the Air."[97] The heavy scent of Catholic incense, by contrast, left him half blind and gagging in a Philadelphia side street. Though he embraced religious tolerance as a popular concept of the Age of Enlightenment he lived in, like many of his generation, John was never entirely prepared to welcome other forms of belief.[98] He found the sensory impact of "Romish" rites too robust. American Catholicism's lavish ritual and ornate appeal made him suspect that its practitioners lacked piety.[99] The "Grandmother Church" flaunted "Every Thing which can charm and bewitch the simple and ignorant," John wrote to Abigail from Congress. "I wonder how Luther ever broke the spell."[100]

If the Revolutionary War strengthened John's and Abigail's Christian resolve, then the difficult peace that followed with Great Britain gave them a good reason to put it on public display. John was appointed an Anglo-American peace commissioner in 1778 and minister to the Netherlands and Great Britain shortly thereafter. Trading the relative quiet of Braintree for cosmopolitan Europe throughout the 1780s, the Adamses joined the first wave of "full" Americans who journeyed off in safer, faster packet ships to sample Old World culture. Before the federal Constitution was drafted or ratified, these itinerant diplomats, artists, thinkers, and writers tested out a new national identity as they made use of expanding routes and rationales for transatlantic travel. Eager to mend cultural ties with Britain, they had to adapt or liberalize their Protestant habits to fit with the European (and mostly Catholic) practices that they encountered.[101] "Tho Seas Mountains and Rivers are geographical boundaries," Abigail wrote home in 1786, "they contract not the benevolence and good will of the Liberal mind which can extend itself beyond the limits of Country and kindred and claim fellowship with Christian jew or Turk."[102]

Reading scripture and reporting on Revolutionary events constituted the first part of the Adamses' religious education. Regional roots in Congregationalist communities and controversies had prepared John and Abigail for intense political participation. Diplomatic work in Europe, however, enabled them to represent American Christianity to a world curious about the piety of God's "chosen nation." In an era when Christianity remained vital but "fragmented" by a host of new denominations, John and Abigail joined other Americans in presenting a united front of middle-class gentility. Abroad in Holland, France, and England from 1780 to 1788, they learned that regular Christian devotion connoted universal respectability, no matter their country of origin.[103] Acting like good Protestants made Americans more palatable to European courtiers and kings.

John's diplomatic work took them to Europe, but it was Abigail who ran the households in Braintree, London, and Auteuil; led the children's religious instruction at home; and served as John's savviest political confidante in Protestant and Catholic courts alike. Abigail's religious explorations were indicative of other Revolutionary-era women who brought about religious change while inculcating a model Christian home.[104] The key difference was that Abigail Adams operated on an international scale. As the prototypical republican mother tasked with the moral education of her children, Abigail threaded her letters of

John Adams (1735–1826). *Portrait by Jane Stuart after Gilbert Stuart, ca. 1800, Adams National Historical Park*

instruction with mash-ups of scripture and popular poetry.[105] At home, she centered the family's life on Christian tenets. Abigail's mulberry-and-ivory Delft tiles bordered the fireplace with biblical scenes, designed at a child's height so that John Quincy and his siblings could comprehend Christian morals long before they read the Bible—a common feature in the early American household where Christianity (literally) governed the hearth and nurturing family piety ensured a reunion in heaven.[106]

Abigail Smith Adams (1744–1818). *Portrait by Jane Stuart after Gilbert Stuart, ca. 1800, Adams National Historical Park*

In keeping with Lemuel Briant's call, Abigail clung to the idea that inculcating a stout Christian character was the best defense against damnation—for self and nation. During the war, Abigail was staunch in her letters to fellow revolutionaries that Christian patriotism would spur independence. "A patriot without religion in my estimation is as great a paradox, as an honest Man without the fear of God. Is it possible that he whom no moral obligations bind, can have any real Good Will towards Man, can he be a patriot who by an openly vicious conduct is undermineing the very bonds of Society, corrupting the Morals of Youth, and by his bad example injuring that very Country he professess to patrionize more than he can possibly compensate by his intrepidity, Generosity and honour? The Scriptures tell us righteousness exaltheth a Nation," she wrote to Mercy Otis Warren in 1775. That idea stuck with Abigail after the peace (though her relationship with the Warrens grew thorny). A decade later, just as her son John Quincy began wrestling with ancient history and Christian patriotism, Abigail resumed the cause in a letter to her sister, noting: "In short their is nothing binding upon the Humane mind, but Religion."[107] To her mind, Christianity meant change. Reinterpreting scripture and testing out new rites were ways to bolster and deepen faith.

John Adams enjoyed new cultural habits while serving abroad, as did Abigail. She savored her sudden flight from the New England countryside. Living in Auteuil and London from 1783 to 1788, and briefly reunited with the whole family, she dug into the local varieties of Old World Christianity. The act of observing British and French rituals, in particular, remade Abigail's aesthetic response to worship and stirred her appetite for experimenting with new theological ideas at home and abroad. She praised the rhetorical skill of the universalist preachers in London's Hackney Street, making the six-mile carriage drive each Sunday through muddy roads.

She brought Thomas Jefferson to hear a royal Te Deum sung at the grand Cathedral of Notre Dame in Paris. She marveled at the soaring Gothic arches. She puzzled over the propriety of whispering through a confessional grate to absolve one's sins. Surprised to find French churches open all day, Abigail returned again and again, polishing her criticism of Catholicism's sensory impact. She hated the hard lock-step of schoolboys pacing through the pews and chanting hymns. She disapproved of the casual way in which worshippers shuffled in at midday, "clattering" to their knees before the altar. Worse, the dank and drafty air of great cathedrals left her sick of prayer. "Their Churches seem rather calculated to damp Devotion than excite it," Abigail wrote to her brother-in-law John Shaw, a Calvinist minister in New Hampshire.[108]

Throughout the 1780s, Abigail slowly came to accept "High Church" worship aesthetics as legitimate manifestations of real faith, even when delivered in a foreign tongue. Hearing European church music became, for example, a potent luxury for her to seek out and enjoy. In letters home, the Yankee clergyman's daughter rhapsodized about the "Solemnity and dignity" of hearing George Frideric Handel's "Sublime" *Messiah* sung in Westminster Abbey in June 1785.[109] "When it came to that part, the Hallelujah, the whole assembly rose and all the Musicians, every person uncoverd," Abigail informed her niece back home. "Only conceive six hundred voices and instruments perfectly chording in one word and one sound! I could scarcly believe myself an inhabitant of Earth. I was one continued shudder from the begining to the end of the performance."[110] At their office/home, the Grosvenor Square legation, she stocked the diplomatic dinner table with nonconformist ministers such as Richard Price and Joseph Priestley. John and Abigail became especially fond of Priestley. "Tho far from being an orator, his words came from the Heart and reached the Heart," she wrote. "So Humble, so diffident, so liberal and Benevolent a Character does honour to that Religion which he both professes and practises."[111]

When Abigail Adams documented the joys and rigors of diplomatic life, she showed how elite American women refashioned religious sensibilities and juggled the duties of a much-prescribed "Christian family" constantly on the go. Abigail's travels led her to reinforce the New England Congregationalism that she so clearly missed. Upon learning that Congress could not fund the construction of a chapel at the first American legation in London, Abigail berated her powerful political friends back home. "Do Congress think that their Ministers have no need of Grace? Or that Religion is not a necessary article for them," she chided.[112] Finding Providence, Abigail saw, meant shoving aside any lingering sectarian interests. On their return trip to Boston in the spring of 1788, John and Abigail served as a favorable test audience for one of the few passengers also traveling aboard the *Lucretia*: the Reverend John Murray, a denominational founder of American Universalism and a strident anti-Calvinist. Murray taught that universal union with Jesus meant greater chances for laity like the Adamses to attain their salvation.[113] On shipboard, Murray frequently rose to preach without notes, delivering the sermon in "a familiar talking without any kind of dignity yet perhaps better calculated to do good to such an audience." The Weymouth clergyman's daughter endorsed the more inclusive aspects of Murray's theology of salvation. Yet the more cosmopolitan Abigail Adams doubted his ability to spin a solid Sunday's performance into lasting literature and thereby achieve any permanent traction in the rich field of American religious culture. "I like to hear a discourse that would read well," she wrote.[114]

Armed with a renewed commitment to Christianity and to the American republic, the Adamses made their odyssey back to Massachusetts in mid-1788. Recalled home to serve as vice president under George Washington, John was elected to a single, fraught term as chief executive in 1796. Cosmopolitan experience had significantly sharpened the Adamses' critiques of American Christianity. The intellectual heft of a sound sermon—no matter the minister's denomination—drew John's scholarly attention in his diary, with notes on rhetoric and oratory. But if clergymen spotted the Honorable John Adams in a front pew, and ventured into pulpit commentary on matters of state, then he tuned them out. "The clergy are too little acquainted with the world and the modes of business, to engage in civil affairs with any advantage," Adams observed. "Those . . . who are really men of learning, have conversed with books so much more than men as to be too much loaded with vanity to be good politicians."[115] Joining John in the critic's perch, Abigail rarely shirked an occasion to praise or pan local preaching—their longtime rector in Quincy, Anthony Wibird, had only ten sermons, she sniffed. She was more interested in nursing piety—to see what holiness felt like—than in parsing theology. In the religious reminiscences scattered across her many letters, Abigail mixed religious sensation and scientific reason with eighteenth-century literary aplomb. As she later lectured her daughter-in-law Louisa Catherine: "I do not profess to be a theologian. I never would puzzle my head with their disputes; but I have endeavoured to exercise my own understanding: *What can we reason, but from what we can know?*"[116]

Despite all the "founders"-related myth-making that swiftly enveloped John and Abigail Adams, they resembled other rural New Englanders who struggled to harmonize Enlightenment-era Christianity with the mysterious sovereignty of Providence over their lives.[117] They wanted to reconcile sensations of faith and doubt with what they heard or read of scripture and science. They seized on clues, large and small, that Providence cared about America's plight. They audited events in the family circle and in political life, monitoring the moments when divine interference finalized new treaties, tempted away suitors, or comforted them after the death of a child. In their speeches and letters, John and Abigail turned to Providence for aid, or to burn off their sinful anger over real and perceived political slights. At home and abroad, they scanned the Bible seeking lessons of martyrdom and revelation to use in their "new Israel."[118] European travel and biblical criticism molded the Adamses into cosmopolitan Christians. A close look at how this famous family employed Christian rhetoric, in turn, offers an elite view of providentialism as a malleable ideology that drove Americans from the Declaration to disunion. It also reveals how Providence disappointed them.

Prestigious diplomatic missions ripped away the chance to raise their family at close quarters, a circumstance that caused John and Abigail to agonize over the moral instruction of their faraway children. In events of great loss, they reminded each other that the whole family would meet again in heaven. An omniscient Providence, Abigail thought, engraved the "terms of existence" for humanity in scripture, prizing endurance and piety above all. Prompted by prayer, Abigail avowed that a real Christian knew to search times of trial for eternal reward. John and Abigail, cast in the roles of president and First Lady, became the most prominent American Christian couple of the post-Revolutionary era. Diligently, they kept up proper Protestant profiles. From his executive pulpit, John fretted that the country's emergent institutions of commerce, government, and faith were all susceptible to "many Seed Plott's of Division Faction, Sedition and Rebellion."[119] Like other liberalizing Protestants who applied reason and the truth of personal experience to religious doctrine, John and Abigail explored other faiths but still saw Congregationalist Christianity as *the* catalyst of self-education and social change.[120] As the eighteenth century waned, the Adamses tried to reinforce and "Americanize" faith through the labor of Christian statesmanship. Yet by upholding *his* Providence, John Adams may also have forfeited his legacy.

Throughout the 1790s, elite New Englanders like John and Abigail Adams forged and maintained high social standards for Protestant piety. On ready display in the public sphere and in national newspapers, they came across as generous, curious, communally minded Christians.

John and his peers heard fast-day sermons in April and sang thanks-giving psalms in December. Back in Braintree, Abigail and her friends slipped stray shillings into the deacon's bucket for the evangelization of Neponset Indians. When winter blizzards blew mounds of snow into the First Church, they left their farms and shoveled out the pricier pews.[121] Like other Congregationalists descended from the Puritans, they thought their religious ecosystem embodied an ideal for national life: a democratic union of souls that enabled inquiry and progress.[122] It helped that New England Christianity, with its core of Harvard- and Yale-trained pulpit talent, attracted a feisty, knowledgeable congrega-tion.[123] John rarely missed reading Harvard's annual Dudleian Lectures on natural religion, and he defended the Puritans in print.[124]

When Abigail considered the rise and formation of young America, she at first perceived a providential design, strongly ingrained among the New England families alongside whom she worked the land. What she came to believe, after a lifetime of shouldering political burdens, was that God made all earth a mere "state of trial" for professing Christians to endure.[125] The Adams family's choice to take root in Massachusetts foretold a long and complex relationship with faith and underlined a multigenerational, transatlantic commitment to non-conformity. Their regional ties, in many ways, doomed them from achieving real popularity in the national political arena. Asked to eval-uate American prospects in the Napoleonic age, John confessed: "My spirit of prophecy reaches no farther than New England *guesses.*"[126] For, as John and Abigail discovered in the 1790s, American voters were less willing to corroborate their views.

A political crisis rattled John's and Abigail's abiding belief that prov-idential Christianity still resonated with the rest of the country. On March 23, 1798, in an effort to soothe concerns about the collapse of Franco-American relations, President John Adams proclaimed that "all Religious congregations" should observe a "day of Solemn Humiliation, Fasting and Prayer" on May 9.[127] Colonial governors and clergy had reg-ularly called for days of fast and thanksgiving, often held on Wednesdays and Thursdays in April and December. On fast days, congregants attended a double church service, refrained from eating and all forms of labor, and repented of their sins.[128] This presidential proclamation was a striking, federal reinvention of the Puritan rite. John Adams's act of "recommending" national religious observance marked a new use of executive power. It also implied that the president was keyed in to a direct dialogue with the workings of Providence—exactly the sort of personal intimacy with holy power that had endangered Anne Hutchinson and other would-be community leaders. Exhorting Americans to heed the "loud call to Repentance and Reformation" occasioned by divine judgment, Adams wrote that the United States was "placed in a hazardous and afflictive situation, by the unfriendly Disposition, Conduct and Demands of a foreign power."[129] A key problem with the proclamation, in his detractors' view, was that he gathered citizens in special worship to resolve a foreign policy crisis. Did the president believe he had a divine right to do so, like the English king they had thrown off? Outraged citizens thought President John Adams's "New England manners" and providentialist rhetoric signified not godly republicanism but the act of a republican who fancied himself God.

Adams's resurrection of a New England rite originally intended for afflictions like war, drought, and cholera—but this time as an event of national penance—ignited controversy and incensed the Democratic-Republican opposition. To Adams's mind, it was the innate function of a shared cultural habit (Protestant Christianity) that informed his diplomatic policymaking, and therefore it seemed to be the right way to invoke his domestic leadership, too.[130] Critics, however, felt that John's proclamation was too high-handed. They sneered that the phrasing of his text bordered on a "death bed repentance." Adams was lampooned in popular caricatures. Newspaper squibs mocked his piety.[131] In the opposition press, the Virginia senator David Brent sniped that he "would not fast a day to save John Adams from an appopletic fit . . . that he would on that day rather introduce a dance."[132] Some ministers, like Adams's ally and prominent Massachusetts Congregationalist Jacob Norton, crafted strong sermons to manufacture support. "I know not what can excite their Wrath to such a degree," Abigail complained to her sister, "but that they think there is yet some Religion left in the Country and that the people will have some respect to it, & to those Rulers who acknowledge an over Ruling Providence."[133]

One spring night in Philadelphia, the protesters brought their quarrel to John Adams's front door. Much later, when he reflected on the 1798 fast-day controversy in an 1813 letter to Thomas Jefferson,

Adams recalled a more violent set of events. "I have no doubt you was fast asleep, in philosophical Tranquility, when ten thousand People, and perhaps many more, were parading the Streets of Philadelphia, on the Evening of my Fast Day," he wrote. As Adams remembered it, angry men thronged Market Street. The mob assembled on his doorstep, where they were held back only by his "Domesticks in Phrenzy, determined to Sacrifice their lives in my defence." Through "bye Lanes and back doors," John called for "Chests of Arms from the War Office," until the rioters subsided.[134] Evidently undeterred by the dissenters' rage, on March 6, 1799 Adams called another fast day for April 25; his unpopularity grew. Party politics baffled and disgusted him. A quasi-war with France, the Alien and Sedition Acts, and the rise of electioneering forced John (and Abigail) into early retirement at the "Peacefield" farm in Quincy.

From his Massachusetts haven, Adams griped to Benjamin Rush that the fast-day debacle had cost him the presidential pulpit and his rightful place in God's unfolding history of America. In John Adams's view, an Anti-Federalist sect of critics had wrongfully charged him with "an hypocritical, Machiavellian, Jesuitical, Pharisaical attempt to promote a national establishment of Presbyterianism in America, whereas I would as soon establish the Episcopal Church, and almost as soon the Catholic Church."[135] John regarded his failure to translate New England Christianity to the national stage as one in an epic series of setbacks that plagued his family circle. His zeal to apply providentialist guidelines and to align Americans with the practices of godly republicanism had, in Adams's mind, triggered his descent from political grace. Like other colonists who relied on a near-mythic sense of Christian unity to solder the Revolutionary cause with providentialist meaning and fervor, John realized that many different Christianities were developing in the new nation.[136] This blossoming sectarianism, and the way that it paralleled party politics' growth, deeply troubled him. "There is no such Thing as human Wisdom," he wrote in 1779 as he sealed the American peace with Britain. "All is the Providence of God."[137] Now, at the nineteenth century's dawn, John Adams sounded less sure about Christianity's social "place" in the new republic.

The period from 1798 to 1813 encapsulated what American preachers would have called a "school of affliction" for John and Abigail Adams.

After departing the capital in 1801 with a tarnished legacy, the first family experienced a wave of tragedies, personal and political, that strengthened John's and Abigail's inward turn to Christianity. When she sat down to address her youngest granddaughter in 1808, Abigail had only one real lesson to impart. "Every moment should be devoted to some useful purpose, that we might ask the moments as they passed, what report they bore to Heaven," she wrote.[138] The eternal gaze of Providence, as Abigail and many early Americans thought, was fixed firmly on their mission of nation-building. Stepping back from public life cemented Abigail's view of the unfolding family events that she cataloged as the "allotments of Providence."[139] John called it a "pretty large dose . . . of distress and pain."[140] Brutal party wars separated John from longtime compatriot Thomas Jefferson, and they severed all ties for a decade. A new historical narrative of the Revolution, crafted by (sometime) friend Mercy Otis Warren, notably excluded John. The sudden death of their alcoholic son Charles, occurring just as Adams left office, dealt an extra blow. Their daughter Nabby (Abigail 2d) underwent a radical mastectomy (without anesthesia) and died of breast cancer in 1813. Another son, Thomas Boylston, rode the court circuit as a Massachusetts chief justice and oversaw the family estate, while battling alcoholism.[141] The most promising Adams scion, John Quincy, angered his father's Federalist cronies by championing Jeffersonian policy and fled to Russia in semi-exile in 1809. When John wrote to tell Dr. Rush—Nabby's doctor in her last days—that Christianity was the force that preserved the Adams "race" in all its glory, it was probably more to remind himself that Providence might heal his mounting afflictions.

The renewal of correspondence with Jefferson in 1812 and an impulsive academic plunge into the study of comparative religions brightened John Adams's remaining years. Theological disputes he still found to be petty and pedantic, worth little more than idle sport. As he quipped, "These things are to me the Marbles and Nine Pins of old Age: I will not Say the Beads and Prayer Books."[142] But in his scholarly excursions into Jewish and Egyptian customs, Adams was exceptional. Comparative religious studies would not fully emerge as a discrete field in American institutions of higher education for another half-century or more. Happily, he retreated to his books.

Religious headlines annoyed the elderly former president. On the national stage, doomsday prophets frequently sputtered on and off, exhorting that the end of the world was near. John Adams watched in chagrin as popular interest surged around itinerant soothsayers ranging from Nimrod Hughes to the Shawnee prophet Tenskwatawa.[143] Caught between mediocre clergy and false prophets, Adams and his New England friends sought to reaffirm Congregationalist authority despite widespread pushback from growing evangelical and Catholic fronts. To Jefferson, Adams ranted that "Sober and sincere Christians" would diagnose the "impious" nature of such prophecies, which threatened "political safety" and undermined faith. "For nothing is clearer from their scriptures than that their prophecies were not intended to make us prophets."[144] Openly, Adams traded this and other thoughts on faith with his longtime colleague. At Jefferson's request, John Adams whittled down his religious credo to four short words: "Be Just and Good."[145]

Occasionally, the Quincy Congregationalist tweaked the Virginia deist with pointed scriptural allusions. And he told long tales of reading outside the usual roads of Protestant enlightenment. "I have been a diligent Student for many years in Books whose Titles you have never Seen," Adams wrote from his estate of "Montezillo" to Jefferson's Monticello.[146] At the end of his life, the Ten Commandments and the Sermon on the Mount summed up Adams's entire creed, he wrote. Adams joined many other Christian republicans who broadened their search for morality far past the pages of instruction preserved in the Bible. With scripture in hand for his proof, John stood by the same concept of Providence that he sketched as a young man: "From a sense of the Government of God, and a Regard to the Laws established by his Providence, should all our Actions for ourselves or for other men, primarily originate."[147]

The Bible was key to absorbing God's plan for America, John Adams thought, but it was not the only sacred book worth a more thoughtful read. Understanding how foreign cultures prayed—and familiarizing himself with other dissenters in other lands—became John Adams's intellectual finale. Overall, John's wide-ranging course of reading had confirmed his perch on the religious spectrum between liberal Congregationalist and Unitarian-adjacent. Adams's annotated books, now housed at the Boston Public Library, show some of his livelier marginalia related to faith. Next to an image of ancient Egyptian ships aligned to conduct a ritual, he scribbled, "Is this Religion? Good God!"[148] Adams, who tallied the Moroccan-American Treaty of Peace and Friendship among his diplomatic wins, was more respectful toward Islam and owned an 1806 edition of the Koran.[149] Happy to be back in conversation with Jefferson, he speculated on the historical parallels between the biblical Exodus of the Israelites and the contemporary migrations of Native American tribes.[150] John Adams yearned for "translations into English and French and Spanish and German and Italian of the Sacred Books of the Persians, the Chinese, the Hindoos &c. &c. &c.," he wrote to a friend in 1815. "Then our grand Children and my great grand Children may compare Notes, and hold fast all that is good."[151]

The loss of Abigail in 1818 from a bout of typhoid fever that rendered her unable to speak for days led to John's decline. Briefly finding her voice in her final hours, Abigail stated that her dying wish was to reprise the last Thanksgiving day celebration—nine of fourteen grandchildren crowding the Quincy table for the feast—then the former First Lady paused, proclaiming that she knew a full family reunion awaited her in heaven.[152] John died eight years later.

What John labeled the Christian "constitution" of human nature, and how colonists-turned-citizens restructured Christian behavior within a new republican model, illuminates a distinctive challenge of American religion.[153] As the founders' generation died out, antebellum thinkers grappled with the question that sparked the last exchange of John Adams and Thomas Jefferson, who debated whether "the Christian Philosophy" was "the most sublime and benevolent, but the most perverted system that ever shone upon man."[154] The question turned on the use of New England providentialism, a Puritan intellectual relic that did not die with the first Henry Adams, within a public sphere dominated by the broader language of Christian republicanism. Adams's own memorial hangs in proof of the struggle. After July 4, 1826, when John Adams was "summoned To the Independence of Immortality, And to the Judgment of His God," his political heir, John Quincy, spent months drafting his father's honorary church plaque. Omitting Puritan ideals, the younger Adams took on an assertive tone of Christian citizenship: "This

House will bear witness to his Piety: This Town, his Birth-Place, to his Munificence: History to his Patriotism: Posterity to the Depth and Compass of his Mind."[155]

In an era when most congregations heard that "good Christians make good citizens," church and state were culturally bound together. For John and his "dearest friend" Abigail, the providentialism of New England Christianity offered the clearest language to reconcile their overlapping duties to family, nation, and God. "The duties of a son, brother, a father, a neighbor, a citizen, I can see and feel," John Adams wrote in 1813, as his eldest son raced ahead into bolder forms of Christian inquiry. "But, I trust the Ruler with the skies."[156] As the new nation took shape around the Adams family, the question of how to be simultaneously Christian and American was the defining challenge of their lives.[157]

2

John Quincy and Louisa Catherine Adams at Prayer

PRIVATELY, HIS FAITH WAS SHAKEN. Preparing to argue the case of the *Amistad* captives before the US Supreme Court in 1840, former president John Quincy Adams prayed in the pages of his diary, anxious for the "mercy of Almighty God, so to controul my temper, to enlighten my Soul, and to give me utterance that I may prove . . . equal to the Task."[1] Publicly, he had never appeared so firm in his convictions and so eager to broadcast Unitarian values to his fellow Americans. That same day, Adams embarked on a winter lecture tour to share his views "On Faith." Drawing on his "intercourse with the world," he described the "many liberal minded and intelligent persons—almost persuaded to become Christians"—whom he had met.[2] For the seventy-three-year-old congressman, it was an arduous trek.[3] And, for a layman who held public office, it was a curious odyssey to undertake. So powerful was Adams's religious message that when his son Charles encountered it years later, he labeled it for the family archive: "Two sermons/JQA." The talk, which he delivered from Boston to Salem and Hartford to Brooklyn, laid out the formation of Adams's faith. Throughout the life he led on the world stage, John Quincy Adams struggled to reinforce his native Unitarianism by chronicling people, places, and religions like no other American statesman of his era. [4]

"Faith must have its bounds, and perhaps the most difficult and delicate question in morals is to define them clearly," Adams told the standing-room-only crowds. "But allow me to say that this unbounded freedom of religious faith, far from absolving any individual from the obligation of believing, does but impose it upon them, with a tenfold force."[5] This insight was especially true of Adams's own itinerant religious history. Seeking among other faiths cemented his Unitarian identity and echoed antebellum Americans' desire to meld scripture with inner spirituality. In a politically divisive era, how did the president pray, and what did he ask for?

John Quincy Adams's intense engagement with the world's believers and skeptics mirrored his generation's shift from rigid Calvinism to a more liberating Arminianism. Essentially, that theological transition widened the path to salvation for Adams and others, as they moved from a model that favored only God's predestined elect to one where all freely accepted or rejected God's grace, progressing to heaven through faith and good works. Adams's religious curiosity, and his lifelong cultivation of it, reflected the individualistic drive of market society.

From an early age, John Quincy was groomed to become a Christian patriot. Thanks to a peripatetic childhood in the 1770s and 1780s, Adams divided his youth between the austere wooden pews of his parents' First Parish Congregational Church of Quincy, Massachusetts, and the grand cathedrals of Europe, where he acted as his father's diplomatic attaché while John served as an American minister to the Netherlands and Great Britain. He spent his formative years in Paris, Amsterdam, and Leiden.

For the budding diplomat, accessing knowledge of local religions became a vital key to understanding national character and relating New England faith to that of the Old World. Adams used his diary, which eventually spanned fifty-one volumes over sixty-eight years, to chronicle foreign practice. Touring the Renaissance humanist Erasmus's hometown of Rotterdam in 1780, for example, the teenager recorded the religious panorama with the same forensic detail that he used to quantify its population, canals, and local government.[6] With his father, John Quincy worshipped in a series of Protestant churches, including a

Presbyterian one in Holland where he was surprised to hear the sermon delivered in English.[7] On a jaunt to Sweden in late 1782, John Quincy did not understand a word of the sermon, so he doodled in his journal throughout the service. His entry for that day—December 5, 1782— bears in the margin his witty sketch of the minister's pulpit harangue. Even if the message sounded foreign, John Quincy learned to seize on what felt familiar: the planted stance of a clergyman bent over the congregation, midlecture, with his brows furrowed in devout concern for their welfare.[8] He was already looking for parallel patterns of faith between Americans and the rest of the world.

After returning to Boston in 1785, John Quincy followed the piety and practices of his New England forebears. He took sermon notes twice each Sunday and studied history, sacred and profane, during his whirlwind education at Harvard. John Quincy's religious education, like that of his Revolutionary peers, was homemade and interlaced with literary pursuits—at times, Virgil's verses, or even *Tristram Shandy*'s directive to answer the "great ends of existence" guided Adams just as much as the family Bible did.[9] Legal apprenticeship followed John Quincy's college graduation in 1787. The young, single attorney passed much of the next decade indulging a mild bout of intellectual crisis. John Quincy Adams spent mornings bored at his Boston law office, flipping through a stack of weighty classics meant to refine his powers of oratory.[10] Frustrated with the dryness and dimness of reading law after a dazzling adolescence abroad, Adams initiated a brief, self-taught course in the literature of antiquity.[11] He lost his first court case but won minor fame for a string of pseudonymous newspaper editorials. His long, contemplative walks in the mall brought "low spirits." Mostly, the eldest and arguably the most promising Adams son sounded lost, and (somehow) overlooked by Providence.

Around John Quincy, the post-Revolutionary glow of excitement had sputtered out. American preachers of the 1790s stepped up to their pulpits intent on re-energizing themes of millennial faith and unifying Protestants in missionary societies and philanthropic efforts to counter suspected threats of religious infidelity.[12] The melancholy John Quincy, often napping through such sermons in a fine family pew, would have made a prime target for their verbal jabs.[13] Friends married, moved, had children—and Adams remained a half day's ride from his Braintree relations, ready for the "smiles of Providence" to elevate his public role, and yet fearing what that ambition might also bring. For John Quincy, his father's political trajectory expressed the ugly truth that even Providence could not control party and press. The twenty-five-year-old John Quincy Adams felt "as obscure as unknown to the world," a man whom Providence neglected while blessing his contemporaries with wealth, sons, and success. Late in May 1792, Adams recalled some advice from a family favorite, Laurence Sterne's bawdy bestseller *Tristram Shandy*. Speculating on his "future Fortunes in Life," Adams declared that he would "adopt some Resolutions, and prescribe . . . some regulations which may enable me as uncle Toby Shandy said of his miniature sieges, *to answer the great ends of my existence*."[14] Four more years passed, quietly.

In 1796, while his parents battled through party politics in the nation's capital, Adams accepted his first major diplomatic post, as minister to the Netherlands. A year later, John Quincy married Louisa Catherine Johnson, the sociable daughter of a Maryland tobacco merchant then living in London. John Quincy's wife claimed a different religious heritage; their interfaith union underlined a transitional moment in American Christianity's wary embrace of pluralism in an age of disestablishment. Louisa's parents were nominally Unitarian but were hardly regular churchgoers, and her religious background was varied. She had been raised first as an Anglican and then tutored at a Catholic convent school in Nantes.[15] Louisa's initial encounter with faith, formed in the grim shadow of the London Tower, was at the ancient Anglican parish of All Hallows Barking. As a girl growing up in the lower- to middle-class neighborhood of Tower Hamlets, Louisa admired the church's seventh-century Saxon arch, rebuilt in Roman tile, and its aura of Gothic grit. Triggered by her father's bankruptcy and the global aftershocks of American independence, the family's abrupt exodus to France in 1778 introduced Louisa to the mysteries of Catholic devotion.[16] One of her first religious memories was kneeling before "the Image of the tortured Jesus and the horror I felt at the thought, of mixing with hereticks."[17]

A few years later, Louisa came back to London and made a rocky return to Protestant ritual at the Unitarian meetinghouse and school in the northeastern borough of Hackney. When her governess instructed the eight-year-old Louisa to kneel and pray, she "fell as it were dead upon the floor." After a two-month reprieve, Louisa returned with "strict orders from my parents that I should not be harried or urged too much upon the subject of going to Church. . . . I was to be accustomed gradually to the prayers of the school, until my fears wore off." A second fainting fit ensued. Thereafter, Louisa committed to the plan and "quietly conformed to the usages and forgot insensibly all the prejud[ic]es which I had so early and so strongly imbibed."[18] Louisa cherished hazy memories of All Hallows during her Ursuline education, and so it became the site where she married the American president's son in the summer of 1797.[19]

When the two expatriates—Unitarian New Englander and Anglican southerner—wed in an ancient London church, their diverse religious backgrounds were not, surprisingly, at issue.[20] John Quincy and Louisa participated in a new wave of American Christianity that welcomed interdenominational marriage, choosing a cultural route that many took without rupturing their households.[21] They adapted the family unit to a radical style of religious individualism that would have jarred ancestral sensibilities. Parents sometimes prayed at different churches, but they still raised their children as Christians, tended house, and made or lost money together. By the time John Quincy met Louisa, Americans had figured out how to detach piety from kinship and thereby loosen the old New England bonds of orthodoxy that once soldered church to home.[22] Adams did not care if he married outside of his denomination, and he put little pressure on Louisa to convert. Her mother-in-law, First Lady Abigail, balked only at her half-British pedigree, proclaiming to John Quincy that she hoped "the siren is at least *half blood*."[23]

Mrs. John Quincy Adams curated her own sense of theology with a critical eye. Privately, in her diary pages, she needled her new "Yankee Unitarian" kin, calling them a "sect enveloped in a cloud of Mist."[24] Yet when Louisa sat down to write her memoirs in the late 1820s, becoming the first First Lady to do so, she recalled a husband for whom she had willingly sacrificed her own mixed set of creeds, so confident and appealing was his outlook on faith. "I likewise joined in the Duties of his religious exercises as a tribute of respect to him, and as an example to my little ones," she wrote.[25] The statesman's wife drafted scriptural reflections and composed religious poetry. Like other readers, she consumed the growing denominational periodicals of the day, which replaced Calvinism with a Christianity born of "benign feeling, good works, and divine benevolence."[26] The Stone Library in Quincy reflects the shared breadth of the couple's reading habits: diverse sermons, hymnals, and Bibles printed in Latin, Greek, French, German, and Hawaiian.[27]

A distinctively American Christianity that mixed scientific curiosity, Scottish Common Sense philosophy, and Protestant piety became the Adamses' great guide in navigating the world. Like their post-Revolutionary peers, John Quincy and Louisa found that practicing Protestantism fulfilled their everyday needs in ways that the prevailing precepts of rational philosophy and Whig ideology did not. Further, religion made daily life meaningful and great tragedy bearable wherever they went.[28] For John Quincy and Louisa, Christianity heralded opportunities for innovation. The Adamses studiously made and remade what Louisa (and her mother-in-law, Abigail) called "true religion," both in the courts of Napoleonic Europe and in the courtrooms of a slaveholding American republic.[29]

From 1809 to 1825, the relentless tug of a diplomatic itinerary uprooted and replanted John Quincy and Louisa along with their three sons, George Washington, John II, and Charles Francis. From 1809 to 1815, Adams acted as the first American minister to Russia, returning to serve as President James Monroe's secretary of state from 1817 to 1825. Like his father, he endured a fraught tenure as president, alienating many with his plans for internal improvements and federal support for the arts and sciences. Known mainly for serving as a Massachusetts congressman from 1831 until his death in 1848, John Quincy opposed the annexation of Texas and war with Mexico. He overturned the gag rule on slave petitions and championed American neutrality in foreign affairs. Louisa, who acted as his confidante and *salonnière* in Washington, DC, maintained her religious preferences to the end, stipulating an Episcopal funeral service for herself, an event for which the entire Congress adjourned in May 1852.[30]

In a century marked by people, goods, and ideas on the move, John Quincy Adams manufactured an eclectic brand of Christianity through the daily exchange of diverse ideas about faith and doubt. He relished traveling through the liturgical seasons and sampling new beliefs.

Reflections on the theology and rites of Catholics, Anglicans, Greek and Russian Orthodox, Hindus, Muslims, and Jews all appear in his diaries, letters, and miscellanies. They are interspersed with his regular updates on Napoleon's advance toward St. Petersburg, the perils of British politics at the Court of St. James, and his own uneasy adjustment to the fishbowl of congressional life in the new capital. Throughout, Adams retained his New England providentialism, believing that the man who adhered to religious duty from infancy would "never be exposed to the resentment of a good and wise god, whatever the mode of his worship may be."[31]

Manuscripts record the Adamses' religious journeys; so, too, does their money trail. Like other Americans who migrated between Protestant sects, John Quincy Adams pronounced denominational differences indistinct and arcane; but he was exceptional in leveraging family wealth to subsidize the message. A survey of his parallel investments in multiple American religions offers additional evidence of Adams's cosmopolitan Christianity. During his time in Washington, John Quincy owned pews at the Second Presbyterian Church and St. John's Episcopal Church, while paying large sums for other pews at the major Unitarian and Episcopal venues in Quincy.[32] Adams mirrored his generation's interest in diluting denominational differences. He was eager to strengthen the American union by proclaiming a shared Protestant identity.[33]

As a "frequent sinner before God," by his own description, Adams felt it vital that his constituents see him in church—*any* church—come Sunday. There, he welcomed admonishment for his sins and an exhortation to virtue, two acts that Adams thought he was "sure of receiving" through prayer in "all the forms of Christian worship."[34] As each new encounter or pew purchase faded into the pages of his diary, the president pensively returned to the faith in which he was raised. By far, Adams concluded in 1846, he preferred the Congregational "essentials of Christianity." He did not join the full communion of his home church in Quincy until 1826, and when he finally did, the famed Christian statesman blamed his itinerant career for the extended delay in committing to one of the more formal aspects of the Adams family's longtime religious tradition: "I ought to have joined it thirty years ago or more; but the tumult of the world, false shame, a distrust of my own worthiness to partake of the communion, and a residence

elsewhere and constantly changing, made me defer it to a more convenient opportunity."[35]

For Louisa, too, sampling and evaluating new religions became a
significant hobby, paving another intellectual path for the First Lady
to consolidate her influence at home or abroad. Louisa entrusted her
life to Providence, subscribed to the idea of Jesus's "superhuman" nature, and served as an agile critic of the clergy. Frequently, Louisa
responded differently (and with less tolerance) to new rites than her
husband did. She disliked Russian Orthodox priests and referred to one
Methodist preacher in Washington as a "miserable Rhapsodist."[36] Like
many Americans, Louisa met and mocked the Shakers of Bordentown,
New Jersey. She saw the community as suffering under an "obviously
imperfect" creed, led by "illiterate and vulgar preachers" in a "highly
ridiculous mode of worship." Later, describing the Shakers in a letter
to John Quincy, Louisa tried to peer beyond contemporary prejudices
and attempted a more tolerant view of the sect. She acknowledged that
the Shakers had shown "disciplined solemnity in their motions" and
that, "as in most creeds, their motives and intentions are pure, however
wrong they may be in practice."[37]

The Anglo-American Louisa, who charmed a sea of nobility at several European courts, also used local religion to read national culture
and assert social influence. Abroad, Louisa performed some diplomatic
maneuvers of her own, and often with religious undertones. Skillfully,
she cultivated queens and noblewomen who grew comfortable sharing
"private history," once they found common ground in discussing the universal Christian duties of motherhood.[38] Delicately, Louisa Catherine
Adams knew when to change the topic (*away* from religion) at a state
dinner.[39] She saved some of her most biting invective, however, for her
Adams kin. Setting foot in America for the first time in 1801, Louisa
gasped: "Quincy! What shall I say of my impressions of Quincy! Had
I stepped into Noah's Ark I do-not think I could have been more utterly
astonished. . . . Even the Church, its forms, The snuffling through the
nose, the Singers . . . were all novelties to me."[40] She never settled into
Unitarianism, and John Quincy happily joined her in journeying away
from their home church, toward God.[41]

Growing up an ocean apart, Louisa and John Quincy came from very
different worlds of faith. A transatlantic teenager, John Quincy grew up

praying whenever and wherever he could. What kind of a Christian and a republican was he? Proudly, Adams hailed from a long family line of nonconformists and innovators who led revolutions in church and state. John Quincy's dominant theology, from his earliest Harvard days, was close to early Unitarianism, with a heavy emphasis on pluralism as the bulwark of the American republic. Both of his parents came from a liberal wing of Congregationalism, where they learned to prioritize ethical training over dogma.[42] Under their quasi-Unitarian tutelage, John Quincy believed in salvation, but he likely never heard a single, clear plan for how to achieve it.

Here is how John Quincy tackled it. He acknowledged Jesus as a gifted teacher, and he blended scientific reason with religious inquiry. When John Quincy pored over scripture or dipped into popular literature, he knit together moral education and social reality, with the end goal of perceiving a "grand design of Christianity" in his own life. For John Quincy and other liberalizing Protestants of his era, that meant living a constant battle between "ought" and "is."[43] Such an approach to Christianity, at once idealistic and realistic, instilled a multigenerational sense of ecumenism within the family. "Ask me not then whether I am a Catholic or Protestant, Calvinist or Arm[i]nian?" his father, John, wrote. "As far as they are Christians, I wish to be a Fellow Disciple with them all."[44] The Adamses' peripatetic nature reinforced the commitment to pluralism within the family circle, leading John Quincy to create a liberal form of portable, patriotic Protestantism.

Intermingling religion with the last remnants of revolutionary sentiment, Americans like John Quincy strained to be good Christians while building a republic. They agonized about the roles of church and state in guiding civic virtue.[45] On the eve of John Quincy's launch into political life, his father issued the definitive multivolume sourcebook on tripartite federal government, *A Defence of the Constitutions of the United States of America* (1787–88), in which he framed American growth within the greater traditions and ideologies of ancient European republics.[46] There, the second president equated American resistance to British tyranny with Ciceronian resistance to Caesar's corruption. The creation of a republic like the United States, where three branches of government held power in check, thus met and symbolized the apogee of classical goals. Flipping through the *Defence*, John Quincy quickly rectified his "monumental" error of (initial) Anti-Federalism, soothed by his father's endorsement of a national constitution that balanced aristocratic and popular interests in a bicameral legislature. Over the course of three volumes, however, the senior Adams barely touched on the singular theme that John Quincy believed to be responsible for the ability of American republicanism to thrive in a largely monarchical world: Protestant Christianity.

The *Defence* made a powerful, provocative argument that resonated with Americans, but it was only one of many texts that fueled the new nation's obsession with what John Adams called the "full-length mirror" of antiquity.[47] Americans devoured Virgil's *Aeneid* and composed mythic odes to the founders. They clashed over the beribboned "aristocracy" of the Society of the Cincinnati. They posed for portraits in Roman dress, imported panoramic wallpaper depicting Minerva's acts, and embroidered Hector's exploits on household linen.[48] Coming of age when strangers claimed his own father as their founder, John Quincy moved in a world where classical allusions like these bolstered notions of American liberalism and challenged the architecture of a new, slaveholding republic. The first portion of Adams's life epitomizes that large-scale social change, namely, his youthful examination of using ancient republican models in the service of American growth. This also marked his first foray into serious religious inquiry. In many ways, this junior scholar's experiment illuminates the dilemmas that early Americans encountered when they tried to mesh the ideologies of Protestant Christianity with classical republicanism.

According to the young John Quincy's investigation, the rise of Protestant Christianity marked a fortunate divergence from the classical republican tradition, one that would serve to benefit the long-term growth of American democracy. So how did he reach this conclusion? Partially in preparation for the Harvard entrance exam and partially out of religious curiosity, from 1784 to 1786 John Quincy absorbed Homer's *Iliad* and *Odyssey* along with the Gospel of Luke.[49] When he began, Adams clung to a popular view that was synthesized in the last act of the Age of Revolutions, based on the claim that the rise of American democracy belonged to a political tradition of liberalism stretching back to classical antiquity. The Greco-Roman past was particularly instructive, John Quincy thought, but it was not wholly predictive of the American future—mainly because classical republics lacked the Protestant Christianity needed to instill a moral ethos and solidify true republican virtue. If popular sovereignty was the great "invention" of the last century, he was determined to identify the real engine— Christianity—that would keep the Constitution running.

In order to grasp how other republics had malfunctioned, the teenage Adams buried himself in a self-assigned syllabus to settle whether the beliefs of antiquity intersected with those of eighteenth-century Protestant Christianity. Could he draw a straight line from ancient Athens to Boston, the "Athens of America"? Did Plato's *Republic* hold new lessons for a close reader of the Gospels? After several months of study, the young Adams's main conclusion was that Christians, "favour'd by revelation," should avoid overreading problematic translations of classical philosophers in conducting their quest for helpful republican "truths." All religion, Adams thought, evolved through the practice of human dissent and discovery rather than through divine revelation. To a degree, this reflected how his father had instructed the Adams children to read the Bible—as an ancient text capable of enduring myriad translations, which was clear proof of Christianity's robust merit.

John Quincy was certain that his New England brand of Christianity, however flawed, featured a kinder, gentler Providence than the pantheon of pagan gods, which, despite imposing arbitrary judgments, were worshipped fervently by Greco-Roman republicans. For example, in weighing Jupiter's appetite for revenge against the omniscient benevolence of the scripture's "Supreme Being," John Quincy Adams was gratified to see that he could not force the gods, ancient and modern, to align. Addressing the earlier Protestant scholars who (mistakenly) situated Greek and Roman gods alongside Christian Providence as the chief agents of change and human progress, John Quincy asked: "Is it not a denial, of his wisdom, and justice, as well as of his Power? Surely our ideas of a God, are much more perfect at this Time."[50]

Like his peers, Adams now understood Christian republicanism as a dialectic that harmonized personal beliefs with the daily duties of America's blossoming civic life.[51] As he picked through Homer and Luke, John Quincy grew convinced that America coalesced at a providential moment in history, just as the Protestant laity became strong and rational enough to support a constitutional republic. To Adams's mind, this historical break between two modes of thought—primitive and Protestant—indicated that people now knew to marshal scientific reason and to distance themselves from harmful, stale beliefs. To the young Adams, the creation of America marked a dual milestone in humankind's religious and political progress: it was, historically, the best possible moment to be both Christian and republican. In Adams's view, the Christian laity, once it passed through the period of Reformation, had been empowered by Providence to shape religion and republic. Further, his generation of Protestants was able to approach Christianity without fear of godly reprisal for indulging in mortal sin or conducting scientific inquiry.

In re-evaluating the popular arguments for Christianity to guide national growth, Adams confronted the question of the day: Could the same Christianity underpinning the American republic also be leveraged to criticize it, and at what cost? Again in line with widely held social thought, Adams believed the answer was yes, although he worried about the toll that might take on Christianity. Even a pious patriot might ruin the fragile republic. Adams's greatest concern, shared by other elites, was binding together faith and progress.[52] Informed by his inquiry into biblical and classical texts, this youthful discovery— that Protestantism powered and preserved American union—became central to John Quincy Adams's lifelong commitment to Christian patriotism.

Traveling with Homer's heroes and antiheroes set Adams on a permanent path away from biblical literalism and enabled him to grow as a lay critic of New England religion. From the beginning, John Quincy's diary reveals an American Christian determined to pray for others and to think for himself. Biblical Christianity, for Adams and others of his generation, was ever relevant. They read avidly, but they also acknowledged that scripture did not supply a total understanding of moral precepts. Hailing Enlightenment-era deism as largely defeated, a handful of Protestant elites, including Adams, grappled next with the advent of German textual criticism on American shores.[53] They believed that the Bible was intellectually sound enough to compete against other systems of faith, but thoroughly unable to predict history. Rather, it was merely prefatory to the greater moral canon that Christians must discover through their own actions.

John Quincy Adams wandered beyond the Bible to search for foreign meditations on ethics. The young Unitarian eschewed literalism for liberal inquiry and seized the chance to translate his personal experiences into an elastic, free-form theology. He joined other inventive thinkers, operating inside and outside of the nation's blossoming seminaries, who placed Protestantism at the core of a broad humanities curriculum. Harvard and Princeton, for example, were two major arenas for the significant debates unfolding on biblical inerrancy and scripture's reply to scientific discoveries. For Adams and his classmates, the Bible was one, special book among many in a burgeoning religious press. They were ready to view religion as a menu of livable Christian directives that invited proficient, *personal* interpretation.

Christian patriotism steered Adams's choices and bolstered the familial instinct that adopting an open-minded approach to religion was the best way of reinforcing the early republic. Although his religious curiosity took root abroad, it was Adams's youthful interactions with New England life that shaped his belief of how religion should operate *within* Providence's newest creation. Reading was one lens for Adams's recurrent study of human nature; the cycle of daily life in small-town New England provided another pivotal perspective for his religious musings. John Quincy reacted to new religious ideas, he wrote, as he did to colors striking his senses. Despite changes in hue, the purity of providentialism was never in doubt. "I desire never to have an Idea, of a god, who is not infinitely good, and merciful, as well as powerfull," Adams wrote.[54] When two young neighbors in Quincy died suddenly, Adams sensed local grief overflowing to communal rage; friends sought to prosecute the "author of Nature" who governed any such loss. He feared that "weak" and "impious fools" might shun God and embrace atheism—a theme that his grandson Henry would take up with acidity in the modern parable *Esther*, a century later. But making such a violent turn to unbelief, for John Quincy, was as inconceivable as tossing a pebble in the air and rejecting the scientific truth of gravity. "Is it not still more absurd to deny, what Nature cries aloud in all her works," he wrote, "when we must, all acknowledge, ourselves, entirely ignorant, of the secret springs that keep the machine of the world in play."[55] Beyond reading assignments and personal experience, family history shows that traces of his father's deism and his mother's providentialism thus gave order to John Quincy's early religious thought.

As the American Revolution gave way to a difficult peace, and ministerial duties carried his parents to distant London, John Quincy deepened his roots in New England intellectual life. He grew more confident about expressing his theological views, joining his peers in denouncing Calvinism and evangelical fervor. His uncle and tutor, the Reverend John Shaw, parried with the teenager on questions of good and evil. Adams's precocious queries demonstrated a youthful irritation with pulpit authority as the final word on theology.[56] Preachers were, to his mind, much as his father and others had struggled to describe them in the Massachusetts Constitution of 1780, the "public Protestant teachers of piety, religion, and morality" who encouraged Christians to be good subjects of the commonwealth.[57] Entering Harvard as a junior in 1786, Adams heeded those teachers' advice that builders of the republic must be "instant in prayer" as they readied American culture for the world's review. At school, however, he found the assigned reading on religion to be tedious and unimaginative. He blasted Philip Doddridge's divinity lectures for being too "mathematical" in refuting challengers to Christianity.[58] Decrying a general scarcity of viable models for moral virtue among the Harvard faculty, John Quincy pored over Terence and the Psalms, turning inward to develop his ideals of Christian humility and heroism.[59]

In evaluating local theology and pulpit talent, young Adams made for an unsparing critic. Adams found it distasteful when preachers, even the stars of the annual Dudleian Lecture series on natural and revealed religion, castigated other sects as a way of promoting their own.[60] As a Harvard student, the future Boylston Professor of Rhetoric and Oratory took close notes on religious instructors who sacrificed content for "too much cant."[61] In their selection of subject and tone, Adams felt that most ministers condescended to address "a lunatic people" in the pews.[62] Like his father, the polymath John Quincy realized fairly early on that religion was not a profession that he cared to attempt. When Ebenezer Learned, a friend of less than "first-rate" genius and a "soul tortured with Ambition," confided his secret hope that a pulpit career might ensure his immortality, John Quincy scoffed at the idea.[63] Adams never could separate the man from the cloth. This may have been the result of John Quincy's enforced sociability with a steady rotation of ministers—for, as an Adams, he was expected to subscribe for sermons, host dinners or teas, and pass along (discreetly) news of his father's missions.

John Quincy Adams was exceptionally harsh toward ministers who promoted resurgent Calvinist doctrines of man's innate depravity. He condemned the histrionics of New Divinity acolytes who visited the campus.[64] Throughout the 1780s, his repeated encounters with these ministers drew John Quincy's special disdain. Championed by the Calvinist Samuel Hopkins, New Divinity adherents believed in double predestination and set "disinterested benevolence" as the corner-stone of Christian morality. By the end of the eighteenth century, the Edwardsean influence in New England had waned somewhat, due to uncharismatic clergy and an admittedly "dreary" message of Christian fate that ran counter to the laity's surge of post-Revolutionary con-fidence.[65] John Quincy heard New Divinity ministers preaching in a moment of theological transition, just as they were testing out the con-cept of a "moral governance," a process that flipped an internal switch, actualizing one's "taste" for good into a real action of will.[66]

To John Quincy's ears, the doctrine felt dissonant and even dan-gerously anti-intellectual, so it was worth decimating in the pages of his diary. Not only had New Divinity ministers co-opted and misinterpreted key precepts of Christianity, Adams thought, but they had done it in a fraught rhetorical style that smeared New England's heritage of clerical eloquence. For example, Newburyport's Samuel Spring preached with devotion, Adams wrote, and all the "enthusiasm of a bigot."[67] Another notable interaction with this brand of theology included John Quincy Adams's cool reception of Tillotson Howe, a New Divinity protégé of Eleazar Wheelock's Dartmouth nursery, who guested in the Quincy pulpit during the winter of 1786. After meeting Howe for tea in a cousin's parlor, Adams decided that Howe's "brain is a little crack'd but the singularity of his behaviour may be owing to the manner in which he has been educated and the Company he has kept." Adams sketched out Howe's upward climb from farmer to student-minister and was impressed that Howe paid for his own college tuition, thereby showing "a spirit of Ambition, and fondness for Study, which argue a mind above the common."

John Quincy's review of Howe's sermons, delivered the next day, was less kind. Of the "impious system" outlined by Howe, Adams objected most to the narrow and "ludicrous" path to salvation that Howe proposed: grace brought belief and hence salvation, *but* that grace was unobtainable by human will alone. What Howe lacked in clear logic, he apparently made up for with a dose of provocative rhetoric. For ten long minutes, Howe drew out what Adams sarcastically labeled an "elegant simile," in which "unregenerate" men savored heaven like swine romping through a palace. Though Howe brandished colorful examples with "a great degree of energy and Propriety," Adams thought the doctrine "opposite to common sense, as well as injurious to the supreme being." Beyond indulging in excessive oratorical flair, Howe's error, Adams wrote, was to carry the theme of man's innate depravity to an unreasonable degree. Once again, Adams used his diary to frame a query that echoed across his generation: What did all this New Divinity preaching mean for the future of American Protestants, who had been so often led by Massachusetts's pulpit stars? "If a Clergyman ventures, not to be quite illiberal," John Quincy wrote, "it is the most he can do."[68] The New England preacher's challenge, Adams concluded, was how to evolve a distinctively American Protestantism for republicans without appearing too Catholic. Liberal sentiments, as he acknowledged, faced an uneasy home in the national pulpit.

By closely evaluating New England religion, young John Quincy Adams refined his intellectual voice as a lay critic. He yearned for a political pulpit of his own to share those views. Emboldened by his initial wanderings, Adams embraced a new stage of religious development that coincided with his transition to husband, father, and professional diplomat. Given the range and scope of his intellectual seeking, the permanence of John Quincy Adams's own commitment to the "spark" of Unitarianism seems somewhat extraordinary in a period when Protestant denominations were rocked by evangelical revivals, the onset of church disestablishment, and bitter splits over slavery. Perhaps the puzzle is best explained by Adams's choice of profession and his inclination to represent American identity as part of a globalizing Protestant influence in nineteenth-century life. During his diplomatic mission in tsarist Russia, he and Louisa used Christianity to weather family tragedy, reconsider the Bible's lessons, and interpret the panorama of St. Petersburg's faiths.

For John Quincy and Louisa Catherine, their fledgling family's spiritual health centered on adhering to general Christian tenets, making it a microcosm of young America's struggle. When they were separated by the hardships of diplomatic travel, letters between husband and wife framed news of daily life around the "blessings of Providence" and lunges at understanding why God afflicted or blessed their small family.[69] Both trusted in an abiding and benevolent God. Each Adams turned to scripture for renewal when affliction roused symptoms of doubt. Largely representational of other citizens who struggled to sustain faith, John Quincy and Louisa were exceptional in where they worked through those issues: the imperial court of tsarist Russia.[70]

Between 1809 and 1815, events and experiences in Russia altered the Adamses' modes of religious practice and led them to write intimately on themes of faith and doubt. Often, Louisa and John Quincy were the sole Americans in a packed ballroom, made exotic by their republican politics and their Protestant-hybrid faith. Repeatedly, John Quincy pledged to be a "profitable" man to his family, mainly through the completion of American foreign service.[71] If, however, diplomacy heightened John Quincy's profile and expanded his religious tolerance, it did not always suit his wife's temperament. The glamor of life abroad took a physical and spiritual toll on Louisa. Her adherence to Protestantism, tinged with quasi-Catholic interest in Marian compassion and the holy virtue of motherhood, acted as a buffer to the aesthetic upheaval that Louisa felt in racing between cultures. "I assure you one of the greatest taxes I have to pay is that of concealing that I am a travelled Lady," she wrote.[72] Their joint depiction as both "profitable" and "travelled" paints John Quincy and Louisa as self-identifying cosmopolitans; in Russia, they learned to deepen their Christian practices, too.

Frequently, the young ambassador spent his New Year's Eve diary entries agonizing over who might improve the soul of John Quincy Adams more: Providence, or the man himself. When Louisa experienced a series of miscarriages—at least four in the first three years of marriage, all suffered abroad—the stress and agony of repeated disappointment caused them to seek out faith to heal. Another tragedy, the death of their infant daughter Louisa in St. Petersburg in the

John Quincy Adams (1767–1848). *Portrait by an unknown artist after John Singleton Copley, 1796, Adams National Historical Park*

fall of 1812, shattered much of John Quincy's mental world. Louisa's namesake was buried on Vasilevsky Island, a Lutheran cemetery for those not of the Russian Orthodox faith.[73] John Quincy could not fathom the providential reasoning that justified so many consecutive episodes of loss. His daughter's death upended Adams's highly intellectualized notions of what constituted good and evil. Her loss triggered some very direct questions in his diary about the kind of

Louisa Catherine Johnson Adams (1775–1852). *Portrait by Edward Savage, ca. 1791–1794, Adams National Historical Park*

God that let it happen. Grappling with the great ends of existence, as he saw in his grief, required a religious dexterity he had yet to achieve. More than once, Adams confessed that he was horrified by his shortcoming as a Christian who would not submit to divine judgment.

Inaugurating what became his characteristic way of coping with family tragedy, John Quincy Adams turned to Christian literature for solace. His poetic effort to address the problem of theodicy, titled "The Death of Children," relayed the sad event in ultra-Romantic imagery, describing the "silent shaft of death, / Which speeds an infant to the tomb."[74] Feeling melancholy and bitter, Adams turned to any and all forms of religion in St. Petersburg to seek peace from his "rebellion of the Heart." He was aware of how such private outbursts of emotion might be interpreted in an age of revival. When Adams looked over his diary, using it as a self-improvement manual of sorts, the Christian self that he saw emerging seemed less than ideal. "Religious Sentiments become from day to day more constantly habitual to my mind. They are perhaps too often seen in this Journal," he wrote. "God alone can make even Religion a Virtue; and to him I look for aid that mine may degenerate into no vicious excess."[75]

By contrast, Louisa's religious writings brimmed over with emotion, full of passionate punctuation ("!!!") and melancholy poetry dedicated to the family tragedies that she endured. Haunted by her daughter's death long after her stay in Russia, she wrote in 1812 that the "babes image pursues me where ever I go bitter reflection adds to my pangs and in religion alone do I find consolation."[76] In Russia, Louisa's role as wife and mother (of a splintered and often damaged family unit) cemented her religious personality. Louisa came to reject affiliations with "Romanism," but, like many American women, she aspired to spread the kind of "family love" that expanded into feelings of social communion—just the sort of "softer" image that a polarizing politician like Adams needed his wife to exhibit in public.[77] Louisa compared her plight to that of a Catholic martyr in search of "true religion."[78] Her providentialist theology of grace, she wrote, was "so simple so clear and so striking that the tawdry dress in which its precepts are sometimes taught to the publick by men who have mistaken their genius, almost always mortifies me as it casts a shade of ridicule on things in themselves the most sacred."[79] Certain that sustaining Christianity at home would guarantee a family reunion in heaven, Louisa sacralized her role as wife and mother.[80]

By John Quincy's generation, the Adams family was famous on two continents. Privately, between bouts of diplomatic service, they struggled to hold the family together. The multiple losses that John Quincy and Louisa suffered abroad led the former to redouble his efforts to instill Christian morality in their surviving children via a transatlantic program of Bible study. "Let us impress that . . . *Education* is the business of human life—that our religion is the religion of a book—and that the meaning of that book is intrusted by divine Providence to the deliberate judgment of our own understandings," he wrote.[81] John Quincy and Louisa felt that Christian nurture was, as the American theologian Horace Bushnell later advised, a way to ensure that the nation maintained a ready supply of godly help.[82] Eyeing the American future, Adams harbored "lively and confident . . . hopes" that his heirs would become "useful citizens to their country, respectable members of society, and a real blessing to their parents."[83]

The painful fact that Adams and his wife spent nearly six years separated from two of their sons did not excuse them from the task of Christian parenting. Dutiful reports from the distant boys, who were shuffled between aunts and uncles in Quincy and Atkinson, New Hampshire, hinted that their religious education was fitful at best. A throwaway line from one of George Washington Adams's letters in 1811, which reached his parents nine months later when the waterways melted enough to allow for mail, prompted great concern. His son's fondness for reading aloud Bible chapters to his elderly aunt was laudable, John Quincy wrote reprovingly, but it was not enough.

The remedy was vintage Adams. Over the course of the next two years, he issued a series of pedantic and personal *Letters on the Bible* describing how his sons should read scripture, when to apply its lessons, and why it merited special distinction in world literature. "No book in the world deserves to be so unceasingly studied, and so profoundly meditated upon as the Bible," he wrote.[84] Here, John Quincy was repeating his own parents' advice, and that of a generation that still relied on scripture as the point of departure for living a moral life. Nor was Adams alone in his quest to reinvent the Bible in popular understanding. The Bible, widely venerated by Americans as a cultural landmark, had attracted a fresh and vigorous round of interest.

Aside from arming Americans to build a Christian republic, there was another reason for the large-scale appeal of biblical inquiry. Among Protestants, Bible reading encouraged the converts who emerged from the Second Great Awakening and subsequent evangelical revivals, from about 1790 to 1840. At the same time, biblical inquiry offered new intellectual projects for the educated laity. President Thomas Jefferson scrap-booked his own version of scripture and created a homemade Bible, and Herman Melville reconsidered biblical themes to form the basis of his novel *Moby-Dick* (1851).[85] In Philadelphia and New York City, the Presbyterian lawyer Elias Boudinot began a campaign to raise the $10,000 he needed to found the American Bible Society in 1816.[86] The Romantic painter Washington Allston overlaid parables on quasi-American landscapes, while scholars—often Harvard-trained Unitarians just like John Quincy—tussled over how to use the Bible as a form of rational, scientific evidence.

His own mastery of biblical scholarship, Adams thought, was amateurish. Sometimes Adams could not find a decent copy to peruse during his travels, even in one of the five or so languages that he could read. And though he rose to study several chapters before breakfast, sometimes his attention slid away. "Sometimes I say to myself, I do not understand what I have read; I can not help it; I did not make my own understanding: there are many things in the Bible 'hard to understand,' as St. Peter expressly says of Paul's epistles," Adams acknowledged.[87] He cautioned his sons to persevere in the task. The Bible, as Adams lectured in his letters home, should be read in four ways: as divine revelation, as historical record, as evolving system of morality, and finally, as an unparalleled literary composition.[88] Further, the Bible provided several layers of history: universal, national, institutional, family, and individual. Rediscovering the Old and New Testaments with the intention of sharing them with his children, John Quincy found fresh illustrations to support his case that the Bible was "an invaluable and inexhaustible mine of knowledge and virtue."[89] He emphasized that the Sermon on the Mount held the most eloquent expression of Christianity's major tenets, including the principles of nonviolence, the Ten Commandments, the Beatitudes, and the Golden Rule. Writing from Russia, John Quincy Adams found special resonance in the history of Abraham, whose trials of character tested his obedience to God as he coped with a childless wife and the divine mandate to build a new nation.

Such was the religious life of the mind for John Quincy Adams in St. Petersburg, as he settled into marriage, fatherhood, and a high-profile diplomatic career. He had first traveled to the city as American agent Francis Dana's translator almost thirty years earlier, part of a failed mission to secure Empress Catherine II's recognition of American independence.[90] Now, as a professional diplomat, Adams keyed into religion to decode Russian culture and press ahead with trade talks. As the American minister labored over a commercial treaty with Alexander I, diverse religious rites captivated his interest, offering Adams a unique way to apprehend Russian civilization. In a three-month stretch, he sampled Sunday services, baptisms, weddings, funerals, and high holy days at a Catholic church, a Kazan church, and the English Factory Church (the Anglican outpost in St. Petersburg). Adams interviewed Greek Orthodox priests, curious as to how they calculated the date for Easter. He interrogated the Jesuit headmaster regarding the academic minutiae of schoolboys' curricula. He documented the retail operations at the "Frozen Market" near the Monastery of St. Alexander Nevsky, noting the commercial accommodations that merchants made for religious observance.[91] He recorded how various laity and clergy marked the life cycle, where the faithful buried their dead, what they wore to service, and the gestures of supplication that they used in prayer. No detail of how people "lived" religion in Russia escaped John Quincy's dogged capacity for scholarly curiosity or outright wonder. One of Adams's chief interests was how new Christians found their way to religion and whether the performance of ritual shored up belief in God. A generation later, his son Charles would seize on the same question, wondering what—if anything—outward shows of piety could "tell" of one's inner faith. John Quincy's rage to quantify varieties of religious experience coalesced in Russia, but it did not end there, and his own international celebrity began to change how Adams prayed.

After a brief stint in Paris to negotiate the Treaty of Ghent that ended the War of 1812, he and Louisa reunited with all their sons in London. The period that John Quincy spent there serving as American minister, from 1815 to 1817, was a relatively happy time. Living eight miles outside of London in the suburb of Ealing, the Adamses attended service at the newly repaired Anglican church of St. Mary's.[92] As a model of American life in miniature, the Adams family respected but largely evaded adopting British ways, seeking out dissenting traditions that challenged the established Church of England. The three Adams boys attended the local Presbyterian school and went to service at the nonconformist chapel there, too.[93] Following New England religious instincts, the Adams family preferred the Presbyterian service as an occasional nonconformist respite from Anglican life. Adams found Presbyterian worship to be nearly the "same form as that of our congregational churches," featuring one-hour sermons that he thought were "written in a very good plain style, and the delivery was above mediocrity."[94] He cast a critical eye on the Anglican pulpit, calling the St. Mary's preachers haughty and obsessed with preventing the "infection of Methodism." He loathed how Anglican clergymen spoke, dressed, and walked. With every step, he thought they conveyed "arrogance, intolerance and all that is the reverse of Christian humility."[95] Once again, Adams derided what he perceived to be manifestations of religious intolerance, lay malaise, and clerical overreach.[96]

In Ealing, the rising son of John Adams learned that his family name was one of the few American connections that most British citizens readily made, for better or for worse. John Quincy's efforts at Christian statesmanship, then, had to extend beyond the Court of St. James in an attempt to charm his reluctant small-town hosts. For the world-traveling Adams, some of his thorniest diplomatic work was excruciatingly local in scope, and it meant mending British perceptions of Americans by reminding them of a shared Protestant pedigree. In one of his frequent chats with John Quincy, St. Mary's elderly pastor, Colston Carr, nearly cited "the rebellion of the colonies" but (barely) reeled himself in before he could give offense. Carr "softened his expressions with an evident effort," Adams wrote, "and called it the time when America was throwing off the yoke."[97] John Quincy, in turn, worshipped at St. Mary's but grumbled privately about its practices: use of the Athanasian creed, lavish pine garlands hung after Advent, and the paltry ten parishioners who lingered after service to receive communion, or, "as they call it the most comfortable sacrifice of the body and blood of Christ."[98] As in Russia, Adams investigated the English holy days' impact on the local marketplace. Minutes after an "indifferent" crowd of Christmas worshippers shuffled out of St. Mary's, Adams wrote wonderingly, the bakers' shops of Ealing were "illuminated" and open for business.[99] An extravagant display of evergreens notwithstanding, John Quincy Adams was never fully persuaded that the daily actions of the Anglican faithful constituted any true Protestant piety.

In 1817, readying to serve as President Monroe's secretary of state and as an officer of the American Bible Society, a mature John Quincy Adams channeled his Christianity toward new beginnings in his native country. In Paris, he hastily purchased six small bronze busts as talismans of republican virtue. At the midpoint of his career, John Quincy had, seemingly, acquired the intellectual balance he craved between Christian instinct and republican ideal. He had married outside of his denomination, immersed himself in biblical scholarship, and surveyed foreign religion. If leaving America had allowed Adams to grasp for a fuller formation of his Unitarian faith, then returning home would test it. John Quincy Adams packed up his household gods and sailed for Boston.

American religion had undergone sweeping changes in his absence, as revolutions in transportation and communication reshaped a nation growing beyond its original boundaries.[100] An admixture of scientific rationalism and lingering providentialism still guided the minds of most Americans, but differences over slavery, party politics, and evangelical revival increasingly divided them.[101] The next major phase of John Quincy Adams's personal religious change centered on his very public production of Christian rhetoric to guide the fractured, industrializing nation. Between his return from Europe in 1817 and the end of his less than successful presidency in 1829, Adams infused political action with religious motivation by crafting a range of Fourth of July orations, town meeting speeches, and antislavery diatribes. Now adroit in adapting the language of Christian citizenship for any audience, John Quincy operated with more religious tolerance than had his Revolutionary forebears, and especially so on the page. He held fast to his belief that Protestant patriotism engendered pluralism and inquiry in ways that would make the nation flourish. Often, Adams rose to address a mechanics' hall or church picnic audience of increasingly diverse Americans who thought, as he did, that Christianity laid the groundwork for a good society, bolstered efforts at public education, and solidified the identity of Americans as God-fearing, hard working, and just.[102] Adams's longtime interest in deploying literature to share these views took a more serious turn. He began to write poetry that connected Christianity with the "wants" of American culture. In a bustling religious marketplace, poetry would offer John Quincy

Adams a rare haven to mull over Providence's plan and to pray for guidance.

Protestant Christianity prevailed in the early American republic, but there was a vast and exhausting set of varieties and practices for the returning Adams to either learn or relearn. Ever inquisitive, the secretary of state resumed his religious journeys. Now, as a prominent player in the federal arena, Adams struggled to balance his own beliefs with the social reality of divergent Protestant groups and to sample their miscellaneous offerings. Returning home had brought John Quincy's private days of religious musings to a sudden end; strangers easily recognized him and Louisa as they traveled through America. Once installed in Washington, DC, in 1817, Adams served as a trustee of the New York Presbyterian Church and purchased thirty pews to support the family's longtime Unitarian home in Quincy. Louisa kept an Episcopal pew as well at Christ Church Quincy and hosted "sociables" to benefit any number of Christian charities, orphan societies, and voluntary associations.[103] From 1818 onward, Adams served as vice president of the newly created American Bible Society. And, at least once, he drafted the cover letter that accompanied mass mailings of Bibles.[104]

Writing in Advent 1825, contending with a deeply bifurcated Congress and barely ten months into his own contentious administration, Adams used the borrowed pulpit to revisit some familiar Old Testament passages on leadership. There is no clear record of John Quincy Adams reading Friedrich Schleiermacher, but Adams employed messages that reflected the German theologian's high reputation among American scholars. Like Schleiermacher, Adams was intrigued by the dual nature of the human soul, where one "drive" ensnares experiences for personal pleasure, and a competing force "longs to extend its own inner self even further . . . while never being exhausted itself."[105] Adams, in turn, defined religion as the "first sentiment . . . . . . impressed . . . upon [the] Soul." That Christmas, voters held their free King James Bibles and read the new president's plea: to receive Solomon's "wise and understanding heart" from America's God.[106]

It was a tough era for John Quincy to endure, one where well-groomed, Harvard-educated statesmen like the Adamses lost their offices to a bumper crop of ambitious, mud-slinging politicos. Poetry helped. As he had done at Harvard and in Russia, Adams turned to literature to reckon with Providence's blurry plan for America and to cope with political disappointments, particularly his loss of a second presidential term in 1829. Just as historians hailed his rival Andrew Jackson as the symbol for an age, a politician who came to represent the introduction of the country's roughest and newest characters into power, so the literary figure of John Quincy Adams stands as the symbolic "pilgrim for an age." At least three of his poems open with pilgrims complaining of weakness, strife, or despair; all of them are perplexed about how to greet God. Adams's literary heroes share a narrative arc: they begin in distress, convene with Providence for aid, and end in thanksgiving. The peak of Adams's poetry writing occurred as he suffered three more sudden tragedies: the deaths of his father (1826) and his sons George (who died in a jump or a fall from a New York steamship in 1829) and John II (who died of complications related to alcoholism in 1834). Adams's own health began to fade, and he suffered a paralytic stroke in the late winter of 1846. Yet, among his prolific and talkative class of lawmakers, Adams's willingness to share the process of aging and to experiment with prayer in poetic form was wholly unique.

In a presidential career marred by nasty personal politics, writing poetry remained one of Adams's great joys. Usually he galloped ahead of his colleagues to set intellectual trends, but for once, Adams was merely following a wave of popular interest in Coleridgian Romanticism.[107] John Quincy, born along with the new nation in an era of literature that celebrated the excessive in tandem with the sublime, epitomized a Romantic generation that saw America as an unfolding adventure.[108] Much of the prevailing excitement over the nation's physical beauty and a desire to resurrect its Puritan past came across in the appreciative religious themes of Adams's poems. He was in good company. New England's prominent Unitarians shared his literary bent, giving rise to a theological controversy that dominated the emerging print culture.[109] Though he did not go so far as William Cullen Bryant or Henry David Thoreau in "worshipping in the woods," Adams's life of seeking convinced him of at least one of their conclusions: that sacred beauty was often found past the meetinghouse, in corners of everyday life.[110]

John Quincy Adams was not a natural poet, but he was a devotee of great literature. Ever a diligent student, Adam's torturous process of writing Romantic poetry showed him to be a fine mimic of the art.

His nuanced appreciation for the literature of antiquity shaped Adams into a gifted translator of the classics and won him the sobriquet "Old Man Eloquent" on the House floor, but few would have expected him to become a best-selling author of original verse.[111] As a diplomat in Prussia, Adams taught himself German by completing a full-scale translation of Wieland's *Oberon*. Later, Adams published a medieval epic in Byronic verse, *Dermot MacMorrogh, or, the Conquest of Ireland: An Historical Tale of the Twelfth Century, in Four Cantos*, which was popular enough to enter a third printing just before he died. He especially admired the "noble and magnificent sentiments" of Plutarch's *Lives* (so "Christian like" in scope, he thought, but marred by an "inattention to Chronology") and the human condition as Shakespeare framed it in *Hamlet*. Like his parents, John Quincy invoked lines from Pope's *Universal Prayer*, Milton's *Paradise Lost*, and anything by Dryden or Sterne. The sixth president went along with prevailing literary trends by composing pastoral odes to sundials, pretty young women, rainbows, and even a hot-air balloon, but a more serious love of the Psalms' melodic language drove his style. Poetry was an enjoyable linguistic maze for Adams to parse, and he approached writing it with all the rigid calculation that he once reserved for drafting his *Report upon Weights and Measures* (1821).

John Quincy Adams's contribution to the Unitarian renaissance was, as he knew, inescapably amateurish. As the president aged into a senior congressman, poetry was something he dashed off quickly with an autograph request; enclosing "a few lines" pleased both the hobbyist and his supporters. Some odes were lighthearted, like the verses he enclosed to son John II, advising him to "Keep Life's steamboat at low pressure."[112] When Adams really began writing in earnest, around the time of his failed reelection campaign in 1829, it was probably because he felt religious poetry to be both challenging and therapeutic. His "rubbish" books and miscellanies, filled with a fair amount of interlocking revisions, show how curled up in editorial anguish he could become over a single line of verse. Often, at first pass, Adams appeared frozen in the familiar writer's dilemma of word choice and, like the lawyer that he was, willing to argue from every angle. But a closer look at his acts of revision suggests that poetry served as the intellectual landscape in which Adams, through wrenching self-examination, puzzled out how to approach his Creator for help. One poem, frayed by endless rewrites, began, "My soul, before thy Maker, stand." Adams crossed out "stand" in favor of "kneel," then proceeded to reconsider his choice, on and off, for some time. When it finally appeared in print as part of *Poems on Religion and Society*, an anthology published shortly after his death, John Quincy Adams had, finally, opted to kneel.

Many worshippers of Adams's generation felt obliged to align religion with the republic, fearing that the national surge of material progress had incited a cultural riptide of immorality.[113] One of the most fascinating aspects of Adams's religious development was his headlong pursuit of an idealized Christian patriotism through the political, intellectual, and institutional channels of a national culture that was steadily ripening and opening to the world. The medium he chose, however, set John Quincy apart from his father. At the center of his poetry lay two themes, the significance of Christian fellowship and the search for American identity. In choosing to approach God as a pilgrim of nineteenth-century America, Adams weighed what form his pilgrimage should take in conjunction with civic duty. Adams's attempts to reconcile political issues with the personal questions that revolved around heartfelt religion were manifested in his poetry drafts. The process of creating poetry functioned as a kind of healing act for Adams, allowing him to re-encounter the young country's recent past and reframe it in a way that would make the republic's future feel less fragile. He marveled at the scientific and technological changes that the market revolution wrought, connecting new cities with railroads and opening lines of communication, but he worried about interpreting Christian responsibility for the American republic. With his political plans for vast internal improvements lying in shambles, it was hard for Adams to point to any real success derived from his agenda. By 1830, after a checkered presidency that saw Adams at war with his cabinet and Congress over efforts to modernize American life, his poetry reflected the trials of a Christian patriot refitting his faith for a republic in peril from forces within.

Preserving the American union was Adams's great cause, but it was difficult to do so when the existence of slavery grossly undermined the republic's lofty Christian ideals. Neither he nor Louisa owned slaves, but her sisters did, so political issues like the Missouri Compromise (1820) rippled through their vast family circle. John Quincy and Louisa were stridently antislavery, but their abolitionist leanings tilted only toward a vague consideration of Thomas Jefferson's derelict plan of education, gradual emancipation, and recolonization in Africa. Throughout the 1830s and 1840s, Adams's Unitarian conscience was tested repeatedly in Congress by legislative wrangling over slavery, Sunday mail service, and issues of public morality. It was most apparent when, from December 1835 to May 1836, the petitions he presented from constituents "praying" for local abolition of slavery intensified from eighteen to three hundred thousand.[114] Joining liberty of religion with the right of petition was a triumph for Adams, personally and politically. As his congressional service was repeatedly extended, the core belief that "good Christians make good citizens" continued to steer Adams through the growing disunion.

John Quincy Adams's successful intervention in 1841 in the case of fifty-three enslaved Mendi captives who had mutinied aboard the Spanish schooner *Amistad* stemmed from an inner crisis of Christian conscience. Aware that by representing them he took on prosecuting the entire slave trade, Adams labored over his nearly eight-hour closing argument to the Supreme Court. Alone with his omnipresent diary, Adams persuaded himself that the frailty of age must not hinder the Christian's siege against slavery. "No one else will undertake it. No one but a Spirit unconquerable by Man Woman or Friend, can undertake it, but with the heart of martyrdom," Adams wrote. "What can I do for the cause of God and man? for the progress of human emancipation? for the suppression of the African Slave-trade? Yet my conscience presses me on—let me but die upon the breach."[115] Writing proudly to family and friends, Adams marked his legal wins in the *Amistad* case and in overturning the gag rule as Christian victories. The *Amistad* crew, in turn, paid Adams's legal fees by giving him a Bible.

This was the kind of godly America that John Quincy navigated: scripture led him to make moral choices about the kind of case he took on, no matter the political fallout, and his Mendi clients knew enough to honor him by paying in scripture. Overall, John Quincy's vision of the rising American republic was powerful, Protestant, and prudent. Professing that the two keys to his political creed were internal union and independence from foreign exploitation, Adams blended his private religion with the national interest.[116] Or, as he put it in an 1837 poem: "Almighty father look in Mercy down, / Oh! grant me Virtues to perform my part / The Patriots favour and The Statesman's art." All of the American religious history that he knew filled out several more stanzas: a judicious (or judicial) Providence that favored this nation above all others, the ancient directive to men and women to refine Christianity through citizenship, and the expectation that heavenly reward depended on the fulfillment of republican duty. He titled it "A Congressman's Prayer." For John Quincy, as for his father's generation, Protestantism represented the first form of early modern nationalism, tethering citizens to their government with a moral cause to save it and a righteous God to guard it. The double yoke of Protestantism and patriotism gave Adams's career its force; writing poetry finally gave him the public grace he sought. In his last years of political life, Adams wrote poems that celebrated the Psalms and made prophecies to other "sons of the Pilgrims," prodding them to recall that a "Nation's living power" corresponded to its people's trust in divine mercy.

The poem for which Adams remains best known, "The Wants of Man," was published in 1841. This mass-market Christian parable coincided with Adams's most significant legal drama, the *Amistad* case. It represented a culmination of the poetic style and subject that Adams had begun rehearsing as a teenager in 1784, and it differed little from the other "album verses" he signed away daily to autograph seekers. His father had played with the same theme twenty years earlier, riffing to one Virginia senator, John Taylor of Caroline, that the "first Want of Man is his Dinner, and the Second his Girl." Such a scenario often led to "rash Marriages" and a "Chapter of Accidents," he warned. "The most religious," the senior Adams added, "very often leave the consideration of all these Wants to him who supplies the young ravens when they cry."[117] John Quincy's take was less snappy, and it was saturated in the melancholia of social ills (such as intemperance of spirit, or spirits) that afflicted various Adamses. Composing the twenty-five stanzas gave Adams a much-needed respite from turbulent congressional debates over slavery, the bequest to found the Smithsonian, and the collection of revenue. Throughout the spring and summer of 1840, the insomnia that Adams had suffered in Russia flared up again, so he kept writing.

D. O. M

To the Omnipotent, All wise, and good God

Walls.

Beneath these Stone

Are deposited the mortal remains of

John Adams.

Son of John and Susanna (Boylston) Adams.

Born 19/30 October 1735.

On the fourth of July

One Thousand seven hundred and seventy-Six

His life His fortune and his sacred Honour

He was One of the Founders of the Freedom

Of His Country.

On the fourth of July

One Thousand eight hundred and twenty-six

(was on The day of Jubile

Emancipated to the Freedom

(We Humbly Hope)

Of a Blessed Immortality.

He This Temple attests his Piety.

He was one of the founders of this Temple

& This Town his beneficence.

And a Benefactor of the his native Town.

At His Side
Sleeps till the Trump shall ~~sound~~ found.
Her only Wife.
Abigail, Daughter of William and Elizabeth (Quincy) Smith
Born 22. November 1744.
Deceased 28. October 1818.
In the Seventy fourth year of Her Age —

Of this Temple
He was a principal Founder
And otherwise a Benefactor of this his native Town.

United through Life
They are not divided in Death.
And to the virtues and Graces
Of the Christian Character
They joined a Spirit and Energy
Suited to the Trials of Their Age and Country
~~and worthy of the~~ ~~days~~
~~of Republican Rome~~
Roll — years of promise, rapidly roll round
Till not a Slave shall on this Earth be found.

Part of the family's public service meant deepening roots in their hometown church and embedding their legacy in local memory. John Quincy Adams, a tireless writer, labored to draft the text for the church's memorial plaques for his parents, John and Abigail, in 1829. *Adams Papers, Massachusetts Historical Society*

In June 1840, Frances Adline Seward, the influential wife of New York's governor, saw a final draft of "The Wants of Man." She sent it, with Adams's permission, to the editor Thurlow Weed. Weed published the poem in the *Albany Evening Journal* on September 3, 1841, and other newspapers rushed to reprint it.[118] Newly returned from his lecture tour "On Faith," the elderly Adams was delighted with his overnight success. The poem was a straightforward diatribe about vanity and greed, an exposition of his conscience indicting the sins of capitalist culture and excess.[119] Adams's rendition of human wants was seemingly endless. There were cashmere shawls, French cooks, marble mansions, "picture-garnish'd rooms," gold tureens, and "a printing press for private use." Adams longed for a wife "of temper sweet—of yielding will— / Of firm, yet placid mind," and a home of "wise and brave" boys and, poignantly, "chaste and fair" girls. His "Wants" ended with "the seals of power and place, / The ensigns of command, / Charg'd by the People's unbought grace, / To rule my native land."

Was the Christian patriot tallying up his life? If so, the pilgrim had found, in poetry, another way to weave his inner religious dilemmas into the fabric of the nation. Man would do well to consult his faith— that "natural and essential denomination of the human soul"—and to realize that the last great want of religion should be first, Adams wrote. As with any Romantic hero constructing the self from Puritan origins, Adams used poetry to reckon with his place in the universe and his relationship to God.[120] At the end of his life, John Quincy was well established in his theological beliefs but curious about how others came to their own parameters of justice, charity, and truth. As he traveled up and down the eastern seaboard in 1840, giving his lectures *On Faith*, Adams called for a widespread renewal of inquiry and a return to crusades of social justice. He urged listeners to make their own journeys through religious culture.

On February 21, 1848, John Quincy Adams took his usual seat in Congress and heard debates for an hour before the vote came up. He had opposed the motion on the floor—to commend victories in the Mexican War—and rose again to press his argument at a little past one o'clock. He suffered another stroke. Adams lingered in a coma in the Speaker's Room before dying two days later. "His own wishes are gratified," one newspaper reported of Adams's final hours, "for it was his wish to die in harness."[121] Americans closed in to mourn Adams's death with scenes of public pomp, shrouding the capital in black crepe and lining the streets for a glimpse of his silver-mounted coffin. A freshman congressman from Illinois, Abraham Lincoln, stepped forward to serve as a pallbearer. The sixth president's sole heir, Charles Francis, left his young family at the first word of his father's illness and hastened to Washington. Charles was concerned about the delicate health of Louisa, who lived for four more years. Delayed en route at the Philadelphia train depot, Charles circled a stranger reading a black-bordered newspaper, too nauseous to approach and confirm the breaking news.

As Washington mourned John Quincy, his family cast around for his successor, Charles. Gazing grief-stricken at his father's writing desk, still strewn with weeks of work—and reluctant to clear the statesman's last notes—Charles at first ran from the room. "The glory of the family is departed and I a solitary and unworthy scion remain overwhelmed with a sense of my responsibilities," Charles wrote in his diary, adding: "I am alone in the generation."[122] Dinner parties and sermons were given in the president's honor, and a stately funeral procession bore his body back to Quincy. Elegiac death notices swept through the cities. "The remarkable history of the Christian Statesman and honored Patriot, whose death the Nation now mourns throughout its length and breadth, should be speedily written," one editor advised.[123] State legislators passed resolutions praising John Quincy's legacy. The Supreme Court adjourned, executive offices were shuttered for two days, and army regiments wore crepe on the left arm and on their swords for the next six months. After the Unitarian William Parsons Lunt, then the minister of Quincy's First Church, eulogized Adams's sacrifice "upon the altar of his country and his God," he directed the pallbearers to "rise up, and take these remains of the patriarch, and bury him with his fathers. There may he rest in peace until the resurrection of the last day."[124]

Six years after his death, John Quincy Adams began to speak again. This, at least, was the belief of Josiah Brigham, a self-described "modern spiritualist" and a long-standing member of Adams's own family church. The popular resurrection of John Quincy in many ways reflected the desire of American Christians to seek God in esoteric places without completely deserting traditional churches. The cultural shift in who led these experiments signaled a sea change in American religious authority; leading seances gave women a greater public speaking role as well as a new platform to discuss politics and propose church/state reforms. When Brigham's wife showed interest in the dead (and less popular) sixth president, people listened—and printed what they heard. Brigham had attended John Quincy's funeral, had even funded publication of Lunt's sermon. As his spiritual interactions with Adams's memory attest, Brigham fit the mold of progressive-minded, industrializing Americans who used spiritualism to apply moral order to the chaos of market society.[125]

Brigham took a special interest in cultivating Adams's afterlife. He knew Adams from summers in Quincy. Well respected in the Congregational community, Josiah Brigham traced his family line back to 1634 in Cambridge, Massachusetts. His estate sat between Northborough and Westborough and offered a stunning view of Little Chauncey Pond. By the time Josiah inherited it, two hundred years of Brighams, five successive generations, had worked the same land. For his father, a Revolutionary War veteran, a good farm represented the pinnacle of Christian success and the lifeblood of republican community. The young Josiah disagreed. In this way, his thinking was very much in step with that of his peers. Since 1815, the market revolution had changed men's and women's paths for professional fulfillment and heightened their expectations.[126] The crumble of patriarchal authority and, with it, notions of how Revolutionary fathers passed along lands or creeds to their sons, reshaped Josiah's generation.[127] Formally, Brigham adopted the family religion of Congregationalism, but he did not stop his seeking there.

Although Josiah Brigham's intellectual travels were not as wide as those of John Quincy Adams's, he represented the archetype of the industrializing New Englander. Brigham taught in a series of Massachusetts public schools and spent the War of 1812 as a Light Infantry volunteer encamped at South Boston. On returning home, Brigham again turned away from agricultural life, this time favoring the "mercantile pursuits" that suddenly felt more attuned to the needs (and profits) of the modernizing nation. By the time of Adams's death, he had risen to impressive heights of civic leadership: chairman of the General Schools Committee, clerk and treasurer of the new and powerful Quincy Canal Corporation, trustee and president of the Board of Investment of the Quincy Savings Bank, and president of the Quincy Stone Bank. Massachusetts governor Edward Everett, who was Charles Francis Adams's brother-in-law, personally selected Brigham to serve as a justice of the peace. Much as John Quincy himself wished to be portrayed, one of Brigham's biographers recalled him as "frank and affable," a "Christian gentleman" who was ever mindful of religious duty and never missed communion. The central Christian lesson to draw from Brigham's life was that "the honorable pursuit of wealth and outward reputation" came only from forming "a character strong in integrity and in that fear of the Lord which is the beginning of wisdom."[128] In a country bedeviled by fears of "Mammon" and the onset of "Christian" wealth—an issue that Charles Francis Adams would battle privately—Josiah Brigham had transformed himself into a model merchant-prince of a *new* New England.

In the early 1850s, the Quincy businessman began hosting private seance circles at his estate to entertain his wife and daughter, who were both "rapping and tipping mediums."[129] Through his web of civic connections Josiah Brigham was always meeting new people, and in June 1854, he made the acquaintance of a "respectable, unassuming young man, of only common-school education, with no pretensions to more than common capabilities." This was Joseph Dutton Stiles, who quit his job as a printer when he "perceived he possessed mediumistic powers," and eventually became a well-known spiritualist.[130] Stiles quickly impressed Brigham by contacting the spirit of the banker's dead brother; then he moved on to the "Sixth Sphere" of the "Spirit Land," where Stiles claimed to encounter John Quincy Adams. According to Stiles's book *Twelve Messages from the Spirit of John Quincy Adams*, Adams took six hours to transform from his physical body and to get his bearings in the celestial plane, his "new sphere of duty." Greeted by his parents and John Hancock, Adams discovered a "celestial telegraph" that allowed him to communicate with the living through mediums, and to control their thoughts via quasi-poetic messages of Christian fellowship. Adams even visited the Brigham family home, identifying its green expanse of farm and sparkling pond.

A pageant of historical figures moved through the scenes, occasionally colliding: Salem witches and Christopher Columbus, Patrick

Henry and Benedict Arnold, enslaved children and early Pilgrims. In a late twist, Stiles's iteration of Adams indicated that heaven was not what he expected, warming to the theme of organized religion as defective and misleading. Adams condemned churches as antiquated institutions that had built up "sectarian platforms" and had not "met the spiritual exigencies of the people."[131] A foray into the "Temple of Peace and Good-Will" with William Penn, Martha Washington, Shakespeare, Hannah More, Jane Grey, Empress Josephine, and Peter Whitney managed to resolve many of Adams's doubts about human nature. A hovering circle of spirits (Thomas Jefferson, Alexander Hamilton, Aaron Burr, and Israel Putnam in that order) descended in the semifinale to bless "Spirit-life, one grand reception day."[132] The rest of the book contained similar adventures of John Quincy Adams in the afterlife as he met Napoleon, debated Confucius, and joined in an impromptu jubilee for emancipated slaves.

Bizarre as it may sound, *Twelve Messages* may be the best testament to John Quincy Adams's appreciation for religious culture; surely few people would have enjoyed reading it as much as he would. Here was his faith bounded and unbounded, American pilgrims and European heretics, Unitarian clergy and Congregationalist counterparts, Calvinist forebears and a generation of free blacks. Adams's religious conscience was just as crowded and his place in American life just as curious. During his stints as ambassador, secretary of state, president, and US congressman, Adams remained committed to the projection of America as a Christian commonwealth. Human will forged belief, Adams argued, and that sense of belief formed the Christian faith needed to counter man's trials. Faith, he concluded, was a "natural and essential denomination of the human soul."[133] Scion of a famous family rooted in New England Congregationalism, Adams has frequently come across in American history exactly as he (correctly) feared colleagues would describe him: cold, awkward, and Calvinist to the core.[134] Yet in reading the nation's leader as an important social historian of religion, we see that Adams's intense pursuit of religious exchange suggested greater stirrings of liberalism within Protestant life, too. As a young man, he borrowed his father's copy of the Marquis de Condorcet's *Outlines of the Progress of the Human Mind* and likely saw the marginal commentary scribbled there, "Philosophers must arrive at perfection *per saltum*." The making of John Quincy Adams's religion happened in much the same way, by a leap or a jump.

How and why John Quincy Adams came to define and redefine religion matters deeply, because often the form of worship that he attended was not his own. Throughout the first three decades of his career he led what he called a "wandering life" through The Hague, Prussia, St. Petersburg, Paris, and London—all sites largely bereft of opportunities to hear Unitarian preaching. When Congress was in session, the chaplains who shaped Adams's moments of reflection between debates were rarely clergy of his own denomination. As a statesman and, later, as an antislavery firebrand, John Quincy valorized political office as the epitome of a Christian patriot's service to Providence. Throughout a contentious career, Christian thought and practice refitted Adams with the moral armor he needed to persevere in politics and to persuade the American public that the work of nation-building must continue. Like other Unitarians, John Quincy enjoyed testing theologies within the dual fields of experience (party politics) and art (Romantic poetry). He was the rare American president who wrote poetry, mainly to interrogate or reinforce his religious beliefs. While he found theological hermeneutics little more than an academic hobby, he was captivated by the world's variety of religious cultures. Though he and other Unitarians were most at home in a faith that, by the Civil War, was snidely described as centered in "the fatherhood of God, the brotherhood of man, and the neighborhood of Boston," Adams's cosmopolitanism set him apart.[135]

As America's sixth president moved through diverse religions, he tried out new language, including poetry, to narrate his pilgrimage. The story of John Quincy's religious life shows the limits of education in early America; his midlife mission, in Russia and elsewhere, to record foreign religions and promote Christian statesmanship; and the literary crusade he undertook to embed Protestant values in American minds. Along with other Americans, John Quincy Adams moved from a theological system that emphasized an elect community of the "saved" to one favoring experiential, individualistic works of grace, born of free will, as the key to salvation. Over time, John Quincy came to care less about using religion for self-perfection and far more about harnessing its social power to defeat "national sins" such as slavery. A lifelong

Unitarian, he set aside demands for evidence of miracles and cautiously embraced the notion of a "superhuman"—but not necessarily divine— view of Jesus.[136]

John Quincy Adams's life was filled with unique trials—children and siblings horribly lost, friendships worn thin by his political principles, and a vicious presidential election race—but in terms of religion, he remained both curious and firm. Eager to explore faiths beyond his Unitarian comfort zone, he embodied the civic humanism that piloted the post-Revolutionary generation.[137] Adams believed in sacrificing self-interest for the greater national good. "A man without religion can never have a very strong feeling of humanity," he wrote in an echo of his mother, Abigail, "nor can one truly be religious without it."[138] Gaining God's forgiveness, and doing so in the eyes of his constituency, became Adams's paramount goal as a Christian patriot. Issues relating to doctrine and denominational identity receded from significance. Religion, Adams declared, was "one of the *wants* of human nature—an appetite which must be indulged, since without its gratification human existence would be a burden rather than a blessing. . . . I cannot reject a doctrine merely because my reason will not sanction it."[139] Often, John Quincy self-identified as the friendly American stranger in a foreign pew, glad to "cheerfully join in social worship with all others willing to receive me in Communion with them."[140]

In their own ways, John Quincy and Louisa Catherine Adams grappled with a shared set of concerns about Christianity's social power and moral authority. On the whole, they were early adopters of the social language and middlebrow literature of nineteenth-century religious liberalism.[141] They reshaped ideas of "godly community" to suit American congregations transformed by sectarian unrest, industrial growth, a burgeoning immigrant population, and the resurgence of evangelical orthodoxy.[142] Reimagining John Quincy Adams at prayer—his private moments of doubt and public messages of faith— illuminates the evolution of the Unitarian conscience in a transitional era that emphasized free will, toleration, and biblical inquiry. Like other liberalizing Protestants, the Adamses combined faith and good works to advance on the widening path to salvation. Holding fast to the Reformation-era legacy of the priesthood of all believers, John Quincy and Louisa molded Christianity into a minimalist set of core teachings that respected Providence, encouraged morality, and upheld the natural order.[143] Overall, they came to champion a universal "religion-of-humanity" model.[144]

Near the end of his life, in the autumn of 1844, John Quincy settled into Pew 54 of the family's Unitarian home church and listened to William P. Lunt preach on how a troubled soul might reconnect with God.[145] The sermon, while "ingenious and impressive," Adams wrote, was too long for his taste. On Sundays like this, when Adams could not shake off the "cares of the world" before receiving communion, he grew reflective. He let his mind drift, past the gray-white republican columns lining the congregation's familiar pews. Sitting in church but again striking out on his own path of religious exploration, Adams reminisced on the course of his spiritual development. When he imagined his own religious autobiography, John Quincy Adams recalled what first guided his steps of religious inquiry away from Quincy. "My soul was like one of those Sheets of antient parchment," Adams reflected, "upon which a poem in monkish rhyme is written over an Oration of Cicero."[146]

3

Charles Francis Adams on Pilgrimage

ON A MAY MORNING IN 1843, Charles Francis Adams handed over his $1.50 fare in a Boston railroad car. Charles, a thirty-six-year-old lawyer and aspiring man of letters, rattled alongside New England roads that would have looked strikingly different and greener a decade earlier. A new set of landmarks—textile mills, tollgates, turnpikes, and clusters of suburban development—now sped by. Cutting the old four-hour stagecoach commute to Worcester in half, the train bore Adams in the first-class carriage, wage laborers in the second-class seats, and a sizable load of freight: everything from manufactured goods due for sale in New York City and Providence, to horses, iron, and mail bound for the South and West.[1] Adams's destination was a prime example of young America's explosive industrial expansion and commercial growth. Thanks to the newly completed Blackstone Canal, an influx of Irish Catholic workers, and the birth of wire-making and industrial firms, Worcester epitomized the rising antebellum metropolis.[2] Hardly relegated to the Boston backwater where Charles's grandfather John was "condemnd to keep School," Worcester citizens of the 1840s presented new scholarship at the American Antiquarian Society, propelled their local representatives into the Massachusetts governor's chair, and debated such national topics as abolitionism and temperance reform.[3]

Despite massive internal improvements, New Englanders still followed the same spring calendar as their colonial forebears. They scheduled their annual benevolent association meetings for the end of May, just as the General Court wrapped up business and adjourned for the summer.[4] At the city's heart, marking the crossroads of three rail lines, lay a low-slung, wooden depot made festive with floral garlands and swags of evergreen. Still lacking a real ticket office, the Worcester depot was the principal venue for major gatherings like the one that Adams had traveled to attend, hosting events for a thousand people in an upstairs hall as the trains rumbled and braked below. Along with eight hundred other prominent churchgoers and clergymen, he filed into the Unitarian "collation," an annual day of feasting, hymnals, and oratory held to honor denominational works and to broadcast piety. It was a fairly new tradition, just a few years old.[5]

Six dutiful hours later, Charles left, dubious of the event's religious payoff. Only recently, he had resumed church attendance after a hiatus from the Unitarian fold, reasoning that "setting apart one day from secular work . . . leads to great improvement of the mind and the affections."[6] Alongside many Victorian Americans, Charles diagnosed in himself the signs of a budding secularism, one that might ruin the republic or denote a surge in widespread religious liberation.[7] Charles was not sure what to make of it. Skeptical gentlemen scholars including Adams hesitated, intellectually and emotionally, when it came to swallowing whole any Christian doctrine. Instead, Adams and the rest of the American gentry tested out secular (mostly Romantic) methods to investigate the dilemmas of self and society that religion no longer resolved.[8] Proclaiming New England Christianity with flowers and speeches at the local depot, Adams thought, was no proof of the piety they used to cope with the deeper changes of an industrializing age. "It was a very curious spectacle and singularly illustrative of New England manners," he wrote of the day's exhibition. "I think all the peculiarities of the character of our people were visible here. Their good nature and their stiffness, their quiet domestic feelings and kind hearts with their utter deficiency in the elegance of life. As soon as I decently could, I escaped from a scene in which my greatest surprise was to find myself."[9]

When it came to religion, Charles Francis Adams often felt like an awkward observer. In history and in his own day—painfully so—Charles was often noticed but rarely seen. Son and grandson of great men, he clung to their Providence for comfort. Religion remained a constant, but cultivating a worldly Christianity became his goal. Inner piety, not pew time, mattered most. "I am not one of those who think that religion is to be formed in particular places alone," he wrote.[10] Diplomatic duty led him through foreign Christianities. Back in Quincy, Charles's travels to and from the family church epitomized generational tensions between local faith and experimental practice.[11] Ostensibly the ideal Christian republican, Charles was locked in a lifelong battle for belief. The pilgrimage he undertook on that spring day in 1843—traveling to a rote performance of Unitarianism and voicing his doubts aloud—indicated a new dividing line between the generations in the field of worship and dissent.[12] How had American Christianity been "made strange" to New England's native son?

Charles Francis Adams was born in Boston in 1807 and raised as a citizen of the world, first babbling in French and then perfecting his English in letters to grandmother Abigail.[13] His changeling childhood, spent in Tsar Alexander I's palace and in the middle-class suburbs of Georgian London, did not wholly prepare him to grasp the "New England manners" that framed his faraway brothers' adolescent years. Sickly and nervous, John Quincy and Louisa Catherine's third son was an unlikely heir apparent to the Adamses' political dynasty, yet the pair cultivated him for public service from an early age. At age two, Charles made his diplomatic debut in the "Savage" dress of a Native American chief, opening a Russian costume ball with another toddler on his tiny arm.[14] At eight, "white-faced," he braved the overland passage from St. Petersburg to Paris with his mother, evading Napoleon's resurgent forces on a forty-day, two-thousand-mile haul through the Russian winter of 1814.[15] When he reunited with his older brothers in London a year later, Charles was a relative stranger to the two loud "Yankee" teenagers who shared his surname. He had little in common with them, especially in terms of religious upbringing. For the first decade of his life, Charles's sole interactions with the family faith of American Unitarianism came either from outdated books or from his father's close instruction.

As a transnational teenager, Charles leveraged his education to nurture a wary pluralism. Charles tried "to act as becomes a member of a high family," as he put it, but he was certain that, as a third son, even his most promising path did not lead as far as the White House doors.[16] It was far more likely, Charles thought, that he would serve as a Massachusetts senator or as a literary man, mining his education to steer the new republic's progress. "I do not expect to make a very great figure in the world," Charles observed. "I cannot get over my dislike to the idea of a political existence. It shackles the independence of mind and feeling which I have always perhaps extravagantly admired, and in this Country it destroys all social ties."[17]

Charles devised the eclectic education that he needed for his future role as another "Christian in heart and life" bound to serve the nation.[18] And, just as his father had done, he completed much of it abroad. Charles studied first with Russia's resident corps of itinerant Jesuit and Orthodox faculty, then attended a Presbyterian boarding school in suburban England. After returning to America in 1817, Charles deviated from the usual Protestant education of his peers, blurring old denominational lines in order to maximize his opportunities for intellectual growth. After a two-year stint at the Boston Latin School, Charles enrolled in the Washington, DC, school of George E. Ironside, a former Episcopal priest and a prominent convert to Roman Catholicism.

As a literary mentor—and Adams's first real teacher on American shores—the Catholic Ironside proved formative to Charles's long-term intellectual habits. Ironside's change of faith made news in the capital, especially once he began advertising the idea that it was "more convenient to live a Protestant, but safer to die in the Catholic church."[19] The Adamses, long accustomed to public battery in the newspapers, did not care about Ironside's colorful press. John Quincy hired him as an undersecretary and Spanish translator for the US Department of State, awarding the Scot an annual salary of $1,750.[20] The new Georgetown Jesuit's second wife, two sons, and three daughters were favorite fixtures at Louisa Catherine's high-end "sociables" and elsewhere on the capital scene.[21] Ironside's small school next to the Treasury office became a second home for Charles.[22] Under the unconventional Ironside's guidance, Charles flourished. His Greek improved. He started and kept up commonplace books of poetry and law.[23] In the early republic, Ironside prospered as a unique figure in religion and politics alike. He was an Aberdeen native handling sensitive documents of American foreign policy; an Episcopal chaplain whose biblical inquiry led to Catholic conversion; and a family man who chose Jesuit life but squired his wife to Washington galas.

The rare example of George Ironside, a Christian republican entrusted with the highest duties of the nation and at least two churches, confirmed to Charles that Protestant tendencies (that is, inquiry) did not always culminate in a commitment to Protestantism. To Charles, the ability to distinguish the finer nuances of beliefs held by his string of Protestant, Orthodox, and Catholic instructors mattered little. Thanks to a polyglot band of tutors, and just in time to enter Harvard's halls, Adams built up a generous definition of what constituted "real" or "useful" Christianity. Early on, Charles Francis Adams arrived at his lifelong credo: "Theology is not religion."[24]

Charles was not alone in modifying his religious views to retrofit intellectual pursuits, and, as with past Adams alumni, his Harvard years were crucial to his next stage of development. "Journeying toward liberalism" with other early Victorians who evinced an all-purpose Christian "worthiness" over denominational dogma, Charles joined his brothers in Cambridge, in 1821, at the heart of the nation's Protestant establishment.[25] Largely unrivaled in the realms of faculty, books, and scientific equipment, Harvard College was where the worldly American came to learn. Harvard's religious ecosystem played an important role in Adams's youthful formulation of faith and doubt. There, the prim young man learned more about Christianity and temperance. He showed some tolerance to religious ideas, though he never warmed up to the people who spread them.

To a degree, the household gods still set the curriculum. From Mondays to Saturdays, metaphysics and natural philosophy filled the hours after morning prayer—except when Charles overslept "shamefully" often and skipped that rite in the campus chapel.[26] When he did make it to one of President John Thornton Kirkland's sermons, Adams's focus drifted off. "I sunk into my usual apathy and was conscious of nothing passing before me," Charles wrote of church services at Harvard.[27] He spent afternoons rotating between lecture topics in Protestant theology, oratory, algebra, and classical literature. Beside him, a charcoal sea of Oxford-suited peers labored away at Homer's *Iliad*, William Enfield's *Institutes of Natural Philosophy, Theoretical and Experimental* (1783), William Paley's *Principles of Moral and Political Philosophy* (1785), Cicero's *De Officiis*, and the political essays of John Locke. Charles excelled at history and literature, and little else. He had a "meditative mind" made for prose, along with the Adams stubbornness for stomaching orthodox instruction. "Charles must teach himself all that he learns," John Quincy wrote wearily. "He will learn nothing from others."[28]

Even as he toiled through ancient church history in class, Charles's attention to personal religion was lackluster. Though he did not journey into doubt as fully as his son Henry would, Charles was an openly apathetic Christian. In 1823, packing for a Christmas sojourn to visit his parents in Washington, DC, for example, young Adams received his fall test results and deemed them fair. He did not linger at Harvard for final word of another grade: his theology exam, which consisted of a written analysis of Paley's tenets, and which Adams was sure he had flunked. He stood fifty-first in a class of fifty-nine and had already tried to talk his way out of a mathematics requirement.

The sheer tedium of studying theology was a particularly sore point with Adams.[29] "I know full well I am no zealous disciple of that school," Charles wrote flatly. "It is not a subject which interests me."[30] Rather, the president's son studied just enough doctrine to pass his classes. He showed up for just enough church services to satisfy expectations. There, following in his forebears' habits, Charles evaluated his religious instructors' oratory. Adams had formed his first religious memories in the grand cathedrals and private boys' schools of Europe. By contrast, New England Unitarianism felt foreign and sounded quaint. But, fated to follow in the family footsteps of public service, Charles knew he could not afford to separate himself outwardly from a mass of God-fearing voters. Admittedly, Charles never learned or appreciated theological distinctions because he did not foresee a career in the pulpit.

Theology and ritual did not attract the awkward young man, but people who professed religious ideas casually—along with those who "canted" doctrine from a pulpit—intrigued him. Charles had a broad spectrum of American Christianity to sample. The Protestant ministers who preached to Adams and his friends sounded nationalistic and highly competitive about what shape a Christian America should take. Jacksonian-era clergy scrambled to reassert social authority and to shore up their cultural relevance. Overall, ministers crusaded with the intent of recruiting laity to serve as ardent reformers.[31] Throughout the 1820s and 1830s, the clergy blamed Native Americans for cholera outbreaks, issued myriad fast and thanksgiving proclamations, and blasted the Bostonians who tasted the exotic "Romanism" of Catholicism. The Adams family faith took a hard hit in the religious marketplace, too: following the evangelical fervor of the Second Great Awakening, led by such dynamos as Timothy Dwight, Francis Asbury, and Charles Grandison Finney, Unitarians' longtime growth wavered while the Baptists and Methodists claimed ground.

Charles and his peers rebelled against the insular nature of *all* ministerial authority when it came to constructing their worldview. Charles, who studied the law but dreamed of a literary career, focused on criticizing pulpit oratory and rhetoric. He sidelined cumbersome theological details. Charles's early sermon notes tallied a minister's rating based on two criteria: Was he a memorable speaker? How did he use scriptural and social evidence to convey his argument? Adams found most visiting Protestant missionaries "arrogant," and, in his private journal, he relished puncturing the swollen reputations of clergymen such as Henry Ware, Ralph Waldo Emerson, and even Harvard's leader, John Thornton Kirkland. Ware he found "highly Metaphysical" and "rather too demonstrative." Charles did "not much like any of the Emerson family," all talented theologians who made, he thought, for "haughty" and weak orators. Adams, further disgusted by what he saw as the provincial clergy's "undue" emotional manipulation of laity, wrote that "there is nothing so wicked to me as to make religion a cover for exciting the passions of the people as there is nothing which can more easily be done and which done, has more pernicious effects."[32]

The reading list and pulpit critiques may have looked familiar, but this was hardly the same Protestant education in godly republicanism that so many Adams ancestors had endured.[33] Rather, Charles's experience at Harvard was of a New England institution in transition. As admission criteria broadened, the college inaugurated an array of "beginner" classes in the arts and sciences. At the same time, it wooed alumni to return as "resident graduates" to undertake advanced study at no cost.[34] The school was eager to bridge gaps in American culture, for the old "New England ways" were in flux.

Beyond Harvard's walls, Charles's America was a nation weighing how to work and pray. Coming of age in the decades when state lawmakers disestablished Congregationalism in Massachusetts, Charles met an industrializing nation riven by physical and spiritual change.[35] Americans' attention was split between dueling arenas of "God and Mammon," producing an evangelical hive of social upheaval and industrial invention. As cities rose, Protestant sects grew diverse and diffuse. The individualistic drive of the market revolution had begun in 1815 and (quite literally) gathered steam over the succeeding decade, minting a batch of freethinking, self-made men and women. In turn, Charles's Jacksonian-era peers strove to fire up and refuel national networks. They funneled tax money, once allotted to clergy, into the industrial endeavors and civic associations that they planned on a new, interurban scale. They kept building steeples, but they also laid down railroads, carved out canals, and set up cities. As they refined the "godly" gifts of Puritan heritage, citizens wondered if America was to become the promised land where, as John Quincy Adams envisioned it, "the race of mankind is advancing towards perfection; where deserts are turning into villages, and forests into cities."[36]

Charles grew up in an era of American life when old providentialist promises of prosperity seemed to be made manifest in the rising traffic of diverse peoples, ideas, and goods. As Charles observed, new modes of transportation and communication improved prospects for rapid intellectual exchange. In 1820, Americans ventured down the Ohio and Mississippi Rivers on 89 steamboats; by 1840, some 536 steamboats jammed the same waterways, carting bulk goods such as cotton and grain at cheaper freight rates.[37] In his "bourgeois republic," literacy bloomed, followed by rising enrollment in higher education. In 1820, Adams and other savvy readers got their news from twelve hundred daily and weekly papers; by 1835, that figure had more than doubled. Trains connected readers, ferrying ideas that upended rural New England's fabled quiet as they tore through each hamlet. The Gothic allegorist Nathaniel Hawthorne, vacationing in Sleepy Hollow, New York, eyed the train's approach—"shrieking . . . comes down on you like fate, swift and inevitable"—with queasy glee. "How much life at once has come into this lonely place!" Hawthorne wrote, echoing Americans' collective shudder and thrill at the change. Such phenomenal progress ignited spiritual concern. How (if at all) did a "railway nation" hail God?

Caught in the press of change, Americans took stock of their Christianities. Eighteenth-century revolutionary life had led families to experiment with different modes of piety and morality, but now industrial demands altered their religious goals. Preserving a Christian America, as Charles and others acknowledged, required at least the appearance of a unified front to combat the rampant "sins" introduced and proliferated by industrialization and urban growth. As the founding fathers of John Adams's generation died out, Americans tried on "selves" that were more flexible to the fluctuations of market society, and to an expanding arena of denominations.[38] "My ideas upon the subject of the Christian Religion are very vague and have compelled me to this," Charles wrote of his diary-keeping, where he led a lifelong search for the "right bent."[39] In many ways, his journal reflects the myriad spiritual wanderings of a generation that, in line with the Unitarian periodical of record, preferred the label of "Christian examiner" as they adapted theology to fit with new urban realities.

For Charles and his peers, the project of shaping a new middle-class morality took several forms, contouring Christianity to ensure that their behavior kept to the "right bent." Challenging traditional ministerial authority, they revised old philosophies of right and wrong. Working within the Protestant and Catholic traditions, the American laity devised a set of Christian solutions meant to resolve the growing list of communal ills. Banding together in tract societies and mutual-aid groups, women and men (often in that order) vied to counter the social sins of intemperance and "ungodly" behavior bred by city life. Everywhere Charles turned, Christian rhetoric crept into the mix. A popular pantheon of women authors—including the Adamses' New England neighbors Louisa May Alcott, Harriet Beecher Stowe, and Julia Ward Howe—infused the literature of the day with parables of fallen ministers and deathbed scenes of pious triumph. Abolitionists addressed biblical justifications for slavery. Utopian pioneers promoted communal living as stewardship of the earth. Sabbatarians upheld the sanctity of Sunday as a day of prayer safe from congressional activity, mail delivery, and profiteering merchants.[40] Charles Francis and his early Victorian peers grew up in an American Christian environment that was republican, reform-minded, and experimental.

For all of young Charles's purported moral superiority, the Adams family circle was not immune to the same sins of intemperance and ungodly behavior that troubled life in the early republic. Two of his uncles—including Thomas, who controlled his inheritance and the Adams estate—suffered from alcoholism. Charles's brothers, John II and George, would succumb, too, by 1834. Charles's Christian neighbors in Boston had a long and contradictory history of suppressing intemperance. In fact, his grandfather John once attempted (fruitlessly) to map out and ban Braintree's taverns.[41] Wider social efforts to curb drinking were, in turn, constrained by mixed messages among reformers; Massachusetts's first temperance society, for example, served wine at most of its meetings.[42] Charles's lack of sociability at first protected him from his brothers' predilection for partygoing. But in the spring of 1824, a teenage Charles was eager to shake off his studies, especially the months-long assigned reading of Johann Lorenz von Mosheim's *Ecclesiastical History*, which he called a doorstop of "dull doctrine."[43] Charles's small circle of Harvard friends supplied entertainment, usually in the form of late-night singing parties and roving card games that crisscrossed the college yard, fueled by cheap wine. Cambridge residents and Harvard presidents took these improprieties somewhat seriously. Since the school's inception in the seventeenth century, a few legions' worth of clergy and lawyers (all on the cusp of a gentlemanly graduation) had incurred large fines for drinking, smoking, or breaking glass.[44]

Charles, more reserved than his peers and slightly priggish, rarely joined in Harvard's binge nights of student mayhem. On May 14, he awoke to a mystery ailment: headache, nausea, disinterest, melancholia. Huddled in his dormitory room, Charles leafed through some family favorites (Voltaire, Laurence Sterne's *Sentimental Journey*) for comfort, then threw aside the "lame poetry" that he read there. Adams could not diagnose the root of his illness, beyond the two bottles of "champagne wine" he drank the night before—a new habit that, he confessed, caused his "blood to be in a heated state." The hungover Charles, naive to the scientific links between alcohol and health, made an interesting vow. "Indeed if I do not feel better I have made up my mind to ask leave of absence from the President for the rest of the term," he wrote. As the day wound down, and Adams improved, he made one more uncharacteristic choice. Charles took out his Bible. He read two chapters, straight through, "for the first time for a great while," he wrote in his diary. "I do not recollect having read one before for three or four years."[45] He sketched out his own Christian temperance plan, deciding that one night's error merited a course of self-reform.

For Charles and many of his Anglo-American peers, then, Christian examination began at home. The primary texts of young Charles's religious life became the Bible and his own diary. Charles's close maintenance of his journal was the act that linked his "writing self" to his "reading self." After the 1824 debacle, he resumed daily Bible reading and he kept a diary in earnest. Diaries, which underscored the privacy of the bourgeois home in contrast to the public frenzy of the marketplace, were hardly private in the Adams household.[46] The Adamses wrote for the archive. Diaries were assigned reading for the next generation to consume, and they were created as such. The journal was Charles's arena to record and refine his behavior, a liminal place to confess the many emotions that fell short of his high Christian ideals. Here, he was very much in line with other Victorian Protestants who enjoyed notching the daily growth of the Christian "self" on the page. A willingness to set down in writing all the ways they sought God's solace—in church or, better, in the wilds of nature—demonstrated true spiritual submission. The thinking man's diary was a medium that allowed a prominent Christian such as Charles Francis Adams to call out differences between the nation's progress and that of his own soul.[47]

And, if those differences incited a change in self or society, then the Victorian diarist went public with the tale. Abolitionist and lawyer Richard Henry Dana Jr. used *Two Years before the Mast* (1840) to garner attention to the plight of sailors. In his eponymous *Narrative* of 1845, orator Frederick Douglass laid out his odyssey from Chesapeake slave to free man. The Transcendentalist Henry Thoreau offered *Walden* (1854) to show how living apart from industrial life fostered self-reliance and spiritual discovery. Later on, reformers such as Jane Addams, a pocket diarist at fourteen years old, used journal writing to stockpile professional confidence and to articulate Christian plans for social change. Even the monarch who came to name the age—Victoria—kept a diary in which she painted an idyllic family life and drafted prayers for divine guidance. Charles, heir to an American political dynasty, kept his diary with the same Christian fervor. Admittedly less eloquent than Thoreau, and "pretty monotonous" in subject matter next to Dana's adventures as a Brahmin seaman, Charles always heard the diary ticking along as his "second conscience."[48] Imitating his Puritan forebears, this Adams treated his diary as a self-improvement manual, an evergreen trap that ensnared his moral triumphs and many failings. Aware that he was considered cold and morose by his peers, Charles committed his diary, from an early age, to monitoring the progress of his Christian self.

Within the pages of his diary, Charles Francis Adams also preserved a unique home study of Christian life in Victorian America. He interspersed religious musings with the episodes of birth, marriage, and death that followed his Harvard graduation and marked out the traditional Adams family cycle of public life. In 1827, Charles noted meeting Abigail Brown Brooks, whom he married after a courtship filled with high melodrama (mostly manufactured by Charles). Lively hostess "Miss Abby" was the third and youngest daughter of Boston's wealthiest merchant, Peter Chardon Brooks, and Nancy Gorham Brooks. Abby's New England roots ran deep, and her Brahmin pedigree easily outshone suitor Charles's: Gorham goldsmith money on her mother's side, and the prestige of colony founders, including the Saltonstalls, Wards, Cottons, and Boylstons, filling out her father's side of the family tree.[49] Charles's mother, First Lady Louisa Catherine Adams, approved of the match, calling Abby "a wonderful favorite of the family" in Washington, DC, and "quite an oddity."[50] Vivacious and chatty, Abby was well-suited to cohost Charles's prospective career as a lawyer and man of letters. She was, as Charles noted with his customary reserve, "gregarious like all other Americans and this is perhaps what I regret most in her."[51] Curdled compliments aside, he was eager to marry Abby.

Charles's father, John Quincy, already battling the family's displeasure over his decision to serve in Congress following the presidency, was less supportive. He ordered Charles to put marriage plans on hold until he finished a two-year clerkship in Daniel Webster's law office and secured a real job. The younger Adams was irate, and he continued to rage against parental intervention as the engagement was extended. Blocking marriage was not, Charles thought, the act of a Christian

Charles Francis Adams (1807–1886). *Portrait by Charles Bird King, 1827, Adams National Historical Park*

father. His mother, often ill or distracted by the alcohol-related antics of her other two sons, seemed numb to Charles's pain. "Indeed I never saw a family which has so little of the associating disposition if it can so be called," Charles grumbled. "I am therefore not much attached to family and much more happy when independent of it."[52] At a time when the home was a safe harbor for Christians to convene, Charles pulled away from his famous parents. By 1829, he and Abby finally won

Abigail Brooks Adams (1808–1889). *Portrait by William E. West, 1847, Adams National Historical Park*

their consent, moving into a spacious Boston townhouse. On the brink of creating a new life with Abby, his mind turned to fatherhood: Was the Christian family really a refuge from political life?

Throughout the 1830s and 1840s, the ideal of the Christian family dominated and joined together America's ever-shifting public and private spheres. Through art and labor, decoration and practice, Victorian homemakers projected Protestant messages of union and progress despite the rising tides of modernity. Charles and Abby had, over time, five sons and two daughters; their notions of Christian family life evolved in tandem with the growth of the family.[53] The home was also Abby's religious turf. Though she was considered subordinate to the "government" of husband Charles, Abby and other Victorian mothers were heralded as the main arbiters of religious nurture at home. On the basis of her writings alone, Abby is a hard woman to know, a keen homemaker who charmed the sour Adams clan despite their family politics. Abby, who left little literary imprint of her spiritual journeys in the archive, seems to have stepped out of one of the glossy Currier and Ives lithographs of her day. Her letters revolved wholly around the welfare of her husband and children. Her brief, mature diary noted only the "perfect days" she spent calling on neighbors with fresh fruit baskets. "Mrs. Charles Adams is a very pleasant young woman," wrote one family visitor in 1842, with "an endless tongue and a great number of small children."[54]

The site to search for Abby's religious influence, then, is not in the archive but at home. There, Abby and other Victorian mothers lined foyers with rich iconography of religious events or stories (heirloom Delft scripture scenes, for example). Proudly, they laid out a handsome, gilt-tipped Bible for visitors to see. Raised in the Brooks tradition of philanthropy, Abby sponsored a number of "ladies' causes" and regularly mailed ten-dollar bills to an ecumenical range of charities. Echoing the "separate spheres" vision of social motherhood that Victorians promoted, Mrs. Charles Adams also made the rounds to sick and dying relatives, dispensing prayers and dinner baskets.[55]

The longest and most lyrical diary entry Abby wrote was an account of a teenage girl's funeral. Graveside, Abby watched as six farmhands raised and lowered the white bier, ivory tuberoses piled high. "We then all walked back across the same green fields without the child," she wrote.[56] On happier days, Abby joined Charles in an hour of hymn singing at home. They recited Psalms with their children, then made the carriage drive to town for several hours of church service. Parents might split up—often, Charles attended Boston's Brattle Street Church (Unitarian) with his sons, where his political connections lay, while Abby went to Trinity Church (Episcopal) with the girls, to reconnect with her father's business associates and their wives.[57] The Adamses used Sundays to burnish the idea of the family unit as a microcosm of national community and progress. Overall, they believed that good Christian citizens who tried out different paths always reunited at home, just as they would in heaven.

Sidelining salvation as an immediate goal, Abby and Charles's generation of Protestants lived in an age of political voluntarism that yielded intense religious change.[58] Increasingly, as Charles noticed during a series of 1830s fast days, the pews felt emptier. The face of New England religion was changing again. Charles attributed it to the bustle and stir of industrial life. New families joined the Unitarian fold, upgrading the silver communion plate and sponsoring reforms.[59] The American Christianity of the 1830s, to Charles, took on a mechanical and inauthentic feel. Around him, religion flourished in a rising sea of specialized periodicals, a Sunday School Union, and missionary drives. New entities such as the American Bible Society and the American Tract Society mass-produced and deluged homes with material: a million Bibles and six million tracts a year, respectively.[60] As Boston's Catholic hierarchy took shape, local Protestants kept busy in politics. Charles and his fellow worshippers invoked Christian language to protest Cherokee Indian removal, debate the national bank's fate, decry slavery, and urge temperance reform. But, Charles fretted, was all this "Christian" talk hollow?

Empty pews, to his way of thinking, were indeed worrisome, but they probably meant Americans were just busy being model Christians somewhere else. A general decline in clerical talent upset him more. Without their storied ministers, how would New Englanders set their moral compass? During one 1831 fast day, Adams sat down in a "thin" church and analyzed the scene. Charles's Providence understood humility, but also man's right to enjoy life. "The doctrine that the mere act of self mortification is meritorious in the sight of God, is somewhat exploded," Adams wrote. "Surely he is not disposed to look harshly upon the moderate use of human enjoyments."[61] He was less kind to the clergy. Pressed to counter evangelical revivalists and to ferry faith to the Western frontier, New England Unitarians were stretched far too thin, Charles thought, and their pulpit work suffered as a result. "Faith is a favourite topic with Unitarian preachers who as a class believe less than almost any Sect of Christians," Adams wrote in his diary. "They consider faith only in its more limited applications to credibility, or to the qualities of humanity."[62] To compensate for bad sermons, Charles began packing his Bible on every business trip.[63]

Still eyeing the "slippery steps of the Presidential palace," Charles pondered his political path and endured what he labeled Boston's "religious gloom" throughout the 1830s. He continued to practice law.[64] On Sundays, Adams tried out a fair number of churches, surprised to find that he far preferred the anonymity of the gallery seats. There, he snagged a better perspective and heard the choir's emphasis more clearly. The sight of old Harvard peers in the pulpit made him grimace. Their iterations of religious ideas such as universalism made Adams mistrustful of how such "liberality" might operate on an impressionable worshipper base. "The world is not open easily to new truth," Adams wrote, and his attitude was no exception.[65] For example, Charles found Transcendentalism—a philosophy based on experiential knowledge and self-reliance, as espoused by acquaintance Ralph Waldo Emerson and other thinkers—to be downright dangerous.[66] Charles accepted holy mysteries, and he loathed preachers who overexplained them. "The mystery of the birth of Christ is one of those things I never pretend to rest upon," Adams wrote with complacent rigidity. "Inexplicable as it is in every point of view, I prefer to let it remain so, satisfied with the divine nature of the mission and its beneficent purpose."[67] To Charles, theological illiteracy was a point of pride, a pious badge of Christian submission.

Painfully, the collapse of a tight-knit Christian community around the itinerant Charles Francis Adams came when he most needed its support, as his own famous family again fell under attack. By the 1840s, his dual careers as a lawyer and writer had coalesced. He was a published essayist and executor of the Adams family estate, but Charles felt professionally idle, barred from pursuing a political career while John Quincy continued on the public stage. One brother, a likely suicide, had died in 1829; by 1834, Charles was "alone in the generation" following his second brother's violent spiral into alcoholism and debt.[68] "I am tossing about in an ocean of nothing," Charles wrote, blaming his fitful Christianity for the drift.[69] A twenty-five-year-old father, he no longer saw a way to revive his original plan of leading a quiet literary life. When he read aloud Bible passages to Abby at home, Charles identified with the parable of Lazarus's resurrection.[70]

Grudgingly, he took up the family's political mantle. Charles discovered that his Protestantism eased the burdensome fact that he was forever "wedded to the soil of Massachusetts."[71] Charles and other pious Americans had acquired strength through the "school of affliction," as past waves of sermonizers suggested. So Adams set to funding new institutions of charity and education, the kind that helped "good men contract localities of feeling" and bolstered self-improvement.[72] Halfheartedly, he trained for public office by observing fast days. Dutifully, he and Abby hosted ministers for dinner. If snow barricaded them inside and kept them away from the church, then Charles skimmed over sermon anthologies or read the Psalms aloud to his children. This was the "numb deism," more political than personal, that son Henry went on to eviscerate in his memoir. And, as the nation grew, Charles and other Americans acknowledged how difficult it was to keep up the old ways of "knowing" God, and God's plan for the nation.

In the swirl of new ideas that suffused 1830s religious life, Charles Francis Adams and many of his republican peers clung to the vestiges of New England's colonial worship habits. One Anglo-American custom, the fast day, became Charles's preferred marker to measure his religious growth. The fast day, with its New England Congregationalist roots, existed as religious tradition and political sacrament from colonial days. The power to designate a fast day rested with local clergy and state governors; presidents could only "recommend" national fasts—as Charles's grandfather John had learned as president.[73] As Americans drew on religion to help build the early republic, days of fasting and thanksgiving allowed them to ritualize spiritual engagement in political life once the Revolution's fervor had passed. Early nineteenth-century calls to the fast day shuttered businesses, legislatures, and schools in order to attract believers to the country's ever-multiplying denominations.

A standard proclamation appointed a day of "solemn humiliation, fasting, and prayer," but it is hard to know if any actual fasting took place among observers. The proclamation language came from the Church of England, and it was issued with few American edits. State fasts were in April or September, with national fasts set for the summer months. They united citizens by reminding them of the Puritan past. In this period, sermons outlined a public Christianity that blended religion with republicanism. Between 1800 and 1850, four themes dominated the fast-day literature that Charles and his Protestant peers heard every year: the impulse of patriotic piety; the sources of national sin; the pulpits' advice on foreign policy and American neutrality; and the public response to afflictions such as cholera.

In 1832, a decade after yellow fever devastated New York, cholera struck at America's rising cities. Municipal regulations and health boards were weak; medical knowledge was scant at best. Residents were advised to stay calm and scrub down infected buildings with quicklime. "King Cholera" claimed nearly a million lives in Europe; the death toll spiked higher throughout the spring and summer, as Canada and then New York City came under siege. Citizens understood little of how the contagion spread—via poor hygiene, polluted water, and a general lack of city sanitation protocols—but they were certain it came from anywhere except America (often they pinned blame on the non-Christian powers of India or Asia).

On August 3, New Yorkers knelt in prayer for a local fast day, called by clergy to still the "hand of God" that administered cholera's retribution for an urban "mother-monster," the rampant sin of atheism.[74] Six days later, Bostonians joined them in a national fast-day service, countering the pandemic's "destroying angel" with a show of Christian solidarity.[75] Many ministers, including the New Bedford Unitarian Orville Dewey, dusted off their old providentialist rhetoric to rouse the crowd. "If you doubt whether your ears hear me rightly, I repeat it, and say it is a *beneficent visitation*," Dewey thundered in his widely circulated sermon. "There is another calamity, another curse, which, as I believe, it is designed to remove, and which impressed me with greater horror. The Cholera, I am firmly persuaded, will prevent more suffering than it will occasion."[76]

To Adams and his Boston neighbors, the scourge of cholera hinted at the vengeful return of an Old Testament God, one that Americans had jettisoned for material gains. Deeply invested in national sins such as slavery and luxury, Christians viewed cholera—a seemingly arbitrary and vastly understudied illness—as divine judgment. Interpretation varied. A worshipper like Charles would not have heard—or appreciated—the same Calvinist jeremiad of "great destiny and sorry failings" that his Puritan ancestors did.[77] Rather, the concerned minister of 1832, who read news accounts of the epidemic and prayed over dying worshippers, confronted a monumental task in composing the August fast-day sermon. For reference, he might have checked Charles Buck's new edition of the *Theological Dictionary.* There, Buck defined sin plainly as "the transgression of the law, or want of conformity to the will of God," and enumerated the recognizable kinds of sin. Buck listed eight types: original sin, actual sin, sins of omission, sins of commission, sins of infirmity, secret sins, presumptuous sins, and the unpardonable sin.[78] In rationalizing cholera as a sacred judgment levied for mortal vice, to which sin(s) should the responsible clergyman refer? Since colonial days, Americans had accepted affliction as admonition for sin and as a way to renew faith, but cholera's pervasiveness and high mortality rate made it difficult for even a model Christian to comprehend.

Just as his undergraduate debauchery served Charles Francis Adams a lesson in Christian temperance, the cholera outbreak of 1832 prompted another sharp turn in his practice and belief. Charles feared that the Christian family circle he had built was vulnerable to providential wrath. Panicked that he could not save Abby and their small children from contracting cholera, Adams tried to inoculate the family with prayer. He transcribed his father's letters concerning the Bible. The family sang an extra round of Psalms, and Charles's Bible drills with the children intensified. On August 9, 1832, he fasted all day but skipped church, opting to stay home and read the Gospel instead.[79] Cholera's march added to Charles's characteristic anxiety over family affairs, and he sought refuge in his diary. "Have I done as much as I ought to have done?" he wrote. "Am I what I should be?"[80] Surrounded by the ornaments and cues of the Christian home so closely curated by Abby, he devoted the next four Sundays to drafting a full exegesis of the Sermon on the Mount, an Adams family favorite. This writing assignment was, to Charles's mind, an exercise meant to sharpen religious reasoning and virtue.[81] Charles laid out his thoughts on the opinions and character of Jesus Christ, compiling a layman's guide to modern morality that wavered remarkably little over the next fifty years. With great labor, he condensed it to two pages.

When Charles began work on the exegesis in the summer of 1832, he still considered himself a shapeless Christian "what" meant to be molded into a useful Christian "who." Though it marked Charles's only foray into deeper theological waters, his observations offer key evidence of how skepticism and belief coexisted in the Unitarian mind. Religion was a constant for Charles, as it had been for past Adamses, because practicing faith served to shape personality and politics. Charles conceived of his own Christian conscience as innate, a pure human instinct that Providence (or people) prodded into growth. "The object of all religion," he wrote, "is to operate upon human conduct."[82] In Christ, Adams looked for another "self" to parse, and possibly to emulate. He was not entirely sold on what he found. First, in step with other Unitarians, Charles admired Christ as a gifted moral teacher, but he demurred from proclaiming Christ's divinity. With a trace of Brahmin elitism, Adams wondered how such "a man issuing from the midst of poor, uneducated people in a state of ignorance and excessive depression, should all at once pour out a flood of the purest morality upon the world?"[83] Second, while he believed that Christ deployed doctrine and popularized morality in a manner that eclipsed Plato and the prophet Muhammad, Adams doubted Christ's utility as the best ethical model to follow. Here, Charles siphoned his reasoning directly from the social arenas of God and Mammon through which he moved.

In his essay, Charles pitted Seneca against Savior, to show that Christ conquered lust and greed where the household gods had not. Adams admired Jesus's "supernatural" ability to renounce pride and wealth, but he charged that Christ's human flaw was "a passion for prosletyism" that bespoke a "purely selfish motive."[84] Christ's power as a moral teacher, to Adams's mind, was undercut by an entrepreneurial avidity for promoting his parables abroad. Next, Charles tackled the dilemma of where else in history to locate models of piety. "There have been many persons claiming precisely the same character in which Christ appears to the world," Adams wrote, comparing and dismissing leaders of Christianity, Judaism, and Islam. "But the mentality sticks in them all. There is a taint of self in every action."[85] To conclude his scriptural analysis, Adams pledged a form of "self-government" that regulated his mind, heart, and actions to Christian piety. In the face of affliction, Charles rationalized that *his* God understood skipping a service or two.

If the "inner man" was a true Christian, Adams wrote, then outward piety was just a rote exercise. "The practice of religion as inculcated by the Saviour," Charles wrote, "is to be found in the every day life of industrious men."[86] Intellectual pilgrimage over, Adams sped back to the familiar fray of local politics.

Following his bout of biblical inquiry, Charles Francis Adams committed wholly to a solo career of politics, publication, and philanthropy, armed with what he called "the force God has given me." For Charles, the period from 1832 to 1861 marked a high tide of literary production and public engagement. His fast-day reflections stirred up a dose of the religious confidence that he so desperately sought, transforming him into the man he thought he should be as a Christian Republican, and as an Adams. Throughout the 1830s and 1840s, Adams authored book reviews and essays for Boston newspapers and the *North American Review*, reaping success as a serious practitioner of belles-lettres.[87]

An ardent bibliophile, he was drawn to the new science of librarianship—the idea that saving and sharing historical documents was a manifestation of American identity and the cultural work of the gentleman scholar.[88] Powered by virtuosic filiopiety, Charles trudged through sorting and reading the family papers: roughly a quarter of a million manuscript pages of diaries and loose letters. As a modern discipline, historical editing was largely underdeveloped. From the archive, Charles mined his transatlantic education, drafting an American genre of experience that differed from the "life-in-letters" models of European biography. Carefully, he wrapped the Adams cosmos around the familiar trajectory of Revolution-to-republic, embedding the family's story within that of the nation and effectively repackaging it for resale.[89] Surveying two generations' worth of the rare manuscript harvest, Charles began preparing the papers for publication. He finished in 1874.

Charles's early education had equipped him to be a man like the father he prized to a cultic degree, "fully imbued with the spirit of Roman fortitude qualified by Christian morals."[90] His Adams lineage also foretold a wanderlust for religious travel, and Charles embraced it. Between 1832 and 1868, as he fought to consolidate political influence in his father's shadow, Charles drew on the popular ideal of the Christian family for moral support. But at heart, he remained a pilgrim, happy to leave Abby's cozy Christian nest and try out other ways of knowing God. Religious travel became an intellectual escape for Charles, a path away from Unitarianism's stifling grip on Boston politics and culture. Charles's "journeyings" north, west, and south brought a much-needed respite from local religious thought and practice. Whenever he tangled with the Quincy pastor William Parsons Lunt over politics, Charles went on hiatus from churchgoing to *save* his faith. "I scarcely know what to do," Adams wrote of one such customary break. "To leave a church with which I am so intimately associated is in the highest degree painful, and yet to subject myself to such trials of Christian temper is spoiling all my religious feeling, and my respect for church forms."[91]

Historical editing was a passion project that Charles fit in when public duties allowed. Elsewhere, he followed the Adams template, serving from 1841 to 1845 in the state legislature, where he emerged as an antislavery leader. By 1846, Charles had found another outlet for his talents, as editor and proprietor of the *Boston Daily Whig*. Two years later, Charles joined the family line of politicians, running (unsuccessfully) as the vice-presidential candidate for the new Free Soil Party. In 1858, Charles was elected to the US House of Representatives, serving until Abraham Lincoln appointed him minister to the Court of St. James's in spring 1861. For the next seven years, he upheld Adams traditions: sampling Europe, enacting diplomacy, and soaking up religious views abroad.

There were other places to seek God in everyday life, he decided. As with many Victorians who sought the sacred and the sublime, Charles marveled at the natural beauty of Niagara Falls. He went west to meet the Mormons and dabbled in Catholic and Anglican aesthetics—along the way, testing his idea of Providence as the agent of progress. In many ways, Charles's travels of self-discovery illustrate a generation of men and women who exuded "parlor piety" at home but who really wanted to engage with God alone, on a foreign road.

Travelers tend to turn inward. They are equally focused on reaching an external goal (for example, a shrine) and on exploring the spiritual change that such an experience causes within (a miracle). Along the way, they identify relics or markers of progress. The routes they take are gridded onto maps as new cultural pathways. In literature, pilgrims appear vulnerable but steadfast. They are lone souls thrown together and bonded by a collective desire to access something greater and eternal. These conflicting Protestant personalities coexisted within Charles and other Victorians. Three pilgrimages were pivotal to Charles Francis's mature Christianity: to Niagara Falls and Catholic Canada in 1836; to Nauvoo, Illinois, in 1844; and, finally, back to High Church England as the Civil War tore America in two.

Niagara Falls, when Charles encountered it in 1836, was the Victorian pilgrim's amusement park of choice. By 1861, hordes of visitors had collected enough evidence to persuade the distant Roman Catholic church that Niagara merited consecration as an official "pilgrim shrine." Striking in its idyllic beauty and ready-built for thrill seekers, the rocky site hunched over the American-Canadian divide. Once the Erie Canal was completed in autumn 1825, "doing the Falls" became a dramatic must-see on the New England version of the gentleman's grand tour. Voyagers such as Charles, taking the "Fashionable Tour" through upstate New York and Canada with a set of Brahmin friends, approached via steamer and train. On arrival, they could buy Indian beadwork or, like the novelist Nathaniel Hawthorne, "pilgrim staffs" at the souvenir shops ringing the site. Hawthorne's purchase was a wise one. Niagara's slippery rocks, weak staircases, and blinding spray all reinforced the physical adversity and emotional turmoil of an actual pilgrimage. Paid "hermits" popped out to startle visitors, lending authenticity to the scene. Tightrope walkers captivated the crowds.

Battered by Niagara's strong wind, Americans clutched their bestselling guidebooks and stumbled on toward the sublime. For a twenty-five-cent general admission fee (some attractions cost extra), Charles hiked a semiwild landscape of fancifully named venues: Horseshoe Falls, Termination Rock, the Cave of the Winds, and Mr. Barnett's "museum of curiosities." Judging by the bloated advertisements and gazetteers of a nascent tourist industry, Niagara's sacred spots (literally) promised to dose Charles with divine enchantment. The Cave of the Winds was, for example, the "*ne plus ultra* of wonders, a visit to which no person of sufficient nerve, ought to omit," one 1840 guidebook rhapsodized, "especially as there is always, in the afternoon, when the sun shines, a very bright rain-bow visible within the cave, and behind the sheet of water."[92]

Despite the circus sideshow and the hyperbolic advertising literature that it relied on for profit, Niagara's splendors and terrors stirred genuine religious reaction in paying pilgrims. For Charles, and for other genteel city dwellers or honeymooners on holiday, Niagara's "wild," prepackaged pilgrimage symbolized the Burkean sublime of the eighteenth century, and the mad rush of industrial change that they lived in.[93] As a walkable parable of beauty and danger, Niagara epitomized the residual lawlessness of America's borderlands, and the young nation's conflicted love of expansion. One prize view that recurred in Victorian lithographs and journals, for example, was the perspective taken "from the top of the American ladder," which bourgeois tourists used in their Niagara memoirs to glorify national progress and to nudge for even more. From that eerie summit, drawing closer to God and with chaos gushing below, many recorded spiritual epiphanies. Adams's initial response was less effusive than that of the American author Caroline Howard Gilman, who "felt the moral influence of the scene," and a great deal more like that of another writer who "stamped" Niagara's peace on his heart, Charles Dickens.[94]

Part of a generation of early Victorians who traveled cross-country and wrote about it, Charles also put down his changing impressions of Niagara's unique spirituality on the page. Adams landed at Niagara in June 1836. Niagara offered a canned pilgrimage for cautious Protestants to experience and record. Unlike many of them, however, he omitted the tiresome details of climbing the Terrapin Tower's faulty steps, of skirting the Whirlpool's rapids, and of earning his Termination Rock Certificate. Rather, he focused his religious self on the sensory experience of the falls. He heard Niagara three miles before he saw it, marveling at the sight of three waterfalls pounding down a wall of rock. He longed to duck under the spray, but he did not want to upset his already nervous children. The whole trip, Adams thought, was therapeutic but impossible to describe. "I looked with that kind of wonder which is not satisfied with seeing and continues under the impression till the mind ceases to be conscious of the cause operating upon it," Charles wrote with customary reserve. "I was under constant excitement while at Niagara, never ceasing to take pleasure at observing the Fall from the various positions, although I could not analyze in what that pleasure consisted."[95]

En route, the train chatter had been about presidential conventions. What Adams loved best about Niagara—its numb peace—soothed his inner spiritual unrest over the grim prospect of an extended bout of political service in New England. The air was softer, Charles wrote. Niagara's tranquility, briefly, spirited him away from party strife. The prickly Charles even managed to make a few friends among fellow pilgrims as they hobbled along the same slippery paths, strangers suddenly "united by scrambles." He disdained patronizing the souvenir sellers, who polluted the sacred site with the "penny-wise projects of man." In his diary, pondering how the epic waterfall placed "man in scale with creation" for the industrializing age, Charles gazed out at Niagara's sheet of blue-brown water in reverie. "To the worldly man, the rivers of God flowing in Paradise with milk and honey would appear only as power to move so many millwheels," Charles wrote bitterly, torn between his cosmopolitanism and his Christianity.[96]

Reluctantly abandoning Niagara's pleasure grounds for the oddities of Catholic Canada, Charles traveled north to Quebec City and Montreal. Again, he expected a religious spectacle. The Bostonian Charles's impressions of North American Catholicism were, in line with those of other elite Protestants, fairly negative. While popular complaints about Catholics hewed to the same old prejudices that his grandfather John once voiced—they favored papal pomp and performance over true piety; they answered to Rome before Washington—an ugly groundswell of anti-Catholic invective shaped the cultural message further. An influx of (mostly Irish) Catholic immigrants stocked new industries and companies with employees.

At the same time, these newcomers disrupted long-established New England notions of class and privilege. For, as the "Catholic hordes" swept up construction jobs and settled in city boarding houses, they also planted churches and schools, in Baltimore, Boston, New York, and Philadelphia. Catholics now nurtured seminaries, convents, and colleges. Nuns, perhaps even more than clergy, reinforced ideals of Christian charity and exerted Catholic authority in regional Protestant strongholds. These far-flung communities of women religious, who between 1727 and 1920 helped to operate five hundred hospitals, fifty colleges, and more than six thousand parochial schools, also attracted the wrath of Victorian critics. Overall, the visible consolidation of

Catholic social power unnerved traditional Protestant elites and upset their political efforts. By the 1850s, this Protestant anxiety manifested in the nativist and anti-Catholic policies of the Know-Nothing Party and others.

It can be hard to see who "made" American Catholicism more in the nineteenth century, Catholic promoters or Protestant critics. Vigorously, Adams's Protestant colleagues debated the religion's theological authenticity in public. Doggedly, they investigated the Anglo-Protestant and Franco-Catholic imperial roots of American history. Thanks to popular literature and new opportunities for steam travel to Canada's Catholic enclaves, Protestants shored up their own "ism" by redefining "Romanism" and its related evils. Certainly, Boston's Brahmin corps was simultaneously perplexed by and disdainful of the "new" Catholics' rise, and convents came under their direct fire. Satirized in print and attacked on city streets, urban Catholics faced a difficult, transitional era in the 1830s and 1840s. In the Boston newspapers that Charles read, for example, he saw ample evidence of Catholic cruelties. The papers frequently cataloged a litany of atrocities committed against young, innocent women by a tyrannical Mother Superior or by a roving Catholic worker.

Charles read shocking extracts of Rebecca Read's 1835 "tell-all" memoir of the horrors she suffered in nearby Charlestown's Ursuline convent (*Six Months in a Convent*), which was burned to the ground by a mob of Protestant rioters in summer 1834. Adams flipped through the juicier bits of Maria Monk's *Awful Disclosures*, an 1836 exposé of Montreal convent life, in which the Mother Superior acted as little more than a brothel director. Monk's and Reed's sensational tales— brimming with lecherous priestcraft, pimping nuns, and overstuffed prose—became instant bestsellers for the wide audience of anti-Catholic agents.[97] As his carriage rolled up to the gates of Maria Monk's former convent/brothel in 1836, Charles's religious curiosity ran high.

Adams had seen Catholics before, and even worshipped alongside them—in Europe. At the Cathedral-Basilica of Notre-Dame de Québec, his gaze lingered on the Gothic rafters longer than on the people in the pews. The architectural beauty of a foreign church attracted Charles far more than its ways of worship, and when he visited in summer 1836, Quebec's neoclassical facade was under reconstruction. Repeatedly ravaged by fire and invaders, the cathedral represented to Charles the inevitability of Christianity's (even Catholic Christianity's) endurance of earthly ills. Adams admired the church's high vaulted ribcage of gold-white arches and gemlike, stained-glass windows. There, and when he attended high mass in Montreal, he found the ornamentalism of most Catholic churches imposing, and the parishioners focused solely on acts of "external piety."[98] While Adams singled out devotion as the lone precept that Catholics excelled at teaching, his private list of complaints about them multiplied. He could barely hear the minister, who stood some distance away from the pews. He thought that the mass, which clocked in at one and a half hours, was overlong. Worship aesthetics—especially the music—disappointed him, reifying his opinion that Catholicism was made for "an ordinary class of minds" that preferred "idolatry" to piety. "The common people in the aisles all seemed to pray," Adams wrote, glancing around the cathedral, "although it might be a matter of doubt if they knew to whom they were praying."[99]

The salacious aspects of Catholicism paled as Charles continued his Canadian journey, yet his interest in other religions grew. He was especially curious to see how cities shaped Christianity. Arriving at Maria Monk's site of the "Grey Nunnery"—where the black-veiled novice/novelist had reportedly lain in her own coffin for a rite of initiation, and then "resolved to submit" to the physical assault of several priests—Adams discovered none of the same lurid rites on display.[100] Rather, the convent and adjoining hospital functioned as a joint gift shop, selling "trifles" to fund their operating costs. "I confess I was puzzled to perceive the wickedness," Adams wrote, with more than a trace of disappointment.[101] Catholicism, Charles concluded, was more of a business than a cult, focused on making profits, not on "stealing" Protestants.

Once back in Boston, Charles watched the onset of urban Catholicism keenly, attending mass at new churches and describing the quality of oratory in his diary. He came to admire the "simple, clear, direct, and affectionate" approach of "paternal" Catholic clergy. He was surprised to hear pastors address their flocks in English, not Latin. "I was not aware that this was within the rules," Charles wrote. "But being so, it explained the sources of influence over the people."[102] Trained to travel through foreign churches and read for aesthetic clues, Adams relied on local religion to teach him how city politics might ebb and flow. One

Easter, for example, lilies and a white cross greeted Charles from the familiar Unitarian altar of the Brattle Street Church. The new Catholics, not old-school Unitarians, would own the city by century's end, he predicted. "The recognition of the papal calendar is complete," Charles observed of the change in tradition. "I foresee that in time Boston will be zealous in Romanism, but it will be long after my day."[103]

Niagara's beauty spoke to Adams's search for the sublime, and visiting Catholic Canada brought a respite from the burdens of New England church history and practice that he inherited. But in contrast to other Adamses, the mature Charles was less agile at integrating foreign religious ideas into the teachings with which he was raised, probably a result of his dim appreciation for learning theology. His religious encounters were just that—awkward and unexpected episodes of amateur discovery. In these meetings, Charles resembled the bulk of Victorian Protestants who were, by turns, fascinated by and fearful of how new prophets and changing liturgical rites transformed God's message for America. Charles held new beliefs, and their caretakers, at a scrupulous distance. Throughout his life, he remained reticent to pursue robust religious inquiry at the intellectual level. As his Protestant peers

After a long career in the political arena, Charles Francis Adams retreated to the ancestral farm of Peacefield with his wife, Abigail. There he edited popular editions of private family letters and memoirs. *Photograph by Marian Hooper Adams, 1883, Massachusetts Historical Society*

grew bogged down in theological battles, Charles purposefully turned away. "The Trinity or the Unity are questions involving so much of unintelligible matter," he wrote, "that I think it is better to trust without discussing the goodness of God."[104] Instead, he worked at mastering the sensory study of religion. He clocked when worshippers sat or stood, and why certain ornaments decked the church. Aesthetics, not creeds, dominated his diary of exploration. Often, the architecture of foreign venues—a cathedral's bones, not the souls gathered inside—was Adams's key to understanding various forms of prayer.

Charles considered these "journeyings" north, south, and west to be acts separate from his regular congregational membership. His pilgrimages away from the family faith were a chance to exhale, often occurring after he took on extra Unitarian duty. Take the spring of 1844: no sooner had he and Abby entered formally into the communion at the family church in Quincy—a step he had weighed since 1832—than Charles began booking a southern and western tour with his cousin Josiah Quincy.[105] Abby, recuperating from a miscarriage, stayed home and read sermons. Together, Charles and Josiah traveled from Boston to Baltimore, then on to the capital for a few days. There, Charles enjoyed Unitarian sermons on "brotherly love," but he thought that the Washington clergy lacked the vehemence to exhort a crowd. "The difference between us and the South seems to be in matters of Oratory," Adams noted, "that their manner is better than their matter, and our matter is better than our manner."[106] Leaving Virginia, the two men steamed down the Ohio River and then looped up the Mississippi, taking in the sights at Cincinnati, Louisville, and St. Louis before landing in the Mormon complex of Joseph Smith's Nauvoo, Illinois, in mid-May.

They were a prominent pair. Charles was serving in the Massachusetts House of Representatives, and his fourth cousin Josiah presided over Boston's city council. They had a religious kinship, too. Both men were Unitarians and highly skeptical of any self-pronounced prophet. "Revelation, I must confess it, never looked to me much beyond the frenzy of an excited imagination," Charles wrote in his diary.[107] But, along with Josiah, he was eager to meet "the celebrated Joe Smith," who had swiftly consolidated both sacred and secular power in a fertile region of the expanding nation. Now a presidential candidate who prophesied and authored scripture from his haven in the American West, Joseph Smith was as far from Unitarianism as Charles Francis Adams could flee in 1844.

When Charles called Smith "celebrated," he did not mean it as a compliment. Adams came to judge the Mormon as a profiteer and "mountebank apostle" of Christianity. In this way, Charles echoed the awe and ire that often characterized American attitudes toward "a peculiar people" who, with their home-made prophet and practice of polygamy, felt too foreign to be claimed by Christians of any stripe.[108] When Adams and Smith met in May—one short month before Joseph and his brother Hyrum died at the hands of an anti-Mormon mob—Adams was familiar with the basic outline of Smith's religious development. Charles had heard of the Mormon leader's angelic visions, which began in the 1820s at his family's farm in upstate New York. He had read of Smith's efforts to set down those heavenly revelations, translated from holy golden plates, in the Book of Mormon, which was first published in 1830. And Charles had some idea of the formalization of Joseph Smith's beliefs into a religious institution, the Church of Jesus Christ of Latter-Day Saints.[109] What Charles did not realize, until he sat down with Joseph Smith in Nauvoo, was how adroitly the Mormon tavern keeper had bonded together religious and political authority on the ground. Josiah Quincy's biting account of the trip, published in 1881, is far better known to scholars. But Adams's reflections on meeting the first generation of Mormons show something else—namely, his drive to understand how religion and politics shaped Americans as they pushed westward.[110]

Working his way toward the frontier, Adams was not entirely sure what to expect. In his journal, he offered up a series of character sketches and notable anecdotes from the trip. By the time he reached Nauvoo, they had been on the road for several weeks. And to a seasoned traveler such as Charles Francis Adams, bad tavern keepers were nothing new. At first glance, he counted Joseph Smith in that number, just another civil but unkempt host who hustled him in and out of a maze of occupied rooms in search of a clean, spare bed. The Mormon founder was, to the Bostonian's eyes, a man of "frank but not coarse vulgarity."[111] To Charles's mortification, Smith woke a dozing tenant, "whom he very abruptly slapped on the shoulder and notified to quit."[112] After providing a generous breakfast, Smith lectured Charles and Josiah on Mormon doctrine. With what Adams called a "cool impudence," he led them down to the private chamber to visit his mother, Lucy Mack Smith. There, the Mormon leader unwrapped four Egyptian mummies and several rolls of yellow papyri. Next, "Joe" explained in detail the related holy manuscripts that he had transcribed. "Of course, we were too polite to prove the negative," Charles wrote in his diary with trademark Unitarian aplomb, "against a man fortified by revelation."[113] He was more interested in Smith's half-finished stone temple, his total control of the Nauvoo courts, and his use of communal tithing to fund Mormonism's national structure and growth. Despite Smith's best efforts at instruction, Charles never grasped the intricacies of Mormon belief, and he resented paying a quarter to Lucy to see the cache of antiquities and hieroglyphics. Smith's ideas of how Mormons marked revelation, conversion, and salvation never really coalesced in Charles's mind.

At first, Adams struggled to view Mormonism as a Christian-ish variation of "the Jewish system." By trip's end, he hazarded (wrongly) that Smith's "theological system is very nearly Christian Unitarianism—with the addition of the power of baptism by the priests of adults to remit sin, and of the new hierarchy of which Smith is the chief by divine appointment."[114] Asked to give an impromptu homily during the easterners' visit, Smith obliged with a sermon on the tavern's front steps, defeating a Methodist heckler in the process. But Charles missed his only chance to hear a Mormon preach. He was upstairs consulting with a US marshal chasing a debtor in Nauvoo, where federal power was often thwarted or superseded by the prophet's authority. For Charles, it was a reminder that harnessing sacred and secular power—as Smith had done—relied on a dangerous amount of charisma. As Smith walked the Brahmins back to their carriage, Adams mulled the Mormon lesson of his high-speed tour through western Christianity. "On the whole I was glad I had been," he wrote. "Such a man is a study not for himself, but as serving to show what turns the human mind will sometimes take."[115]

Back in Boston, politics and publishing absorbed Charles's attention. From 1841 to 1845, he served in the Massachusetts state legislature, gaining a reputation for his antislavery orations. Although he was the vice-presidential candidate of the newly formed Free Soil Party in 1848, Charles did not hold office again until 1858, when he was elected as a

Republican member of the House of Representatives. He served in that post until early 1861. With less time for long-distance junkets, Adams committed himself to raising a Christian family. Charles always chose to renew his faith, but, like most Adamses, he returned home with a distinctly critical edge. Charles gloomily projected that Unitarian talent— and, therefore, denominational influence on American thought and culture—was in steep decline. "As a consequence I fully expect they will die out by the end of the century," he wrote.[116] Charles began to worry, looking at his growing children, that he was the last of the "Adams race" to view religion as a constant.

Around him, evidence mounted that the Christian family ideal was dissolving along with the American union. His youngest daughter, Louisa, could recall just three commandments out of ten. Sons Henry, Charles Francis Jr., and John Quincy II showed faint interest in reciting their Psalms.[117] An occasional Sunday school teacher throughout the summers of the 1850s, Charles tried to reconnect his children with the Bible, just as his father had done. Charles walked them through chapters of Jeremiah and the prophets, desperate to sow "habit and familiarity with the sacred book."[118] Early on, he declared it a losing battle, but he persisted with the Bible drills: "I fear that in this endeavour of mine to promote the religious culture of my children I have very nearly failed. Probably not many parents have persevered with more steadiness than I in efforts to advance those who have been placed under my care, but I regret to feel that I have not been successful," Charles wrote in his diary. "My children do not show the smallest sign of religious feeling— much less than I did at their age, although I was left much more to myself."[119] Once a caustic critic of Boston's "religious gloom," Charles now seemed to embody it.

Diplomatic duty called Charles and his family back to England in the spring of 1861. Appointed American minister to Britain just as the Civil War erupted, he mostly relished the opportunity to step (finally) into the family spotlight of public service. Speeding away from what he called "the terrible explosion of the sad moral volcano of American slavery," Charles sheltered, with wife Abby and most of their family, in the buoyant culture of Queen Victoria's London.[120] In 1863, he scored a major diplomatic win, persuading the British foreign ministry to halt the production of Confederate ironclad ships, built in Liverpool. His act stemmed a tide of British support for the South, just as a ring of Confederate agents pressured Victoria's ministry for aid. Adams, who loathed the pomp and parade of diplomatic life at the Court of St. James's, resigned his post in 1868. While the seven years in England were personally and professional stressful to Charles—the livelihood of both his nation and his Union soldier son were in constant, grinding doubt—his time in England was, by far, the most fulfilling pilgrimage of Charles's life. An American statesman who felt more at home in cosmopolitan Europe, Charles mined every scrap of free time to indulge his aesthetic curiosity in foreign modes of Christianity and culture.

Charles Francis Adams's "journeyings" through English religion had, at first, a theme. His plan was to locate and catalog the work of the country's quintessential church architect, Christopher Wren, who rebuilt London's religious landscape after the Great Fire of 1666. Charles had no pretensions of becoming a professional architect, but beauty was holy to him. The Victorian statesman found religious art to be highly therapeutic. Trekking from St. Paul's Cathedral to a set of lesser-known chapels, Charles learned to spot Wren's signature motif: the cruciform layout with spare design, capped with a broad white dome that rose, more of a castle than a church, against London's gritty skyline. With his sons Henry and Brooks in tow, Charles methodically worked his way through most of Wren's fifty-two churches. His notes were brief, and he focused on the quality of light in each house of worship. "We value this so little in America, that we make cellars of our churches," Charles wrote after a stop at St. Michael Bassishaw.[121] Just as the Civil War fractured Charles's world and shredded old ideas of Providence, he took his cues from Wren to rebuild his Christianity.

Often, the city expanded and intruded on Charles's enjoyment of religious beauty. He loathed the park crowds. Italian opera blared loudly from a theater near his legation office, and gin shops gaped open for early-morning business on the Sabbath. "Think of this on a Sunday in New England," Adams exclaimed.[122] Yet Charles, undeterred, resumed his religious wanderings. He sampled mesmerism and Christian "parlor games" alongside his English peers.[123] He tried out the British versions of Unitarian, Presbyterian, Anglican, and Baptist denominations. Overall, Adams decided that British clergymen possessed "more fervor" and less talent than their American cousins.[124] Filiopiety, too, guided his steps back to boyhood haunts. Charles knelt in prayer at All Hallows Barking, where his parents wed, and wept quietly at the wonder of it. "Life has rolled away since I was here," he wrote, with his customary blend of melancholy and nostalgia.[125] At Ealing, where he and his brothers (long dead) had reunited, Charles circled their old rooms. "My spirit was softened all day as if I had accomplished a pious pilgrimage," Adams observed, "and as if I could lay up the remembrance of a cheering vision of the distant past, as one of the compensations of my in some respects painful present state."[126] In 1868, with the city at his back, Charles felt he had mastered a new stage of Christian pilgrimage.

Suffering from ill health and dementia in the late 1870s and early 1880s, Charles receded from public view and died in 1886. Abby followed three years later. To the world, Charles Francis Adams seemed to be the ultimate all-American insider: scion to a political dynasty, a Bostonian who honed his aesthetics in the royal courts of Europe. He was far from it. As his religious journeys show, Charles never felt that blessed. He was most at home in a strange city, and violently uncomfortable in a roomful of Americans. New England religion baffled and at times repulsed him enough to flee. Charles journeyed away from the family church not because he suddenly stopped being Christian but because he thought his Christian instinct might grow dull from the low quality of liturgy that he heard there. Overall, Charles's most deeply felt spiritual actions came from the bone-deep certainty that he was born with a religious instinct. Christianity was always *his*, Charles believed, and that preset condition merely needed his steady nurture to thrive. Pilgrimage helped. By the end of his life, Charles was convinced that skepticism was a healthy intellectual attitude as well; his natural Christianity made him immune to unbelief. "I believe so fully in Christianity that I have little fear of discussion of Atheism in any form it may take," Charles wrote in his omnipresent diary.[127]

As the first descendant to tackle publishing the Adams archive while attending to diplomatic duties, Charles spent his life hunting for the religious confidence to live up to recent history and to play down family scandals. As his father and grandfather had done, Charles dutifully attended Harvard, manned a post as the American minister in London's court, and dabbled somewhat successfully in the twin spheres of local and national politics. He was the family's last providentialist, determined to see God's hand in American history and to examine Christianity for republican adaptability. Charles's "journeyings" into Christian aesthetics inspired his son Henry to understand religion from the outside in—no need to suffer over studying theology. And, as his youngest son, Brooks, would do, Charles evinced a cultic adherence to the family as a form of religion, a clan that demanded his protection and preservation to meet providential goals.

Statesman and political scion Charles Francis Adams stands in as a Christian pilgrim in the age of American Victorianism. It was an era when, as Anne C. Rose has framed it, Adams and others "sought careers that shaped identities, leisure that engaged imagination, family life that evoked resonant feeling, and a political process that explored ideals."[128] Among members of Adams's generation, the substance of faith's appeal dimmed, eclipsed by massive social changes in communication, transportation, and intellectual exchange. Church membership became more of a formality, or a beacon to indicate social status, rather than a proof of deep piety. Adams, at first nonchalant about this change, became increasingly distressed about how Christian republicans might properly behave. Adams grew perplexed as to how—if at all—his family legacy of Enlightenment Christianity operated in the industrial society through which he traveled. Along with other well-educated Victorians, Charles audited troves of moral philosophy to shape his self-identity. Unlike many, he did so in the shade of two less-loved presidents. Charles's close account of the Victorian commoditization of Christianity, then, forms another link in the long chain of Adams family faith. In John Quincy's America, Christianity was a unifying force for those who pursued temperate, disciplined lives. In Charles's America, the new opportunities created by market society bucked against those norms as talk of disunion swelled. Political fractures made men and women move against old religious currents.

Charles's own religious biography, always at hand in his diary, disappointed him most. Adams traveled widely through foreign faiths but never fully shouldered New England practice. To his death in 1886, Charles was perplexed as to how (if at all) the family heritage of liberal Protestantism fit into the American republic. Despite all the Bible drills, Charles knew he never imprinted Christianity on his children. And that failure of faith—more than any political injury—gutted him to the core. "Their total neglect of religious services is a source of profound regret to me," he wrote, "as it is the first departure of the race since it removed from the old country for free worship."[129] His ancestors grappled with institutionalizing the ideologies of providentialism and Christian republicanism. They drew on New England tenets of church and state to build revolution, then government. Charles, in turn, led a host of critics who quantified and questioned religion's value. Behind him trailed a boy who savored his tales of Niagara's roar and made his own notes on Wren's rafters. The real payoff of Charles's life of pilgrimage and Christian examination came, perhaps, a generation later, with the rise of son and skeptic Henry Adams.

4

The Cosmopolitan Christianity of Henry Adams

FOR THE CURIOUS AMERICAN OF 1886 seeking a glimpse of the Great Buddha in Kamakura's full autumn splendor, the journey to Japan had to begin in late spring. The historian Henry Adams, still mourning the suicide of his wife, Clover, packed a handful of books on Buddhism and left his new H Street townhouse in May.[1] From Washington, DC, Henry traveled to his native Boston to pack and then doubled back to New York, where he "dragged" friend and artist John La Farge aboard the Albany express bound for San Francisco.

Both men were grateful for the opportunity to escape recent setbacks. La Farge's bankruptcy had tarnished his fame as muralist of Boston's new Trinity Church, and the Catholic artist hoped that a three-month tour of Shinto temples would rejuvenate work on his next commission, an altarpiece in New York City entitled *The Ascension of Our Lord*. Turning eastward, Henry thought, would "right" his point of view and hasten completion of his multivolume *History of the United States 1801–1817*.[2]

The pair traveled in high style. For the next eight days, they enjoyed skimming through the western landscape in the comfort of a luxurious private car—La Farge sketching the plains in watercolor and Adams reading about the rites of Buddhism between naps. Outside, rumors swirled that they were on a mysterious "railroad-related" mission to Japan for the American government. Then, in Omaha, as Henry remembered it, "A young reporter got the better of us; for when in reply to his inquiry as to our purpose in visiting Japan, La Farge beamed through his spectacles the answer that we were in search of Nirvana, the youth looked up like a meteor, and rejoined: 'It's out of season!' "[3]

Fashionable or not, the journey suited a seeker like Henry Adams, who epitomized the "confused Christianity" of the Gilded Age and centered his life on looking for a usable nirvana.[4] Henry made an assault on the two central faiths—Christianity and republicanism—that had set (and mostly kept) the Adams dynasty in political office for two centuries. For, in a rogue departure from family history, the skeptic Henry proved far more cosmopolitan than Christian. The rise of Henry's unbelief reveals how Gilded Age skeptics flourished: by setting aside the search for God's existence; by making a "nontheistic morality"; and by elevating new ideals or non-Western faiths above those of Christianity.[5] Deliberately, year by year, Henry sloughed off the family heritage of godly republicanism. His religious disenchantment, however, was more complex than a simple "subtraction story."[6] Rather, Henry embraced the "purity" of modern science and, later, Buddhism, transforming himself into a savage critic of American manners. "Every church mouse will write autobiography in another generation," Henry predicted in 1883, "in order to prove that it never believed in religion."[7] Henry's trajectory from lukewarm Christian to full-on skeptic exposed a deepening rift in the busy landscape of American religious thought.

More than a millstone that cramped scientific understanding, religion was to Henry a crippling force, one that often toppled statesmen and obliterated the world's finer forms of culture. Paradoxically, the ritualistic act of consuming religious culture—rather than *being* religious—fueled Adams's masterworks. Henry came to believe that modern Christianity, in its familiar American Protestant format, corrupted progress. Crafting a worldview that rejected his father's corrosive Providence, Henry embodied a nascent agnosticism, or suspension of belief in God, that shaded many scholars' thought as the nineteenth century motored to a close.[8] By 1914, bracing for war, he self-identified as a "faithless" St. Augustine of Hippo, trapped "like an octogenarian rat" in a world "whose social, political, scientific and moral systems rests on a religion of high explosives."[9] How Henry Adams got there—and why he still pursued nirvana—mirrored a major plot twist in late

Victorian life: for a growing number of Americans, Christianity was no longer a constant.

Henry Adams, third son of Charles Francis and Abigail Brooks Adams, was born in 1838. A Harvard professor of medieval history and the author of a provocative autobiography, he spent most of his life on the road. He honed his critical edge at the helm of the *North American Review* and issued (anonymously) two novels satirizing American culture. Turning his pen past the Puritans to vet the preindustrial soul, Adams took an approach to building historical narrative that was, increasingly, cemented by his day job reading medieval chronicles, admiring stained glass, and hunting down jongleurs' ditties. He traveled widely, soaking up foreign experiences and reveling in aesthetic journeys through Europe, Latin America, Japan, and the South Seas. He steamed off to Samoa, Cuba, Mexico, and Tahiti with friends, books, lavish wardrobes, photography equipment, journals, and prized watercolors in tow. Partly inspired by his wife Clover's photography, Adams spent the last decades of his life capturing the sights and scenes of the late Victorian world as he traveled through it. He died in 1918, leaving behind a religious legacy that was wholly unique within the Adams clan.

Shearing away from his Puritan namesake, young Henry Adams displayed none of the usual, familial instinct to uphold and administer God's government in New England. Henry's story is one of curiosity and deliberate destruction. As a cultural critic, he was forceful in addressing issues of church and state. Henry was one of the intellectual leaders of a pivotal generation of modernizing Americans who abandoned providentialism, decentered biblical influence, and unapologetically reframed social values.[10] Like other Victorians who came of age in the Civil War era, he grew up practicing a "mild deism" under the guidance of the nation's first family.[11] In his memoir, *The Education of Henry Adams* (1918), he described that "large and overpowering" family as "rather an atmosphere than an influence."[12] By his account, each child was indoctrinated into the Adams/Brooks legacy with a bound Bible and a silver christening mug.[13] Little Henry, the middle child of seven, mumbled through his weekly recitation of the Psalms for his parents, Charles Francis and Abigail Brooks Adams. Early on, Henry questioned scripture's historical accuracy.[14] He suffered through Sunday services at the old Unitarian church in Quincy.

Henry Adams (1838–1918). *Harvard College class of 1858 photograph album, Massachusetts Historical Society*

Along with his peers, Henry rejected the idea of an omniscient Providence—the Civil War's horror confirmed that he had no real clue what God "did," for either North or South. Raised Christian in America, Henry showed no interest in using Protestantism as a means

Marian Hooper "Clover" Adams (1843–1885). *Massachusetts Historical Society*

of reform. Later, he produced *Democracy: An American Novel* (1880) to satirize the other family faith, republicanism. "He went through all the forms; but neither to him nor to his brothers or sisters was religion real," Henry wrote of his first dealings with faith and doubt. "The children reached manhood without knowing religion, and with the certainty that dogma, metaphysics, and abstract philosophy were not worth knowing."[15] Christianity never felt authentic to Adams, even as a young man. His great-grandfather John, that "church-going animal," would have been shocked to hear Henry's brazen confession (or boast) of faithlessness. The sudden death of "real" religious instinct haunted his *Education*, and splintered Henry's intellectual attention along parallel lines of interest in medieval and modern life. In counterpoint to his Puritan ancestor, then, it is worth seizing on Henry Adams's own query: Where did the roots of his *un*belief lie?

It can be hard for biographers to recall that Henry was once a child, and that his landmark work, *The Education of Henry Adams,* is not the sole source—or even an accurate one—for reconstructing his religious life.[16] In fact, Henry Adams's *Education* may be the greatest con in American history writing. There, his self-invention (and subsequent self-annihilation) begins at baptism, when Henry conjures up a fictional preacher, venue, and guest list for his own christening.[17] In fact, the First Church parish registers show that pastor William Parsons Lunt baptized Henry before the Unitarian congregation in Quincy on September 23, 1838. After that, the church record falls silent.[18] So what kind of faith had Henry accepted through baptism? Moments after Henry's welcome to Unitarianism, Lunt preached that sin ruined the mind. He emphasized that performing religious duty was the hallmark of a truly "moral" person. Henry's father, Charles, who prized inner morality over outward piety, bridled at the pastor's advice. Charles found most clergy "irksome" and out of touch. Religious leaders like Lunt, in Charles's eyes, blinked past the dilemmas incurred by chasing success in Victorian America. "Mind is not moral," Charles grumbled that evening. "If it was, the world would be a less difficult place to live correctly in."[19]

Broad doctrines of Christian community prevailed in New England culture and shaped Henry's early development. In keeping with mainstream Unitarian thought, Henry was to be seen "not only as a religious, but as a social being."[20] Churches, as Henry heard throughout his childhood, were therefore noble but wholly voluntary associations.[21] He grew up in a well-to-do household where the rigors of theology never really held sway. "Men are not *born* into the church, but into the *world*: though volumes have been written to the contrary," one prominent minister advised in his bestselling religious manual. "Nor can any act of power, ecclesiastical, or civil; or any parish, or diocesan, or other geographical lines, make them members. It must be by their own intelligent act."[22] This, then, was the Unitarian community that first claimed Henry Adams as a Christian in baptism: individualistic, voluntary, and experiential.

Coming of age in the 1840s and 1850s, Henry experienced a home church in transition. Throughout New England, the influence of the Unitarian church's suburban membership ebbed, while central Boston's fast-rising Unitarian churches drew larger crowds, better preachers, and wealthier donors. Following Lunt's death in 1857, the Quincy parish sank into eclipse.[23] A half-century cycle of Transcendentalist utopias and reform movements had rejuvenated some American Unitarians with the spiritual energy of philosophical idealism.[24] But as the new Universalist congregations encroached on Unitarian turf in Quincy, the Adams family's preferred sect seemed to hit an intellectual plateau. Exhausted from theological battles, the antebellum Unitarian establishment, at the local level, was simply too depleted to excite Henry's generation.

Henry was aware of these great structural changes in American religion, but wholly uninterested. The theological controversies that habitually gripped New Englanders flew past. Rather, Henry blamed the "irksome" Unitarian clergy when his religious instinct, ever weak, sank further. He loathed the Bible drills that his father led at home. He scoffed at pulpit oratory. Around him, the Unitarian parish still moved with stately tradition. But Henry sensed a hollowing out of piety in reciting creeds, and he resented wasting hours in worship that might be spent in literary pursuits. As the First Church withdrew from denominational preeminence, young Henry quietly called off his search for God. His experience echoed that of other disillusioned Victorians who pulled away from faith.[25]

From an early age, Henry Adams prioritized searching for "self" over searching for God. After arriving at Harvard in 1854, he followed the well-worn family path and dabbled in Christian metaphysics, but he deemed that system of ideas wanting.[26] He felt that the metaphysics of his father's day—still a staple of most Quincy pulpit orations — was ill-suited to inform his intellectual journey. The central problem of American faith, Henry thought, was the same that afflicted any religion: clergymen failed to account for the laborious process of fashioning self-identity, and when they did address the relationship between religion and society, ministers tended to treat God as the sole agent of human development. Henry Adams dissented. He thought that what he called the metaphysical "god Whirl" and the secular authority of science wrote people *out* of the story of human progress by decentering the role of individual will.[27] "I AM is the starting point and goal of metaphysics and logic, but the church alone has pointed out that this starting-point is not human but divine. The philosopher says—I am, and the church scouts his philosophy," Adams later wrote of the drawbacks of Christian metaphysics. He confessed that taking the skeptic's path triggered repercussions. "She answers NO! You are NOT, you have no existence of your own," he continued. "You were and are and ever will be only a part of the supreme I AM, of which the church is the emblem."[28]

Gradually, Unitarians and Unitarianism grew more fragmented in Henry's home town. In New England, where the "visible saints" of his Puritan namesake's era once governed church and town, many Protestants now took an inward turn. This trend accelerated the rise of less visible saints, who valued the search for grace over the exculpation of sin.[29] Interdenominational mobility, a feature of the new normal of "common-core Protestantism," meant that many prayed at a mix of old and new houses of worship.[30] They maintained Protestant power by performing benevolence. If they skipped services, then young Henry and his peers kept the ascendant spiritual market alive by bankrolling Christian charities, buying tracts, funding missionaries, and merging reform societies.

So long as he marked *some* holy days in the presidential pew at Quincy, Henry's mounting lack of interest in organized religion did not rile the family circle. After all, to be a doubter did not mean making a permanent disconnection from Christian culture. Many American Victorians, echoing the activities of their British counterparts, used doubt as a method to re-engineer hereditary concepts of good and evil that fit with industrial society. Amid such soul-shaking concerns, church membership was no longer a habit that Henry Adams and his peers felt they must maintain. Little had changed a few decades later, when Henry quipped to a longtime friend that he was "now going to church every day, that is to the church door as the young women come from afternoon service. You know me better than to expect more."[31] The two, world and church, did not connect for him—yet.

After graduating in 1856, Henry set out to become a scientific historian and gentleman scholar in the English model.[32] Adrift on the eve of the Civil War, Henry celebrated his Harvard commencement with a grand tour of England, Austria, Italy, and France, pausing to study civil law in Berlin and Dresden. A series of changes in the Adamses' fortune made possible Henry's flight. His mother, Abigail Brown Brooks, had cemented the family wealth with a dowry from the China trade. A railroad enterprise in Quincy proposed cutting through several underused acres of family land, and the Adamses brokered a tidy profit from the sale. As one of the highest-paid members of the American diplomatic corps, which was supported by the State Department's bureaucrats, his father, Charles, enjoyed a hefty income. Two centuries after his namesake bolted from England, Henry became the first Adams son who could afford the return trip in high style.

The heroes of Henry's life (Charles Sumner, grandmother Louisa) were Continental travelers. Henry pined for colorful experiences like theirs, and for the aesthete's life that lay beyond the old Adams triangle of Washington duty, Boston law, and Quincy leisure. Henry knew he would remain wealthy enough to continue traveling indefinitely for research—good news for any budding scholar. Hearing how unhappy his brothers John Quincy II and Charles Francis Jr. were in their Court Street law offices, Henry fled to Europe in 1858. At first, he planned to edit his grandfather's papers for publication. Then Henry shoved aside family duty for foreign pleasures.

Henry's first solo European jaunt in many ways exemplified his generation's avidity for consuming world culture in grand tours, university exchange programs, and exotic pilgrimages.[33] Just a half-century earlier, John Quincy Adams expressed reluctance at printing his *Letters on Silesia* in the *Port Folio*, believing that few Americans cared to read about Bohemian castle ghosts and Prussian military maneuvers.[34] Grandson Henry likely found his travelogue downright dull. Antebellum Americans had completed the intellectual project of "unbecoming British," and thus Henry's generation greeted Europe with heightened expectations. In their letters and novels, Gilded Age narrators like Henry Adams heroicized (or, in Mark Twain's case, lampooned) Americans' ability to "fill in the blanks" of the world's uncharted places, thus reifying "modern" views of racial ideology, advertising, and commercial tourism.[35] Raised on British books that emphasized the travelogue as an affirmation of education and self-improvement, influential tastemakers like Henry Adams plied (better) travel routes to invent a literary canon of their own. Free of institutional restraints, they reflected on the "American" characteristics that came to light in the European wild.[36] Washington Irving, James Fenimore Cooper, Frederick Law Olmsted, Nathaniel Hawthorne, Wendell Phillips, Bayard Taylor, and Ralph Waldo Emerson all produced travel literature starring Americans abroad. Their books and lecture tours advertised that Americans were inquisitive and mobile purveyors of intellectual life.[37]

The new vogue for literary tourism stirred writers like Henry Adams to memorialize their contact with ancient wonders and foreign cultures while creating new, transatlantic reform networks.[38] Often, religion supplied the road map. Visits to churches, religious sites, artworks, and clerics formed popular itineraries. At the same time, tourists experimented with other, more daring personalities abroad. Descendant of two presidents, Henry had idolized his grandmother Louisa Catherine, a London-born First Lady, for "try as she might, the Madam could never be Bostonian, and it was her cross in life, but to the boy it was her charm."[39] His father, Charles, worried privately that such European overexposure "unfitted Americans for America."[40]

Those who could afford a grand tour returned laden with souvenirs, new political affiliations, and, strikingly, with changes wrought on their Western brands of thought. Some, like Henry Wadsworth Longfellow's son Charles, an occasional parishioner at the Adamses' congregation, ventured far beyond "le tour du monde" set by Continental borders and sampled life in Asia. There, the young Longfellow and his peers literally committed themselves to the Unitarian ideal of experiential self-knowledge with a tattoo tapestry of their travels, inking themselves with souvenir designs.[41] By century's end, these encounters fostered a high tide of cross-cultural exchange, widened Americans' reading habits, and evolved ideas of citizenship and universal rights.[42]

Americans on a grand tour—which could run for several years—picked over saints' bones, ogled royalty, shopped for art, dined at mineral springs, and holed up in alpine retreats.[43] On his grand tour of 1858–60, Henry followed the privileged path set down by young English aristocrats a century earlier.[44] He landed in Europe shortly after abolitionist headliner Harriet Beecher Stowe's triumphant tour, hungry to sample the "real" Old World after years of study. Aside from good steak and claret, however, Henry was (fashionably) disappointed in the offerings that he encountered abroad. Berlin society he called "profane" and more isolating than "the society of the twelve Apostles." Significantly, he went out of his way to entertain a pair of Jewish American women whom he saw repeatedly ostracized at social events.

Church attendance did not factor into his routine other than touring famous chapels and cathedral libraries. First dazzled and then dazed, Henry grew jaded from the sensory overload. "I get so bored by all these sights that I only want to get out of their way," he complained.[45] Notably, family letters gathered from his grand tour plot a more colorful mosaic of culture than the mournful portrait he painted in the *Education*. For, in company with other antiprovincial intellectuals and artists, Henry moved easily between disparate worlds, in a way that transcended the commitment to the American exceptionalism or extreme Anglophilia of his parents' generation. Henry came to savor Europe as a living museum, and he used the trip to sharpen his tone as a critic.

Henry's encounters and exchanges on his grand tour reinforced his self-identity as an erudite critic and jettisoned much of the Christian instinct that the Adams clan so prized. In letters home, Henry vented plenty of glib, twenty-something angst over his unformed moral character. Then, neatly, he turned around and skewered European clergy as too rotten to restore his molting spirituality. "The tone that I hear is so low, so selfish and so irreligious, that it compels me more and more to a love for what is pure and good," he wrote. "I should become a fanatic, I believe, and go into the pulpit if I remained here long."[46] Henry did not say what was pure and good to him. Perhaps he was reluctant to diagram his moral philosophy in stale Christian rhetoric. Or perhaps he did not know. In any event, Adams's pessimism took sturdy root abroad, alongside his scholarly interest in Christianity's functionality.

The first step in asserting an independent intellect, he decided, was shedding the religious frameworks that historians used to interpret culture. Henry also repudiated his grandfather John Quincy's model of the transatlantic Christian patriot, trampling long-held intellectual traditions as he did so. Henry used his grand tour to evict three religious ideas formative to the family's string of statesmen: Providence, patriotism, and a thick haze of Christian metaphysics.

When it came to observing foreign faith, however, Henry drew on the family's customary modes of exploration and simultaneously chose to indulge in the aesthetic odysseys of his era. He was fascinated by foreign ritual. In letters home, Henry recorded stray bits of evidence: the diameter of a saint's tomb, a seating plan for a Dresden wedding reception, the distance between long-martyred dissenters' homes. Adams began amassing religious artifacts to flaunt before his Brahmin friends, hunting down a rare engraving of Raphael's *Madonna di San Sisto*, for example. In many ways, Henry's new mania to collect religious art typified Americans' mission to share Protestant, middle-class values through the acquisition and contemplation of Christian themes in popular art.[47] Again, Henry Adams lunged at the world of religion with seemingly contrary purpose—as his distaste for blind piety grew, so too did his vast display collection of religious art, books, and talismans.[48]

In January 1861, Henry returned to Washington, DC, to serve as his father's diplomatic attaché. He rediscovered America as it was on the brink of the Civil War. Angling away from the search for God, Henry saw that Providence would shield neither his family nor his nation from the coming fracture. Around him, Americans struggled to balance regionalized Christianities with millennialist perspectives on the conflict. As it unfolded, multiple religious interpretations of the Civil War enveloped the Adamses, gathering momentum within the reflective sphere of Anglo-American print culture.[49] But in what language should the skeptic-as-citizen address this or any other republican dilemma? Despite his glamorous European tour, Henry was too inexperienced to manufacture real political eloquence. On the editorial page, he retreated from quoting doctrine but still exercised Christian rhetoric to stage the hostilities.[50]

Though he believed its social force was frail, Henry attempted to use Christianity to frame his thoughts on the projected secessions of

Maryland and Virginia. Then, he pivoted to prophesy how the Civil War would eradicate American Christianity. "I do not want to fight them. Is thy servant a South Carolinian that he should do this thing?" Henry ranted, likening Confederates to dogs. "I claim to be sufficiently philanthropic to dread it, and sufficiently Christian to wish to avoid it. . . . Men . . . will come with their bibles as well as their rifles and . . . will pray God to forgive them for every life they take."[51] Already, he showed a mature skeptic's talent in blurring sacred and secular lines for public consumption. And at the moment of national disunion, just as the Adams family's two-hundred-year-old legacy of godly republicanism gave way, this was Henry's self-identity: "sufficiently Christian."

On the Union side, one of those Bible-toting men was Henry's brother, Charles Francis Jr., who longed for a career in the First Massachusetts Cavalry in place of predictably genteel skirmishes in the family field of law. Charles's late 1861 enlistment enraged Henry. He claimed that Charles was "throwing" himself away thanks to the "madness" of the times, which no longer offered "any chance of settled lives and Christian careers."[52] Henry never bothered to expand on what he meant by "Christian" livelihoods, beyond the usual New England paths of clergy, law, and medicine.[53] But both brothers knew that political careers hinged on service in Congress, not the cavalry, and Henry's words stung. In Charles's blustery rebuke, a two-page harangue written on picket in the Carolinas, he lashed out at Henry's lack of "faith in God and the spirit of [the] age." It was the brothers' first real argument, and the only time they clashed over religion. Charles reasserted some of the old Christian certainty about the American future that Henry saw peeling away: "We shall come out all right," the elder brother wrote, "and if we don't, the world will."[54] Fighting for the Union army foretold a providential path of service, Charles wrote, and the Adamses' hard-won political gains must be preserved. He advised the petulant Henry to find his own course of duty. Henry took up his family post in London as the American legation secretary and sent dispatches or pro-Union editorials to the *New York Times* for anonymous publication.[55]

As it was for many Americans, the Civil War was a religious event that engraved a boundary line in the brothers' intellectual formation. Charles reaffirmed his faith, and Henry left it behind. By 1862, Henry professed, his belief in nearly everything—hopes for American

Charles Francis Adams Jr. (1835–1915), third from left, savors a rare moment of relaxation with his fellow Union cavalrymen in Virginia in August 1864. Adams, who fought at the bloody battles of Gettysburg and Antietam, wrote vital reports of the Civil War's progress to his family in Europe. *Library of Congress, LC-DIG-cwpb-03797*

union, the surety of his father's diplomatic skill, and his own future prospects—had dissolved in the tumult of war. Henry's always tentative faith in God wilted further, even as Charles's spirituality blossomed on the battlefield. Rebuffing one family faith—Christianity—Henry anxiously turned toward another, republicanism. Religious tidbits armed Henry with cocktail party chatter, but church history was only a superficial interest that augmented his more serious reading of democratic theorists such as Alexis de Tocqueville and John Stuart Mill. Democracy, young Henry informed his family, was all the religion he would ever need. Viewing America from London, Henry declared that Mill and Tocqueville alone reigned as the "two high priests of our faith" in republican democracy. He remained steadfast in his belief that the democracy was "still capable of rewarding a conscientious servant."[56] So he trailed after his father, taking notes on Christopher Wren's churches and parliamentary debates, but Henry's professional passions for religious tourism and political critique remained shallow in his twenties.

By contrast, his brother Charles's commitment to a robust American form of Protestantism grew. It was Henry, safe in London, who made a strategic retreat to the more skeptical realm of scholarship on historical Christianity.

The young Adams brothers confronted old Christian certainties, and each man chose a markedly different approach. Why? Like most Americans, both men saw that Providence would not carry them out of the war's horror.[57] They accepted, then, that reshaping Christianity—or rejecting religion outright—might help them find a way to live through it. At war, Charles latched on to faith as solace. Back at the American legation in London, Henry experimented with a secular approach when religious topics arose. Their intellectual activities in the spring of 1863, for example, predicted divergent paths. Henry pored over Mill's works on democracy. He debated Calvinism's "brutalized and degraded Christians" with poet Robert Browning at a dinner party. To his parents, Henry declared that Tocqueville's life and writings supplied the "Gospel of my private religion."[58]

Meanwhile, the Christian soldier Charles's reliance on authority, local and divine, wavered more than once. A few miles outside Boston, his commander had proved too drunk to lead the handpicked corps of Brahmin rookies, and Charles found himself at the regiment's head.[59] Encamped near Harpers Ferry, Virginia, the "boy-captain" struggled to incorporate the "7000 masterless slaves [who] have joined the line." To brother Henry alone, Charles deplored Americans' reluctance to undertake the "Christian and tedious effort to patiently undo the wrongs they had done, and to restore to the African his attributes."[60]

Family correspondence again serves as a better key to indexing *how* Henry Adams left the Unitarian "brotherhood of man" and overrode scriptural authority. For, at a critical juncture in his religious development, Charles's voice was the loudest in Henry's head. At the American legation, the entire Adams family shared and discussed Charles's dispatches from the Southern front. Letters to and from Charles stitched together literary quotes, philosophical mottoes culled from old Harvard drills, and, critically, snippets of scripture. For the Victorian Adamses, the Bible was many things: a great literary opus, a historical record, a symbol of human progress, and a moral resource to be used in times of crisis. Like great-grandmother Abigail, Charles quoted Milton's

Paradise Lost and *Paradise Regain'd*, at one point asking Henry to replace the chorus lines he had forgotten from *Samson Agonistes*. Stumbling at what followed from "Though we oft doubt," Charles finished his troubled thought on the Civil War—"to live to see the philosophy of this struggle"—by drawing on Matthew's Parable of the Talents.[61]

Charles reported on the war in religious language, but Henry never replied in kind. Writing on the anniversary of the Battle of Bunker Hill (June 17), father Charles Sr. addressed his soldier son in the providentialist rhetoric leveraged by Northerners and Southerners alike. The "great trial," he wrote, was a way of "purifying and exalting us in futurity," and the sole means of paying slavery's penalty to a righteous God.[62] When Charles Sr. and his namesake defaulted to providentialism to rationalize the war and its aftermath, Henry pointedly refrained from joining in. In Henry's eyes, his brother's renewal of Christianity marked him for a mundane life. "You work for power. I work for my own satisfaction," Henry wrote to Charles Jr., appraising the war's toll on their family. "You like roughness and strength; I like taste and dexterity. For God's sake, let us go our ways and not try to be like each other."[63]

For Henry, Christian civilizations older than the American republic now held greater scholarly appeal. The Civil War that endangered his brother daily gifted Henry with a profitable career as a freelance journalist and gentleman scholar. A few episodes drawn from Henry's tenure in Europe of 1861–68 illustrate his path. He shipped off to Palermo (minus credentials) to interview the Italian revolutionary Giuseppe Garibaldi. "Ye Gods what an escapade and won't the parients howl," he bragged to Charles.[64] Next, he fired off a series of screeds against the Southern cotton interest for the *Boston Advertiser*. He watched William Wetmore Story sculpt Union general George B. McClellan from life. Then Henry steamed back to the capital in time to earn notice as "one of Washington's three best dancers." On sabbatical in 1863, Henry poked through the ruins of Wenlock Abbey. He picnicked on champagne and partridge near the former Roman baths. An ocean away, Charles wrote of enduring Virginia's "Carnival of Death."

As the Civil War and his father's mission shuddered to a close, Henry Adams publicly swore off the "family go-cart" of politics, instead hoisting his profile as a deft critic of culture.[65] Mentioning President Lincoln's death only in passing, Henry openly mourned the new and sorely needed grid of steel railways that scarred the ancient charm of Florentine roads. The young traveler was showing real signs of wear, too. He had no tattoos to brandish, but after several years on tour, dusty carriage trips to visit medieval mountain towns had badly thinned Henry's dove-brown hair. And there was a serious intellectual change at work. Finally feeling free of Christianity's encumbrance, Henry would return from Europe, as he told Charles, a "violent radical, inclined towards every 'ism' in the faint hope of detecting within it some key to the everlasting enigma of progress."[66]

May 1865 found the fledgling historian Henry Adams plotting a return to his American roots, and a greatly changed family circle. "This scattering of our family has left curious marks on us," Adams observed from the Continent, where he lingered for three more years in a pseudo-diplomatic capacity. "For my part I can only promise to be liberal and tolerant towards other people's ideas; let them leave me equally to mine."[67] Cavalryman Charles Jr. entered the railroad industry, eventually rising to the presidency of the Union Pacific Railroad. Brooks practiced and taught law. The eldest brother, John Quincy II, took up experimental farming and dipped into Democratic (!) state politics. Sisters Louisa Catherine Kuhn and Mary Parker Ogden settled into motherhood, philanthropy, and seasonal grand tours. Henry dove back into American culture, honing his reputation as a razor-sharp critic of politics, art, and literature. Arguably more liberal but no longer a standard-issue Protestant, Henry Adams came home to Quincy in 1868.

Henry's interest in religion now was purely academic in scope. Spending several years out in the world had made him confident enough to manage the family faith on his own terms. For example, he did not regularly receive communion at First Church, but he sustained the Adams Temple and School Fund that funded Quincy's centers for educational and religious development. He made payments on the family's Unitarian pew but rarely used it. Publicly, he had no interest in exploring the many denominational roads of Victorian life. Privately, he kept up old lines of correspondence with Harvard classmates-turned-clergy. He loaded up his bookshelves with teachings on Buddhism, Hinduism, and the history of the early church.

Using Christianity was part of Henry's shortcut to reading Berlin's social ranks and charming the peers who so intimidated his parents in

London. His actual theological attachment to it was superficial at best, but Henry's acknowledgment of Christianity as a cultural language had never faltered abroad. Now he sought to translate that discovery into American scholarship on the preindustrial soul. Henry accepted a professorship at Harvard, where he was, as he said, "pitchforked" into the field of medieval history.[68] Professor Adams was assigned nine hours a week to lecture a hundred upperclassmen and was given the syllabus start date of AD 987.[69] Teaching a specialization that was utterly foreign, and gleeful to do it, Henry mined his grand tour memories for material. He took up editing the *North American Review* and opened a long series of editorial volleys sparring with and criticizing presidents, artists, and social reformers.[70]

Henry's pledge of ideological liberalism evaporated before his new field of study and the happy prospect, in 1872, of marrying a "charming blue," Marian ("Clover") Hooper. "She knows her own mind uncommon well," Henry wrote, heaping on worldly praise for his bride. "She does not talk *very* American."[71] In Clover, Henry Adams found the ideal partner for his globetrotting lifestyle: another well-educated skeptic eager to sample religious culture from New England to the Nile, minus any fruitless search for God.

Henry Adams's longest correspondence was with his brothers, but it was the women in his life—medieval and modern—who refined his scholarly sense of religion and next helped him to construct a nontheistic morality. A closer analysis of his marriage to Clover, their travels, and his 1880 parable, *Democracy*, reveals Henry to be a skeptic bent on shredding all family faiths. Here, Henry's literary fame set him apart, but in his confused approach to Christianity, he was just following the American crowd. As he embarked on the next phase of his journey away from God and Unitarian membership, Henry joined other seekers of the 1870s and 1880s who worked to remake morality without certain Protestant precepts. To do so, they used Christianity as a point of departure rather than as a destination. They sidelined conversion as a goal and surveyed different ways to practice spirituality. They experimented with "exchanging selves" to ensure that American religion "bore the signs of contact with those who were other and different."[72] Postbellum Protestants pursued this intellectual and cultural project widely, in print and in prayer, emphasizing that what made the

American religious experience distinctive was its vibrant dynamic of encounter and exchange. Henry and Clover cultivated an acid skepticism regarding organized faith and its purported moral virtue. They were openly disenchanted with the Protestant Christianity that they inherited. Henry and Clover Adams never fully invested in the Gilded Age reinvention of America as a Christian nation.

Clover's earliest religious life was, like Henry's, tilted toward doubt. Clover was the youngest child of the Transcendentalist poet Ellen Sturgis and physician Robert Hooper.[73] Ellen was an active contributor to *The Dial* and a friend of Margaret Fuller. Her death at thirty-six devastated the family and launched Clover into the role of hostess for her father, leaving little time for prayer. The first editor of her published letters enshrined Clover at the heart of a "Washington Circle" of *salonnières*, describing her genealogical pedigree as "half Puritan and half Pilgrim."[74] She attended James Freeman Clarke's Unitarian church in Boston as a child but shared Henry's aversion to organized faith. Like Henry, Clover read Latin, Greek, and German. Later, when Adams conducted historical research at the Library of Congress, Clover assisted him. Well read, curious about religion—but not wholly committed to Christianity—and by all accounts as eloquent as Henry, Clover made a feisty intellectual match. She studied widely on her own; frequent house guest Henry James dubbed her "a perfect Voltaire in petticoats."[75] Along with many of the Hooper women, Clover battled mood swings and bouts of depression.

The neurasthenic Henry considered her an ideal wife, and they honeymooned on the Nile in summer 1872.[76] Their first journal letters home were joint narratives, in which Clover huddled in a fringed luxury cabin, seasick and homesick for the distant "heaven" of New England.[77] In the skeptical Clover, Henry had found a unique intellectual partner to share and debate his discoveries. She was equally willing to explore and proof out new forms of faith. With Clover in tow, Henry Adams resumed his intensive course of self-discovery around the world. The pair kept up a costly whirlwind of foreign travel throughout the 1870s.

A bare half-century after John Adams and Thomas Jefferson traded daydreams of Cairo's call, Henry and Clover steamed, stylishly, into port. Henry's flight into Egypt, along with a sea of other blue-blooded travelers who lugged their new Kodak cameras on "donkeyback" to the pyramids, represented a shift in how modernizing Americans documented such encounters.[78] Egypt, nominally a province of the Ottoman Empire, was awash in debt following the American Civil War boom years of cotton trade with Britain.[79] After weathering waves of English and French occupation, Egyptians mostly welcomed the onslaught of rich, literary-minded visitors like the Adamses. The Victorian genre of Far East travel writing, in turn, split Americans into two camps: either tourists (passive clients of expert-led trips) or travelers (active intellectuals who chased experience).[80] The Adamses were a bit of both. Travelers like Clover slotted a stray Anglo-Arabic phrase into letters home as evidence of their worldliness. Tourists like Henry groused about the price of desert lodging and lamented the absence of little modern luxuries. Whether diligent or pretentious in their labor to comprehend the exotic, Gilded Age writers like the Adamses reshaped American readers into reformers, using foreign adventures to nourish new conversations about universal human rights and religious pluralism.[81]

The Adamses and their transatlantic peers reached across religious neighborhoods to picture the world anew. The idols and byways of Cairo invited them to road-test new behavior free of their era's hidebound etiquette manuals.[82] Henry and Clover made a great effort to photograph ruins, to befriend imams and visit mosques, and to learn a variety of the local customs. Ever inquisitive, they were not always kind to foreign ways of faith, nor to people living outside Christianity. Occasionally, the Adamses evoked the characterizations of shallow American tourists that Twain parodied in *The Innocents Abroad* (1869). It was no accident that Twain's subtitle—*The New Pilgrim's Progress*—jabbed at wealthy Yankees who relaxed their old sensibilities once free of New England's strictures. Money helped. Henry and Clover could afford the novelty of constant travel, and it filled a sensory void. Even dire news from home could not curb their extravagant gallop. Alerted to a $9,000 loss arising from a mill fire, Clover joked she would "buy a big Japanese teapot and put everything in it—a fireproof one. I still buy clothes, for . . . we may as well die game."[83] Clover grew as jaded as Henry. To pass the time at Karnak, she printed photographs: panoramas of the sacred space pocketing the Pyramids, and not a worshipper in sight save her five-foot-four husband. Clover lacked the education, she claimed, to appreciate the idols as Henry did.[84] Eye to eye with the Temple of Dendur—and with the very gods that John Adams had once rifled past in Christian dismay—Clover glazed over. Even the ornate shadow-play of the tall sandstone registers, alive with lotus-bound believers praising Isis and Osiris, failed to move her. "One gets so blasé and anything less than three thousand years seem[s] quite too modern to be worth much," Clover wrote home.[85]

After Karnak, the religious sites that drew Henry and Clover were multidimensional, as complex to experience as any of the lavishly illustrated books lining the Adams library in Quincy. From the beginning, it was Clover, operating as the domestic manager, who kept their itinerary on track by navigating religious proprieties abroad. In this respect she suffered few of the budget constraints or condescensions that Abigail or Louisa Catherine had endured. As Henry swept toward the Sphinx, for example, it was Clover who stayed behind to hire guides and to ease the delays brought about by the observance of Ramadan.[86] Following the route that most Westerners took, Clover and Henry spent Christmas in Asyut. As the crew baked bread, Clover dressed the barge with what she described as "palm branches in default of the orthodox hemloc" and shopped for last-minute pottery gifts in the bazaars.[87] Henry, restless to see how a world without Christianity thrived, roamed from site to site. Every revelation made him giddy. In Luxor, he photographed Abu Simbel and planned a treatise on the complex legacy of Egyptian law. Spain beckoned, too. Near Cordova, John Adams's great-grandson entered the "glorious" Great Mosque and fell in epiphany: "But whether my name is now Abd-el-adem, or Ben-shadams, or Don Enrique Adamo, I couldn't take oath, for I have been utterly bewildered to know what has become of my identity, and the Spaniards have been so kind to us that I feel as though I owed them a name."[88]

For Henry, religion was emerging as a transitory force in history, one that remade nation and self. His most vivid ideas about faith often "came home" to Henry Adams on the road, and the full realization of that philosophy struck him first in Egypt. Peeling back the historical strata of Christian, Jewish, and Muslim growth prodded Henry to think that religion supplied scholars with markers, or fixed points, when human progress accelerated toward change.[89] Certainly, by the late

1870s, he perceived that energy at work in his own life. For, overwriting the family's religious tradition, Henry and Clover's odysseys untethered the last remnants of their hereditary Christian character. And, increasingly, Henry was drawn to researching notions of female divinity. He questioned why the premodern ideal of a miracle-working Sainte Vierge (Virgin Mary), emblazoned in mosaic form at the Chartres cathedral, had fallen so far out of favor. Past generations of Adamses had used explorations of foreign faith to reinforce American Protestantism, publicly and privately. By contrast, Henry and Clover Adams embraced new religious knowledge as a way to get around the world, not into heaven.

On their return, Clover and Henry hosted gatherings in Boston and Washington, but they abstained from formal church membership. In this, they were not alone. Pew demographics remain blurry at best, but after a dip in the 1870s and 1880s, American Christian membership did not rebound until the 1890s.[90] From the skeptics' perch, Henry and Clover witnessed a religious marketplace in flux. They watched as interest in Catholic, Baptist, and Methodist communities swelled. From the sidelines, they saw an influx of Protestant immigrants transform common-core worship. They noticed that Western churches had institutionalized beyond their frontier roots.[91] Henry and Clover did not care to join in any of it. Now and then, they walked the one block up from Lafayette Square to St. John's Episcopal Church for Christmas or Easter services.

God was never a part of how Clover framed the Washington world. For most of her life, Clover's only Sunday morning ritual was to write a long letter to her father. Her dispatches were lighthearted reminiscences of cocktail party repartee, museum trips, and political gossip. Glancing out the screen window onto posh H Street, just beyond a tangle of heliotrope and rose, Clover recorded her neighbors—those "miserable sinners"—making their way to church in "very good clothes." She mocked the "look" if not the "feel" of practicing Christians of her own class. "I fancy no prayer-book repentance would bring them to confess that their Sunday clothes are bad," Clover quipped. "Those are no matter of heredity, but so very personal."[92] Even religion-minded friends, such as the philosopher and psychologist William James, failed to change the Adamses' views about the potential benefits of committing to Christian

An accomplished photographer, Clover Adams captured the couple's foreign odysseys in sweeping panoramas. Like Henry, she used art to jab at American elites, as in "Gossips," which features a posh trio of dogs (Marquis, Possum, and Boojum) posed for a garden tea party. *Photograph by Marian Hooper Adams, 1883, Massachusetts Historical Society*

membership. And, for a time, Adams pronounced Clover "quite converted" by James's philanthropy; the pair doled out substantial sums to Christian causes.[93] Henry Adams respected James's notion that the "great men" who improved society were recognized by God—"if there is a God," Henry taunted.

But charity did not reawaken belief, and in the Adams household, a stylish agnosticism prevailed throughout the 1870s and 1880s. Family letters again string together the story of the Adamses' exit from faith. Past correspondents like John Quincy and Louisa plied Christian language to discuss public or private duty; by contrast, Henry and Clover deployed it only in irony. Clover, renowned for her wit on the Washington dinner circuit, parodied the old New England rhetoric of Christian virtue for comedic effect. "A merciful Providence" freed her from social obligations, and Henry James's visits promised debauchery of a biblical hue. A divorce epidemic in the capital's ranks forced the weary hostess to rewrite her place cards, as she could not "legally open a 'Home for Sinners' without a license from the District."[94] For Henry and Clover Adams, Christianity was no longer a viable practice. It was a punchline.

By 1880, Henry Adams felt bold enough to profess his satire of American faiths—Christianity and republicanism—on the page, under the mask of anonymity.[95] The founder's heir chose to ridicule America's federal machinery in novel fashion. With *Democracy: An American Novel*, Adams amplified the popular critiques of political corruption put forth by other bestselling writers such as Twain and Charles Dudley Warner (*The Gilded Age*, 1873), Marion Crawford (*An American Politician*, 1884), and Edward Bellamy (*Looking Backward*, 1889). Adams also joined with the Victorian authors who geared up to puncture the profile of the Protestant establishment, a literary crusade later championed by the likes of Harold Frederic (*The Damnation of Theron Ware*, 1896), Samuel Butler (*The Way of All Flesh*, 1903), and Sinclair Lewis (*Elmer Gantry*, 1926). More focused on personalities than on plots, this literary cohort used character studies and literary "types" to assess the features that sealed American identity.[96] By turns exploitative or earnest, these authors mocked the upper class and, simultaneously, drafted a manual for new arrivals to follow as they joined industrial America.[97]

Popular literary trends aside, Adams ripped the bittersweet ethos of his own Washington tell-all from the cache of family letters that he had pored over as a bored young man in Quincy. Required reading for any Adams son on the path to statesman, the archive spilled over with musty scandals and political parables. "Remember Democracy never lasts long. It soon wastes exhausts and murders itself," Henry's great-grandfather John had warned in 1814. "There never was a Democracy Yet, that did not commit suicide."[98] The American Civil War, to Henry's mind, capped the self-annihilation of godly republicanism. So Henry set *Democracy* amid the gritty failure of Reconstruction-era Washington. Adams modeled his leading lady, the northerner Madeleine Lee, on a hybrid of wife Clover and grandmother Louisa Catherine.

The wealthy widow Madeleine, spiritually bereft after losing her Confederate husband and her only son, relocates to the capital after years wandering on the European grand tour trail. Hungry to "measure with her own mind the capacity of the motive power" of politics, Madeleine bypasses New York society and settles into the whirl of a

Lafayette Square kingmaker's life. Immediately, she is "bent upon getting to the heart of the great American mystery of democracy and government."[99] Two suitors—the upstanding Virginia republican John Carrington and the sleazier Illinois senator Silas P. Ratcliffe—vie for her affection as wife and patron. On a side trip to Mount Vernon, to their great chagrin, they learn that what Madeleine really wants in a second husband is no less than "George Washington at thirty."[100] Her devout sister, Sybil Ross, fills in as the standard-bearer of Protestant virtue. Through Madeleine's eyes, readers also view "President Jacob" (no surname), one of "nature's noblemen" who ascends easily to the White House, but effects little real change once installed.[101] In receiving-line banter, dinner debates, and Senate gallery snapshots, Madeleine records her utter loss of a once rosy faith in American republicanism. Disgusted with Ratcliffe's drive and underwhelmed by Carrington's dogmatic grip on eighteenth-century moral philosophy, Madeleine makes a dramatic exit to the Holy Land.

Henry's canonical tweak—taking the standard freshman senator's disenchantment saga and awarding the lead to a single woman who cannot vote—was a dress rehearsal for his much weightier critique of church/state/gender relations within the American elite that he later expanded on in *Esther*. The plot of the skeptic-citizen's exodus and journey, according to Henry Adams, was already set in place: a doubter's social task (marriage) compels her to choose between religion, science, and self; she chooses self. Notably, in his first rendering of a new, nontheistic morality where "justice is the soul of good criticism," Adams elects women to the authority role.[102]

In a family where it was customary to announce political creeds, Henry used his first novel to echo great-grandmother Abigail's famed plea, to redefine the duties of women in a democracy. It is precisely because of Madeleine's nonvoting status that Adams assigns such narrative value to her exegesis of American politics. To be a single woman and a skeptic makes Madeleine an outsider twice over. As a social entity whom Victorian churches claimed to aid—the new widow—her repulsion toward Christianity thus becomes especially significant. Madeleine has "not entered a church for years," since such visits only stir up "unchristian feelings." *Democracy*'s heroine is proud *not* to be "an orthodox member of the church; sermons bored her, and clergymen never failed to irritate every nerve in her excitable system." Pious Sybil, on the other hand, quotes scripture, sings in the choir, and sends up novenas for eligible dance partners. Madeleine stifles a laugh at her sister's piety, but she never forces her grim agnosticism onto friends or kin. " 'Time enough,' said she, 'for her to forget religion when religion fails her.' "[103]

If religion failed Madeleine Lee—and Henry, and Clover—might science help? Madeleine Lee's amateurish efforts at applying scientific theory to historical progress are, like those of her creator, extremely unwieldy. There is little talk of "warfare" between God and science in Henry's novels; neither science nor faith can sate his characters' needs. Appraising congressmen thick in debate, Madeleine identifies herself as an alchemist of political talent: "One by one, she passed them through her crucibles, and tested them by acids and by fire. A few survived her tests and came out alive, though more or less disfigured, where she had found impurities."[104] Madeleine, who reads the English biologist Herbert Spencer's works on evolution, tries repeatedly to align Darwinian ideas with unfolding events. Proving an apt and self-taught pupil of political science, she yields to one senator's glib "confession" of support for Darwinian evolution. However, she shares his twinge of fatalism, expressed here, that parroting theories can feel as foolish as reciting the old creeds. Ratcliffe answers:

> I have faith; not perhaps in the old dogmas, but in the new ones; faith in human nature; faith in science; faith in the survival of the fittest. Let us be true to our time, Mrs. Lee! If our age is to be beaten, let us die in the ranks. . . . There! have I repeated my catechism correctly? You would have it! Now oblige me by forgetting it. I should lose my character at home if it got out.[105]

By contrast, her suitor Ratcliffe scoffs at the notion that humankind "descended from monkeys," although his political machinations (ironically) underline Ratcliffe's frenzy to adapt and survive. Via Madeleine, Henry lashes out at the culture of "confused Christianity" in which he moved.

Democracy is an angry book. Henry racks up family feuds, society wars, and a near duel. Far from the well-ordered Christian republic of his ancestors' days, America has run wild with corruption, ambition, and greed on a newly global scale. With no "personal God" but a vague "democracy" to guide her, Madeleine tries to formulate a modern moral philosophy that patches up these social wounds. First, she queries congressmen and is nonplussed at their replies. "Half of our wise men declare that the world is going straight to perdition; the other half that it is fast becoming perfect. Both cannot be right," Madeleine observes. "I must know whether America is right or wrong."[106] Torn, she turns to gathering social clues. She is sickened by the "dance of democracy" around the "automata" of the "waxen" president and his wife, which accelerates daily with "wilder energy." Such a display dampens the heroine's gusto for real political inquiry, despite having turned her "disadvantage" (womanhood) into a democratic role—that of a minority prophet indicating the structure's weak moral foundations.[107] Like Henry, Madeleine senses little ideological substance operating behind the White House curtain.

The pessimistic Adams, more gifted at beginnings than endings, has written himself into a corner. So, near the book's fitful end, the origin story of Madeleine's agnosticism tumbles out. Sybil recalls how Madeleine, devastated by the deaths of her husband and son, raved memorably for days "about religion and resignation and God."[108] Voicing Henry's own discovery, Madeleine perceives that she has sinned by exchanging one dead faith (Christianity) for another (republicanism). She labels the United States a failed experiment. While she has "atoned for want of devotion to God, by devotion to man," she remains hazy about how to resume her course of moral education without attracting more dogma.[109] "I want to go to Egypt," Madeleine concludes. "Democracy has shaken my nerves to pieces."[110] And Henry Adams, persuaded by his own *Democracy* that a skeptic of Christian republicanism would never fit the desirable "American" mold, threw himself into becoming a modern citizen of the world.

At the midpoint of his career, Henry's aesthetic cultivation triggered a violent rejection of the classical precepts of Christian republicanism that his ancestors venerated. Europe, long the Adams family's finishing school for political thought, held few bankable charms beyond good weather and fine ruins. Throughout the winters of the 1870s and early 1880s, Henry and his wife defected to ancient, sunny Venice. Encountering the lavish barbarism of a former model republic—identified as such by John Adams in 1786—*Democracy's* secret author dispensed with the lessons of classical history and pursued aesthetic idylls instead. The pair settled into an easy routine, joining other expatriates to savor the moody beauty of the city's palazzos and lagoons, then captured best by American John Singer Sargent's busy paintbrush.[111] After a lazy breakfast "à la française," they boarded the fleet of overpriced gondolas. Then, as Clover recalled, they would "hunt up churches, where we often turn sadly from pictures which we had wanted to see, getting nothing for our search."[112]

Henry's initial design of a nontheistic morality, based on tattered republican tenets and European travel, soured. Protestant ideas of right and wrong—so clearly reflected back to John Quincy in Erasmus's home town, and to Charles Francis Sr. in the barren pews of a fast-day service—tasted too stale for Henry Adams to use. The Socratic directive to "know thyself" fell especially flat. "We can't prove even that we are," Henry wrote.[113] The family seat of Quincy, Henry's summer home, bore the marks of that ennui. On the library mantel where the household gods still presided, Adams pushed aside the old busts of Homer and Cicero. Slyly, Henry planted his new totem center stage: a colossal bronze trio of half-nudes carousing in Dionysian excess. Between his literary tasks and her amateur photography, the Adamses of the early 1880s were successful, even happy. Eschewing church membership, they bought religious art and used Christian rhetoric. At home and abroad, Henry and Clover found ways to use Christianity without being Christian. Then, in 1884, Clover's father grew ill, and Henry Adams struggled to prepare his wife for the death of her only parent.[114] He settled on writing a novel.

At first pass the plot of *Esther* (1884), published under the pseudonym Frances Snow Compton, is deceptively popular in tone. Yet it was, as Henry recalled, "written in one's heart's blood."[115] He published 1,000 copies, sold 514, and bought up the balance to destroy. Scholars have long associated the protagonist, freethinker Esther Dudley, with Clover Adams.[116] A Puritan heiress and New York society "name," Esther falls in love with the Episcopal clergyman Stephen Hazard. She also fights an attraction to her paleontologist cousin, the skeptic George Strong. Adams keeps the reader guessing as to where he lands in the "warfare" talk of his day; he gives the man of science and the man of faith an even number of choice lines as they pursue Esther. Created by a vigorously agnostic author, Stephen Hazard turns out to be a surprisingly likable prelate. In his first sermon, he reconciles science, Christianity, and civilization. "The hymns of David, the plays of Shakespeare, the metaphysics of Descartes, the crimes of Borgia, the virtues of Antonine, the atheism of yesterday and the materialism of to-day, were all emanations of divine thought, doing their appointed work," he preaches. "It was the duty of the church to deal with them all."[117] His choice of homily, tinged with popular philosophical idealism, suggests that even Clover might find Hazard sympathetic enough to attend Henry Adams's fantasy church.[118]

Again, it is a corps of imaginary women who best advance Henry's nontheistic morality. "The proper study of mankind is woman and, by common agreement since the time of Adam, it is the most complex and arduous," Henry later wrote.[119] To an unusual degree within his profession at the time, Henry took a special interest in the impact of political change on women. He identified religion as the main sphere where they reinterpreted and enacted social power.[120] As "real" women envisaged amid the juvenilia, satire, and sensationalism of Gilded Age fiction, Henry's female characters display a refreshing amount of intellectual panache and religious depth.[121] Esther, named for a biblical queen but increasingly distrustful of scriptural authority, is clearly a reference to Clover. Her status as a skeptic is somewhat shielded by her class and wealth. The roots of Esther's doubt are murky. She delights in the social ritual of churchgoing and finds the notion of congregationalism attractive. And she instinctively welcomes a man named Hazard (Adams's irony!) in the initial guise of Christian solace.

Marriage plans eventually force Esther's religious doubts out into the open. Rather than seeking wisdom from the church, she turns to other laywomen for advice. A "sage hen"—the beautiful and "authentic" Colorado orphan Catherine Brook—arrives to wrench the love triangle further. Made wise by her "Westernness" and ultrafemininity, Henry's native bird makes a stir in the city flock. The sage hen remains a strikingly liberal ingénue for Adams to create, and she likely served as a model for the characters cast in popular fictions by Frederic, Butler, and Lewis.[122] A former Presbyterian, Catherine is a Christian subversive, too, but of a milder variety; she sneaks Charles Dickens novels into service.[123] She is an American innocent who will neither lose her hold on the Christian church nor judge those who choose to leave it—she is a progressive.

With *Esther*, Henry used the production of Christian culture as a plot device to provide a more full-bodied critique of American religion than he had sketched in *Democracy* four years earlier. Rounding out Adams's avatars of religion, science, and "Americanness" is Wharton, a bohemian artist and dimming Catholic. Wharton's lack of a first name hints at his ultraliberal nature, thus ruling him out as a real suitor. Yet it is the creation of his religious art that drives Henry's tale. Wharton recruits Esther and Catherine to paint murals for Hazard's new Fifth Avenue church. Henry pulled the plot from his own life, having spent the winter of 1883 observing John La Farge at work on the walls of a roofless Trinity Church. Adams watched La Farge set three massive stained-glass window scenes—*Resurrection, Christ in Majesty*, and *New Jerusalem*. Fixed on making a "color church" to shake up the dowdy Boston palette of white and gray, La Farge translated favorite Protestant themes into neo-Byzantine shades of Pompeian red and Ravennese teal.[124] In Henry's retelling, the same commission is executed mainly by women. Esther and Catherine embrace the opportunity to join the previously all-male artists' club, indicating their moral commitment to build up the church for future parishioners in a meaningful way.

Modern American women, to Henry, were copies of the Sainte Vierge: holy, emotional, and able to rule others (wisely) by feeling as well.[125] A closer analysis of *Esther* suggests that in the Victorian contest for moral purity, to be won either by masculine intellect or by feminine emotion, Henry again finds Christianity torn asunder. Abigail Adams's great-grandson leans closer to calling a victory for the ladies. For, like Henry's own female friends, Esther is imbued with an emotional intelligence that outstrips conventional notions of male superiority. That makes her a formidable intellectual rival, and especially so to her suitors. Clever Esther/Clover, in Adams's formulation, is the literary rebuttal to a sea of Gilded Age heroines ruined by goopy "sentiment." Esther never weeps. She never laments. Empowering Esther is Henry's rejoinder to an American religious establishment phobic about "feminization" at the hands of pious women.[126]

Esther Dudley cannot focus heart and mind in prayer, and she feels no remorse about it. Complacent in her lukewarm Christianity, she uses sermon time to rank her neighbors' outfits. Slowly, she distances herself from the ideas behind the rites. Adams depicts Esther's retreat from organized faith as rational and deliberate, a necessary tragedy of modernity. Viewed as a literary idol, Esther is Adam's finest monument to the elegant "lady skeptic" of the Victorian era. Inside, she is another confused and "sufficiently Christian" member of the American elite. Her mind whirls in speculation about competing perspectives offered by science and/or faith. After her father's death, Esther experiences a wave of doubt—first in herself, then in God. Mere steps from the funeral, Esther panics and accepts clergyman Hazard's offer of marriage. They embark on a rocky engagement. Minister Hazard, writes Adams, in "calling up the divinity which lies hidden in a woman's heart, is startled to find that he must obey the God he summoned."[127]

Esther dives into a course of self-taught theology, but she cannot master burgeoning doubts. Sage hen Catherine acts as a friendly foil, trying to soothe Esther's mounting agitation. And Adams, more agnostic than ever, finally unlocks the narrative skill needed to explain a crisis of faith. Adams invents some stunning scenes between Esther and Catherine. His dialogue yields a unique portrait of female skeptics discussing Christian doctrine and legitimating their motives for doubt. In staging these conversations, Adams's "female" tone is grave and focused—a throwback to the women theologians who drove the novels of Harriet Beecher Stowe. According to Henry's narrative, Christianity is unraveling in real time across the bands of American society that Esther and Catherine represent.[128] If she weds Hazard, then Esther fears she will be discovered as a doubter and ruin them both. Catherine flings off her friend's deepest worry with a casual put-down of the congregation's relative piety. Esther's doubt, the sage hen observes, is normal, respectable—even laudable. Here is the exchange:

"But I must go to his church," said Esther, "and sit at his communion."

"How many people at his church could tell you what they believe?" asked Catherine. "Your religion is just as good as theirs as long as you don't know what it is."[129]

Esther realizes her inability to commit to Christian devotion except on her own terms. She cannot make a wholehearted leap backward to accept dogma. Like Adams, she is more drawn to church aesthetics than to theology. Along with many of her real-world peers in the American gentry, Esther turns to the physical beauty of religion as a strategy to redeem her ebbing faith.[130] But, in her big-city "color church," Esther cannot find a Yankee corollary to match the great blue majesty of Henry's Chartres. Esther's inward turn, to inventory and judge the precepts of American Protestantism, strengthens her resolve to reject it—no matter how many more murals of divine femininity Wharton commissions her to create. Esther breaks off the engagement in order to defend her status as a skeptic, and similarly puts an end to her cousin's chances, too. She remains in love with Hazard, who acknowledges Esther's Christianity to be a lost cause, and quickly departs for . . . anywhere else (Adams does not say).

Admittedly, Henry Adams's intellectual goals here were high. But the oddball literary form that he chose—an overlong novella or a too-short novel, with a La Farge–based bankruptcy subplot—makes the whole religious dilemma feel rushed, with no satisfactory ending for Esther. Henry, stumbling over how to end it, nearly seized on a much darker suggestion from his friends. At a pivotal moment, Esther stands in the shadow of Niagara Falls, explaining to the clergyman that what irks her most about organized faith is the act (real or pretended) of total submission. Aloft before Hazard she is a powerful profile: the forthright skeptic, defiant against nature's flood and resistant to the social tide of Christian membership. But, as Clarence King recalled to John Hay, Henry nearly flipped the scene another way. King thought that Esther should have jumped to her death, "as that was what she would have done," and he told Adams so. "Certainly she would," Henry agreed, "but I could not suggest it."[131] Pointedly, Henry used *Esther* to show Clover that religion did not offer the only path out of grief. Clover, always better at finishing projects than Henry, never mentioned the novel in her correspondence. Like Esther, she fled to art.

Imagining and writing *Esther* proved therapeutic for Henry's historical craftsmanship. His academic interests remained permanently focused on the subject of female divinity: specifically, how to reinterpret the role of women in church development. Outwardly critical of modern religion's utility throughout the 1880s and 1890s, Henry Adams became obsessed with comprehending how the Catholic Church had made and manufactured the preindustrial soul. More and more, the self-invented medievalist relied on religion to explain episodic change in history.

At Harvard, Adams focused his history seminars on medieval institutions, notably record-laden churches, in order to collect more evidence. How, he wondered, had Christianity atrophied from the glory of Mont-Saint-Michel and Chartres? The church history that Adams sought to tell was a wholly new draft of how Christianity rose and fell in the Western world. He shunted aside the Puritans and reintroduced Gilded Age Americans to the Sainte Vierge, emphasizing the significance and sensation of medieval female divinity. "Christ the Trinity might judge as much as He pleased," Henry wrote of the Virgin enthroned at Chartres, "but Christ the Mother would rescue; and her servants could look boldly into the flames."[132] After *Esther*, restaging republican or religious dramas as novels no longer intrigued Adams. Recovering the "limitless will" of women, soldered by history to the "limitless conscience" of medieval Christianity—that project consumed the rest of Henry Adams's professional energy.

Henry's anonymous novel sold well but, sadly, his effort failed at home. On December 6, 1885, nearly ten months after her father's death, Clover drank the potassium cyanide stored in her Chestnut Street darkroom. The newspapers were kind, discreetly noting that she "dropped dead . . . due to a sudden paralysis of the heart."[133] After an Episcopal funeral service, Henry buried his wife at Rock Creek Cemetery in Washington, DC. He made contact with the sculptor Augustus Saint-Gaudens, then wrapping up work on the Robert Gould Shaw memorial on Boston Common, and the architect Stanford White. Henry Adams wanted Clover's tomb (and, later, his own) to mark the convergence of several religious cultures, like the many sites they had experienced together. At the same time, Henry wanted the monument to summon up something nameless and dateless enough to appeal to his fellow travelers in grief. The grave marker, Adams thought, must demonstrate the acceptance of death but not be overruled by loss. Peacefield's household gods likely stirred in his imagination, for Adams requested something "Socratic" for the tomb, with a touch of Michelangelo's Sistine glory, a sexless figure that would evoke the "peace of God" and "mental repose." For Clover, Henry commissioned "Nirvana."[134]

Puzzled, Saint-Gaudens made a few sketches and scribbled in his notebook, "Amplify." He pressed Adams to assign "any book

Inspired by ideals of Buddhist compassion, Augustus Saint-Gaudens and Stanford White designed this memorial to serve as Clover and Henry Adams's final resting place in Washington's Rock Creek Cemetery. In his *Education,* Henry wrote that he "was apt to stop there often to see what the figure had to tell him that was new; but, in all that it had to say, he never once thought of questioning what it meant. . . . The interest of the figure was not in its meaning, but in the response of the observer." *Library of Congress, photograph by Camilo José Vergara, LC-DIG-ppmsca-23707*

not long" so he could study the subject of nirvana first. Distraught, Henry declined. He might have offered a few words of definition from Clover's childhood pastor, James Freeman Clarke, who had just published *Ten Great Religions* (1884). There, Clarke epitomized Victorian Americans' fuzzy understanding of Buddhism as "the Protestantism of the East."[135] Adams might have articulated an understanding of nirvana as Clover's cousin William Sturgis Bigelow later defined it: a "peace that passeth understanding trained on material things . . . the peace of limitless consciousness unified with limitless will."[136] Or Henry might have quoted back the words of his own bohemian artist Wharton in *Esther*: "Nirvana is what I mean by Paradise. . . . It is eternal life, which, my poet says, consists in seeing God."[137] Perhaps the medievalist did not know what to suggest as an introductory text, given his own odd pastiche of intellectual encounters with non-Western religion. Scouring sacred Buddhist texts did not reveal nirvana's "mysterious *Nothing*," nor how Adams might conquer "that highest state of absolute quiescence" through, as his generation understood it, committing to a sort of self-annihilation or "Asiatic atheism."[138] Buddhistic notions of compassion, Adams guessed, might connect to his historical vision of the Virgin Mary's unifying power over medieval society—but he was far too grief-stricken to investigate how or why. Henry, convinced that American culture had poisoned Clover, gravitated for comfort to the most foreign philosophy that he could find.

The cub reporter who intercepted Adams on the Nebraska prairie in 1886 was entirely right—nirvana had a "season," and Henry was not alone in his quest. Increasingly, nirvana appealed to many seeking a neutral alternative to the constant sectarian storms over what made up "Christian" heaven. For those shaken by the Civil War's carnage and enticed by the chance of spiritual regrowth, Buddhist passivity offered a therapeutic option to the militaristic Christian optimism manifested by the Social Gospel movement's budding reform culture.[139] For Henry and other Victorians who dabbled in grafting Eastern religion onto Western science, nirvana came to represent a scholarly state of mind beyond joy or sorrow.[140] The efforts of main-line Protestants (and skeptics like Henry) to understand the theological principles of nirvana, however, rarely penetrated farther than a vague, imperialist-tinged sympathy for a "passive" race of believers.

As it progressed over several decades, Henry's concept of nirvana most approached Clarke's early grasp of it as "that profound inward rest" of nothingness. Losing Clover—and, in the next year, his father, Charles Francis Sr.—reinvigorated Henry's search for religious truth, but only to achieve the mystical heights of nirvana. "I have not had the good luck to attend my own funeral, but with that exception I have buried pretty nearly everything I lived for," Henry wrote before the first anniversary of Clover's death.[141] He groped for the peace that such "nothingness" offered, though he never put that sentiment in print.

Instead, Henry recruited the aesthetic counsel of John La Farge and set off on a marathon grand tour of the world for the rest of his life. If Henry served as an "exceptional normal" case study of the curious Victorian skeptic before Clover's death, then his religious travels now veered—permanently—away from the household gods and toward truly "exceptional" territory. He promised to send Saint-Gaudens photographs of Buddhas and nirvanas from their next stop: Kamakura, Japan.

Once aboard the San Francisco steamer in June 1886, Henry was distressed to learn that his fellow passengers included four female missionaries. His great-grandparents John and Abigail relished crossing oceans with clergymen. But several weeks into the Pacific voyage and still a thousand miles from Yokohama, Henry Adams—historical champion of holy women—refused to speak to them and fled the cabin when service began. "They sing and talk theology, two practices I abhor," he wrote.[142] Finally arriving in Kamakura, an exhausted Henry insisted on scaling the rooftop of a local priest's home. Borrowed Kodak in hand, he wobbled on the wooden slope, cursing the physical work it took for him to properly shoot the forty-foot bronze Buddha. Right there, "standing on my head at an angle of impossibility," Henry recalled, "[I] perpetrated a number of libels on Buddha and Buddhism."[143] Fighting for balance in the Great Buddha's shadow, Henry Adams entered a new and final phase of his religious development, eager to explore and elevate non-Western religious ideals that might enliven and inform the world.

Despite washed-out roads and a cholera outbreak, Henry's quest for nirvana continued daily.[144] A survey of Adams's Japanese sojourn shows how deftly Gilded Age cosmopolitanism eroded the "mild deism" in which he was raised. Henry's three months in Japan established his new, more professional pattern of religious inquiry. By trip's end, it was clear that the skeptic had grown into an avid collector of all things touched by faith: ideas, records, lands, and objects. In Japan, Henry Adams refined his approach of studying religion from the outside in. "Images are not arguments, rarely even lead to proof, but the mind craves them," Adams wrote.[145] His mature understanding of faith hinged more on image and perspective than on feeling or doctrine.

Adams maintained a few quirks of the gentleman traveler, but his method of documenting Japanese religion in words and photographs made him into an all-new brand of church historian. Every morning, Henry brewed his own Chinese tea. Then he photographed monks and mortuary gates, temples and tombs. La Farge tarried in a temple entryway for an hour or more. Adams tore through, then spent hours struggling to convey the unique scale of Buddhist faith in his letters home. Henry's view soared up to seek the infinite. The visual record of religion that he created is extraordinary. It is simultaneously an inner war for perspective on a new world, and a statement of agnostic bewilderment that such believers exist. Traveling on to Latin America, the South Seas, and back to Europe, Henry let his camera talk. His photographs restage lost landscapes of Gilded Age faith, as one American encountered it: Shinto priests resplendent in full robes, mosque spires rimmed in sepia, dusty workmen resting at Ramesses's toes, Tahitian royals at play, and a company of Fijian women dancing right off the page.[146] From Tokyo, Henry mirrored American popular interest in home-made sacred art. Many saw this as part of a "therapeutic culture" of religious devotion that sheltered them, if only for a lunch hour, from the secular mayhem of industrial change that brought managers, mergers, mechanization, and the metropolis.[147] From Kyoto, Henry saw it as vital to the historian's craft.

Religion and art, for the scholar Henry Adams, were one. In Japan, Henry absorbed the visual language of religious iconography, learning to "read" temples as he did Gothic cathedrals. The trappings, symbols, and folkways that the Japanese used to build religion indicated their past and future as a culture, Adams thought. Sketches of crenellated pagodas dot his "Japan Expenses" notebook, where he recorded spending the modern equivalent of $250,000 on Japanese netsuke, brocades, kimonos, and bric-a-brac.[148] He bought as much as he could

Avid traveler Henry Adams relished his time viewing the Bake Jizō, or "Ghost Jizō," Trail. The statutes of the Jizō deity, a revered Bodhisattva, line the path by a narrow gorge near Nikko, Japan, and are known for their otherworldly antics. In 1902, a flood ripped away or broke a number of the protector statues. *Henry Adams Photographs, Massachusetts Historical Society*

carry away via rickshaw, cornering markets' worth of religious "stuff" and then rushing back at the first word of a new salesman's lot.

The avid shopper was slightly less generous in his criticism of Japanese religion. Far away from the familiar flying buttresses of Gothic France, Adams dismissed the scarlet-and-gold curlicues of Shinto temples as too "baroque." The temples looked like "toys," he wrote, with the same sting he gave Chartres's enfeebled laity. Among many Japanese, "religion was a high old joke," he wrote, mocking Tokyo's upper-class piety with the same whiplike tone he honed in *Esther*. He loved the landscape—dreamier and greener than he expected, stirring a sublime pleasure when other sights underwhelmed the aging traveler. In Japan, however, Adams never found an Asian apogee of religious culture to equate with his Western discoveries. Kamakura's Great Buddha lacked the great blue of Chartres, he thought, and Adams suddenly missed the neo-Byzantine exuberance of Trinity Church. Henry's carefully wrought photographs, though, eventually served as a vital artistic aid.

It is his Mount Fuji skyline that La Farge used for the asymmetrical, rose-gold haze backing Christ in his final *Ascension*. It was the artistic expression of a religious idea that Henry Adams now appreciated and endorsed as his own: Buddhism rising over Christianity.

Like his far-flung peers, Adams saw the fin de siècle as a cultural bookend. He mulled over which religion might carry them into a gainful American Century. This intricate project—a pluralistic survey of multiple religions that, in turn, challenged the "democratization of American Christianity" ushered in during the antebellum period— took place across the overlapping levels of national culture and social class that Henry Adams traversed. Back in the United States, many heard the shift before they saw it. Abruptly, in the 1880s, America's religious soundscape changed key. Streetcars, once hushed by state courts to appease the clergy, clattered along on Sabbath days. Pealing church bells, once sheltered by the same local lawmakers, were frequently deemed a public nuisance.[149] In Henry's home town, the family church still sat at the town's center, but the heart of the public square had shifted. World's fairs, leisure communities, and trade union activities now dominated as the venues for civic discussion and debate. Communal events like the 1893 World's Columbian Exposition restaged questions of identity, race, and gender to ask who made up "we the people," and why global empire was, definitively, to be "our" goal. An increasingly critical working class, attracted to the solidarity and benefits of membership in industrial unions, experimented with riots, strikes, socialism, and contracts.

Christian leaders, trying to synchronize episodes of national change with lessons in morality, hastened to keep pace with each cycle. Protestant churches had, arguably, governed the early republic's mission and regularly put forward their clergy to settle social questions for a mass of Christian citizenry. By the 1890s, however, Christianity was one option among many. Judaism, Hinduism, and Buddhism all drew popular interest and the scholarly spotlight. Fresh dilemmas arose: How might these new faith communities vote? What kind of social behavior did these religions shape? Against such a busy backdrop, the drama of a few well-heeled doubters fretting over either inner Christianity or outward republicanism felt insignificant, and even irresponsibly so. Within a decade, Henry Adams's *Democracy* fossilized into a religious artifact.

After Clover's death, Henry never really returned to America, or to Western Christianity. New England society repulsed him. Perhaps he feared that a return would confirm that he was right on trend with his generation rather than racing ahead of it, and therefore already lost "in the ranks." Like his peers, Henry grappled with a moral crisis born of the Civil War and encroaching modernity. To many Americans, the national Christian conscience that pressed on his grandfather had been overdiluted by constant sectarian reinventions. With evangelical revivals cooling down and main-line churchgoers ceding to what William James labeled an inner unrest, Adams's generation wrestled anew with ways to reinterpret the world. As analysis of Henry's literary output and religious travels has shown, the philosophies of naturalism, scientism (or positivism), and agnosticism all gained ground, part of a broader effort to determine the basis of existence and action.[150] Like a scientific naturalist, Henry believed that nature and nurture combined to mold irrevocable characteristics and choices, so he wrote novels meant to unlatch the motives of religious behavior. His attraction to positivism—the idea that scientific theory revealed general laws of human action—grew, too. Mostly, Adams felt alone in the crusade to understand humanity's (or even his) purpose in society. "I am still in the religious epoch of blind and silent recognition of the will of God—or of the Devil," he wrote to his younger brother Brooks from Paris, "anyway, of the helplessness of insects and polyps like us."[151]

During his frenetic rounds of travel in the 1880s and 1890s—to the South Seas, Latin America, India, and Russia—Adams formalized his commitment to a functionalist view of religion. He worked out an intellectual hierarchy of creeds that he held, more or less, until his death in 1918. Overall, Henry viewed Christianity as a historical system that effectively powered bygone civilizations. Once the primary operator of political growth and self-development, modern Christianity was, in Adams's view, corpselike at best: good only for an occasional fright. Christianity's traction in America was dubious, he pronounced, since the "dynamo" of science loomed to supplant the church's desiccated authority.

Most "Asiatic" religions were too passive to present a serious threat, Adams decided, reserving a special rancor for Hinduism. Throughout the Gilded Age era, as steady waves of Vedanta Society speakers descended on New York City and Boston to articulate philanthropic agendas, or to attend the World's Parliament of Religions in Chicago in 1893, Henry turned away in disgust.[152] Before the 1890s, his knowledge of Hinduism came from skimming Rudyard Kipling's tales. He had little interest in reading the sacred Hindu texts first translated and made available in his boyhood, courtesy of Ralph Waldo Emerson and Henry David Thoreau, whom he considered dilettantes.[153] "It is a nameless horror, tempered by Buddhistic illusions," Henry wrote to Brooks, traveling through India. "It is a huge nightmare, with cobras and cows."[154] Henry's main complaint with Hinduism, however, was economic. To Adams, religious "success" hinged on "survival of the cheapest," and monotheism therefore always triumphed, since its adherents owed fewer tributes to one god.[155]

Judging showcases of faith at century's close, Henry devalued Hinduism and Judaism—two "dysfunctional" and "corrupt" religions that he stuck firmly at the bottom of his rankings. Originally, Henry's frequent use of "Jew" as an epithet was likely not intended to be religious in nature for, unlike those of his ancestors, Henry's private library did not contain a single work explicitly focused on Judaism. The Adams family fortune sank in the panic of 1893, and the shock killed Henry's eldest brother within a year. Thereafter, when Henry or Brooks took aim at bankers, "Jew" operated as a replacement for "moneylender." Idly, they laced family letters with a virulent undertone of anti-Semitism. One of Henry's stray publishing communiqués to Brooks, for example, alluded to "your friend Jew No. 2." When his overstuffed townhouse felt devoid of new acquisitions or pleasant company, Henry complained of living in a "Jew atmosphere."

Henry Adams was not alone in his anti-Semitism. Russian pogroms, implemented in 1881, sent waves of Eastern European Jews to American shores. Jewish synagogues, periodicals, and benevolent societies—all routes of assimilation that Henry would have recognized—were fairly common by the 1890s, but not necessarily welcomed in American cities, where social and ethnic discrimination was rife. Often, proponents of Jewish heritage came into conflict with the Social Gospel movement's militant conceptualization of Christlike behavior.[156] Henry's casual anti-Semitism tainted otherwise thoughtful critiques of world economy with ugly screeds against the Jewish "pig" bankers allegedly engaged in a vast global conspiracy. "I plunge into a horde of Jews, the most terrible since the middle-ages," Henry wrote from London. "They are secret and banded together; they lie; they cheat the Christian; they are gutter-Jews at that, the new lot; and they own us all."[157] In Paris, Adams read and praised the work of Édouard Drumont, founder of the Anti-Semitic League of France. For an editor who advised his *North American Review* contributors to write in "bald" style, one wonders if anti-Semitic sentiment flooded Henry Adam's conversation, too, since he freely granted it so much space on the page.

Sensory appreciation of ritual—a bright wedge of stained glass, the swaying chant of prayers to the Sainte Vierge—led Henry Adams to other household gods. And, in any given letter, Henry was as liable to curse a religious discovery as to gush about it. The American skeptic was surprised and even charmed by the persistence of faith in others. In Fiji with John La Farge, Adams was struck by the religious pluralism espoused by Protestant missionaries, who acknowledged that rites of ancestor worship would never totally melt away from local culture. "Everyone knows that the natives are all Christians only in form; they try any sort of God that comes handy, on the idea that it can't do harm and may do good," he wrote.[158]

In his own quest for nirvana, begun "out of season" several years earlier, Henry Adams openly emphasized the elevation of non-Western ideals to replace Christianity. More and more, a hazy Buddhism guided Adams's work and gave new purpose to his travels.[159] Busy completing an ox-cart pilgrimage through Sri Lanka in 1891, Adams declined Augustus Saint-Gaudens's many pleas for supervision on the Rock Creek monument to Clover. At Anuradhapura, Henry inspected the great plain of brick dagoba shrines marking fallen temples. He searched out the sacred Bodhi Tree where Buddha attained nirvana, saddened to see that only "a sickly shoot or two from the original trunk" remained. Henry Adams was further disappointed when, after a half hour sitting meditation, he failed to achieve nirvana. "The place was a big bazaar of religion, made for show and profit. Any country shrine has more feeling in it than this whole city seems to have shown," he wrote. "I am rather glad the jackals and monkeys own it, for they at least are not religious formalists, and they give a moral and emotion to the empty doorways and broken thresholds."[160] Once again, Henry had "missed" nirvana, but he identified two items on his short list of what constituted "pure and good": morality and emotion.

Many Adamses wrote most when they were deeply embedded in a foreign faith, and Henry was no exception. His next mode of exploration—writing poetry—followed family custom in all but theme. In curly script, Adams scribbled a poem, "Buddha and Brāhma," for a niece's enjoyment. He did not mail it for twenty years. Like John Quincy, Henry drafted and revised stanzas, rejiggering the words on sheets the size of index cards to sum up his mature system of nontheistic morality. John Quincy had recorded his religious poetry in a private miscellany book that he dubbed "The Chaos," but for Henry, the phenomenal chaos of modernity was real, and inescapably public. Composed in an ox-cart at century's end, the poem is Henry's attempt to compare the relative truths of Hinduism and Buddhism—the same project that his Unitarian predecessors plied earlier as antebellum missionaries and merchants drawn to the Bengal Renaissance. His poem, carved out of Buddhist catechism, describes the dilemma of Malunka, a pilgrim torn between the systems of (native) Hinduism and (acquired) Buddhism. Malunka asks Buddha if the world is eternal. The teacher admires and lets drift a single lotus blossom in reply—and the student is thoroughly lost. Malunka asks his Brahman father to decode the Buddha's meaning. The elderly man narrates the saga of Buddha's enlightenment, outlining the "silent thought, abstraction, purity" of the Eightfold Way to nirvana. Henry's ode to Buddhistic suffering is focused and calm in tone—akin to that of *Esther*'s women, who must dwell in doubt.

"Buddha and Brāhma" is the clearest statement of what Henry finally deemed "pure and good." It is his renunciation of the filiopiety that he thought clouded the Adams family mind. Henry's depiction of the encounter is staged like a classical epic; such an open-minded, open-hearted exchange would not have been possible with his own father. Even more intriguing is Henry's assumption that Eastern religions are broken parts of a whole, with Hinduism refracting multiple morals also found in the comparative unity of Buddhism. One faith can act to explain another, Henry suggests. In the poem, Adams writes that the thoughts and acts of Buddha have been "to me a mirror, clearer far / Than to himself, for no man sees himself." Henry drew on his scattershot, kaleidoscopic knowledge of "Veda . . . the alphabet of all philosophy," and underlined his desire to study the Buddha's Dharma Wheels of existence. Henry's poem ended worlds away from his grandfather's effort, "A Congressman's Prayer," offered a century earlier. Plainly choosing Buddhist ideals over Christian precepts, Henry wrote: "Gautama tells me my way too is good; / Life, Time, Space, Thought, the World, the Universe / End where they first begin, in one sole Thought / Of Purity in Silence."[161]

The globetrotting Henry saw, by 1892, that he must cycle back to his commissioned nirvana. He returned to Washington, anxious to see the Rock Creek monument. He agreed with the Paris art critic who called it "the image of Eternity and Meditation. . . . I know of no analogous work so profound in sentiment, so exalted in its art, and executed by methods so simple and broad, since the most telling sculpture of the Middle Ages. In me personally it awakens a deeper emotion than any other modern work of art."[162] Henry's blank reverie before that bronze monument of nirvana marks Clover's sole cameo in the *Education*.

Certain political duties came with being an Adams, and Christianity was part of the family brand in Henry's day. His presidential pedigree made Henry a prominent skeptic in an era when main-line church membership floundered and spiritual tourism led Americans to take non-Western faith seriously. Soured by New England Unitarianism, an itinerant youth introduced him to the wonders of older Christian civilizations. Henry and Clover, taken as skeptical interpreters of the country's evolving religious cultures, made a unique pair. Previous Christian generations of Adamses explored other religions and returned home to liberal Unitarianism. Henry and Clover, by contrast, encountered new faiths with surprise, mistrust, enjoyment, and doubt; they had no Christian home to return to, and they reveled in it.

Henry's creation of popular literature reflected his view that Christianity and republicanism—the twin pillars of Adams family faith—were too ruined to salvage. Fortunately, he began to flourish as a writer in middle age, just as American worshippers' interest swiveled from pantheistic Hinduism to Buddhism. An expensive passion for researching historical Christianity ran Henry around the world in eighty years—through Tokyo, Tahiti, Cuba, the Rockies, Russia, Greece, and Egypt. In the course of his religious travels, the medievalist also produced two anonymous novels that censured national touchstones of church and state. Unlike many other skeptics who traveled between denominations, he rejected modern Christianity whole. And, most notably, Adams delivered a searing indictment of New England's moral decay in his self-titled *Education*. By 1905, what was left for Henry Adams to criticize?

As the twentieth century's first spring bloomed across Washington, a childless Henry Adams reflected on his legacy. The family had always written for the archive, and Henry was nervous that they said too much, and that his own personal habits were so finely etched there. "Our dogmatism is certainly odious, but it was not extravagant until we made it a record. The world is going so fast, now, that dogmatism or marked individuality has become economically unprofitable and socially obstructive," he wrote to Brooks. "Types are fast changing even here. . . . The new century is already a new world."[163] Desperate to grab hold of it, the medievalist grew uneasy, and then reckless. For, if the familiar work of history writing was not exactly the nirvana he still hoped to find, it did offer Henry a dose of intellectual relief. Using Christianity to explain life—what father Charles had called the "religious confidence" to go about *his* life a generation earlier—spurred Henry to depart from tradition and adapt methods of scientific determinism to produce scholarship. Choosing to be free of a denominational anchor, Henry Adams next drew on his skepticism in order to undertake the scientific study of medieval religious life. Perhaps, like his academic peers, he generalized about Christianity's ills in order to reject it and thus grasp for the scientific objectivity needed to write "good" history.[164] Though he was not a churchgoer, Henry held to faith (and, particularly, to Christianity) as a way to trace human progress and its inevitable degeneration. As his later work shows, Adams presented a new hybrid of religion for his readers: a blend of what he called his prized "twelfth-century instincts," quasi-Buddhist passivity, positivist experimentation, and a general feeling of disillusionment about his Christian education. A great deal of Henry's outlook manifested itself in his last religious studies, not all of it kind, balanced, or well-informed. He was a cultural omnivore and dilettante who frequented transatlantic constellations of thought.[165] Henry's final, key reflections on faith arise in his scientific history on the female soul of medieval architecture, in *Mont-Saint-Michel and Chartres* (1905).

Scholarliness was next to godliness, in Henry's mind. From the 1890s and until his death in 1918, Henry promoted the "hard pan of science" as the best method to make history, stating that "science cannot be played with."[166] The payoff of being a philosopher and a scientist of history, as Adams thought, was the "pleasure . . . to work as though he were a small God and immortal and possibly omniscient."[167] From the South Sea beach that served as his household, the "small god" accepted the presidency of the American Historical Association in 1894. That winter, Adams forwarded his annual address from Guadalajara, Panama. His speech, "The Tendency of History," later expanded and published as "A Letter to American Teachers of History," is a curious artifact, studded with all the ornaments of late nineteenth-century thought. Filled with Darwinian vigor, Henry argued that his colleagues must "necessarily raise history to the rank of a science." This approach, he wrote, incurred the wrath of two powerful institutions, church and state. The "church," as Adams predicted in cautiously liberal terms, would resist "any science of history, because science, by its definition, must exclude the idea of a personal and active providence." A thorny patrilineal history of service to the state made Henry even sharper on the second point. He warned that the American government would move against such a doctrine with real muscle. Among Henry's distant audience sat scholars primed by the Enlightenment legacy of scientific rationalism, long divided over how to implement his theory. Was history to be science, or art?

Back at the American Historical Association, Adams's dream of scientific history was not an entirely new vision—merely a more eloquent pitch of themes that had preoccupied scholars throughout the century. Energized by the age of Darwin, modernizing Americans had spent recent decades endeavoring to place their experiences within the context of a longer, liberal tradition.[168] The appeal of using scientific tools to conduct credible historical investigations that legitimated their finds naturally grew. Simultaneously, science-minded historians faced a public battery of new ideologies that tested their scholarly work. At the same time, Henry put his own twist on the old family religion by rejecting the prototypical Victorian search for "unity, comfort, inspiration" in both his personal and professional spheres.[169] Christianity was a relic to be studied, with Henry's own scholarship as the model, but never an intellectual tradition to be fully revived. Henry's "Letter" was strident, yet he demonstrated genuine affection for other gentlemen scholars—a love of professional fellowship that evoked the Victorian academic ideal, a tranquil Protestant community of "small gods" bent in inquiry. Adams sized up the circle and sped away, diving into a colorful twelfth-century Catholic past that marked, for him, the lost heights of godly civilization emblazoned in feminine, mosaic form.

Henry Adams returned from his exotic sojourns set on gathering and cataloging symbols of morality and emotion, seeding what became the academic field of scientific study of religion. No biography of Adams can omit his *Education*, but it is the companion volume, *Mont-Saint-Michel and Chartres*, that articulates the final phase of his religious thought. Focused on the sensory appreciation of ritual, *Mont-Saint-Michel* succeeds as a melodrama of the medieval soul. Men, women, the infinite—this is the moral inquiry of Henry's life in sixteen chapters, and it is a lively example of the scientific scripture of history writing that he obsessively promoted.[170] While the *Education* asserts that a multiplicity of selves must suffer through modern life, *Mont-Saint-Michel* offers a glorious prequel of forfeited Christian unity and Marian compassion. In *Mont-Saint-Michel*, Adams plays his hunch that the second law of thermodynamics steers history, causing humanity to accelerate between fixed points of progress or decay.[171] The results of his trial are beautifully uneven. As scholars have frequently noted, *Mont-Saint-Michel* is not a particularly well-researched work of art history, nor is it the handy guidebook that Henry, still imitating travelogues, meant it to be.[172] Rather, *Mont-Saint-Michel* says a great deal about Henry Adams's inner fantasy of religion. It is the moral *Education* that the skeptic longed for, and that homemade Unitarianism failed to stock.

Perhaps it was a latent, ironic effect of his upbringing, but Adams's medieval scholarship evinced his desire to rebel against the tendency of American Protestant historians. He was not interested in replicating their soft, weak notions of female divinity while privileging the goals of male self-interest.[173] The iconoclastic Adams was not the average medievalist, for the writer of *Esther* and the widower to Clover chose to enshrine female intellect in the Church. For a functionalist like Adams, the project offered a dual case study in the juxtaposition of two refuges for the religious: the masculine, mountain island abbey of Mont-Saint-Michel, and the grand, feminine cathedral of Chartres.

Both holy sites recall a bygone era when, as Adams writes in skeptical wonder, Christianity was stout enough to solve "the whole problem of the universe."[174]

From the opening, Henry's narrative voice in *Mont-Saint-Michel* is one of a small god (or a young Buddha?) marveling at medieval creation. "The Archangel loved heights," Adams begins, carrying the reader "nearest to God," to share Michael's perspective on earth.[175] Knowing Adams from the *Education*, though, his angels will fall. And so, rather than gazing up at God in rapture, the reader is sent wheeling wildly and plunging back to earth. It is a vicious reminder of man's inevitable moral descent and an artful symbol of the normative social structure that Adams describes as religious rule in Mont-Saint-Michel: warlike and rough, versus Chartres's peaceable reign of bourgeois progress, afflicted by the rise of monastic schools and an occasional Crusade. Henry's innovative use of popular and material culture, such as jongleurs' ditties and architectural figures, allows him to construct a cathedral-sized narrative of impeccable detail. To the middlebrow reader who could not afford the pilgrimage to isolated Mont-Saint-Michel, Henry recreated a lost world to stir twentieth-century Americans' interest in medieval life. He strips off the courtly fairy tale and assigns moral complexity to its brutality.

Piecing together French ballads and stained glass, Henry managed to say at least as much about the moral crises of Gilded Age America as either his brother Brooks (a critic of Western civilization's decay) or Charles Francis Jr. (a critic of railroad monopolies and capitalism). The senior scholar Henry Adams appreciated the French version of a Catholic past where women reigned, but he did not go so far as to forecast a Catholic future for America. That inquiry remained for others to explore. Henry idolized his grandmother Louisa and her Marian qualities, but he separated himself from brother Brooks in adopting a wholehearted stance for or against Catholic modernity. "As a religious and conservative anarchist I have had much to thank God for. . . . Indeed God has been good to me," Henry wrote, adding: "Bishop Keane has hopes that I may join the true church, and truly I would like to be a cardinal."[176] Nor was the childless Henry invested in passing along faith to the next generation. Religious education, as the self-proclaimed "conservative Christian

Anarchist" instructed one niece, was "a means of holding oneself up in faith and feeling. Therefore it tends to what is called Jesuitism, or practiced evasion of difficulties. What it is intended to help, it then helps to destroy."[177]

At the end of Henry Adams's well-traveled life, long after his religious tours shifted from dusty carriage to Mercedes motorcar, a religious sentimentalism took over his daily routine in Lafayette Square. When Henry's health began to fail, his nieces arranged to send him a live-in secretary on trial. Learning that Miss Aileen Tone could sing Thibaut's chansons de geste in a rotating program of six per night for two weeks straight or more, he hired her on the spot. Henry opened the American Century with daily recitals culled from his favorite "Hundred Men and Women" of medieval myth. In a cache of letters to his nieces, the old cosmopolitan delighted in overlaying modern marvels with medieval norms. "My idea of paradise," Adams wrote, "is a perfect automobile going thirty miles an hour on a smooth road to a twelfth-century cathedral."[178]

Once restricted to a few chosen friends, his *Mont-Saint-Michel* was published to critical acclaim. Medieval Christianity kept the skeptic alive and wholly engaged in the past. Thanks to the recovered beauty of his premodern "glass," he was "at home here and everywhere," Adams wrote from St. Rèmy, France. Facing the world war that he and Brooks had long predicted, Henry turned back to familiar medieval supports. By mid-1914, Adams claimed to have reached a nirvana of sorts, when he returned to his New Hampshire summer cottage after a season entertaining old friends. Convinced that religion and art were one, he speculated as to the next form that an American skeptic's story, like his own, might take. "It is astonishing that no one of rank and breeding has ever since said anything worth repeating—except me, of course, and a few dead-beats like us," Henry Adams wrote to a friend in July 1914. "But it only proves my theory that the whole show is—what do they call it now, a movie?"[179]

5

Higher Than a City upon a Hill

HENRY ADAMS'S BETTER ANGELS—FROZEN IN sepia prints made at Mont-Saint-Michel and framed in New England oak—hung over the bed of his youngest brother, Brooks.[1] Like his *Education*, the pictures were meant for Henry's reference or for family eyes only, filling out the unique religious landscape that Brooks made of his sanctuary in the Adams home.[2] Great-grandmother Abigail's Gospel tiles bordered the hearth. Charles Sr.'s novels and church histories hugged hallway shelves. Within easy reach lay a dog-eared King James Bible that Brooks had owned since the age of nine. A gravel path led Jazz Age visitors into the Stone Library, where three hundred thousand Adams manuscripts were tucked away from the country damp, with the household gods keeping watch. Brooks toured guests past the bronzes and through the colonial garden. Proudly, he pointed out First Ladies' china and presidents' diaries. Keeping house in a shrine, Brooks and his wife, Daisy, were cocooned in a Christianized version of the American past. Heirloom quilts blanketed John Quincy's pine bed, where they slept. Underfoot, red Turkish rugs rounded out the room with tree-of-life motifs. In an unlocked drawer, Brooks kept candles and matches close for late-night reading, along with a loaded pistol. It was there in Quincy, as family legend went, that Brooks Adams greeted every day with his acid hymn: "God damn it! God damn it! God damn it!"[3]

Often overlooked except by economic historians who lionized his critique of capitalism, Brooks Adams offers a slippery and surprising bend in the family's religious road.[4] Born in 1848, four months after John Quincy's death, the sickly Brooks seemed prone to buckle under the ancestral mantle. He attended Harvard, toured Europe, and worshipped at Quincy's First Church. In his religious path, the contrarian Brooks seceded from the Adams tribe. At first agnostic, he reached out to the world's "others," initiating a slow burn of discovery that kindled his mature, public recommitment to organized faith. Groomed for a political arena that no longer welcomed Adams presidents, he was, in the words of his contemporaries, "an unusable man" who wrote "damnably superfluous" prose—a cultural critic who felt overqualified yet unappreciated by his people and by his God.[5] A single-minded theorist who barbed his best arguments with paradoxes and rants, Brooks wrote brilliant but tortured text.[6] Brooks's bylines outnumbered those of Henry, who won far more praise. To kin, Brooks came across as a bitter, haunted man who preached daily of pessimism and catastrophe. Powerful admirers like Theodore Roosevelt and Henry Cabot Lodge acknowledged Brooks's work, yet they did not apply his parables to political life. Painfully, he was an intellectual without a public. "I shouldn't wonder if I had quite a reputation after I'm dead," Brooks guessed.[7]

Like his Puritan ancestors, Brooks strove to connect Christianity with American culture. Bringing the family story full circle, Brooks battled to renew his faith and then use it to critique the rise of urban capitalism. Along with other modernizing Protestant elites, Brooks eyed warily the blossoming of Christian fundamentalism, the growth of foreign missions, and the assimilation of Catholic and Jewish communities into American culture. He judged New England's Unitarian ecosystem to be suffocating, dull, and unimaginative. But Brooks grew up minus the providentialist proclivities of his ancestors. So his worldview tilted when he considered life without—and then with—God. Seer-like, Brooks marshaled Christianity to serve the sweeping claims he made in two major works: *The Emancipation of Massachusetts: The Dream and the Reality* (1887, 1919) and *The Law of Civilization and Decay* (1895). These volumes represent the hinge in Brooks's thought as he transitioned from agnostic to believer, from Victorian failure to modern prophet.

In sorting out his Christianity, Brooks joined with other mainstays of the Unitarian flock who merged old-fashioned piety, historical scrutiny, and social justice to bind up the postbellum republic.[8] The main-line Protestants of Brooks's day carried the Puritan past with them, acutely aware of the burden of New England church history.[9] Brooks's struggle is a prime case study in how Gilded Age elites dealt with that weight.

The story of Brooks's "failed" New England education mirrored that of his brother Henry. Religion was, to Brooks, a tiresome form of family duty rather than an instinct to nurture. Throughout the 1850s, Sundays in Quincy were, for all the children of Charles Francis Sr. and Abigail Brooks Adams, a special torment. As Brooks's brother Charles Francis Jr. recalled, it meant an onerous recitation of Psalms, followed by a dreary stretch of homily at the same church a short ride away. At midday, between services, the Adamses often hosted a leaden roast beef lunch for the pastor. "I was glad when Monday came; for me it wasn't 'black Monday,' for it was six days before another Sunday. I remember now the silence, the sombre idleness, the sanctified atmosphere of restraint of those days, with their church-bells, their sedate walk and their special duties," Charles Jr., wrote many decades later. "The recollection of those Sundays haunts me now."[10] The hyperactive Brooks, at odds with his siblings, fidgeted throughout the day and bristled at his parents' plan of Christian nurture. A poor pupil, Brooks failed at reciting scripture, spelling, and saying his prayers. He ruined his father's evening reading with "screams, & laughs, & rants, & twists, & jumps," his mother reported.[11] Abby labeled him "very backward," telling Henry that Brooks was "good, dutiful, & honest as the day, lovely tempered as you know full well, & in intellect about like the generality of boys, but not so clever as you three."[12] By April 1861, when the clan decamped to England for Charles Sr.'s diplomatic duties, Brooks had channeled his mania into an obsessive appetite for collecting exotic stamps.

Along for the adventure, thirteen-year-old Brooks took the related change of culture in stride. Around him, Europe was increasingly more than a private playroom for well-heeled Americans. The Adamses' penchant for foreign travel neither set them apart nor marked them as members of the monied class. Any bourgeois tourist could book a first-class passage for an affordable $200 or, by the century's end, stay home and roll the dice on an eighty-five-cent board game that simulated Continental glamor.[13] In Brooks's day, affluent Bostonians believed that firsthand exposure to British culture was particularly vital for New England's sons and daughters to experience. For the Puritans' descendants, the trip was a cultural keyhole through which they might glimpse the feudal past. Raised on the cardinal lesson that their forebears had fled for liberty's sake, the men and women of Brooks's era regarded Old World travel as a useful historical contrast with American life. They greeted Europe with a national self-identity hardened by industrialization, urbanization, and war. Part filiopiety and part fun, visiting England allowed Americans to explore and to preen.

When Brooks first crossed the Atlantic, he hoped to supplement the highbrow culture of his famed home town, then dubbed the "Athens of America." Busy London suited Brooks's rapacious intellect; his Christian education remained haphazard at best. Brooks kept little record of it, though, since the grand tour narrative as a genre had fallen out of vogue by midcentury. But in family letters from England, flashes of Brooks appear. An "innocent abroad," much like Mark Twain's (anti) heroes, Brooks evidently learned to parrot the Boston Brahmin's take on daily life in 1860s Europe: simple yet slow; majestic but far too feudal for the archetypal American go-getter; tranquil to the point of tranquilizing. Underwhelmed by Old World culture, a sullen Brooks tagged along on his father's pilgrimages to Gothic churches.[14] He tried out Anglican, Catholic, and Presbyterian rites. He shadowed a few legs of his idol Henry's tour. The tattered repertoire of holy bones and sacred sites failed to ignite any spiritual interest in the youngest Adams. Harvard-bound, he returned to the heart of Unitarianism in July 1865. Brooks carried back, as a souvenir, the lightly clipped English accent with which he spoke for the rest of his life.[15]

When the *Africa* docked in Boston three weeks later, at the same Rowes Wharf where his Puritan kin once bought timber to build their meetinghouses, Brooks encountered a home town under construction. As he drove up from the waterfront, new German, Irish, and Italian arrivals all pressed into view. Like their modernizing peers in Baltimore, Chicago, and Philadelphia, Bostonians sought to create a walkable, industrial center that embodied Christian, middle-class values and embedded natural beauty in the daily pedestrian experience. Between 1860 and 1870, the city's population surged from 177,840 to 250,526.

Brooks Adams (1848–1927). *Carte de visite by C. Silvy,
ca. 1865, Massachusetts Historical Society*

The self-styled "Hub of the Universe" bustled with change, and the
mayor annexed several harbor islands to accommodate its growth.
A quartet of new bridges knit together old neighborhoods. Thanks to
the genesis of a metropolitan park system, Frederick Law Olmsted's
leafy green pathways arched through a half-finished network of
monuments, department stores, apartment buildings, and civic gathering spots like the Romanesque showstopper of Horticultural Hall.
Catholic (Boston College) and Methodist (Boston University) college
campuses emerged. Horsecars pulled along shoppers at a laggardly (and
aromatic) five miles an hour, while local engineers raced New York
rivals to develop an underground subway and thereby end the traffic

mayhem. Wealthy city dwellers like the Adamses bankrolled a pipeline of new institutions (museums, libraries, academic societies) and technological marvels (railroads, transatlantic steamers) that ferried their cultural goods abroad. These urban efforts, in part, united the genteel tradition of Brahmin writers and thinkers who upheld social hierarchies and adhered to conservative political views. When Brooks landed in the new Boston of 1865, that was the intellectual club he longed to join.

Venerable Puritan-era institutions like Harvard University showed change, too. University overseers shifted around resources to accommodate a swollen population of scholars. In President John Adams's day, for example, the college made do with only ten or twelve faculty members to guide 100 students. By contrast, his great-grandson Brooks was one of 1,097 undergraduate and graduate scholars steered by forty professors. The old red-brick quadrangles melted into cityscape. Side by side, two new spires rose to scratch the Cambridge sky. Echoing postbellum Americans' parallel interests in religion and science, the Peabody Museum of Archaeology and Ethnology broke ground adjacent to the new Episcopal Theological School.

Brooks's tutors adjusted their goals, too. As the modern university program superseded worn, antebellum modes of apprenticeship, the task of pursuing higher education meant refining a personal sense of morality. An army of men emerged from Cambridge with empty but unbiased and "supple" minds, Henry Adams noted in one *Education* rant. "Four years of Harvard College, if successful, resulted in an autobiographical blank," he wrote, "a mind on which only a water-mark has been stamped."[16] Imprinting intellectual and cultural standards on staple students like Brooks, Harvard labored on.

A popular student there until 1870, Brooks followed the family pattern of youthful agnosticism, and Harvard's increasingly secular curriculum enabled his way forward. In his formative academic choices, Brooks represented a transitional generation of Americans who met a modern campus reshaped by three factors: the explosive growth of respectable public universities, engendered by the land-use terms of the Morrill Act (1862); a fleet of faculty who imported formats of European (especially German) pedagogy; and the widespread application of scientific research methods and tools by fledgling humanities scholars like Henry and Brooks.[17]

In tandem with the professoriate, Brooks's approach to achieving a liberal education thus meant shedding New England orthodoxy on two key points. First, he rejected God's—and also Protestant Christianity's—power to unify knowledge and instead embraced specialized fields of study. Second, Brooks relied on science to explain episodes of human progress and historical failure. This method, Brooks thought, would mold him into the fair and principled civic man he hoped to be. Even the president of Harvard, the educational pioneer Charles William Eliot, agreed. "The whole work of a university is uplifting, refining, and spiritualizing," he lectured Brooks's class in 1869. In the "New Education" Eliot championed, one theme resounded: "A university cannot be built upon a sect, unless indeed, it be a sect which includes the whole of the educated portion of the nation."[18]

A bright but unfocused student, Brooks partied a lot, cheated on a Latin exam, and vied in vain at the local racing regattas. To win admission to the exclusive Hasty Pudding Club, he pranked a classmate by expertly forging private notes from a star professor—Henry Adams.[19] Notably few courses made an impression on Brooks, save history. At first he resented Harvard's "pigheaded" insistence on studying classical republics, but by his senior year Brooks had grown to accept the intellectual value of analyzing the household gods.[20] His own life course was harder to discern. "I have no particular leaning toward any one kind," he wrote as graduation loomed, "and my education has not been such as to give me any reason to hope that I should succeed."[21] Presented with eight whole pages in the class yearbook to sketch his biography and future plans, Henry's little brother panicked and blanked. He mustered the minimum three lines. "Brooks Adams born 1848 at Quincy Mass. Entered college in Sept. 1866," he wrote. "I intend to study law."[22] Proceeding on to Harvard's heavily professionalized law school, where professors now taught via the new format of case studies, Brooks developed more of his long-term intellectual outlook on ethics. Slowly, he began to find his footing within the family dynasty of lawyers.

After a short stint in Geneva to aid his father with Anglo-American arbitration claims, Brooks set up residence in Boston in 1872.[23] The old family path of letters and law beckoned. He passed the bar one year later and moved into the Adamses' Pemberton Square law offices. On the side, he served as assistant editor of the *North American Review*. Over the next two decades, Brooks published a series of critical essays on American government, history, and culture there and in other reform outlets of the Gilded Age press.[24] His protean work shows traces of the political and economic theories for which he would earn attention, but national notoriety eluded Brooks during his twenties and thirties.

In 1877, Brooks lost a bid for the Massachusetts legislature by two votes (and two of his uncles had voted against him).[25] Straining to meet monumental family standards, he suffered a series of physical and emotional breakdowns due to overwork. Brooks traveled south and west for "rest cures," then sank into escapist reading.[26] At his lowest points, wholly uninterested in God and the therapeutic possibilities of communal religion, Brooks prayed to Henry for guidance. Anxious about how this melodrama might be portrayed in the growing family archive, his big brother heartily sympathized with Brooks's troubles. Then Henry burned up the letters pleading for his help.[27] By the summer of 1885, Brooks Adams was ready to go his own way. He hunted for a history project.

Prolific Adams statesmen of the long nineteenth century had legitimated their scholarly credentials by examining the American past, and Brooks yearned to do the same. Rashly, he chose the first case study at his fingertips: the rise and fall of the Puritan patriarchy. "I am, for my sins, trying to write something about this state," Brooks told a friend in July 1885.[28] In many ways, city life had supplied Adams with his subject. For as the modern metropolis rose up around him, vestiges of its seventeenth-century residue clung fast to cultural memory. Olmsted's city parks adopted old Native American names. At the Massachusetts Historical Society, the Boston Athenaeum, and the new Museum of Fine Arts, scholars collected piles of Puritan genealogies, artifacts, maps, diaries, and manuscripts. Those troves were open for research to members only, and so popular literature—much of it manufactured a few blocks from Brooks's old dormitory—guided visions of the early American saga. Schoolchildren of the 1860s and 1870s learned early American history via poems such as "The Courtship of Miles Standish," "Evangeline," and "Paul Revere's Ride" thanks to the busy pen of Cambridge native Henry Wadsworth Longfellow and a crew of Fireside Poets who more than matched the skillful prose and record sales of British and French authors.[29]

Squinting at the past, Brooks's Harvard tutors and neighbors perceived of the Puritans as bigoted "witch-burners" who must be, for propriety's sake, quietly elided within a nobler cohort of colony-builders known simply as "The Pilgrims."[30] When the Congregational churches met in Boston for a national council in 1865, even the local clergymen wavered over how to celebrate their seventeenth-century roots. "Standing by the Rock where the Pilgrims set foot upon these shores," the Massachusetts ministers equivocated in issuing a full Declaration of Faith that made modern use of the "grand peculiarity of our Puritan Fathers, that they held this Gospel."[31] Some clergy lashed out at the Puritan creed and warned that Salem's sequel lay on the horizon, should religious toleration falter. "It is a creed that has done an immense amount of harm," the *Boston Investigator* opined, "and it is time that it was laid to rest forever in the grave of its first teacher John Calvin."[32]

Fifteen years later, the same newspaper swung around on the topic with renewed vigor, observing that the "Puritan Sunday," thankfully, had been made extinct by the "progress of the age." Any restoration of Puritan thought might retrigger a darker time, when "no boy was allowed to live in Massachusetts unless he was dipped and salted down in Hopkinsian Orthodox brine."[33] Elsewhere, other American Christians peered back for lost lessons of piety. As the new city church model, laden with lavish art and fine music (but relatively light on good theology), morphed into a private clubhouse, several lay critics resurrected the hoary Puritan example as a way to measure modern forms of morality. "Congregationalists have lost much of the self-absorption in a holy cause that distinguished their Puritan ancestors," one editorial writer chided in 1868, managing to sound both horrified and relieved by the historical slippage.[34]

Bostonians like Brooks were at the heart of the battle over how to evaluate the Puritan legacy, but the question was hardly confined to New England. The prudent curation of a shared past was essential for the nation's survival. Professional history writing, like Brooks's, was another form of the cultural labor that Victorians did to mend the fissures made by Reconstruction politics, union strikes, and conflicting crusades for social reform. So what did the Puritans look like to Adams's

Gilded Age audiences reincarnated "The Puritan" as a popular character in plays, novels, and artwork. Augustus Saint-Gaudens, the
same sculptor commissioned by Henry to make the Rock Creek
Cemetery memorial, created a tabletop version that came to adorn
many American homes. *Bequest of Jacob Ruppert, 1939, Metropolitan
Museum of Art*

prospective readers beyond New England? In print, Victorians praised
Puritan congregationalism as an ideal that anticipated democracy. They
were less committed, however, to modern Congregationalism as a
denominational force.

Led by Longfellow's odes and a glitzy Centennial Exposition in 1876,
Victorian Americans dragged the Puritans back into the cultural spotlight. With ambivalence, they lauded the great-great-grandfathers of

"Revolutionary stock." Like one South Dakota clergyman, many saw the Puritans as a stern people who dared "all that human nature was capable of enduring, and even more for the sake of freedom to worship God—men who might be tyrants but could never be slaves."[35] The Puritan trope was so deeply entrenched in the national consciousness that when a dramatized version of Longfellow's "Courtship of Miles Standish" hit the Texas stage in 1880, it was sufficient for the local newspaper to report that it starred "a characteristic Puritan, who will not suffer the rules of his household to be amended."[36] The rest of the plot unspooled easily enough. Despite the Puritans' sober, sour, and Salem-tainted legacy, most Victorians discovered they were reluctant to let go. Many, like Brooks, did not know how. To do so meant cutting cherished ties to ancient ideals of liberty and dissent, as well as England's commonwealth tradition and the precepts of constitutional law. "Shall we give up our Puritan faith?" one newspaper editor thundered. "We say no! a thousand times NO! No, because this would be treason to the memory of the holy and heroic men from whom we have derived our ecclesiastical lineage."[37] Small-minded but hardy, the Puritans resisted real analysis.

Lawyer and editor Brooks Adams waded into the fray in July 1885, mostly by accident. Over the past two decades, Brooks had experimented with a new formula for understanding history, and he was ready to test it on the page. Brooks's plan for his *Emancipation of Massachusetts* (1887) bore the stamp of his secularized liberal education, and his intellectual goals were high. First, like his fellow founders of the new American Social Science Association, Brooks was concerned that academics had ceded the presentation of historical "facts" to popular authors. According to Brooks, evidence-based arguments and rigorous analysis must replace sentimental vignettes (like Longfellow's) of the American past. The *Emancipation* was his chance to reclaim cultural authority for genteel Brahmin scholars and to shape future forms of history writing.

Brooks also had a pet theory to promote, and he needed the Puritan case study to prove it. To Adams's way of thinking, civilizations were Darwinian by nature, in which people adapted to different but cyclical phases of thought. Most societies underwent a bleak theocratic period, when an "autocratic priesthood" deadened a society's souls with their barbaric insistence on mechanical piety, superstition, and dogmatic instruction.[38] Once a civilization ran through Brooks's phases— including democracy—it achieved imperial wealth and then fell inevitably into moral decay.[39] The golden republics of the household gods, by Brooks's lights, were born to die. If Brooks could solder his theory of history to a discrete case study, he thought, then he would identify all the phases and laws that governed the human mind and, in turn, piloted American progress. Luckily, he had an easy target at hand. The native drama of early Massachusetts, brimming with issues of orthodoxy and liberty, suited his plan. He did not set out to write a fair history, nor even to offer a half-decent analysis of Puritan theology. Brooks intended to blueprint his way of writing highly deterministic, scientific history by using the Puritan clergy's trajectory as an "illustration" of the use and abuse of law. Diving blindly into the "gloomy bondage" of Puritan life, he reframed how people broke free of orthodoxy's restraints.[40]

Laden down with unwieldy agendas, Brooks encountered a new roadblock: he did not know enough about religion to begin. "There are of course, to a man so ignorant of church history, in particular, as I, a number of points I should much like to get cleared up, on which I can't find much light in the books," Brooks wrote to local antiquarian and dry-goods heir Charles Deane.[41] With his mentor Henry far away on nirvana's trail in Japan, he begged Deane and a few other scholars to meet, either at the Historical Society or at the Athenaeum, for tea and research assistance. In the end, Brooks's citations stemmed from a set of well-trod sources, including John Winthrop's journal, the Massachusetts Bay court records, and the sermons and testimony of the Mather clergymen and suspected witches. Brooks wrote like the amateur historian that he was, pasting in blocks of primary-source text when he lacked the analytical dexterity to place Puritan voices in broader cultural context. Chunks of Anne Hutchinson's cross-examination, for example, glossed the theological nuances of the Antinomian Controversy.[42] An embedded chronology of Quaker persecution and transcriptions of related correspondence, more research notes than polished text, padded the book's middle.[43] Much of the scientific rigor that Brooks intended was undermined by his agitated tone in the text. The *Emancipation* rattled along at a hysterical pitch, as Adams feverishly indicted clergy for shuttering American minds and perverting Christianity in the process. Far from his purported scientific history, the *Emancipation* became Brooks's fiery prosecution of his Puritan kin for the sins of stifling free inquiry and dissolving social bonds.[44]

Brooks launched his opening arguments of the *Emancipation* at a wide audience of savvy readers who already knew how to spot "a characteristic Puritan" from several centuries away. He spent the first part of the *Emancipation* sketching the English traditions, legal and religious alike, in which the Puritans flourished before they fled.[45] Next, he demonstrated the organizational significance of their guild charters and the theological ingenuity of the Protestant Reformation, crediting the first Puritans as catalysts for larger religious change. When it came to the Adamses' old nemesis, Archbishop William Laud, Brooks turned surprisingly softer. Finding the prelate to be a maligned man "as reasonable as Calvin," Brooks forgave Laud, who "only did what all have done who have attempted to impose a creed on men."[46] Here, Brooks paused on the same historical ground that his great-grandfather John had passed through in 1765, and he imparted a strikingly different perspective. Brooks, a nascent economist, saw in the Puritans' Great Migration another facet, namely, the inherent value of transferring successful English business models to uncolonized American shores. In his origin story of Massachusetts, the Puritans' creation of companies, charters, and the regulations of the General Court showed them to be transatlantic entrepreneurs. To Brooks, this was the part of the Puritan paradox that connected to the urban realities of his own day, the rabid drive to consolidate temporal and spiritual power at any cost. Enter the clergy.

The Puritan priesthood, mainly signified by Increase and Cotton Mather, served as villain. A well-educated but power-hungry lot, these "party orators" dominated an early America that lacked newspapers, roads, and a solid sense of community.[47] Their influence, even for the seventeenth century, eclipsed the normal bounds of church and state. In Brooks's retelling of events, Puritan clergymen served as trusted government consultants without holding office, and they rivaled the Massachusetts Bay magistrates in dispensing justice. By disciplining dissenters (Antinomians, Quakers, Baptists) and practicing tactics of exclusion via their baptismal rites, the Puritan clergymen chose to "keep alive unreasoning prejudice . . . to serve their selfish ends."[48] Brooks abhorred the rule that prospective church members give a public testi-mony of faith and receive communal consensus before earning admis-sion into the local Christian parish. Joining the "visible saints" meant enduring months of social and spiritual limbo. "To sensitive natures the initiation was appalling," he wrote, adding that clergy duly investigated every protest against admission.[49]

Puritan life, to Brooks's mind, was an age of priestly oppression. Promoting superstition over enlightenment, the clergy fined, branded, whipped, mutilated, banished, and hanged any fellow Christians who challenged their power. Nodding briefly to the horrors of the Salem witchcraft trials, Brooks set his bloodiest chapter in Boston, describing in graphic detail the physical and psychic torture that early Quakers suffered.[50] Significantly, when he reintroduced their stories, Brooks sympathized with the female martyrs.[51] The ugly hardships of Margaret Brewster, Mary Dyer, Sarah Gibbons, Mary Prince, and Elizabeth Hooton featured in his tale. Often, Brooks sounded more like a pros-ecutor than an objective historian. When he narrated the bouts of Cambridge imprisonment and public whipping that Hooton endured for her Quaker beliefs, Adams pointed at the Puritan clergy's "savage-professors" and declared, "The intent to kill is obvious."[52] No detail was too gruesome for Brooks to shock readers with; he reminded them that when winter weather made hangings difficult, the clergymen mandated that floggings be staged across three towns in order to "properly" afflict a dissenter's frozen, striped skin as she lay naked in an open cart.[53] If the reader just shuddered and recoiled, then Brooks made his point: to perceive both the Puritan priesthood's instinct for raw cruelty, and the need for the laity to rise up in social revolution and end it. "This, then, has been the fiercest battle of mankind," he wrote, "the heroic struggle to break down the sacerdotal barrier, to popularize knowledge, and to liberate the mind, began ages before the crucifixion upon Calvary; it still goes on."[54]

By the time he arrived at the events of 1692 and 1693, in a chapter ominously titled "The Witchcraft," Brooks had built a persuasive saga of depraved clergy who preyed on the faithful. Adams needed to find a hero to counter the clergy's actions and to prove his theory that a civi-lization could surmount a theocratic phase and move into democracy. He returned to Salem. As the first accusations of witchcraft sped across

Danvers, Ipswich, and Andover, the bulk of the village worshippers turned to their educated priest "caste" to confirm or dispel spectral evidence. And at this moment, Brooks decided, the Puritan clergymen precipitated the final social crisis that led to their downfall—a historical view that many scholars after Brooks would support.[55] For when "the people stood poised upon the panic's brink, their pastors lashed them in," he wrote.[56] Amid the mania of mob brutality, Brooks managed to identify a few level-headed saviors of early American Christianity, praising the Brattle Street Church leadership, the Harvard faculty, and the Boston-born lawyers who contested the witch-hunters' work.[57]

Brooks's pet theory, not research, drove the final sociology of religion that he produced. "My book is not a history, it is not intended for one," he explained. "It is an attempt to set forth a scientific theory of the action of the mind, illustrated by a section of history which happens to be taken from Massachusetts, but which might as well be taken from India."[58] Rushing from Salem's atrocities to the Boston Massacre, Brooks hastily pinned together several historical developments to hold up his theory. At *Emancipation*'s end, Brooks wrapped up his case by annihilating the Puritans' dual legacy of religion and education. Reviewing his own forebears' historical contributions in a new light, he ruled that the cultural differences between theological ("conservative") and scientific ("liberal") training were "irreconcilable." Pulpits harbored the dogmatists who stifled human curiosity. By contrast, universities nurtured the pioneers who led inquiry and invention.[59] In the course of civilization, he concluded, liberal communities prospered (for a time) by displacing the religious rites that cemented a corrupt priesthood. Such a long-term commitment to liberty, Brooks claimed, characterized his native region well into the Civil War era, "for it is her children's heritage that, wheresoever on this continent blood shall flow in defence of personal freedom, there must the sons of Massachusetts be."[60]

Not all of Brooks's reasoning was firm in the *Emancipation*, and most reviewers deemed the result to be more provocation than scholarship. Many passages caused historical whiplash. Take Adams's nonchalant logic in the statement that "gradually the secular thought of New England grew to be coincident with that of the other colonies," thereby achieving the "phase" of the American mind needed to secure independence.[61] Or his blanket assertion that all of the Puritan clergy's "strong but narrow minds burned with fanaticism and love of power."[62] Brooks knew he had stitched his sources together in an intellectual patchwork, but he liked the overall effect and was stunned when reviewers panned it. "I wanted to make a small book," Brooks retorted. "And I do not pretend to large reading."[63] The criticism mounted. Throughout the late 1880s, more than fifty scholars weighed in on the book's merits and flaws, marking out the *Emancipation* as a Puritan attack piece. Many, like his good friend E. L. Godkin, then at the helm of *The Nation*, were staggered to see a revolutionary scion like Brooks lacing the early American past with such venom. "It may be that Massachusetts needed to be scourged," *The Nation* reflected, "but it does not follow that an Adams should wield the rod."[64] Brooks grew irate. Readers had seized on his *Emancipation* as a quarrelsome book about Puritans and thoroughly missed the new, high-flying theories of history writing and civilization that he put on trial there. Brooks implored Henry to intervene, since he "could by about ten lines to *The Nation* put me in the position which I want to hold."[65] Again, Henry refused.

The *Emancipation* earned Brooks a measure of notoriety, just as family duties closed in. His mother, Abigail, died in 1889. Brooks began to court Evelyn ("Daisy") Davis, the Episcopalian daughter of a well-known US Navy admiral. Despite his nervous disposition, the two seemed to suit each other, and they wed in the autumn of 1889.[66] Daisy left a light shadow in the family archive, likely a result of her husband's methodical purging of their papers. Childless, the pair spent the 1890s flitting between exotic destinations as Brooks researched his next book. The *Emancipation* had not won Brooks the professional recognition he desired from historians, but he became a marketable author and, like many Adamses before, a popular speaker on key questions of government, culture, and currency.[67] As the new century dawned, Brooks tunneled even farther into his theory of history. He amassed data on ancient civilizations via European archival work and long exchanges with Henry, then traveling in the South Seas.

Balancing supervision of the Adams family estate with his own intellectual pursuits, Brooks turned back to fill in the gaps of religious knowledge that had plagued his *Emancipation*. His new work, *The Law of Civilization and Decay* (1895), demanded greater familiarity with basic theological principles. Brooks tried to mend the error and fill in the gaps by following old Harvard guidelines. He asked Henry to put him in touch with "any German swells who know ecclesiastical history."[68] Henry, turning eastward to chase after Buddhas, came up empty. Brooks, beset by tedious family responsibilities and obsessed with his new project, did what many Adamses had done. He ran.

Europe was a second home for America's first family, and Brooks embraced it in the 1890s, relishing side trips with Daisy to their vacation home near Mumbai for rest cures.[69] Brooks's opportunities for travel were curtailed by the Adams estate's crumbling wealth, but he found India's warmer climate soothed his health, and he shared Henry's breakneck wanderlust for sampling foreign faiths.[70] It was Brooks, after all, who visited the cathedral of Le Mans in 1895 and prompted Henry's landmark survey of medieval church life in northwestern France.[71] Wandering in with Daisy, the forty-year-old Brooks realized he had never heard a great mass in a Gothic church. He sat down in the nave to listen. Sunshine sifted in through the twelfth-century windows. The boys' choir sang its hymns. And, as Brooks wrote in wonder, he suddenly sensed a spiritual communion that transcended the usual sacrament of wafers and wine. "I felt for half an hour as I know the men must have felt who stained those windows, and built those arches. I really and truly did believe the miracle, and as I sat and blubbered in the nave, and knelt at the elevation I did receive the body of God," Brooks recalled. "That . . . was the day on which I resolved to go to Palestine, and to see there at Jerusalem, what it was that had made the crusades."[72] Beginning in the 1890s, odd bits of Brooks's "lived religion" seeped into his scholarship on world economy and history, transforming how he analyzed faith and civilization.

Henry mocked him, but as Brooks kept touring Gothic churches, his agnosticism melted. Along the way, he looked for signs of urban blight. It was an odd confluence of interests, even for Brooks, but he was determined that his second book would better reflect the operation of religion—not necessarily religious truths—in world history. For, to his surprise, a mature Brooks savored the sensation of "being Christian" at Le Mans. In the cathedral's mix of prehistoric stone and bright glass, he sourced new evidence to illustrate his economic and historical theories. "To fill the brush I have had to read so much theology from the earliest days that I know more divinity than I do history,"

Brooks Adams and his wife, Evelyn "Daisy" Davis, often fled New England's winter weather and traveled to India in the 1890s. There, Brooks was able to rest and to write. *Adams National Historical Park*

he wrote to a friend at *Emancipation*'s end.[73] The publication and its mixed reviews had pushed Brooks to rethink how religion played into the laws and sequences of history that he wished to set down. Traveling through North Africa, India, Asia, Russia, and Europe, Adams mined foreign cultures for research. He collected currency rates and tallied several centuries' worth of religious membership statistics. He mapped ancient borders.

The result, *The Law of Civilization and Decay*, was a compact tour de force of economic theory and early modern history that described how urban communities rose and fell. As Brooks tracked backward from Puritans to Palestine throughout the spring and summer of 1895, he isolated *The Law*'s main argument. There he observed that "religious enthusiasm" was the motivating factor that drove pilgrimage, created communication networks, and built up centers of trade. These phenomena bloomed briefly and then "phased" into bloody crusades, priestly oppression, and social disintegration.[74] Vaulting from Roman case studies to Tudor commerce, Brooks's finale endorsed a new socio-political model of "modern centralization."

Cloaked in pseudoscientific jargon, Brooks's work on world economy was prophetic but it was also nearly unreadable, and exceedingly grim.[75] Daisy read the raw chapters and proposed as a title *The Path to Hell: A Story Book*.[76] Brooks, busy polishing drafts at the ancestral farm in Quincy, sounded glib in his report to Henry. "I rather like the title only I think it promises too much," he wrote. "How can I assure my readers that I will show them anything so good as a path to 'Hell.'"[77] Written on the cusp of Brooks Adams's reassessment of religion's utility in his own life, his *Law* also reveals a Victorian scholar who abruptly cared, in contrast to his idol Henry, that he might not be "sufficiently Christian" for the grand "American Century" that lay ahead.

In reinterpreting how cities formed and why that process mattered for the American soul, Brooks joined with other Gilded Age laity and church leaders to debate where to anchor modern Christianity amid a rising tide of unions, mergers, and monopolies. By the time Brooks got to work on his project in earnest, around 1893, a host of Protestant-authored books, articles, and reform campaigns had blossomed, the bulk of them centering on the application of Christian ethics to social sins.[78] In nearby Springfield, Massachusetts, for example, the Congregationalist pastor Washington Gladden exhorted workers to unionize and thereby improve living conditions. Modernity bred chaos, and it followed that nurturing all forms of communal membership, sacred and spiritual alike, instilled some form of social order. There was, Gladden warned in 1876, a "fissure now running through the social world, and threatening to become a great gulf fixed between the employing and the laboring classes" that would "divide the church as well."[79]

Setting up shop in the hardscrabble New York City neighborhood of Hell's Kitchen in 1886, the new pastor Walter Rauschenbusch struggled to aid his flock at the Second German Baptist Church. He found many congregants to be "out of work, out of clothes, out of shoes, and out of hope."[80] From coast to coast, women reformers of the Social Gospel movement joined the greater cause to save the American city from vice. "Common-core" Christian rhetoric permeated the Chicago settlement houses founded by Jane Addams, the temperance crusades of Frances

Willard, the Methodist-inflected suffrage work of the Reverend Anna Howard Shaw, the labor activism of Florence Kelley, and the tireless efforts of welfare activist Vita D. Scudder.[81]

When Brooks wrote his *Law*, then, he took aim at a nationful of metropolitan readers who were broadly Christian, ardently American, and deeply reform-minded. Many, like Brooks, were still reeling from a widespread depression caused by the railroads' overreach. As gold drained away, roughly five hundred banks closed and some fifteen hundred companies failed, all factors that ripened Adams's readership for his pessimistic view of history.[82] Rather than crafting another positive appeal to citizens by heralding American adaptability and ingenuity, he turned to a different Darwinian notion—extinction—to chart how religious fear and commercial greed repeatedly ground down humanity into "automata."[83] For the agnostic Henry and others, Brooks's *Law* became the "Bible of Anarchy" with which to navigate the social crises of modern life.[84] Why?

In contrast to most Gilded Age takedowns of city life, Brooks abandoned the prospect of reform and embraced the concept of degradation. Tracing the social "place" of religion in cities of the past, he explained why civilizations, including America, were fated to fail. This time, he knew better than to bill his *Law* as a work of history. "I can't masquerade as a scholar seeking truth at the bottom of a well," Brooks wrote to Henry as the book took shape. "I am dealing with all the burning questions of our time, and I must just face the music."[85] Over the course of a dozen chapters, Brooks demonstrated that human progress accelerated around the creation of cities. Energy, money, people, and culture clustered around such big centers of trade as Athens, London, and New York. Two forms of cultural authority—the soldier and the monk—then battled for control of the popular mind. As Brooks explained to the psychologist William James, these two forces dueled to operate on the soft social intellect: "Fear of the unseen, the spiritual worlds, represented by the priest; fear of the tangible world represented by the soldier. It is the conflict between these forces which has made civilisation."[86] Moral damages naturally ensued.

In each episode of Brooks's *Law*, then, capitalist greed and poverty surged as priests or soldiers laid ruin to urban progress. Adams's downward cycle experienced eternal rotation, as the agents of God and trade succumbed to profit and vice. One of Brooks's most eloquent examples lay in Istanbul, a center of trade and a clearinghouse for ancient faiths. Pointing to the Hagia Sophia—by turns an Orthodox showpiece, a Roman Catholic cathedral, a mosque when Brooks saw it, and soon after that a public museum—Adams inclined again to his theory that both sacred and secular civilizations were destined for dust. Byzantine beauty aside, Brooks wrote, "the most significant phenomenon about the church is its loneliness; nothing like it was built elsewhere."[87]

Brooks's narrative tone in his *Law* was noticeably calmer than that of the *Emancipation*, but his prognosis of human progress was much darker and indicated his deepening pessimism. Brooks wrote with an oddly robotic fury, wholly persuaded of world doom by his own limited data. The language of his *Law* resonated with fin-de-siècle readers, who often felt they were living in a slow-motion catastrophe. His message on how the country should proceed was muddier. Brooks made little effort to counteract the *Law* that he presented, gesturing hazily at a plan of "centralized administration" that might make America's downfall feel slightly softer. Three years after Ellis Island opened as the federal immigration center, Brooks's readers likely puzzled over the *Law*'s visceral advice to pump in a new "stream of barbarian blood" and fuel progress.[88] They resisted Brooks's idea to hire on the militaristic officers of a centralized civil administration in order to lead them through the global emergencies that he (correctly) predicted: American competition with Russia and Asia, two world wars, and the rise of several African independence movements. Against a tide of Gilded Age writers who preached reform, Brooks Adams looked at the last days of the American republic and prophesied that positive change was futile.

As a masterpiece meant to feature his theory more than history, Brooks's *Law* provoked strong reactions, notably in the genteel intellectual circles that he and Henry inhabited at home. Referencing the contemporary nocturnes painted by James Abbott McNeil Whistler and Frederic Remington—controversial for their lack of light and worthiness as artworks—the jurist Oliver Wendell Holmes Jr. struggled with what it was that his friend's second major work elucidated about the long-promised "phases" of the human mind. Brooks's *Law* "hardly strikes me as a science," Holmes wrote, "but rather as a somewhat grotesque world poem, or symphony in blue and gray, but the story of the modern world is told so strikingly that while you read you believe it."[89] Brooks's nocturne divided the critics. Still holding fast to the idea that history must be organized around his *Law*, Brooks ran stacks of archival research, mechanically, through the theory he had programmed. Stitched together with his notion that history swung in cycles, the *Law*'s prophecy turned out "blacker and gloomier" than even Brooks expected. "My book works out this time in such a ghastly way that it knocks the stuffing out of me," he wrote, revising for the London and Paris editions. "I am not aware that I am anything more than an automaton, I certainly have no conscious volition, and yet the stuff comes one way, only always more so."[90]

Reviewers called it a forced triumph, reliant on Adams's inexorable contortions of history and snarled syntax. In his authorship of a *Law* enslaved by theory, Brooks embodied "a certain class of economic writers who have treated history somewhat as the old theologians used to treat the Scriptures," one critic observed, "as a sort of rusty nail box out of which they selected odds and ends . . . to tack some framework of doctrine together, the likeness of which was never to be found in the thought of God or man."[91] Henry loved it. Brooks's *Law* marked "the first time that serious history has ever been written," the senior Adams wrote to friends in Washington, DC.[92] Emboldened, Brooks Adams rushed to reassert his theory in three more works: *America's Economic Supremacy* (1900), *The New Empire* (1902), and *The Theory of Social Revolutions* (1913). As the *Law* was reprinted around the world, Brooks soaked up his success while Henry's literary fame went into a final eclipse. Editors at the *Boston Daily Globe* finally heralded Brooks as a hometown Socrates, the sharp-eyed critic who kept the Athens of America in line. "One of the principal occupations of the Adams family has been to tell the community what it needed to know, but did not desire to hear," the *Globe* wrote of Brooks's many "essays on history" in 1915. "All honor to the gadfly. Let him sting us again."[93]

Brooks's treatment of faith as part of civilization's downfall in *The Law* was sobering, and it coincided with his personal revaluation of Christianity's role in a cosmopolitan lifestyle. Religion was a mobile force in Brooks's approach to crafting historical critique, a public evolution that aligned with his private seeking in the early part of the twentieth century. As for many Adamses, overseas travel regenerated his curiosity, and *The Law*'s generous book sales funded Brooks's exotic journeys to Russia, India, and Europe. Abroad, Brooks acquired new devotional habits from itinerant contact with Hindus, Catholics, and Episcopalians. With Daisy, the gentleman scholar and habitual neurasthenic traveled widely in the 1910s and 1920s, becoming a citizen of the world who unearthed iterations of American identity among the ruins of foreign faith. He bypassed Boston winters to monitor forms of coal development in India. He "wallowed" in Cairo's new museums, seizing on Howard Carter's impromptu offer to attend a preview opening of the Egyptian pharaoh Tutankhamen's tomb. To Brooks, sampling foreign faith only gave more credence to his economic theory and, thus, world history. Religious tourism helped to build up his case studies.

From 1904 to 1911, Brooks imparted his radical geopolitical views to the younger generation by serving as a full-time faculty member of Boston University's new School of Law and raising his profile as a participant in the old family church. "The nineteenth century abandoned unity and elected chaos," Professor Brooks Adams told his students as the centuries changed hands.[94] The subject of God rarely (if ever) made it into his lectures, but, increasingly, Brooks now relied on an admixture of Protestant and Catholic practices to cope privately with greater social change.[95] "We are nationally approaching, very rapidly, our culmination . . . to be greater in our particular way than we ever dreamed it possible for us to be,—and by God, I like it," Brooks wrote in 1901. "I'm for the new world. I go with it, electric cars, mobiles, plutocracy and all."[96]

On weekends away from the university, Brooks began to worship again at the family church in Quincy. Privately, his rediscovered sense of Christianity gave Brooks a fresh outlook on family duties. Religion, once a terse "illustration" to bolster Brooks's historical theories, became his solace when Henry's long decline began in April 1912. Between 1900 and 1927, Brooks criticized the reigning theology at First Church, but he bailed out the impoverished congregation when a wave of panics threatened its closure. As his siblings slipped away, Brooks clung to old Boston ways and pews. He was not sure why. More than anyone, Brooks was dazed by the depth and breadth of his piety.

By 1907, Brooks had gone public in prodding church leaders to do more than "scavenge" for followers. He insisted that they reclaim an ecumenical place at the "headwaters" of civic affairs.[97] Shortly after witnessing the mobilization of Paris in summer 1914, Brooks returned to Quincy, sure that his theories of central administration must be planted firmly in American Christianity. In October, to express his support for new minister Adelbert Lathrop Hudson, the ultraprivate Brooks Adams delivered an extraordinary public testimony of faith, proclaiming his support for "revealed religion" in the same breath that he declared Americans must accept a new mode of "civil administration."[98] Given Brooks's contrarian nature, it is hard to know why he embraced the same Puritan initiation rite he had damned so effectively in the *Emancipation* as "appalling."

Perhaps he saw some similarities between his own religious biography and that of Adelbert Hudson. A Brahmin scion who initially rejected the old Unitarian pulpit for a booming Sioux City law practice, Hudson traced his roots back to 1638 and a cohort of London forebears who had fled Archbishop Laud's tyranny. Religion and liberal education ran in the Hudson family lines, too. Six of his relatives currently served as Unitarian ministers, and five sat on Harvard's faculty. Adelbert reignited his interest in theology around the same time that Brooks had, and for some of the same reasons. Hudson perceived that while he "could not honestly teach the old creeds," modern Unitarianism opened a new intellectual door. Venturing inside, Hudson "found himself in a church whose attitude toward truth was in entire harmony with the scientific progress of the time," allowing him to "use all his energies in noble service without sacrificing his individual convictions."[99] Adelbert quit his law firm and enrolled in the Harvard Divinity School, where he studied from 1893 to 1895. After stints at parishes in Salt Lake City, Buffalo, and Florida, the lawyer-turned-prelate was called to Quincy in March 1912. Hudson was greeted by a refurbished church, a solidly bourgeois membership, and, in pew 54, patron Brooks Adams, a presidential descendant and the sole proprietor of a $20,000 annual fund promised to Hudson's new home.[100] A sharp-eyed pastor and businessman, Hudson called on Brooks Adams to stand and profess his faith.

When he borrowed the Quincy pulpit for his remarkable oration, world events had shifted Brooks onto firmer Christian ground, and he spied a chance to promote his theories once more. To fellow congregants, Brooks renounced the "false" agnostic philosophy of his youth. Adams pledged to adhere to Protestant Christianity—not to the agnostic scientific ideals endorsed by brother Henry—in order to sustain his morality as he explored the gross decay of civilization. The author of the *Emancipation* reminded fellow worshippers that they need not "cavil to the ecclesiastical tradition" in order to prevent American decline. A society must have religion in order to cohere, he argued, echoing a common plea of his Christian peers. Family bonds, he added, were vital to that relationship. To press his point, Brooks invoked examples from family and local history. "In this church we stand at the very core and heart of protestantism, but well I know that John Wheelwright protested not against Christ and his revelation, but against the performance of their trust by the guardians of his law," Brooks stated in his profession of faith, which he printed and circulated as World War I lit up Europe. "I rest tranquil in the conviction that [the Church] will, to her utmost, defend that moral standard which I believe to be vital to my country and my age."[101] Quoting from the Gospel of Mark, Brooks drew his final plea: "Lord, I believe; help thou mine unbelief."[102] Anxious to continue seeking God beyond Quincy's familiar borders, Brooks mailed checks to Hudson and let his religious interest magnetize in a new direction.

Catholic and Episcopalian rites sparked Brooks's interest as he entered his final years. Back in Boston throughout the 1920s, Brooks began to spend regular weekly retreats at an Episcopal monastery near Harvard Square. Henry would not willingly cross a church threshold to worship, but Brooks longed for a sincere invitation to join new forms of Christian community, a religious trait that he shared with his great-grandfather John. Donating a crisp twenty-dollar bill wherever he paused to pray, Brooks apologized to Roman Catholic clergy (whom he called his "benefactors") with characteristic gloom: "I have no real belief. I stand at the door—I prefer to stand outside—and I am then one of yourselves. When I talk with you apart from your chapel I am a pagan."[103] While researching and writing his *Law*, Brooks began to take religion seriously. He chose to experiment with his innate skepticism, ready for a reprieve from the pressure of agnosticism. Brooks's halfhearted quest for Catholic conversion reflected a generation of Americans who journeyed between Christianities, anxious to incorporate some spirituality into modernity.[104] Around him, other Americans joined in the cultural project, scouring a "free market" of faiths that invited them to speak in tongues, attend fundamentalist Bible colleges, and mull over the meaning of a nascent "muscular Christianity."[105] Brooks's religious universe grew vast.

Once again it was the well-traveled Adamses' connections to other laity, and not what they heard from stray pulpits, that connected them with new religious ideas and foreign rites. At home, Brooks used Boston's religious ecosystem to establish social credentials and keep his centuries-old political networks current. Daisy participated in lector duties at the high-society Episcopal cathedral of St. Paul's in downtown Boston, steps away from Brooks's law school.[106] Between 1910 and 1922, Brooks struck up a friendship with US congressman Bellamy Storer, a well-known Roman Catholic convert and Massachusetts Republican.[107] As Storer recalled, the pair traded thoughts on faith and doubt. In Adams, Storer glimpsed another American soul "homesick" for God. Storer diagnosed Brooks as an intellectual who was "the product of New England Puritanism—its forbidding doctrines converted into Unitarian formlessness, yet their old poison lingering on." By 1920, and within his closest circle of Brahmin friends, the seventy-two-year-old Brooks found he could not shed the old burden of New England church history.

Storer recommended Brooks to the religious care of Dom Leonard Sargent, who was then inaugurating a Benedictine friary of Anglo-American monks in Portsmouth, Rhode Island. In long talks with Sargent, a former Episcopalian, Brooks's queries about Christianity resonated.[108] "The whole world is upset. Nobody seems to know how to set it right," Brooks grumbled to Sargent, who threw open the monastery's doors. "Why shouldn't I come," the Unitarian stalwart replied, "as you tell me others do, and try to catch a little of your peace?" Once arrived at the Catholic retreat, Brooks hovered in the chapel doorway to observe, refusing to partake in the sacrament of Holy Communion. As his grandfather John Quincy had done a century earlier in St. Petersburg, Brooks was content to stand and watch a foreign faith unfold. Throughout the summers of the 1920s, Brooks became a familiar figure at Portsmouth Abbey, dining with the black-robed monks every night in full evening dress. He carried around the *Fioretti*, a set of popular legends about St. Francis of Assisi's works.

The Brahmin critic stirred up few theological debates. Brooks Adams confessed to Sargent that he and others longed to "leap the chasm," if only the Catholic clergy could somehow "help us over."[109] As the American Century gave way to world war and popular struggle, Brooks continued the family's long traditions of public service, congregational membership, and religious research. In 1917, he served as a delegate to the Massachusetts constitutional convention. In the debates, Brooks spoke out as a conservative reformer who upheld his great-great-grandfather's original legislative design of 1780.[110] Back in Quincy, mostly alone in his guardianship of the colonial farm and its priceless papers, Brooks revised portions of his misunderstood *Emancipation*. In July 1919, he reissued the book with a lengthy biographical preface about Moses, intended to be a shadow portrait of grandfather John Quincy. To Brooks and too many Adamses, Moses was the biblical figure with whom they identified most: an itinerant lawgiver, the shepherd to a fractious people, and God's sometime favorite.[111] At the end, Brooks segued into the themes of modern centralization and civil administration once espoused in his *Law*. It was an awkward new starting point for a story that condemned Puritan theocracy. "For it has become self-evident that the democrat cannot change himself," Brooks wrote, decreeing that "democracy in America has conspicuously and decisively failed."[112] In 1926, aping Henry's fictional heroine Madeleine Lee, Brooks Adams fled to the Holy Land.

He was joined in Jerusalem by a wave of Anglo-American antiquities hunters, pilgrims, and investors who saw the chance to "walk the Bible" and rejuvenate their faith in a sacred land. Visiting the Holy Land was a religious rite of passage that many Americans would continue throughout Brooks's quarter of the twentieth century, and well beyond.[113] Brooks carted along his father's books for use on the trip, referring often to the same cumbersome volumes of Johann Lorenz von Mosheim's *Ecclesiastical History* that Charles Sr. had so despised studying at Harvard.[114] Standing on the summit of the Mount of Olives, the elderly Brooks paused to recite, from memory, one of his great-grandfather John's favorite lessons from scripture, the Sermon on the Mount. Brooks had found a way to pay tribute to ancient family memories, while testing out a new hybrid faith that incorporated strands of both Protestant and Catholic experience. Completing his political and private pilgrimages, Brooks Adams returned home to sign over the house and family papers to the National Park Service before his death in February 1927.[115]

Overall, Brooks's flickers of faith and doubt illuminate a last shift in what he and Henry called "the family mind." His "Christianization" saga, from Puritans to Palestine, suggests that even the inherited Protestant processes of liberal education and finding faith through inquiry could not remedy the cracks in American culture. Brooks's vision of godly republicanism, led by civil administrators and preset cycles of wealth and decline, was a far cry from his forebears' ideas of a providentially blessed nation. As a result of his scholarship, travel, and work to enshrine America's first family in the Quincy homestead, Brooks journeyed from frigid skeptic to rigorous seeker. He offered a distinctively American—if highly pessimistic—perspective on how to "keep the faith" as social norms changed. Brooks fought to reconcile modern life with Christian practice. By his measure, he failed. Yet Brooks's religious interests and related dilemmas illustrate how many Puritan heirs—erudite, liberal Protestants who disdained theology and traveled widely across religious worlds—met the modern era with murky faith.

Like Henry, Brooks praised the purity and beauty of Gothic architecture. The two scholars diverged, though, on how they experienced forms of religious beauty. Henry preferred to contextualize artistic emotion in the medieval past; Brooks longed to feel its power in the present. Take how each man walked up to the same church and recorded it for history. Henry's approach to the Gothic glory of Chartres varied little from how he juggled perspectives on Japan's roofs. His *Mont-Saint-Michel and Chartres* opens from the archangel's view and sweeps down across farmland. Years after Henry's death, Brooks carried that book to France as his guide. But Brooks approached Chartres from the low road, eager to retrace how the town's farmers, tradesmen, and their families must have climbed up, from the heart of civilization, to receive Holy Communion. In 1922, Brooks and his social secretary Wilhelmina Harris returned to Chartres. Harris recalled: "One morning he looked at the two eleventh- and fourteenth-century bell towers with spires, as he said, rising higher than the hill upon which the city stands and pointing to Unity beyond space."[116] Brooks's fondness for lay prophecy and his casual reference to the Puritan John Winthrop's message reveal him to be a complex critic of capitalism who still found solace in religion as a triumphant force. Poised between his Puritan past and an uncertain American future, Brooks Adams gains new meaning, as a modern man who found greater purpose in "crossing" between faiths while "dwelling" on the doorstep of Christianity.[117]

Epilogue

AMERICA'S FIRST FAMILY WAS ALWAYS on the move, and they had to pray somewhere. Their religious views ranged across the Christian spectrum. Tirelessly planting and pulling up their New England roots for three hundred years, the Adamses as a group felt most at home on the road. Nourishing Christianity was a constant challenge, with or without Providence's help. In and out of political office, Adams family members saw their own story reflected in that of the nation. Most Americans have experienced religion not through high theology and clerical instruction but via vibrant episodes of personal encounter and cultural exchange. The traditions that many nineteenth-century families like the Adamses chose to create depended mainly on how and why other laity introduced them to new ways of worship. Nineteenth-century America has often been heralded as a triumph of congregationalism as a practice, one that successfully gathered in disparate social classes and granted the clergy some measure of cultural authority, while encouraging individual spiritual exploration.

As the Adamses' family history of faith and doubt indicates, most Americans learned about new religious ideas from other laypeople, as well as the pulpit. The prism to understand American Christianity, as the country evolved from colonies to republic, is that complex process of personal encounter, experience, and exchange. The unique way in which America's liberalizing Protestants met the world was a multifaceted practice evident in the cosmopolitan Christianity of this well-traveled family. Prolific statesmen and critics who consolidated

Protestant power, the Adamses emerge as leading interpreters of a democratic culture in which citizens remade their worship politics to meet the needs of the nation.

A distinctively American form of Protestant Christianity, one born of a dissenting heritage and political disunion from England, was the first lens that most Adamses reached for in order to view the world. In this way, John and Abigail's descendants operated, along with their well-educated American peers, as liberalizing Protestants. Biblical inquiry, comparative religious studies, philanthropic efforts, and an inner drive to reconcile the goals of church and state steered their lives. Claiming Puritan ancestry and preferring to practice a liberal form of Unitarianism, the Adamses were unusually forthright in their exploration of a subject as private and provocative as personal faith. Like many Americans, most Adamses accepted organized Christianity as a public good. They filled letters and lives with the effort to answer one query: What was it good *for*?

As longtime servants of the state and elite critics of culture, the Adamses worked to raise America's standing in the world, drawing criticism and praise for their wide-ranging efforts. In tandem, the Adamses and their Harvard-educated peers drove the complex process of "unbecoming British," placing themselves within a longer historical tradition that tied together American Protestant worship and rational inquiry with human progress.[1] These twin projects required a regular, full-scale review of the Christianities that the family might leverage in order to condition moral behavior, support democracy, and ensure the fulfillment of God's special plan for the "chosen" nation.

The spur of constant travel stimulated the family appetite to sample new religions. The Adamses were exceptionally privileged observers of foreign cultures, and they knew it. Such a remarkable head start inspired them to share the knowledge they acquired abroad. As a young John Quincy packed up for Harvard, Abigail tartly reminded her eldest son that he had never been denied a book nor missed a chance to mix with great thinkers on two continents, and thus "how unpardonable would it have been in you, to have been a Blockhead."[2] Most of the Adamses, conscious of their joint legacy as history-makers, took care to write down and transmit what they experienced of the world's religious cultures. Encounters with Old World religion and New World practice appear throughout their extensive diaries, letters, literary efforts, photographs, and historic homes. Whenever John Adams and his descendants turned to survey the American past, they had a unique family archive of religious experience to consult. Simply, the Adams family prayed—and told.

At first glance, the intellectual and cultural history of Adams family religion seems to be quintessentially nineteenth-century New England in scope: Puritans ceding to Congregationalists, a bend toward Unitarian ideology at midcentury, capped by Victorian neurasthenia and the angst of modernity. International travel encouraged the Adamses to develop religious tolerance by bringing them in close contact with foreign cultures. Over some three centuries of civil service, as diplomats who acclimated to new rites with every mission, the Adamses learned that respecting religious differences was key to early American statesmanship. Yet the Adamses' experiences also led them to become leading lay critics of New England religion. They fought to find the social "place" of Protestant Christianity within an American republic troubled by slavery, market politics, and the death of providentialism.

Avowedly Unitarian, the Adamses were constantly on the move toward Christianity, but away from their home church in Quincy. What sort of Christian inheritance did they claim as Americans abroad? When did religious expression or exploration raise the stakes intellectually, presenting new choices for them to make? And what was the role of religion, foreign and familiar, in forming what the critic Henry Adams casually referred to in conversation with his brother Brooks as "the family mind"?

One effect of the Adamses' constant travel was to sharpen their thought on the quality of American religion, once they were back home. Like most of their nineteenth-century peers, they shook off the last restraints of Calvinism, explored foreign faiths, dabbled in biblical exegesis, and rejected theological hermeneutics in favor of aesthetic pursuits that infused Christian precepts and personalities into an emergent canon of national arts and letters. Few families, however, purposefully created a working archive of intellectual culture as this one did. Generations read, reread, and edited each other's writings for publication. They created and cataloged several libraries' worth of religious literature and art. A passion for the family's Revolutionary past guided their projects, reminding them at every step that being part of a presidential family was, as one biographer noted, "both inspiration and obstacle."[3]

Overall, the dilemma of what it meant to be Christian (and famous) in America marked every stage of the Adamses' well-traveled lives, especially once the market revolution entrenched the sins of wealth and worldliness. Often, the religious dilemmas that the Adamses faced centered on how they should operate in a diversifying community of believers. As modern scholars of American religion have reconstructed the nineteenth century, a wild and unpredictable pulse of emotion piloted the Victorian American soul. Laity sought to institutionalize successive (and often conflicting) impulses and innovations, yielding in turn a dramatic landscape of new religious roads for the Adamses to explore.

The dynamic coexistence of Protestant duty and theological innovation set the fast pace of American religious life, leading to the establishment of the nation's blossoming networks of education, culture, and reform.[4] Old Puritan rites, such as fast and thanksgiving days, appeared on the American calendar but, increasingly, families like the Adamses observed them with little real fervor.[5] The polymath John Quincy Adams worried that he had taken biblical exegesis to a sinfully indulgent level, stuffing his private journal with a potentially "vicious excess" of religious sentiment.[6] Seeking a balance between a religion "of the heart" and "of the head," American Christians legitimated and made both personal experience and the claims of science more central to their theological proclamations. Innovative laity competed to claim the American mind with new doctrines, including Mormonism and Christian Science. They founded utopias, promoting the communal ownership of goods and plural marriage, in the backcountry of New York, Indiana, Missouri, and New England. Aided by clergy, some turned away from biblical inerrancy. They opened seminaries and burned convents. They funded foreign missionary societies meant to spread a new, global Christianity. Armed with Gospel rhetoric, they advocated for temperance, women's rights, and the abolition of slavery. Rediscovering the Puritan intelligentsia in the mid-nineteenth century, Protestant laity lit up the public sphere with liturgical controversies and sectarian feuds that mirrored or offset their equally ambitious displays of party politics. This was the hothouse of American religious culture in which the Adamses thrived, and moved through, always taking notes.[7]

The Adamses' religious story reminds us of the American Victorians who sought God in eclectic places and then made their return, greatly changed, to the family pew. As new religions multiplied, the overarching Protestant mission to articulate "true" faith encouraged the Adamses to take the priesthood of all believers to a new level, by arguing with "their" God and society about what constituted true piety.[8] Any construction of national identity or self-identity began by asking Providence: "Am I what I should be?"[9]

As prominent Unitarians acknowledged, the eighteenth-century heritage of American religion, which yoked together evangelical fervor, Scottish Common Sense philosophy, and scientific reason, presented a few shortcomings to the nineteenth-century Adamses.[10] Enduring waves of national expansion and internal fracture, American congregations spent much of the Victorian era struggling with the old colonial directive that "good Christians make good citizens."[11] Though they gained political independence in the eighteenth century, Protestants like the Adamses really made America in the nineteenth century, embedding broadly Christian values into a usable national culture. Their efforts to do so reflect the consolidation of lay leadership, one of American religion's most distinctive characteristics. The church remained a key site for liberalizing Protestants to re-evaluate religion's functionality in fostering growth. At century's end, this line of thinking led Protestant-raised critics like Henry and Brooks Adams to attempt new "Christian" arguments about the nature of industrial progress.

As they used Christian language to criticize government and culture, Victorian Protestants turned inward, questioning how to cultivate piety. Like the Adamses, many rejected conversion as a primary goal. They embraced pluralistic journeys through other faiths, largely as a method of courting and overcoming doubt.[12] Their relationship with God became more intimate, as they pushed past clergy for a closer communion with holy precepts. Just as the Adamses did, many families picked through a catalog of Protestant traditions and compiled an admixture of ideas and practices that felt most American, often through a lifelong process of trial and error. As Reconstruction-era waves of immigration and change swept through the nation, lay seekers added

Catholic, Jewish, and Eastern rites to the list. Charles Francis Adams's sons, Henry and Brooks, dissenting from the numb deism in which they were raised, easily justified "crossing but not dwelling" on the doorstep of foreign faiths like Catholicism, Hinduism, and Buddhism.[13]

Christianity, as American Victorians like the Adamses came to interpret it, shaped individual and national identity, but in ways that no single Protestant sect could either anticipate or claim to master fully. Again, the Victorian Adamses' shift in religious behavior echoed a greater social change; to most Americans, it seemed less vital to maintain orthodoxy in an era marked by events that did not synchronize with biblical predictions or platitudes. Throughout the long nineteenth century, Protestants made and remade American religious identity, exhibiting a spectrum of feeling and scientific inquiry that challenged their forebears' providentialist plans for nationhood. The revised rites of modern Christianity, glimpsed here from the family's-eye view, bear the marks of that struggle. Henry Adams's self-inflicted tragedy of an *Education*—in which he replaced the dead pulpits of New England Christianity with a mash-up of scientific Buddhism and medieval Catholicism—resonated with his generation of American seekers for a reason.[14]

The experience of the Adams family exemplifies how people tried to balance sacred and secular lives in a rapidly changing America. The Adams women ran the estates and speculated in bonds (Abigail), hosted salons in Washington, DC, and on the Continent (Louisa Catherine), widened the family's networks beyond Unitarian circles (Abigail Brooks), and experimented with new media such as photography (Marion Hooper, "Clover"). In keeping with the "first family" pedigree, Adams men followed a fairly common program of attending Harvard and suffering through early careers in law before turning to the farm, the state, the military, or private enterprise to foster reform. More than anything else, it was each generation's sustained commitment to government service and social improvement that brought about their phases of personal religious change.[15]

This family's history of faith and doubts reminds us what is so distinctive about American religion in the new republic, namely, that religious voluntarism meant more than denominational mobility; it carried the intellectual freedom to sample many gods. Gradually, the Adamses imprinted their own template of American religious experience. They were surprised, startled, amused, and enticed by the new faiths they saw and heard. They pursued liberal education at Harvard and toured foreign religions in conjunction with prestigious diplomatic work. Then they returned to their native ecosystem of New England Unitarianism, maturing into fierce critics of national government, faith, and culture. Worldliness and appreciation for higher forms of culture, culled from their nonstop travel, sharpened the literature that they produced. Either on the page or in a July Fourth town-hall speech, the Adamses deployed Christian rhetoric with innovative flexibility, using it to muster political power or to express curiosity, irony, or shame. Religion gave structure to home life, too, and outlined the duties of Christian mothers. And, although they enjoyed roaming beyond Unitarian roads of thought, Christianity remained the political dynasty's constant for three centuries, just as John Adams believed in 1812.

Religion was the main arena in which each generation of Adamses grappled with the successive ideologies that swept through the nineteenth-century American republic: providentialism, Christian republicanism, and agnosticism. Repeatedly, they reconsidered what church membership meant for the American citizenry. To a degree, these decades of intense deliberation culminated in the religious path of Brooks Adams. Indeed, his trajectory highlights a guiding question of American life, namely, how to belong to a community without sacrificing individualism.[16] Over the course of several generations, this was a particularly knotty issue for a train of public officeholders like the Adamses, who thought of their family's service as both the root and vine of national growth. Even an 1875 mayoral race, to Brooks, signified a "trial of strength between those who have a stake in the community and those who have none."[17] The question of how church and state might partner in modern society was one that Brooks thought he had finally settled—for himself and for the Adams family—by the busy spring of 1912. But within the next few weeks, Brooks's world would be upended. All of it lay just ahead: the sinking of the *Titanic*, the wild chaos of a four-way presidential race, the Boston Red Sox World Series Championship, and his brother Henry's final decline.

On April 7, 1912, Brooks sat in the family pew at the Unitarian church in Quincy. He listened to the new pastor, Adelbert Hudson, give a rousing Palm Sunday sermon. There was big church news, too. For the first time since 1639, when their Puritan heirs had regathered the church, the community had revised its covenant. Now the language was more in keeping with that of other twentieth-century Unitarians, as crafted by Charles Gordon Ames (a distant Adams cousin) in 1880. "In the freedom of truth, and in the spirit of Jesus Christ, we unite for the worship of God and the service of man," ran the text. Six feet from Brooks's pew, at the pulpit, lay the marbled book where worshippers could, if they chose, initial their assent to the new pledge after the communion service.[18] It was a step that Brooks, like his forebears, weighed with each faith he encountered—whether or not to commit to that particular version of Christianity, or even to commit to any at all. Around him, families filed out of the pews, putting their names to the text in the shadow of John Adams's memorial plaque. In a few decades, many of the signatures bore new annotations, like "moved" or "killed in World War I." When Brooks rose, he did so as a seeker who chose to join the Unitarian community, and as an Adams who trusted that Christianity yet steered the American republic. His decision represented the three centuries' worth of religious explorers who had resolved, finally, to rest in modern Unitarianism. Brooks walked toward the pulpit and picked up the minister's pen. Adams signed the covenant.

APPENDIX

THE ADAMS FAMILY GENEALOGY

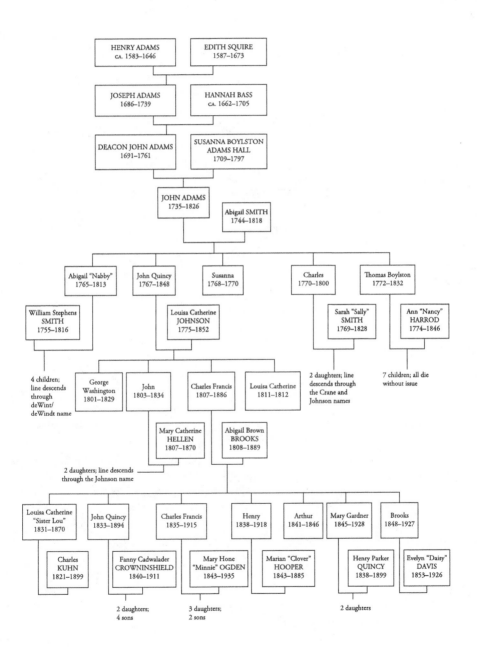

NOTES

Introduction

1. John Quincy Adams, May 10, 1815, Diary, Adams Papers, Massachusetts Historical Society, Boston, Massachusetts.

2. Ravrio (1759–1814) designed ormolu clocks, lamps, and bronze ornaments for Napoleon's chateaux at Saint-Cloud, Compiègne, and the Tuileries; his adopted son, Louis Stanilas Lenoir, continued the firm. According to John Quincy's diary, he visited the studio a few months after Ravrio's death. At the time, the bronze-maker's will was the talk of Paris. Ravrio had bequeathed a prize of 3,000 francs to the inventor of a patent to gild bronze without mercury, as a way to save workmen dying from the fumes. On Ravrio, see Glenn Campbell, ed., *The Grove Encyclopedia of Decorative Arts* (New York: Oxford University Press, 2006); and Edouard Foucaud, *The Book of Illustrious Mechanics of Europe and America*, trans. John Frost (New York: D. Appleton, 1846), 229–232.

3. Aida DiPace Donald and David Donald, eds., *The Diary of Charles Francis Adams*, 8 vols. (Cambridge, MA: Belknap Press of Harvard University Press, 1964–1986), 5:vii, 124. See also Laurel A. Racine, *Historic Furnishings Report: The Birthplaces of Presidents John Adams and John Quincy Adams*, 10 vols. (Charlestown, MA: Northeast Museum Services Center, National Park Service, 2001), 8:723–744.

4. Wilhelmina S. Harris, *Adams National Historic Site: A Family's Legacy to America* (Washington, DC: US Department of the Interior, National Park Service, 1983), 1–64. For Harris, who was Brooks's social secretary and the first superintendent of the Adams National Historical Park, see chapter 5.

5. The few works that exist on multigenerational family religion have significantly broadened scholarly understanding of how Americans have dealt with intellectual crisis and cultural change; some of these historians have also offered new insights regarding religion's effect on family structure. Spanning a dozen Beechers (or more) who lived from 1738 to 1907, Lyman Beecher Stowe's *Saints, Sinners and Beechers* (Indianapolis: Bobbs-Merrill, 1934) chronicled family history in a light, conversational manner that avoided deep theological waters. As a counterpoint, Marie Caskey's latter approach to the same subject, *Chariot of Fire: Religion and the Beecher Family* (New Haven, CT: Yale University Press, 1978), demonstrated the dilemmas that religion caused for the family's intellectual growth. A more substantial effort at incorporating family history came with Emily Bingham's *Mordecai: An Early American Family* (New York: Hill and Wang, 2003). Bingham follows three generations of Jewish immigrants in North Carolina, describing the "protective covenant" of "bourgeois domesticity, intellectual cultivation, and religious liberalism" that grounded the family's newly acquired American patriotism. And for a very different take, on how religion can rupture the family bond, see Craig Harline, *Conversions: Two Family Stories from the Reformation and Modern America* (Ann Arbor, MI: Sheridan Books, 2011).

6. Colleen McDannell, *The Christian Home in Victorian America, 1800–1940* (Bloomington: Indiana University Press, 1994).

7. In intellectual biographies and cultural studies, many scholars have employed family history to tell a larger story. Notable examples are F. O. Matthiessen, *The James Family* (New York: Knopf, 1947); John Demos, *A Little Commonwealth: Family Life in Plymouth Colony* (London: Oxford University Press, 1970); Phyllis Cole, *Mary Moody Emerson and the Origins of Transcendentalism: A Family History* (New York: Oxford University Press, 1998); George Howe Colt, *The Big House: A Century in the Life of an American Summer Home* (New York: Scribner, 2003); Paul Fisher, *House of Wits: An Intimate Portrait of the James Family* (New York: Henry Holt, 2008); Annette Gordon-Reed, *The Hemingses of Monticello: An American Family* (New York: Norton, 2008); Emma Rothschild, *The Inner Life of Empires: An Eighteenth-Century History* (Princeton, NJ: Princeton University Press, 2011); and Jehanne Wake, *Sisters of Fortune: America's Caton Sisters at Home and Abroad* (New York: Simon and Schuster, 2011).

8. Ronald A. Simkins and Gail A. Risch, eds., *Religion and the Family* (Omaha, NE: Creighton University Press, 2006), ix.

9. On the significance of using family history to tell the American story and the methodological challenges of constructing that narrative, see Michael Grossberg, *Governing the Hearth: Law and the Family in Nineteenth-Century America* (Chapel Hill: University of North Carolina Press, 1985); John Demos, *Past, Present, and Personal: The Family and Life Course in America* (New York: Oxford University Press, 1986); Tamara K. Hareven and Andrejs

Plakans, eds., *Family History at the Crossroads: A* Journal of Family History *Reader* (Princeton, NJ: Princeton University Press, 1987), vii–xxi; Elisabeth Donaghy Garrett, *At Home: The American Family, 1750–1870* (New York: Abrams, 1990); Jean E. Hunter and Paul T. Mason, eds., *The American Family: Historical Perspectives* (Pittsburgh: Duquesne University Press, 1991); Gerald F. Moran, *Religion, Family, and the Life Course: Explorations in the Social History of Early America* (Ann Arbor: University of Michigan Press, 1992); Rosemary Radford Ruether, *Christianity and the Making of the Modern Family* (Boston: Beacon Press, 2000); Annette Atkins, *We Grew Up Together: Brothers and Sisters in Nineteenth-Century America* (Urbana: University of Illinois Press, 2001); James Volo and Dorothy Denneen Volo, *Family Life in 17th- and 18th-Century America* (Westport, CT: Greenwood Press, 2006); Marilyn Coleman, Lawrence H. Ganong, and Kelly Warzinik, *Family Life in 20th-Century America* (Westport, CT: Greenwood Press, 2007); and C. Dallett Hemphill, *Siblings: Brothers and Sisters in American History* (New York: Oxford University Press, 2011).

10. These religious biographies served as models: Peter Brown, *Augustine of Hippo: A Biography* (Berkeley: University of California Press, 1967); Edwin S. Gaustad, *Sworn on the Altar of God: A Religious Biography of Thomas Jefferson* (Grand Rapids, MI: Eerdmans, 1996); Jon F. Sensbach, *Rebecca's Revival: Creating Black Christianity in the Atlantic World* (Cambridge, MA: Harvard University Press, 2005); David Hempton, *Evangelical Disenchantment: Nine Portraits of Faith and Doubt* (New Haven, CT: Yale University Press, 2008); and Catherine A. Brekus, *Sarah Osborn's World: The Rise of Evangelical Christianity in Early America* (New Haven, CT: Yale University Press, 2013).

11. On the significance of family discourse and the development of American Christianity, see David D. Hall, ed., *Lived Religion in America: Toward a History of Practice* (Princeton, NJ: Princeton University Press, 1997), and Laurie F. Maffly-Kipp, Leigh E. Schmidt, and Mark Valeri, eds., *Practicing Protestants: Histories of Christian Life in America, 1630–1965* (Baltimore: Johns Hopkins University Press, 2006).

This work draws mainly on the Adams Family Papers held at the Massachusetts Historical Society, Boston, Massachusetts. With material dating from 1638 to the present, the collection includes family correspondence, letterbooks, diaries, literary manuscripts, speeches, legal and business papers, photographs, and other documents.

12. John Quincy Adams, December 25, 1779, in *The Diary of John Quincy Adams*, 2 vols., ed. David Grayson Allen et al. (Cambridge, MA: Belknap Press of Harvard University Press, 1981), 1:18.

13. This anecdote of Edith Forbes Perkins and Charles Perkins appears in Henry Davis Minot's October 26, 1887 letter to William Minot, Henry Davis Minot Papers, Massachusetts Historical Society.

Chapter 1

1. Gathered by Puritans in 1636 and established as an independent Congregationalist church in 1639, the Adams family church became Unitarian in 1750; it has been Unitarian Universalist since 1961. By "Unitarian," I refer to the church's liberal Congregationalist (Arminian) theology and cultural attitudes throughout the eighteenth century.

2. Henry Adams monument, John Hancock Cemetery, Quincy, Massachusetts; John Adams, "Inscription on the tombstone of Henry Adams," March 1822, Adams Papers.

3. Various scholars and Adamses, including John Adams, have conducted genealogical research on the family's Anglo-Welsh origins. See, for example, Andrew N. Adams, *A Genealogical History of Henry Adams, of Braintree, Mass., and His Descendants; Also John Adams, of Cambridge, Mass., 1632–1897*, 2 vols. (Rutland, VT: Tuttle Co. Printers, 1898); Daniel Munro Wilson, *Where American Independence Began: Quincy, Its Famous Group of Patriots; Their Deeds, Homes, and Descendants* (Boston: Houghton, Mifflin, 1902); J. Gardner Bartlett, comp., *Henry Adams of Somersetshire, England, and Braintree, Mass.: His English Ancestry and Some of His Descendants* (New York: privately printed, 1927); Henry Adams, *John Adams's Book: Being Notes on a Record of the Births, Marriages and Deaths of Three Generations of the Adams Family, 1734–1807* (Boston: Boston Athenaeum, 1934); and Hugh Brogan and Charles Mosley, *American Presidential Families* (New York: Macmillan, 1993).

4. Here I rely on the definitions of historical, national, and personal providentialism outlined in Nicholas S. Guyatt, *Providence and the Invention of the United States, 1607–1876* (Cambridge: Cambridge University Press, 2007), 2–6. See also Sacvan Bercovitch, *The Puritan Origins of the American Self* (New Haven, CT: Yale University Press, 1975); E. Brooks Holifield, *Theology in America: Christian Thought from the Age of the Puritans to the Civil War* (New Haven, CT: Yale University Press, 2003); and Harry S. Stout, *The New England Soul: Preaching and Religious Culture in Colonial New England* (New York: Oxford University Press, 2012).

5. John White, *The Planter's Plea; or, The Grounds of Plantations Examined, and Usuall Objections Answered* (London: William Jones, 1630), 3.

6. David F. Holland, *Sacred Borders: Continuing Revelation and Canonical Restraint in Early America* (New York: Oxford University Press, 2011), 40–43.

7. See, for example, James F. Cooper Jr., *Tenacious of Their Liberties: The Congregationalists in Colonial Massachusetts* (New York: Oxford University Press, 1999); and Michael P. Winship, *Godly Republicanism: Puritans, Pilgrims, and a City on a Hill* (Cambridge, MA: Harvard University Press, 2002).

8. John Adams, "Genealogical Note," August 7, 1773, in *The Papers of John Adams*, 19 vols., ed. Sara Georgini et al. (Cambridge, MA: Belknap Press of Harvard University Press, 1977–), 1:351–352; John Adams, "Ancestry," October 5, 1802,

in *The Diary and Autobiography of John Adams*, 4 vols., ed. L. H. Butterfield et al. (Cambridge, MA: Belknap Press of Harvard University Press, 1961–1966), 3:253–257.

9. Charles Francis Adams, May 26, 1824, in *The Diary of Charles Francis Adams*, 8 vols., ed. Aida DiPace Donald and David Donald (Cambridge, MA: Belknap Press of Harvard University Press, 1964), 1:158–159.

10. Bartlett, *Henry Adams*, xiv–xv.

11. Henry Adams to Charles Francis Adams Jr., January 24, 1894, in *The Letters of Henry Adams*, 6 vols., ed. J. C. Levenson et al. (Cambridge, MA: Belknap Press of Harvard University Press, 1982–1988), 3:11–12; 4:158.

12. For liberal Protestants' manifold reinterpretations and eventual rejection of "Puritan" ideals and rhetoric, see Jan C. Dawson, *The Unusable Past: America's Puritan Tradition, 1830 to 1930* (Chico, CA: Scholars Press, 1984); Dean Hammer, *The Puritan Tradition in Revolutionary, Federalist, and Whig Political Theory: A Rhetoric of Origins* (New York: P. Lang, 1998); and Elizabeth A. Clark, *Founding the Fathers: Early Church History and Protestant Professors in Nineteenth-Century America* (Philadelphia: University of Pennsylvania Press, 2011).

On nineteenth-century Americans' interest in genealogical research as the "social glue" needed to reify or to "reproduce contemporary power relations relating to class, gender, and race," see Francesca Morgan, "A Noble Pursuit? Bourgeois America's Uses of Lineage," in *The American Bourgeoisie: Distinction and Identity in the Nineteenth Century*, ed. Sven Beckert and Julia B. Rosenbaum (New York: Palgrave Macmillan, 2010), 135–151.

13. John Adams, December 19, 1779, *Diary*, 4:209–210.

14. Some of the clearest genealogical information about Henry Adams and Edith Squire Adams Fussell, and the family's life in rural England and early Braintree, Massachusetts, appears in Bartlett, *Henry Adams*, 10–13, 28–35, 38, 46–73.

15. John Adams, July 21, 1786, *Diary*, 3:195–196.

16. John Quincy Adams to Edward H. Adams, Washington, DC, December 3, 1843, Schaffner Collection, Harvard College Library, Cambridge, Massachusetts.

17. Henry Adams, Will and Inventory of Estate, Braintree, Massachusetts, June 8, 1647, Adams Papers.

18. Fueling criticism of the church's bureaucratic woes, Barton St. David's vicar of 1668 earned the same salary as his predecessor of 1535, for which see Margaret Steig, *Laud's Laboratory: The Diocese of Bath and Wells in the Early Seventeenth Century* (Lewisburg, PA: Bucknell University Press, 1982), 125–127.

19. Carl Hamilton, *Some Account of the Parishes of Charlton Adam and Charlton Mackrell* (Taunton, MA: privately printed, 1961), 3, 10, 11, 16.

20. Pamela Sambrook, *Country House Brewing in England, 1500–1900* (Rio Grande, OH: Hambledon Press, 1996); Peter Dyer, "Randle Holme and 17th Century Brewing, Malting and Coopering Terminology," *Journal of the Brewery History Society* 126 (2007): 62–73.

21. Robert Dunning, *A History of Somerset* (Guildford: Biddles, 1983), 54–55, 60–61; Phyllis M. Hembry, *The Bishops of Bath and Wells, 1540–1640: Social and Economic Problems* (London: Athlone Press, 1976), 42–78.

22. For the connections, made here and later, between the Laudian reforms, lay persecution, and Somerset dissent, as well as American emigration, see Henry B. Bell, *Archbishop Laud and Priestly Government* (London: A. Constable, 1905), 134–161; Margaret Stieg, *Laud's Laboratory: The Diocese of Bath and Wells in the Early Seventeenth Century* (Lewisburg, PA: Bucknell University Press, 1982); Leo F. Solt, *Church and State in Early Modern England, 1509–1640* (New York: Oxford University Press, 1990); Alison Games, *Migration and the Origins of the English Atlantic World* (Cambridge, MA: Harvard University Press, 1999), 18–20, 132–162; David Underdown, *Fire from Heaven: Life in an English Town in the Seventeenth Century* (London: HarperCollins, 1992); Dunning, *History of Somerset*; and Hembry, *Bishops of Bath and Wells*, 220–221.

23. Stieg, *Laud's Laboratory*, 358–373.

24. Bell, *Archbishop Laud*, 138–139.

25. Solt, *Church and State in Early Modern England*, 178–182.

26. David D. Hall, "Narrating Puritanism," in *New Directions in American Religious History*, ed. Harry S. Stout and D. G. Hart (New York: Oxford University Press, 1997), 51–83.

27. Underdown, *Fire from Heaven*, 113, 140. Aquila Purchase (1589–1633) wed Edith Adams's sister Ann Squire (later Oliver, 1591–1662), for which see Clarence Almon Torrey, *New England Marriages Prior to 1700* (Baltimore: Genealogical Pub. Co., 1985), 607.

28. Virginia DeJohn Anderson, *New England's Generation: The Great Migration and the Formation of Society and Culture in the Seventeenth Century* (New York: Cambridge University Press, 1991), 38–45; David Hackett Fischer, *Albion's Seed: British Folkways in America* (New York: Oxford University Press, 1992), 13–42; Darren Staloff, *The Making of an American Thinking Class: Intellectuals and Intelligentsia in Puritan Massachusetts* (New York: Oxford University Press, 1998), 3–4; John White, *Directions for the Profitable Reading of the Scriptures* (London: s.n., 1647), 1–338; and Frances Rose-Troup, *John White, The Patriarch of Dorchester and the Founder of Massachusetts, 1575–1648: With an Account of the Early Settlements in Massachusetts, 1620–1630* (New York: G. P. Putnam's Sons, 1930).

29. On the range of statistics and motives associated with the Great Migration, see Francis J. Bremer, *The Puritan Experiment: New England Society from Bradford to Edwards* (Hanover, NH: University Press of New England, 1995), 39–47; David Grayson Allen, *In English Ways: The Movement of Societies and the Transfer of English Local Law and Custom to Massachusetts Bay, 1600–1690* (Chapel Hill: University of North Carolina Press, 1981); and Bernard Bailyn, *The Barbarous Years: The Peopling of British North America: The Conflict of Civilizations, 1600–1675* (New York: Knopf, 2012), 365–416.

30. Bailyn, *The Barbarous Years*, 379–383; Guyatt, *Providence and the Invention of the United States*, 28–31; White, *The Planter's Plea*, 1–84.

31. White, *The Planter's Plea*, 3, 5.

32. White, *The Planter's Plea*, 5.

33. White, *The Planter's Plea*, 8.

34. White, *The Planter's Plea*, 10.

35. Burton W. Spear, *Search for the Passengers of the Mary & John, 1630*, 27 vols. (Toledo, OH: B. W. Spear, 1985), 17:7, 124.

36. Roger Thompson, *Mobility and Migration: East Anglian Founders of New England, 1629–1640* (Amherst: University of Massachusetts Press, 1994); Scott Rohrer, *Wandering Souls: Protestant Migrations in America, 1630–1865* (Chapel Hill: University of North Carolina Press, 2010), 8; Fischer, *Albion's Seed*, 36–49.

37. David Cressy, *Coming Over: Migration and Communication between England and New England in the Seventeenth Century* (New York: Cambridge University Press, 1987), 1–36, 74–106, 213–234, 263–291; Malcolm Gaskill, *Between Two Worlds: How the English Became Americans* (New York: Basic Books, 2014), ix–xi.

38. Rebecca Fraser, *A People's History of Britain* (London: Chatto and Windus, 2003), 327–331.

39. Alvin Rabushka, *Taxation in Colonial America* (Princeton, NJ: Princeton University Press, 2008), 84–87. Laud was imprisoned in the Tower for treason in 1641, and he stood trial in 1644. Despite the lack of a verdict and a subsequent royal pardon, Parliament passed a special bill of attainder to sanction Laud's beheading on January 10, 1645. The longtime Puritan nemesis was buried in the crypt of nearby All Hallows Barking Church, where Henry's Unitarian descendant John Quincy Adams wed Louisa Catherine Johnson in 1797.

40. Andrew B. Appleby, "Grain Prices and Subsistence Crises in England and France, 1590–1740," *Journal of Economic History* 39 (1979): 865–887; Bartlett, *Henry Adams*.

41. Cressy, *Coming Over*, 263–291.

42. William Richard Cutter, *Genealogical and Personal Memoirs Relating to the Families of Boston and Eastern Massachusetts*, 4 vols. (New York: Lewis Historical Publishing, 1908), 1:823–824.

43. Mark A. Noll, *The Old Religion in a New World: The History of North American Christianity* (Grand Rapids, MI: Eerdmans, 2002), 29–32.

44. Joseph A. Conforti, *Saints and Strangers: New England in British North America* (Baltimore: Johns Hopkins University Press, 2006); Virginia DeJohn Anderson, *New England's Generation: The Great Migration and the Formation of Society and Culture in the Seventeenth Century* (Cambridge: Cambridge University Press, 1991); David D. Hall, *Puritans in the New World: A Critical Anthology* (Princeton, NJ: Princeton University Press, 2004); and Alden T. Vaughan, ed., *The Puritan Tradition in America, 1620–1730*, rev. ed. (Hanover, NH: University Press of New England, 1972).

45. John Adams, *Diary*, 3:254, 257; Topical Supplements: Wills and Deeds, Adams Papers.

46. The major historical surveys of what became the United First Parish Congregational Church of Quincy—and served as the Adamses' home church for the next three centuries—are Sheldon W. Bennett, *Freedom, Friendship, and Faith: A Noble Heritage through 350 Years* (Quincy, MA: United First Parish Church [Unitarian], 350th Anniversary Booklet, 1989); Peggy A. Albee et al., *United First Parish Church (Unitarian) Church of the Presidents Historic Structure Report* (Lowell, MA: Northeast Cultural Resources Center for National Park Service); Charles Francis Adams Jr., "A Church's Retrospect," *New England Magazine* 7 (1889): 263–265; Charles Francis Adams Jr., *History of Braintree, Massachusetts (1639–1708): The North Precinct of Braintree (1708–1792) and the Town of Quincy (1792–1889)* (Cambridge, MA: Riverside Press, 1891), 129–157; Charles Francis Adams Jr., *Three Episodes of Massachusetts History: The Settlement of Boston Bay; The Antinomian Controversy; A Study of Church and Town Government*, 2 vols. (Boston: Houghton, Mifflin, 1892); and William P. Lunt, *Two Discourses, Delivered September 29, 1839, on Occasion of the Two Hundredth Anniversary of the Gathering of the First Congregational Church, Quincy: With an Appendix* (Boston: James Munroe, 1840), 1–147.

47. Charles Francis Adams Jr., *History of Braintree*, 12–22.

48. Peter Benes, *Meetinghouses of Early New England* (Amherst: University of Massachusetts Press, 2012), 2.

49. Benes, *Meetinghouses*, 13.

50. Benes, *Meetinghouses*, 13–28. The Adams family church was a longtime venue where sinners made public confessions and "suffered the law"; the last such confession (for leading "an unchristian life") took place there on January 20, 1740, for which see Charles Francis Adams Jr., *History of Braintree*, 144–157.

51. Charles Francis Adams Jr., *Three Episodes*, 517.

52. Andrew Delbanco, *The Puritan Ordeal* (Cambridge, MA: Harvard University Press, 1989); Jon Butler, *Awash in a Sea of Faith: Christianizing the American People* (Cambridge, MA: Harvard University Press, 1992), 26–66; Francis J. Bremer, ed., *Puritanism: Transatlantic Perspectives on a Seventeenth-Century Anglo-American Faith* (Boston: Northeastern University Press, 1993); Philip F. Gura, *A Glimpse of Sion's Glory: Puritan Radicalism in New England, 1620–1660* (Middletown, CT: Wesleyan University Press, 1994); and George Macgregor Waller, ed., *Puritanism in Early America* (Boston: Heath, 1950).

53. David D. Hall, ed., *The Antinomian Controversy, 1636–1638: A Documentary History* (Durham, NC: Duke University Press, 1990), i–xvii; Timothy D. Hall, "Assurance, Community, and the Puritan Self in the Antinomian Controversy, 1636–38," in *Puritanism and Its Discontents*, ed. Laura Lunger Knoppers (Newark: University of Delaware Press, 2003), 197–209.

54. John Wheelwright preached from Matthew 9:15: "And Jesus said unto them, Can the children of the bridechamber mourn, as long as the bridegroom is with them? But the days will come, when the bridegroom shall be taken from them, and then shall they fast." While it does not appear to be a particularly pointed sermon, Wheelwright's staging of it before the royal colonial audience—just as social support for Anne Hutchinson began to sour—fueled growing complaints and brought him before the Puritan magistrates. See *John Wheelwright, His Writings, Including His Fast-Day Sermon, 1637, and His Mercurius Americanus, 1645, with a Paper upon the Genuineness of the Indiana Deed of 1629 and a Memoir, by Charles H. Bell, A.M.* (Boston: Prince Society, 1876); and Sargent Bush Jr., "John Wheelwright's Forgotten Apology: The Last Word in the Antinomian Controversy," *New England Quarterly* 64 (1991): 22–45.

55. Charles H. Bell, *John Wheelwright*, 158.

56. Wheelwright's banishment was later lifted, but he never returned to Massachusetts. His daughter Esther continued the practice of religious dissent, rising to become Mother Superior of the Ursuline convent in Quebec, Canada.

57. Most of the First Parish Church records predating the tenure of Rev. John Hancock are no longer extant, but Hancock drew on them for his centennial sermon, for which see William Parsons Lunt, *Two Discourses, Delivered September 29, 1839: On Occasion of the Two Hundredth Anniversary of the Gathering of the First Congregational Church, Quincy; with Appendix* (Boston: James Munroe, 1840). Hancock served as pastor from 1726 to 1744.

58. Andrew N. Adams, *Genealogical History of Henry Adams*; Wilson, *Where American Independence Began*; Bartlett, *Henry Adams*; and Henry Adams, *John Adams's Book*.

59. Francis J. Bremer, *The Puritan Experiment: New England Society from Bradford to Edwards* (Hanover, NH: University Press of New England, 1995); Conforti, *Saints and Strangers*, 178–199; and Noll, *The Old Religion in a New World*, 37–55.

60. Charles Francis Adams Jr., *History of Braintree*, 145.

61. Wilhelmina S. Harris, "The Association of the Adams Family with the Stone Temple" (transcript of presentation at United First Parish Church, Quincy, Massachusetts, November 19, 1972, Adams Papers Editorial Files).

62. Inventory of UFPC Safe Deposit Box, November 21, 2006, Memorandum, UFPC Records. Two volumes of records, from 172 to 1856, are extant offsite. To reconstruct the church's earliest history, I have relied on the UFPC transcriptions as well as Lunt's 1839 bicentennial sermon, which covered a few record gaps.

63. Charles Francis Adams Jr., *History of Braintree*, 145.

64. "Will of Deacon John Adams, with Comments by His Son John," January 8, 1760–April 29, 1774, in *Papers of John Adams*, 1:34–36.

65. Sacvan Bercovitch, "How the Puritans Won the American Revolution," *Massachusetts Review* 17 (1976): 597–630; Winship, *Godly Republicanism*; George McKenna, *The Puritan Origins of American Patriotism* (New Haven CT: Yale

University Press, 2007); and Mark A. Noll, *America's God: From Jonathan Edwards to Abraham Lincoln* (Oxford: Oxford University Press, 1992).

66. Delbanco, *The Puritan Ordeal*, 240; 235–254.

67. John Adams, "A Dissertation on the Canon and the Feudal Law, No. 1" [August as, 1765], in *Papers of John Adams*, 1:112–115.

68. Abigail Adams to Elizabeth Cranch, September 2, 1785, in *Adams Family Correspondence*, 13 vols., ed. Sara Martin et al. (Cambridge, MA: Belknap Press of Harvard University Press, 1963–), 6:328.

69. John Adams to Dr. Benjamin Rush, August 28, 1811, Benjamin Franklin Papers, Yale University Library, New Haven, CT, Connecticut.

70. Of the numerous biographies of John Adams, the key surveys are Gilbert Chinard, *Honest John Adams* (Boston: Little, Brown, 1933); Zoltán Haraszti, *John Adams and the Prophets of Progress* (Cambridge, MA: Harvard University Press, 1952); Page Smith, *John Adams* (Garden City, NY: Doubleday, 1962); Ralph A. Brown, *The Presidency of John Adams* (Lawrence: University Press of Kansas, 1975); Peter Shaw, *The Character of John Adams* (Chapel Hill: University of North Carolina Press, 1976); John E. Ferling, *John Adams: A Life* (Knoxville: University of Tennessee Press, 1992); Joseph P. Ellis, *Passionate Sage: The Character and Legacy of John Adams* (New York: Norton, 1993); C. Bradley Thompson, *John Adams and the Spirit of Liberty* (Lawrence: University Press of Kansas, 1998); David G. McCullough, *John Adams* (New York: Simon and Schuster, 2001); John P. Diggins, *John Adams* (New York: Times Books, 2003); and James Grant, *John Adams: Party of One* (New York: Farrar, Straus and Giroux, 2005).

Several recent works on the founders' religiosity (as a group) exist, but few feature Adams's development in depth. See, for example, David L. Holmes, *The Faiths of the Founding Fathers* (Oxford: Oxford University Press, 2006); Gary A. Kowalski, *Revolutionary Spirits: The Enlightened Faith of America's Founding Fathers* (New York: Bluebridge, 2008); Gregg L. Frazer, *The Religious Beliefs of America's Founders: Reason, Revelation, and Revolution* (Lawrence: University Press of Kansas, 2012); and Daniel L. Dreisbach and Mark David Hall, eds., *Faith and the Founders of the American Republic* (New York: Oxford University Press, 2014).

71. John Adams to Dr. Benjamin Rush, July 19, 1812, Alexander Biddle Papers, Boston Public Library.

72. John Adams, *Diary*, 3:262. For an excellent analysis of how John Adams's diarywriting exemplified the wider religious shift of a culture moving from a Puritan habit (of self-perfection) to an Arminian task (of enlightened inquiry), see C. Bradley Thompson, "Young John Adams and the New Philosophic Rationalism," *William and Mary Quarterly* 55 (1998): 259–280.

73. Deacon John Adams attended Harvard, and sold ten acres of land in Braintree so that his son John could do the same. The younger Adams entered his Harvard class at a high rank thanks to the socioeconomic influence of his mother, Susanna Boylston Adams Hall. See John Langdon Sibley and Clifford K. Shipton, *Sibley's*

Harvard Graduates, 18 vols. (Boston: Massachusetts Historical Society, 1873–1999), 13:513–520.

74. "Introduction," in *The Earliest Diary of John Adams*, ed. L. H. Butterfield et al. (Cambridge, MA: Belknap Press of Harvard University Press, 1966), 37.

75. For the biography of Lemuel Briant and his short but tumultuous career, see Clifford K. Shipton, *New England Life in the Eighteenth Century: Representative Biographies from Sibley's Harvard Graduates* (Cambridge, MA: Belknap Press of Harvard University Press, 1963), 449–455; Duane Hamilton Hurd, ed., *History of Norfolk County, Massachusetts, with Biographical Sketches of Many of Its Pioneers and Prominent Men* (Philadelphia: J. W. Lewis, 1884), 291–293; Charles Francis Adams Jr., *Massachusetts: Its Historians and Its History, An Object Lesson* (Boston: Houghton, Mifflin, 1893), 98–99; and Bennett, *Freedom, Friendship, and Faith*.

76. John Adams to Thomas Jefferson, April 19, 1817, Thomas Jefferson Papers, Library of Congress.

77. John Adams to Thomas Jefferson, April 19, 1817.

78. Lemuel Briant, *The Absurdity and Blasphemy of Depreciating Moral Virtue: A Sermon Preached at the West-Church in Boston, June 18th, 1749* (Boston: J. Green, 1749).

79. Briant, *Moral Virtue*, 18–19.

80. James Levernier and Douglas R. Wimes, *American Writers before 1800: A Biographical and Critical Dictionary*, 3 vols. (Westport, CT: Greenwood Press, 1983), 1:208. Briant married Abigail Barstow, and in 1753, had two young sons.

81. Hurd, *History of Norfolk County*, 292.

82. See, for example, James William Jones, *The Shattered Synthesis: New England Puritanism before the Great Awakening* (New Haven, CT: Yale University Press, 1973); Philip J. Greven, *The Protestant Temperament: Patterns of Child-Rearing, Religious Experience, and the Self in Early America* (New York: Knopf, 1977); and Perry Miller, *Errand into the Wilderness* (Cambridge, MA: Belknap Press of Harvard University Press, 1956).

83. John Adams to Aaron Bancroft, January 21, 1823, printed in *Massachusetts Spy* (Worcester, MA), April 23, 1823.

84. John Adams, *Earliest Diary*, 37.

85. John Adams, *Earliest Diary*, 37.

86. Abigail has drawn an equal share of biographers' attention. The key surveys are Charles W. Akers, *Abigail Adams, an American Woman* (Boston: Little, Brown, 1980); Phyllis Lee Levin, *Abigail Adams: A Biography* (New York: St. Martin's, 1987); Edith B. Gelles, *Portia: The World of Abigail Adams* (Bloomington: Indiana University Press, 1992); Woody Holton, *Abigail Adams* (New York: Free Press, 2009); G. J. Barker-Benfield, *John and Abigail Adams: The Americanization of Sensibility* (Chicago: University of Chicago Press, 2010); and Joseph J. Ellis, *First Family: Abigail and John* (New York: Knopf, 2010).

87. "Diaries of Rev. William Smith," *Proceedings of the Massachusetts Historical Society* 42 (1908–1909): 444–470.

88. "Diaries of Rev. William Smith," 444–470.

89. "Reverend William Smith's Inventory of Property, 1784," Suffolk County Registry of Probate, Vol. 83:724; Doc. 18039, Boston, Massachusetts; "William Smith Diaries, 1728–1778," 444–470. For the long pulpit career of Smith (1707–1783), see First Church (Weymouth, Mass.) Records, 1724–1839, Massachusetts Historical Society; Sibley and Shipton, *Sibley's Harvard Graduates*, 7:588–591; and John Adams, *Diary*, 2:72.

90. "Reverend William Smith's Inventory of Property, 1784," Vol. 83:724; Doc. 18039, Boston, Massachusetts; "William Smith Diaries, 1728–1778," 444–470.

91. These were the four children who survived to adulthood: Abigail 2d (Nabby, 1765–1813), John Quincy (1767–1848), Charles (1770–1800), and Thomas Boylston (1772–1832).

92. Guyatt, *Providence and the Invention of the United States*; Bercovitch, *Puritan Origins*; Holifield, *Theology in America*; and Stout, *The New England Soul*.

93. John Adams to Abigail Adams, May 8, 1775, in *Adams Family Correspondence*, 1:195–196.

94. Abigail Adams to John Adams, June 18–20, 1775, in *Adams Family Correspondence*, 12 vols., ed. L. H. Butterfield et al. (Cambridge, MA: Belknap Press of Harvard University Press, 1963–), 1:222–224. In this letter, Abigail announced the death of General Joseph Warren, the family physician, at the Battle of Bunker Hill. She quoted from Ecclesiastes 9:11: "I returned, and saw under the sun, that the race *is* not to the swift, nor the battle to the strong, neither yet bread to the wise, nor yet riches to men of understanding, nor yet favour to men of skill; but time and chance happeneth to them all."

95. Bernard Bailyn, *Faces of Revolution: Personalities and Themes in the Struggle for American Independence* (New York: Knopf, 1990), 9.

96. John Adams, *Diary*, vols. 1–3, passim.

97. John Adams, August [7/4], 1766, in *Diary*, 1:319.

98. See, for example, Chris Beneke and Christopher S. Grenda, eds., *The First Prejudice: Religious Tolerance and Intolerance in Early America* (Philadelphia: University of Pennsylvania Press, 2011); Eric R. Schlereth, *An Age of Infidels: The Politics of Religious Controversy in the Early United States* (Philadelphia: University of Pennsylvania Press, 2013); Marilyn J. Westerkamp, *Women and Religion in Early America, 1600–1850: The Puritan and Evangelical Traditions* (London: Routledge, 1999); and John Corrigan and Lynn S. Neale, eds., *Religious Intolerance in America: A Documentary History* (Chapel Hill: University of North Carolina Press, 2010).

99. Jenny Franchot, *Roads to Rome: The Antebellum Protestant Encounter with Catholicism* (Berkeley: University of California Press, 1994).

100. John Adams to Abigail Adams, October 9, 1774, in *Adams Family Correspondence*, 1:166–167.

101. Daniel Kilbride, *Being American in Europe, 1750–1860* (Baltimore: Johns Hopkins University Press, 2013), 2–8.

102. Abigail Adams to Elizabeth Smith Shaw, November 21, 1786, in *Adams Family Correspondence*, 7:392.

103. Gordon S. Wood, *The Radicalism of the American Revolution* (New York: Knopf, 1992), 331–334; Richard L. Bushman, *The Refinement of America: Persons, Houses, Cities* (New York: Knopf, 1992), 401–448; Leslie Butler, *Critical Americans: Victorian Intellectuals and Transatlantic Liberal Reform* (Chapel Hill: University of North Carolina Press, 2000), 3–8; Caroll Smith-Rosenberg, *This Violent Empire: The Birth of an American National Identity* (Chapel Hill: University of North Carolina Press, 2010), 1–44; and Yokota, *Unbecoming British*, 8–12.

104. Joan R. Gundersen, *To Be Useful to the World: Women in Revolutionary America, 1740–1790* (Chapel Hill: University of North Carolina Press, 1996), 118–119.

105. For key surveys of the social, economic, and political opportunities for women in the early republic, see Linda K. Kerber, *Women of the Republic: Intellect and Ideology in Revolutionary America* (New York: Norton, 1986); Jeanne Boydston, *Home and Work: Housework, Wages, and the Ideology of Labor in the Early Republic* (New York: Oxford University Press, 1990); Mary Beth Norton, *Liberty's Daughter's: The Revolutionary Experience of American Women, 1750–1800* (Ithaca, NY: Cornell University Press, 1996); Nancy F. Cott, *The Bonds of Womanhood: "Woman's Sphere" in New England, 1780–1835* (New Haven, CT: Yale University Press, 1997); Bruce Burgett, *Sentimental Bodies: Sex, Gender, and Citizenship in the Early Republic* (Princeton, NJ: Princeton University Press, 1998); Joan R. Gundersen, *To Be Useful to the World: Women in Revolutionary America, 1740–1790* (Chapel Hill: University of North Carolina Press, 2006); and Rosemarie Zagarri, *Revolutionary Backlash: Women and Politics in the Early American Republic* (Philadelphia: University of Pennsylvania Press, 2007).

    Increasingly, scholars have focused on recovering and documenting the range of educational opportunities available to Abigail Adams and her early American peers, for which see Margaret A. Nash, *Women's Education in the United States, 1780–1840* (New York: Palgrave Macmillan, 2005); Mary Kelley, *Learning to Stand and Speak: Women, Education, and Public Life in America's Republic* (Chapel Hill: University of North Carolina Press, 2006); and Lucia McMahon, *Mere Equals: The Paradox of Educated Women in the Early American Republic* (Ithaca, NY: Cornell University Press, 2012).

106. Horace Townsend and the Metropolitan Museum of Art, "Early Dutch Tiles," *Art & Life* 11 (1919): 253–261; Colleen McDannell, *The Christian Home in Victorian America, 1840–1900* (Bloomington: Indiana University Press,

1986); Elisabeth Donaghy Garrett, *At Home: The American Family, 1750–1870* (New York: Abrams, 1990).

107. Abigail Adams to Mercy Otis Warren, November [ca. 5], 1775; Abigail Adams to Mary Smith Cranch, September 11, 1785, both in *Adams Family Correspondence*, 1:323; 6:358.

108. Abigail Adams to John Shaw, January 18, 1785, in *Adams Family Correspondence*, 6:62–64, 491. With Jefferson, husband John, and the Lafayette family, Abigail attended the April 1, 1785, Te Deum celebrated in honor of the March 27 birth of Louis Charles, the second son of King Louis XVI and Queen Marie Antoinette.

109. Abigail Adams to Thomas Jefferson, June 6, 1785, in *Adams Family Correspondence*, 6:171–172.

110. Abigail Adams to Elizabeth Cranch, September 2, 1785, in *Adams Family Correspondence*, 6:328–329.

111. Abigail Adams, "Diary of Her Return Voyage to America, 30 March–1 May 1788," in John Adams, *Diary*, 3:214–216. Later, the Adamses distanced themselves from Priestley due to his support of the French Revolution during the Terror.

112. John Adams, *Diary*, 3:214–216.

113. For John Murray, a founder of American Universalism and later minister of the Church of Christ in Gloucester, Massachusetts, see Holifield, *Theology in America*, 221–226; Richard Eddy, *Universalism in America: A History*, 2 vols. (Boston: Universalist Publishing House, 1884–1886).

114. Abigail Adams, in John Adams, *Diary*, 3:214–216.

115. John Adams to Abigail Adams, September 17, 1775, in *Adams Family Correspondence*, 1:280–281.

116. Abigail Adams to Louisa Catherine Adams, April 14, 1818, Adams Papers.

117. Donald H. Meyer, *The Democratic Enlightenment* (New York: Putnam, 1976); Patricia U. Bonomi, *Under the Cope of Heaven: Religion, Society, and Politics in Colonial America* (New York: Oxford University Press, 1986); Guyatt, *Providence and the Invention of the United States*.

118. James P. Byrd, *Sacred Scripture, Sacred War: The Bible and the American Revolution* (New York: Oxford University Press, 2013).

119. John Adams to Thomas Jefferson, February–March 3, 1814, Thomas Jefferson Papers, Library of Congress.

120. Holifield, *Theology in America*, 197–219; Conrad Edick Wright, ed., *American Unitarianism, 1805–1865* (Boston: Massachusetts Historical Society and Northeastern University Press, 1989); and J. D. Bowers, *Joseph Priestley and English Unitarianism in America* (University Park: Pennsylvania State University Press, 2007), 1–27.

121. On colonial worship habits, see Bonomi, *Under the Cope of Heaven;* Stout, *The New England Soul;* Butler, *Awash in a Sea of Faith.*

122. David D. Hall, *Worlds of Wonder, Days of Judgment: Popular Religious Belief in Early New England* (New York: Knopf, 1989), 10; Cooper, *Tenacious of Their Liberties*.

123. Nathan O. Hatch, *The Democratization of American Christianity* (New Haven, CT: Yale University Press, 1989), 15.

124. See John Adams, "A Dissertation on the Canon and the Feudal Law, No. 2," [August 19, 1765], in *Papers of John Adams*, 1:115–118.

125. Abigail Adams to Ann Harrod Adams, February 16, 1806, Adams Papers.

126. John Adams to Thomas Jefferson, February 2, 1816, Thomas Jefferson Papers, Library of Congress.

127. "Proclamation," March 27, 1798, *Gazette of the United States*; Charles Ellis Dickson, "Jeremiads in the New American Republic: The Case of National Fasts in the John Adams Administration," *New England Quarterly* 60 (1987): 187–207. On the decline of Franco-American relations and the public blowup of the XYZ Affair, see Thomas M. Ray, "'Not One Cent for Tribute': The Public Addresses and American Popular Reaction to the XYZ Affair, 1798–1799," *Journal of the Early Republic* 3 (1983): 389–412; and William Stinchcombe, *The XYZ Affair* (Westport, CT: Greenwood Press, 1980).

128. William DeLoss Love, *The Fast and Thanksgiving Days of New England* (Boston: Houghton, Mifflin, 1895); David Waldstreicher, *In the Midst of Perpetual Fetes: The Making of American Nationalism, 1776–1820* (Chapel Hill: University of North Carolina Press, 1997).

129. March 27, 1798, *Gazette of the United States*; Dickson, "Jeremiads in the New American Republic."

130. On religion as a "cultural habit" that informed John Adams and other early American diplomats, see Andrew Preston, *Sword of the Spirit, Shield of Faith: Religion in American War and Diplomacy* (New York: Knopf, 2012).

131. Dickson, "Jeremiads in the New American Republic."

132. March 30, 1798, *Porcupine's Gazette*.

133. Abigail Adams to Mary Smith Cranch, March 31, 1798, in *Adams Family Correspondence*, 12:470–472. Norton married Abigail's niece, Elizabeth Cranch, in 1789.

134. John Adams to Thomas Jefferson, June 30, 1813, in *The Papers of Thomas Jefferson*, Retirement Series, 9 vols., ed. J. Jefferson Looney et al. (Princeton, NJ: Princeton University Press, 2004–), 6:254–255.

135. John Adams to Dr. Benjamin Rush, August 28, 1811, Benjamin Franklin Papers, Yale University Library.

136. Brent Gilchrist, *Cultus Americanus: Varieties of the Liberal Tradition in American Political Culture, 1600–1865* (Lanham, MD: Lexington Books, 2006), 219–254.

137. John Adams, February 13, 1779, *Diary*, 2:354.

138. Abigail Adams to Catherine Smith, January 24, 1808, Adams Papers.

139. Abigail Adams to Abigail Adams 2d, February 21, 1791, in *Adams Family Correspondence*, 9:193–194.

140. John Adams to Thomas Jefferson, May 3, 1816, Thomas Jefferson Papers, Library of Congress.

141. For general biographies of the family, see James Truslow Adams, *The Adams Family* (Boston: Little, Brown, and Company, 1930); Richard Brookhiser, *America's First Dynasty: The Adamses, 1735–1918* (New York: Free Press, 2002); Abigail Adams Homans, *Education by Uncles* (Boston: Houghton Mifflin, 1966); Paul C. Nagel, *Descent from Glory: Four Generations of the John Adams Family* (New York: Oxford University Press, 1983); Francis Russell, *Adams: An American Dynasty* (New York: McGraw-Hill, 1976); Katharine Metcalf Roof, *Colonel William Smith and Lady: The Romance of Washington's Aide and the Young Abigail Adams* (Boston: Riverside Press, 1929); and Jack Shepherd, *The Adams Chronicles: Four Generations of Greatness* (Boston: Little, Brown, 1975).

142. John Adams to Thomas Jefferson, July 18, 1813, Thomas Jefferson Papers, Library of Congress.

143. On prophecy and antebellum Bible readership, see Holland, *Sacred Borders*; and Susan Juster, *Doomsayers: Anglo-American Prophecy in the Age of Revolution* (Philadelphia: University of Pennsylvania Press, 2003).

144. John Adams to Thomas Jefferson, February 10, 1812, Thomas Jefferson Papers, Library of Congress. For a representative sample of these exchanges, see also Bruce Braden, ed., *"Ye Will Say I Am No Christian": The Thomas Jefferson/John Adams Correspondence on Religion, Morals, and Values* (Amherst, MA: Prometheus Books, 2006).

145. John Adams to Thomas Jefferson, December 12, 1816, *Papers of Thomas Jefferson*, Retirement Series, 10:573.

146. John Adams to Thomas Jefferson, December 12, 1816.

147. John Adams, June 14, 1756, *Diary*, 1:34.

148. See John Adams's copy at the Boston Public Library of Jacob Bryant, *A New System, or, An Analysis of Ancient Mythology* (London: T. Payne, 1775–1776).

149. *Catalogue of the John Adams Library in the Public Library of the City of Boston* (Boston: Published by the Trustees, 1917).

150. See, for example, Thomas Jefferson to John Adams, June 11, 1812, in *Papers of Thomas Jefferson*, Retirement Series, 5:122–125.

151. John Adams to David Sewall, November 4, 1815, Adams Papers. For further analysis of how the subsequent Adams generations read the Bible, see especially chapters 2, 3, and 5.

152. Harriet Welsh to Caroline de Windt, November [1], 1818, Adams Papers.

153. John Adams to Thomas Jefferson, July 13, 1813, Thomas Jefferson Papers, Library of Congress; Hatch, *Democratization of American Christianity*, 3–16, 180–182, 210–219.

154. John Adams to Thomas Jefferson, July 16, 1813, Thomas Jefferson Papers, Library of Congress.

155. John Adams plaque, United First Parish Church, Quincy, Massachusetts.

156. John Adams to Thomas Jefferson, September 15, 1813. Thomas Jefferson Papers, Library of Congress.

157. Solomon Williams, *Three Sermons, Preached at Northampton, on the 31st of March—The Other Two on the Annual State Fast, April 4, 1805* (Northampton, MA: William Butler, 1805), 35.

Chapter 2

1. John Quincy Adams, October 27, 1840, Diary, Adams Papers.

2. John Quincy Adams, *On Faith*, draft in Adams's hand, listing lecture dates from October 27 through November 20, 1840; reprised on March 24, 1841, and November 1 [2?], 1842, Adams Papers.

3. John Adams to Abigail Adams, July 26, 1784, in *Adams Family Correspondence*, 12 vols., ed. L. H. Butterfield et al. (Cambridge, MA: Belknap Press of Harvard University Press, 1963–), 5:399–400.

4. The classic biography is Samuel Flagg Bemis's two-volume work, *John Quincy Adams and the Foundations of American Foreign Policy* and *John Quincy Adams and the Union* (New York: Knopf, 1949, 1956). Paul C. Nagel's biography, *John Quincy Adams: A Public Life, A Private Life* (New York: Knopf, 1998), blames John and, in particular, Abigail Adams for overburdening their sons with lofty political expectations. More succinct summaries of Adams's career appear in two other fine works, by Lynn Hudson Parsons, *John Quincy Adams* (Madison, WI: Madison House, 1998), and Robert V. Remini, *John Quincy Adams* (New York: Times Books, 2002), but they, too, offer brief mentions of religion as a shaping factor in the president's thoughts and actions. In *Cannibals of the Heart: A Personal Biography of Louisa Catherine and John Quincy Adams* (New York: McGraw-Hill, 1980), Jack Shepherd offers a richer discussion of the statesman's marriage and the religious reflections of his wife.

Despite the intriguing opportunity to show *how* a president prayed for national and personal salvation, most biographers have approached Adams's religious life gingerly, generally, or not at all. Instead, scholars have chided John Quincy for his "Puritan" habit of declining opulent gifts amid the diplomatic revelry of foreign courts. They have used his Unitarianism as moral shorthand to explain his antislavery stance, and glossed over his ultra-Romantic (and markedly less successful) effort at writing popular religious verse like "The Wants of Man." They are even more reticent on the topic of Louisa's religious convictions, which often wavered between her High Church, Episcopal disdain for Unitarianism and her guilty fascination with Roman Catholicism. Two recent biographies provide fuller portraits: Fred Kaplan, *John Quincy Adams: American Visionary*

(New York: Harper, 2014), and Margery M. Heffron, *Louisa Catherine: The Other Mrs. Adams* (New Haven, CT: Yale University Press, 2014).

5. John Quincy Adams, *On Faith*.

6. For the significance of the Dutch republican example to American revolutionaries like John Adams, see Simon Schama, *Patriots and Liberators: Revolution in the Netherlands, 1780–1813* (New York: Knopf, 1977).

7. John Quincy Adams, in *The Diary of John Quincy Adams*, 2 vols., ed. David Grayson Allen et al. (Cambridge, MA: Belknap Press of Harvard University Press, 1981), 1:41, 71, 73, 76, 80, 86–87. He made note of, but apparently did not attend, the two Roman Catholic churches then extant in Rotterdam.

8. John Quincy Adams, December 5, 1782, *Diary*, 1:163.

9. John Quincy Adams, May 16, 1792, Diary.

10. John Quincy Adams, May 4, 1792, Diary.

11. John Quincy Adams, 14 April 1792, Diary.

12. Ruth H. Bloch, *Visionary Republic: Millennial Themes in American Thought, 1756–1800* (Cambridge: Cambridge University Press, 1985), 117–149; Clive Bush, *The Dream of Reason: American Consciousness and Cultural Achievement from Independence to the Civil War* (London: Edward Arnold, 1977), ix; Richard W. Pointer, *Protestant Pluralism and the New York Experience: A Study of Eighteenth-Century Religious Diversity* (Bloomington: Indiana University Press, 1986), 74–144.

13. John Quincy Adams, March 23, 1794, Diary: "Mr. Clark A.M. Mr. Thacher P.M. Funeral Sermon. I slept, was it my fault? Walk with Frazier, over Cambridge bridge, in the Mall &c. Evening at Mr. Gore's; and very pleasant. T. Amory quite facetious. Welles in Spirits &c."

14. John Quincy Adams, May 16, 1792, Diary.

15. Louisa Catherine Adams, "Record of a Life" and "The Adventures of a Nobody," in *The Diary and Autobiographical Writings of Louisa Catherine Adams*, 2 vols., ed. Judith S. Graham et al. (Cambridge, MA: Belknap Press of Harvard University Press, 2013), 1:1–356.

16. For the bankruptcy of US consul and Maryland entrepreneur Joshua Johnson's tobacco firm, see Edward C. Papenfuse, *In Pursuit of Profit: The Annapolis Merchants in the Age of American Revolution, 1763–1805* (Baltimore: Johns Hopkins University Press, 1975), 53, 73–75, 93, 108, 234.

17. Louisa Catherine Adams, "Record of a Life," *Diary*, 1:3–4.

18. Louisa Catherine Adams, "Record of a Life," *Diary*, 1:7.

19. Certificate, July 26, 1797, Marriage Register, All Hallows Barking Parish, London, England. Documentation of the wedding, witnessed by John Quincy's brother Thomas Boylston, is on permanent display in the crypt museum near the remains of clergy executed at Tower Hill, including the Catholic bishop John Fisher, the Puritan Adamses' nemesis William Laud, and the Renaissance humanist Sir Thomas More. I am grateful to Angie Poppitt, vicar's assistant and

finance manager, for sharing records as well as her expert knowledge on a tour of All Hallows.

20. Louisa bore the brunt of the press attacks on her marriage throughout John Quincy's career—mainly, allegations that she was a money-hungry foreigner who ensnared the president's son in marriage to resolve her father's debt. The greater religion-related scandal for the Adamses in this period was the political fallout from President John Adams's March 23, 1798, fast-day proclamation, which exacerbated the XYZ Affair mess.

21. Dickson D. Bruce Jr., *Earnestly Contending: Religious Freedom and Pluralism in Antebellum America* (Charlottesville: University of Virginia Press, 2013), 9–31.

22. Anne C. Rose, "Religious Individualism in Nineteenth-Century American Families," in *Perspectives on American Religion and Culture*, ed. Peter W. Williams (Malden, MA: Blackwell, 1999), 319–330.

23. Abigail Adams to John Quincy Adams, May 20, 1796, in *Adams Family Correspondence*, 11:297–298.

24. *Diary and Autobiographical Writings of Louisa Catherine Adams*, ed. Judith S. Graham et al., 2 vols. (Cambridge, MA: Belknap Press of Harvard University Press, 2013), 1:xxx.

25. Louisa Catherine Adams, February 3, 1803, *Diary*, 1:184–185.

26. David S. Reynolds, "From Periodical Writer to Poet: Whitman's Journey through Popular Culture," in *Periodical Literature in Nineteenth-Century America*, ed. Kenneth M. Price and Susan Belasco Smith (Charlottesville: University Press of Virginia, 1995), 35–50.

27. John Quincy made close lists of his book and pamphlet acquisitions throughout his life. The sermons mentioned here are cited at his Miscellany for the years 1803 to 1825 (Adams Papers), next to his New Testament chapter summaries. See also Henry Adams, *A Catalogue of the Books of John Quincy Adams, Deposited in the Boston Athenaeum* (Boston: Printed for the Athenaeum, 1938). The 1843 Hawaiian Bible, printed in Oahu and presented in late May 1845, bears an inscription of gratitude to Adams from the American Board of Commissioners for Foreign Missions, "for the kind interest he has taken in the Sandwich Islands."

28. Gordon S. Wood, "Religion and the American Revolution," in *New Directions in American Religious History*, ed. Harry S. Stout and D. G. Hart (New York: Oxford University Press, 1997), 175; Patricia U. Bonomi, *Under the Cope of Heaven: Religion, Society, and Politics in Colonial America* (New York: Oxford University Press 1986), 3.

29. Louisa Catherine Adams, February 27, 1820, *Diary*, 2:477–478; Abigail Adams to Louisa Catherine Adams, January 3, 1818, Adams Papers.

30. This marked the first time that the US Congress conferred this honor on a woman in light of her "public regard." For a representative sample of the press coverage of Louisa's death, see the notices for "Congress" and "The Funeral of Mrs. Adams," printed in *The Republic* on May 18 and 19, 1852.

31. John Quincy Adams, *Diary*, 1:362, 2:391–392.

32. Interview with Daniel A. Stokes, Archivist, the New York Avenue (formerly Second) Presbyterian Church; Organizational Records, Scrapbooks, and Pew Plans, United First Parish Church of Quincy, Massachusetts; Organizational Records, Christ Church Episcopal of Quincy. See also George E. Backer, "John Quincy Adams as a Unitarian," *Unitarian Review and Religious Magazine* 16 (1881): 135–153.

33. Jenny Franchot, *Roads to Rome: The Antebellum Protestant Encounter with Catholicism* (Berkeley: University of California Press, 1994), 6.

34. John Quincy Adams, January 19, 1843, Diary.

35. John Quincy Adams, September 8, 1826, Diary.

36. Louisa Catherine Adams, *Diary*, 1:xxix–xxxi; see also her February 15, 1806, entry, 1:234.

37. Louisa Catherine Adams to John Quincy Adams, August 21, 1826, Adams Papers.

38. Louisa Catherine Adams, "Adventures of a Nobody," *Diary*, 1:144.

39. Louisa Catherine Adams, "Adventures of a Nobody," *Diary*, 1:174.

40. Louisa Catherine Adams, *Diary*, 1:xxi.

41. Louisa Catherine Adams, *Diary*, xxx. For Henry Adams's reflections on Louisa in his *Education*, see chapter 4.

42. Donald G. Bloesch, *The Church: Sacraments, Worship, Ministry, Mission* (Downers Grove, IL: InterVarsity Press, 2002), 111; Martin Fitzpatrick, "Latitudinarianism at the Parting of the Ways: A Suggestion," in *The Church of England c. 1689–c. 1833: From Toleration to Tractarianism*, John Walsh, Colin Haydon, and Stephen Taylor, eds. (Cambridge: Cambridge University Press, 1993), 209–227.

43. Patrick Müller, *Latitudinarianism and Didacticism in Eighteenth-Century Literature: Moral Theology in Fielding, Sterne, and Goldsmith* (New York: Peter Lang, 2009), 207–208.

44. John Adams to Benjamin Rush, January 21, 1810, Adams Papers.

45. Gordon S. Wood, *The Creation of the American Republic, 1776–1787* (Chapel Hill: University of North Carolina Press, 1998); Mark A. Noll, *America's God: From Jonathan Edwards to Abraham Lincoln* (Oxford: Oxford University Press, 1992), 53–157; and Mark Y. Hanley, *Beyond a Christian Commonwealth: The Protestant Quarrel with the American Republic, 1830–1860* (Chapel Hill: University of North Carolina Press, 1994).

46. On the composition, reception, and impact of John Adams's *Defence*, see *The Papers of John Adams*, ed. Sara Georgini et al., 19 vols. (Cambridge, MA: Belknap Press of Harvard University Press, 2016), 18:546–550, 19:130–132; C. Bradley Thompson, *John Adams and the Spirit of Liberty* (Lawrence: University Press of Kansas, 1998); Thompson, "John Adams's Machiavellian Moment," *Review of Politics* 57 (1995): 389–417; Zoltán Haraszti, *John Adams and the Prophets of Progress* (Cambridge, MA: Harvard University Press, 1992); and Mortimer N. S. Sellers, *American Republicanism: Roman Ideology in the United States Constitution*

(New York: New York University Press, 1994), 33–40. A modern reprint of the *Defence* was issued by Da Capo Press (New York) in 1971.

47. John Adams, *A Defence of the Constitutions of the United States of America*, 3 vols. (repr., New York: Da Capo Press, 1971), 1:210.

48. Brent Gilchrist, *Cultus Americanus: Varieties of the Liberal Tradition in American Political Culture, 1600–1865* (Lanham, MD: Lexington Books, 2006), 159–244; Michael Meckler, ed., *Classical Antiquity and the Politics of America: From George Washington to George W. Bush* (Waco, TX: Baylor University Press, 2006), 1–54; Joseph Farrell and Michael C. J. Putnam, eds., *A Companion to Vergil's Aeneid and Its Tradition* (Malden, MA: Wiley-Blackwell, 2010), 353–418; Bush, *Dream of Reason*, 2–57.

49. Details of John Quincy's intense preparation for the Harvard exam (1780–1785), which began under his father's tutelage at The Hague, appear in *Adams Family Correspondence*, 6:98, 405, 408–409, 412; 7:3, 129–130, 372–373.

50. John Quincy Adams, *Diary*, 1:400.

51. Hanley, *Beyond a Christian Commonwealth*, 7.

52. Hanley, *Beyond a Christian Commonwealth*, 57; 32–56.

53. Gordon S. Wood, *Empire of Liberty: A History of the Early Republic, 1789–1815* (New York: Oxford University Press, 2009), 612–619; and Michael J. Lee, *The Erosion of Biblical Certainty: Battles over Authority and Interpretation in America* (New York: Palgrave Macmillan, 2013), 111–172.

54. John Quincy Adams, *Diary*, 1:413.

55. The metaphor equating religious instinct with gravity was John Quincy's, for which see his *Diary*, 1:359–360.

56. Robert A. East, *John Quincy Adams: The Critical Years, 1785–1794* (New York: Bookman Associates, 1962), 31–34.

57. For John Adams's drafting of the Massachusetts Constitution of 1780, especially the fourth article of the Declaration of Rights, which sought to define "religion" and the citizenry's responsibility to support it, see *Papers of John Adams*, 8:228–271.

58. John Quincy Adams, *Diary*, 2:9, 12, 28, 189; *Papers of John Adams*, 1:91, 94.

59. John Quincy Adams, *Diary*, 2:29.

60. John Quincy Adams, *Diary*, 2:91; Pauline Maier, "The Pope at Harvard: The Dudleian Lectures, Anti-Catholicism, and the Politics of Protestantism," *Proceedings of the Massachusetts Historical Society*, 3d ser., 97 (1985): 16–41.

61. John Quincy Adams, *Diary*, 2:122. He served in the Harvard professoriate from 1806 to 1810.

62. John Quincy Adams, *Diary*, 2:111.

63. John Quincy Adams, *Diary*, 2:217.

64. John Quincy Adams, *Diary*, 2:11.

65. Gary J. Dorrien, *The Making of American Liberal Theology: Imagining Progressive Religion, 1805–1900* (Louisville, KY: Westminster John Knox Press, 2001), 6–15.

66. E. Brooks Holifield, *Theology in America: Christian Thought from the Age of the Puritans to the Civil War* (New Haven, CT: Yale University Press, 2003), 135–149, 342–352.

67. John Quincy Adams, *Diary*, 2:317.

68. John Quincy Adams, *Diary*, 1:403, 412–413.

69. As she prepared her memoirs, Louisa referred to John Quincy's more precise diary entries to sharpen recollections of people or events. While we cannot know if Adams ever read his wife's diary, it is worth noting that most of her entries took the form of "journal letters" that she edited and sent either to John Quincy or to her father-in-law, John.

70. Nathan O. Hatch, *Democratization of American Christianity* (New Haven, CT: Yale University Press, 1989), 3–48.

71. John Quincy Adams, November 11, 1813, Diary.

72. Louisa Catherine Adams, February 9, 1821, *Diary*, 2:556.

73. Louisa Catherine Adams, *Diary*, 1:xxx.

74. John Quincy Adams, "The Death of Children," in *Poems of Religion and Society* (Auburn, NY: Miller, Orton and Mulligan, 1854), 58–59.

75. John Quincy Adams, December 31, 1812, Diary.

76. Louisa Catherine Adams, October 23, 1812, *Diary*, 1:357.

77. Franchot, *Roads to Rome*.

78. Louisa Catherine Adams, February 27, 1820, *Diary*, 2:477–478.

79. Louisa Catherine Adams, February 27, 1820, *Diary*, 2:477–478.

80. Colleen McDannell, *The Christian Home in Victorian America, 1840–1900* (Bloomington: Indiana University Press, 1986), 105, 128, 139, 147, 159–160.

81. John Quincy Adams, *A Discourse on Education. Delivered at Braintree, Thursday, Oct. 24, 1839* (Boston: Perkins and Marvin, 1840), 36.

82. Horace Bushnell, *Christian Virtue* (New York: C. Scribner, 1861); David L. Smith, ed., *Horace Bushnell: Selected Writings on Language, Religion, and American Culture* (Chico, CA: Scholars Press, 1984).

83. John Quincy Adams, *Letters of John Quincy Adams, to His Son, on the Bible and Its Teachings* (Auburn, NY: Derby, Miller, 1848), 10. The letters were first gathered for publication by his son Charles and printed in the *New-York Tribune* shortly after Adams's death in 1848. Hereafter cited as John Quincy Adams, *Letters*.

84. John Quincy Adams, *Letters*, 119.

85. Thomas Jefferson, *The Jefferson Bible, or The Life and Morals of Jesus of Nazareth Extracted Textually from the Gospels in Greek, Latin French & English* (repr., New York: Akashic Books, 2004).

86. William Peter Strickland, *History of the American Bible Society, from Its Organization to the Present Time* (New York: Harper and Brothers, 1849).

87. John Quincy Adams, *Letters*, 13.

88. John Quincy Adams, *Letters*, 120.

89. John Quincy Adams, *Letters*, 20.

90. For the unsuccessful Dana mission of 1781–1782, see volumes 12 and 13, passim, of *Papers of John Adams*.

91. John Quincy Adams, January 2, 1812, Diary.

92. Beyond John Quincy Adams's diary entries of his London tenure, held in the Adams Papers, see also Duncan Cameron et al., *An American President in Ealing* (Ealing: Little Ealing History Group, 2014), 56–84.

93. John Quincy Adams, October 1816, Diary.

94. John Quincy Adams, January 26, 1817, Diary.

95. John Quincy Adams, August 20, 1815, Diary.

96. John Quincy Adams, August 20, 1815, Diary.

97. John Quincy Adams, December 15, 1815, Diary.

98. John Quincy Adams, December 25, 1815, Diary.

99. John Quincy Adams, December 25, 1815, Diary.

100. David R. Meyer, *The Roots of American Industrialization* (Baltimore: Johns Hopkins University Press, 2003), 23–41; Charles Sellers, *The Market Revolution: Jacksonian America, 1815–1846* (New York: Oxford University Press, 1991), 3–33; Harry L. Watson, *Liberty and Power: The Politics of Jacksonian America* (New York: Hill and Wang, 2006), 17–41.

101. Gilchrist, *Cultus Americanus*, 130.

102. Gilchrist, *Cultus Americanus*, 159–218.

103. Margaret Bayard Smith, *The First Forty Years of Washington Society* (New York: C. Scribner's Sons, 1906); Catherine Allgor, *Parlor Politics: In Which the Ladies of Washington Help Build a City and a Government* (Charlottesville: University Press of Virginia, 2000).

104. John Quincy Adams, *On Faith*.

105. Richard Crouter, ed., *Schleiermacher: On Religion: Speeches to Its Cultured Despisers* (Cambridge: Cambridge University Press, 2003), 5.

106. John Quincy Adams, *On Faith*.

107. Wendell Glick, "The Best Possible World of John Quincy Adams," *New England Quarterly* 37 (1964): 3–17.

108. David Morse, *American Romanticism*, vol. 1, *From Cooper to Hawthorne* (Totowa, NJ: Barnes and Noble Books, 1987), 2.

109. Lawrence Buell, "The Literary Significance of the Unitarian Movement," in *American Unitarianism, 1805–1865*, ed. Conrad Edick Wright (Boston: Massachusetts Historical Society and Northeastern University Press, 1989), 19.

110. John Gatta, *Making Nature Sacred: Literature, Religion, and Environment in America from the Puritans to the Present* (New York: Oxford University Press, 2004), 73–75.

111. Adam S. Potkay, "Theorizing Civic Eloquence in the Early Republic: The Road from David Hume to John Quincy Adams," *Early American Literature* 34 (1999): 147–170.

112. "Steamboat Verses," enclosed in John Quincy Adams to John Adams 2d, October 13, 1823, Adams Papers.

113. Paul E. Johnson, *The Early American Republic, 1789–1829* (New York: Oxford University Press, 2007), 114.

114. David C. Frederick, "John Quincy Adams, Slavery, and the Disappearance of the Right of Petition," *Law and History Review* 9 (1991): 113–155.

115. John Quincy Adams, March 29, 1841, Diary.

116. John Quincy Adams to Skelton Jones, April 17, 1809, Adams Papers.

117. John Adams to John Taylor of Carolina, January 24, 1815, Washburn Papers, Massachusetts Historical Society.

118. Lyman H. Butterfield, "Introduction," in John Quincy Adams, *The Wants of Man* (Worcester, MA: Achille J. St. Onge, 1962).

119. Adams drew his inspiration from the opening lines of Oliver Goldsmith's Hermit in *The Deserted Village*, "Man wants but little, here below . . ." (London: W. Griffin, 1770).

120. Harold P. Simonson, *Radical Discontinuities: American Romanticism and Christian Consciousness* (Rutherford, NJ: Fairleigh Dickinson University Press, 1983), 154.

121. "Mr. Adams's Illness," *Daily Republican* (Springfield, MA), February 24, 1848.

122. Charles Francis Adams, entries for February 23, 24, and 25, 1848, Diary, Adams Papers.

123. "John Quincy Adams," *Daily Republican* (Springfield, MA), February 28, 1848.

124. William P. Lunt, *A Discourse Delivered in Quincy, March 11, 1848, at the Interment of John Quincy Adams, Sixth President of the United States* (Boston: Dutton and Wentworth, State Printers, 1848), 1–44.

125. Bret E. Carroll, *Spiritualism in Antebellum America* (Bloomington: Indiana University Press, 1997), 3–4.

126. Hatch, *Democratization of American Christianity*, 206–219; Watson, *Liberty and Power*, 3–86, 178–179, 185, 222–223; Lewis Perry, *Boats against the Current: American Culture between Revolution and Modernity, 1820–1860* (New York: Oxford University Press, 1993), 177–178.

127. Amy S. Greenberg, *Manifest Manhood and the Antebellum American Empire* (Cambridge: Cambridge University Press, 2005); Johnson, *Early American Republic*, 113–116.

128. "Josiah Brigham, Esq.," in John Livingston, *Biographical Sketches of Distinguished Americans, Now Living* (New York, 1853), 66–69.

129. Molly McGarry, *Ghosts of Future Past: Spiritualists and the Cultural Politics of Nineteenth-Century America* (Berkeley: University of California Press, 2008), 1–93.

130. "Preface," in *Twelve Messages from the Spirit of John Quincy Adams, through Joseph D. Stiles, Medium, to Josiah Brigham* (Boston: Bela Marsh, 1859).

131. *Twelve Messages*, 180.

132. *Twelve Messages*, 191, 202.

133. John Quincy Adams, *On Faith*.

134. John Quincy Adams confided to his diary on June 4, 1819, that he often appeared to be "a man of reserved, cold, austere, and forbidding manners; my political adversaries say, a gloomy misanthropist, and my personal enemies, an unsocial savage. With a knowledge of the actual defect in my character, I have not the pliability to reform it."

135. The wording of this insult riffed on a common formulation of Unitarianism that, due mainly to James Freeman Clarke's influence, held as creedal through the 1890s, "We believe in: The Fatherhood of God; The Brotherhood of Man; The Leadership of Jesus; Salvation by Character; The Progress of Mankind onward and upward forever." See, for example, Unitarian Sunday-School Society, "Our Faith," *Every Other Sunday* 13 (1897): 147; David Robinson, *The Unitarians and the Universalists* (Westport, CT: Greenwood Press, 1985), 101–106; Michael McGloughlin, *Dead Letters to the New World: Melville, Emerson, and American Transcendentalism* (New York: Routledge, 2003), 20; and Gary Dorrien, *Social Ethics in the Making: Interpreting an American Tradition* (Malden, MA: Wiley-Blackwell, 2009), 327. By 1880, Unitarians ratified it in the "Ames Covenant" introduced by Charles Gordon Ames, an Adams cousin: "In the freedom of truth, and in the spirit of Jesus Christ, we unite for the worship of God and the service of man."

136. John Quincy Adams, March 13, 1828, Diary. As John Quincy told his son George Washington Adams: "I believed the nature of Jesus Christ was superhuman; but whether he was God or only the first of created beings was not clearly revealed to me in the Scriptures."

137. Mark A. Noll and Luke E. Harlow, eds., *Religion and American Politics: From the Colonial Period to the Present* (Oxford: Oxford University Press, 2007), 27.

138. John Quincy Adams, July 12, 1812, Diary.

139. John Quincy Adams, April 12, 1812, Diary.

140. John Quincy Adams to Reverend Alvan Lamson, September 25, 1846, Adams Papers.

141. Leigh Eric Schmidt, *Restless Souls: The Making of American Spirituality* (San Francisco: HarperSanFrancisco, 2005), 10–12; Matthew S. Hedstrom, *The Rise of Liberal Religion: Book Culture and American Spirituality in the Twentieth Century* (New York: Oxford University Press, 2013), 13–17.

142. Conrad Wright, *Congregational Polity: A Historical Survey of Unitarian Universalist Practice* (Boston: Skinner House, 1997), 32–65; James E. Block, *Nation of Agents: The American Path to a Modern Self and Society* (Cambridge, MA: Belknap Press of Harvard University Press, 2002), 424–458; Daniel Walker Howe, *What Hath God Wrought: The American Path to a Modern Self and Society* (Cambridge, MA: Belknap Press of Harvard University Press, 2002), 164–202.

143. Michael J. Langford, *The Tradition of Liberal Theology* (Grand Rapids, MI: Eerdmans, 2014), 19–58.

144. William R. Hutchison, *The Modernist Impulse in American Protestantism* (Durham, NC: Duke University Press, 1992), 12–40.

145. Lunt preached from John 12:27: "Now is my soul troubled; and what shall I say? Father, save me from this hour: but for this cause came I unto this hour."

146. John Quincy Adams, October 6, 1844, Diary.

Chapter 3

1. On the rates, freights, and history of the Boston & Worcester Railroad, see *Report of the Directors of the Boston & Worcester Rail-Road, to the Stockholders, at Their Annual Meeting, June 3, 1844* (Boston: I. R. Butts, 1844); Charles J. Kennedy, "The Early Business History of Four Massachusetts Railroads–IV," *Bulletin of the Business Historical Society* 25 (1951): 207–229; and Edward C. Kirkland, "The 'Railroad Scheme' of Massachusetts," *Journal of Economic History* 5 (1945): 145–171.

2. David R. Meyer, *The Roots of American Industrialization* (Baltimore: Johns Hopkins University Press, 2003), 23–41; Thomas Bender, *Toward an Urban Vision: Ideas and Institutions in Nineteenth-Century America* (Lexington: University Press of Kentucky, 1975); Robert W. Doherty, *Society and Power: Five New England Towns, 1800–1860* (Amherst: University of Massachusetts Press, 1977); Charles Sellers, *The Market Revolution: Jacksonian America, 1815–1846* (New York: Oxford University Press, 1991), 3–33; and Harry L. Watson, *Liberty and Power: The Politics of Jacksonian America* (New York: Hill and Wang, 2006), 17–41.

3. John Adams to Richard Cranch, August 26, 1756, Worcester, in *The Papers of John Adams*, 19 vols., ed. Sara Georgini et al. (Cambridge, MA: Belknap Press of Harvard University Press, 1977–), 1:15; and Kenneth J. Moynihan, *A History of Worcester, 1674–1848* (Charleston: History Press, 2007), 129–153.

4. John Quincy Adams, May 31, 1845, Diary, Adams Papers.

5. "Unitarian Festival," *Boston Daily Atlas*, May 31, 1843; "Exercises at the Collation Furnished by the Unitarian Laymen of Boston, to the Clergy of Their Denomination, on Tuesday, May 30, 1843," American Broadsides and Ephemera, Series 1, No. 6158. On May 27, 1845, John Quincy Adams presided over the same collation, recording in his diary that he "sat up until one o'clock in the morning" to write and polish his two-hour address the night before; Adams Papers.

6. Charles Francis Adams, Diary, November 22, 1842, Adams Papers.

7. John Lardas Modern, *Secularism in Antebellum America* (Chicago: University of Chicago Press, 2011), 4–48; Charles Taylor, *A Secular Age* (Cambridge, MA: Belknap Press of Harvard University Press, 2007); and James Turner, *Without God, without Creed: The Origins of Unbelief in America* (Baltimore: Johns Hopkins University Press, 1985).

8. Jeffrey P. Sklansky, *The Soul's Economy: Market Society and Selfhood in American Thought, 1820–1920* (Chapel Hill: University of North Carolina Press, 2002); Daniel Walker Howe, "American Victorianism as a Culture," *American Quarterly*

27 (1975): 507–532; and Mark A. Noll, ed., *God and Mammon: Protestants, Money, and the Market, 1790–1860* (Oxford: Oxford University Press, 2002).

9. Charles Francis Adams, Diary, May 30, 1843, Adams Papers.

10. Charles Francis Adams, *Diary*, 3:13–14.

11. Daniel Walker Howe, *Making the American Self: Jonathan Edwards to Abraham Lincoln* (Cambridge, MA: Harvard University Press, 1997), 111.

12. Anne C. Rose, *Victorian America and the Civil War* (New York: Cambridge University Press, 1992), 17–67; Daniel Walker Howe, "The Market Revolution and the Shaping of Identity in Whig-Jacksonian America," in *The Market Revolution in America: Social, Political, and Religious Expressions, 1800–1880*, ed. Melvyn Stokes and Stephen Conway (Charlottesville: University Press of Virginia, 1996), 259–281.

13. Charles is undersung in Adams historiography, claiming one full-scale biography that charts his political career and literary efforts, but with little emphasis on religion: Martin B. Duberman, *Charles Francis Adams, 1807–1886* (Boston: Houghton Mifflin, 1961). Sketches of his editorial life appear in Peter Shaw, "The Apprenticeship of Charles Francis Adams," *American Scholar* 2 (1969): 312–322, and Earl N. Harbert, "Charles Francis Adams (1807–1886): A Forgotten Family Man of Letters," *Journal of American Studies* 6 (1972): 249–265. Charles's diplomatic career received new attention in Amanda Foreman, *A World on Fire: Britain's Crucial Role in the American Civil War* (New York: Random House, 2010).

14. John Quincy Adams's account of his mission as the first American minister to Russia comprises his diary entries from June 27, 1809, to June 24, 1814, Adams Papers. For Louisa's version of the children's ball, see Louisa Catherine Adams, *Diary and Autobiographical Writings of Louisa Catherine Adams*, ed. Judith S. Graham et al., 2 vols. (Cambridge, MA: Belknap Press of Harvard University Press, 2013), 1:297–299, 303–304, 316, 326.

15. Louisa Catherine Adams, *Diary*, 1:283–406.

16. Aida DiPace Donald and David Donald, eds., *The Diary of Charles Francis Adams*, 8 vols. (Cambridge, MA: Belknap Press of Harvard University Press, 1964–1986), 1:184.

17. Charles Francis Adams to John Quincy Adams, January 22, 1828, Adams Papers. In his reply of March 26, the elder Adams fired back: "If you *prefer* to remain in private life, stand aloof—you may be sure not to be disturbed in your privacy" (Adams Papers).

18. "Priestley's Life and Correspondence," *Christian Examiner and Theological Review* 12 (1832): 258.

19. "Bishop Hobart's Views of the Catholic Church," *United States Catholic and Monthly Review Magazine* 7 (1848): 661.

20. Thomas Hughes, *History of the Society of Jesus in North America, Colonial and Federal*, 3 vols. (London: Longman, Greens, 1907–1917), 1:1078.

21. On the transatlantic career of George Edmund Ironside (1766–1827), see William M. MacBean, *Biographical Register of Saint Andrew's Society of the State of New York*, 2 vols. (New York: Printed for the Society, 1922–1925), 2:763. The Scottish-American clergyman's diplomatic posting came at the recommendation of Henry Clay. Regular mention of Ironside's contributions appears in John Quincy Adams, Diary, passim, 1821–1825, Adams Papers.

22. For a description of Ironside's school, techniques, and disciplinary measures, see John Quincy Adams, Diary, October 17–18, November 1, and December 22, 1819, Adams Papers.

23. Charles Francis Adams, Literary and Legal Commonplace Books, 1822, 1825, 1827–1829, Adams Papers. In honor of Ironside's memory as an intellectual role model and to ease the "distressed condition" of his family after his death, Adams purchased several of his mentor's books at public auction in June 1828 (*Diary*, 2:134–135).

24. Charles Francis Adams, *Diary*, 5:18.

25. George M. Marsden, *The Soul of the American University: From Protestant Establishment to Established Unbelief* (New York: Oxford University Press, 1994), 3–9, 183–186.

26. Charles Francis Adams, *Diary*, 1:39, 99–104, 211, 220, 290.

27. Charles Francis Adams, *Diary*, 1:353.

28. John Quincy Adams, Diary, December 25, 1825, Adams Papers.

29. Charles Francis Adams, *Diary*, 1:10–13.

30. Charles Francis Adams, *Diary*, 1:10–13. No record of his final theology grade has been found.

31. Sellers, *The Market Revolution*, 209.

32. Charles Francis Adams, *Diary*, 1:15–16.

33. J. David Hoeveler, *Creating the American Mind: Intellect and Politics in the Colonial Colleges* (Lanham, MD: Rowman and Littlefield, 2002), 213–239.

34. Hoeveler, *Creating the American Mind*, 213–239.

35. John D. Cushing, "Notes on Disestablishment in Massachusetts, 1780–1833," *William and Mary Quarterly* 26 (1969): 169–190; Kelly Olds, "Privatizing the Church: Disestablishment in Connecticut and Massachusetts," *Journal of Political Economy* 102 (1994): 277–297.

36. John Quincy Adams to Abigail Adams, June 30, 1811, Adams Papers.

37. Allen C. Guelzo, *Fateful Lightning: A New History of the Civil War and Reconstruction* (Oxford: Oxford University Press, 2012), 188.

38. Sklansky, *The Soul's Economy*, 1–13; Nathan O. Hatch, *The Democratization of American Christianity* (New Haven, CT: Yale University Press, 1989); Meyer, *Instructed Conscience*; and Wilson Smith, *Professors and Public Ethics: Studies of Northern Moral Philosophers before the Civil War* (Ithaca, NY: Cornell University Press, 1956).

39. Charles Francis Adams, *Diary*, 1:105, 108–109.

40. Alexis McCrossen, "Sabbatarianism: The Intersection of Church and State in the Orchestration of Everyday Life in Nineteenth-Century America," in *Religious and Secular Reform in America: Ideas, Beliefs, and Social Change*, ed. David Keith Adams and Cornelis A. van Minnen (New York: New York University Press, 1999), 133–158.

41. *The Diary and Autobiography of John Adams*, 4 vols., ed. L. H. Butterfield et al. (Cambridge, MA: Belknap Press of Harvard University Press, 1961–1966), 1:128–130, 190–192, 204–206, 210–211, 212–216.

42. Christopher G. Bates, ed., *The Early Republic and Antebellum America: An Encyclopedia of Social, Political, Cultural, and Economic History*, 4 vols. (New York: Routledge, 2015), 1:72–76.

43. For his reading of Mosheim's *An Ecclesiastical History, from the Birth of Christ to the Beginning of the Eighteenth Century: In Which the Rise, Progress and Variation of Church Power Are Considered in Their Connection with the State of Learning and Philosophy, and the Political History of Europe during that Period*, 4 vols. (New York: E. Duyckinck, 1824), see Charles Francis Adams, *Diary*, 1:108–149, passim.

44. Bernard Bailyn, *Glimpses of the Harvard Past* (Cambridge, MA: Harvard University Press, 1986); and Samuel Eliot Morison, *Three Centuries of Harvard, 1636–1936* (Cambridge: Harvard University Press, 1936).

45. For the full account of his epic hangover in 1824 and the resulting efforts to resume his daily Bible reading, see Charles Francis Adams, *Diary*, 1:137–139. On links between alcohol and ill health made in the early republic, see Sharon V. Salinger, *Taverns and Drinking in Early America* (Baltimore: Johns Hopkins University Press, 2002); and Matthew Warner Osborn, *Rum Maniacs: Alcoholic Insanity in the Early Republic* (Chicago: University of Chicago Press, 2014).

46. On Anglo-American diarists as "private" intellectuals, see Anne-Marie Millim, *The Victorian Diary: Authorship and Emotional Labour* (Burlington, VT: Ashgate, 2013); Kathryn Carter, "The Cultural Work of Diaries in Mid-century Victorian Britain," *Victorian Review* 23 (1997): 251–267; Jane H. Hunter, "Inscribing the Self in the Heart of the Family: Diaries and Girlhood in Late-Victorian America," *American Quarterly* 44 (1992): 51–81; Molly McCarthy, "A Pocketful of Days: Pocket Diaries and Daily Record Keeping among Nineteenth-Century New England Women," *New England Quarterly* 73 (2000): 274–296; and Ronald J. Zboray, *Everyday Ideas: Socioliterary Experience among Antebellum New Englanders* (Knoxville: University of Tennessee Press, 2006).

47. Rose, *Victorian America and the Civil War*, 253–255.

48. In a letter of November 28, 1827, John Quincy Adams advised Charles's brother George Washington Adams that for any man, "A Diary is the Time Piece of Life. . . . His Record is a second Conscience" (Adams Papers). Charles was typically morose about his skill as a diarist, calling it "a pretty monotonous record of the very even tenour of my life," in Charles Francis Adams, *Diary*, 4:235.

49. William Everett, "Abigail Brown Adams," Obituary, *New England Historic and Genealogical Register*, July 1889, 343; *Quincy Patriot*, June 8 and 15, 1889.

50. Louisa Catherine Adams to George Washington Adams, January 29, 1827, Adams Papers.

51. Charles Francis Adams, Diary, July 17, 1835, Adams Papers.

52. Charles Francis Adams, *Diary*, 2:51.

53. The Adamses' fifth son, Arthur (b. 1841), died suddenly at the age of five.

54. William Clarkson Johnson to Alexander B. Johnson, October 3, 1842, Adams-Johnson-Clements Papers, Massachusetts Historical Society. W. C. Johnson sued Charles for his wife Mary Louisa's share of the Adams estate.

55. Barbara Welter, "The Cult of True Womanhood: 1820–1860," *American Quarterly* (1966): 151–174; Nancy M. Theriot, *The Biosocial Construction of Femininity: Mothers and Daughters in Nineteenth-Century America* (New York: Greenwood Press, 1988); C. Dallett Hemphill, *Bowing to Necessities: A History of Manners in America, 1620–1860* (New York: Oxford University Press, 1999); Nancy F. Cott, *The Bonds of Womanhood: "Woman's Sphere" in New England, 1780–1835* (New Haven, CT: Yale University Press, 1997); Jeanne Boydston, *Home and Work: Housework, Wages, and the Ideology of Labor in the Early Republic* (New York: Oxford University Press, 1990); Stevenson, *The Victorian Homefront: American Thought and Culture, 1860–1880* (Ithaca: Cornell University Press, 2001); and Stokes and Conway, *The Market Revolution*.

56. Abigail Brooks Adams, Diary, October 9, 1861, Adams Family Papers, Massachusetts Historical Society.

57. Together, the Adamses frequently attended service at Boston's First Church (Unitarian), where Abby's brother-in-law Nathaniel Langdon Frothingham served as pastor from 1815 to 1850.

58. Edwin S. Gaustad, *Faith of Our Fathers: Religion and the New Nation* (San Francisco: Harper and Row, 1987), 122.

59. On the growth of Unitarianism in nineteenth-century New England, see Conrad Wright, *A Stream of Light: A Short History of American Unitarianism* (Boston: Skinner House Books, 1989); John A. Buehrens, *Universalists and Unitarians in America: A People's History* (Boston: Skinner House Books, 2011); and David Robinson, *The Unitarians and the Universalists* (Westport, CT: Greenwood Press, 1985).

60. David Turley, ed., *American Religion: Literary Sources and Documents* (The Banks, England: Helm Information, 1998), 35.

61. Charles Francis Adams, *Diary*, 4:23.

62. Charles Francis Adams, *Diary*, 8:16–17.

63. Charles Francis Adams, *Diary*, 4:81–82, 86.

64. Charles Francis Adams, *Diary*, 5:187, 234; 6:9, 25, 107.

65. Charles Francis Adams, *Diary*, 5:55.

66. For the roots and growth of this philosophy, see Charles Capper and Conrad Edick Wright, eds., *Transient and Permanent: The Transcendentalist Movement and Its Contexts* (Boston: Northeastern University Press, 1999); and Philip F. Gura, *American Transcendentalism: A History* (New York: Hill and Wang, 2007).

67. Charles Francis Adams, *Diary*, 5:87.

68. Charles Francis Adams, Diary, February 25, 1848, Adams Papers.

69. Charles Francis Adams, *Diary*, 4:313.

70. Charles Francis Adams, *Diary*, 4:293.

71. Charles Francis Adams, *Diary*, 2:396.

72. Ebenezer Porter, *Signs of the Times: A Sermon Preached in the Chapel of the Theological Seminary, Andover, on the Public Fast, April 3, 1822* (Andover, MA: Flagg and Gould, 1823), 5–6, 9, 15, 23.

73. For John Adams's fast-day controversy, see chapter 1.

74. See, for example, Orville Dewey, *A Sermon on the Moral Uses of the Pestilence, Denominated Asiatic Cholera: Delivered on Fast-Day, August 9, 1832* (New Bedford, MA: B. T. Congdon, 1832). In time, Charles found Dewey "more pretentious than pious" (*Diary*, 8:328).

75. F. W. P. Greenwood, *Prayer for the Sick: A Sermon Preached at King's Chapel, Boston, on Thursday, August 9, 1832, Being the Fast Day Appointed by the Governor of Massachusetts, on Account of the Appearance of Cholera in the United States* (Boston: Leonard C. Bowles, 1832).

76. Dewey, *A Sermon on the Moral Uses of the Pestilence*.

77. Henry F. May, "The Religion of the Republic," in *Ideas, Faiths, and Feelings: Essays on American Intellectual and Religious History, 1952–1982* (New York: Oxford University Press, 1983), 163–186.

78. See "Sin," in Charles Buck, *A Theological Dictionary* (Philadelphia: J. J. Woodward, 1831), 422–423.

79. Charles Francis Adams, *Diary*, 4:343. The national fast day for cholera was called for August 9, 1832.

80. Charles Francis Adams, *Diary*, 4:348–349.

81. Charles Francis Adams, *Diary*, 4:412.

82. Charles Francis Adams, Literary Miscellany, 1841–1875, Adams Family Papers Additions, Massachusetts Historical Society.

83. Charles Francis Adams, Literary Miscellany, 1841–1875.

84. Charles Francis Adams, Literary Miscellany, 1841–1875.

85. Charles Francis Adams, Literary Miscellany, 1841–1875.

86. Charles Francis Adams, Literary Miscellany, 1841–1875.

87. On Charles's literary career, see Duberman, *Charles Francis Adams*; Peter Shaw, "The Apprenticeship of Charles Francis Adams," *American Scholar* 2 (1969): 312–322; and Harbert, "Charles Francis Adams" 249–265.

88. Eugene Charlton Black, ed., *Victorian Culture and Society* (New York: Harper and Row, 1973); Daniel Walker Howe, "The Victorian Period in American History,"

in *The Victorian World*, ed. Martin Hewitt (London: Routledge, 2012), 708–724; and Edmund Richardson, *Classical Victorians: Scholars, Scoundrels and Generals in the Pursuit of Antiquity* (Cambridge: Cambridge University Press, 2013), 58–60.

89. Shrewdly, Charles reintroduced the clan to a critical American public by deploying his tart, quotable grandmother Abigail in *Letters of Mrs. Adams: The Wife of John Adams*, 2 vols. (Boston: C. C. Little and J. Brown, 1840).

90. Charles Francis Adams, Diary, February 26, 1848, Adams Papers.

91. Charles Francis Adams, Diary, November 3, 1850, Adams Papers. He returned to regular service in Quincy on May 4, 1851.

92. Oliver G. Steele, *Steele's Book of Niagara Falls*, 7th ed. (Buffalo: Oliver G. Steele, 1840), 38.

93. John F. Sears, *Sacred Places: American Tourist Attractions in the Nineteenth Century* (New York: Oxford University Press, 1989); Patrick McGreevy, *Imagining Niagara: The Meaning and Making of Niagara Falls* (Amherst: University of Massachusetts Press, 1994); Chistopher Mulvey, "New York to Niagara by Way of the Hudson and the Erie," in *The Cambridge Companion to American Travel Writing*, eds. Alfred Bendixen and Judith Hamera (Cambridge: Cambridge University Press, 2009); Richard H. Gassan, *The Birth of American Tourism: New York, the Hudson Valley, and American Culture, 1790–1830* (Amherst, MA: University of Massachusetts Press, 2008); and Elizabeth R. McKinsey, *Niagara Falls: Icon of the American Sublime* (New York: Cambridge University Press, 1985).

94. Sears, *Sacred Places*; Jane Smiley, *Charles Dickens: A Life* (New York: Viking, 2002).

95. Charles Francis Adams, *Diary*, 8:20–30.

96. Charles Francis Adams, *Diary*, 8:27.

97. In March 1835, Read, a former Episcopalian and Ursuline novice, published her Gothic novel, *Six Months in a Convent, or, The Narrative of Rebecca Theresa Reed, Who Was under the Influence of the Roman Catholics About Two Years, and An Inmate of the Ursuline Convent on Mount Benedict, Charlestown, Mass., Nearly Six Months, in the Years 1831–2* (Boston). Maria Monk published *Awful Disclosures of Maria Monk, or, The Hidden Secrets of a Nun's Life in a Convent Exposed* (New York) in January 1836. Scholars continue to debate both works' authorship.

98. Charles Francis Adams, *Diary*, 8:37–49.

99. Charles Francis Adams, *Diary*, 8:39.

100. Monk, *Awful Disclosures*.

101. Charles Francis Adams, *Diary*, 8:37.

102. Charles Francis Adams, Diary, November 13, 1853, Adams Papers.

103. Charles Francis Adams, Diary, April 17, 1870, Adams Papers.

104. Charles Francis Adams, *Diary*, 8:142.

105. Charles Francis Adams, Diary, February 4, 1844, Adams Papers. Aside from Charles's diary and Josiah Quincy's letters home, the most comprehensive account of this trip appears in Henry Adams II, "Charles Francis Adams Visits

the Mormons in 1844," *Proceedings of the Massachusetts Historical Society*, 3d ser. (1944–1947): 267–300.

106. Charles Francis Adams, *Diary*, 8:47.

107. Charles Francis Adams, *Diary*, 8:74.

108. J. Spencer Fluhman, *"A Peculiar People": Anti-Mormonism and the Making of Religion in Nineteenth-Century America* (Chapel Hill: University of North Carolina Press, 2012); and Patrick Q. Mason, *The Mormon Menace: Violence and Anti-Mormonism in the Postbellum South* (New York: Oxford University Press, 2011).

109. Matthew Burton Bowman, *The Mormon People: The Making of an American Faith* (New York: Random House, 2012), 3–31.

110. Josiah Quincy published his version of the Nauvoo trip in two editions of the *New York Independent* on December 29, 1881 ("Leaves from Old Journals"), and January 9, 1882 ("Leaves from My Journal"). For a thorough, modern reappraisal of Quincy's account, see John J. Hammond, "Re-examining the Adams/ Quincy May 1844 Visit to Nauvoo," *John Whitmer Historical Association Journal* 30 (2010): 66–95.

111. Charles Francis Adams, Diary, May 15, 1844, Adams Papers.

112. Charles Francis Adams, Diary, May 15, 1844.

113. Charles Francis Adams, Diary, May 15, 1844.

114. Charles Francis Adams, Diary, May 15, 1844.

115. Charles Francis Adams, Diary, May 15, 1844.

116. Charles Francis Adams, Diary, December 12, 1869, Adams Papers.

117. Charles Francis Adams, Diary, 1840–1850, passim, Adams Papers.

118. Charles Francis Adams, Diary, February 5, 1843, Adams Papers.

119. Charles Francis Adams, Diary, October 10, 1847, Adams Papers.

120. Charles Francis Adams, Diary, December 31, 1861, Adams Papers.

121. This church was demolished in 1900. St. Michael Bassishaw's former site is now the Barbican Centre.

122. Charles Francis Adams, Diary, June 23, 1861, Adams Papers.

123. Charles Francis Adams, Diary, November 17, 1861, Adams Papers.

124. Charles Francis Adams, Diary, 1861–1868, passim, Adams Papers.

125. Charles Francis Adams, Diary, March 24, 1862, Adams Papers.

126. Charles Francis Adams, Diary, March 24, 1862.

127. Charles Francis Adams, Diary, November 15, 1870.

128. Rose, *Victorian America and the Civil War*, 4.

129. Charles Francis Adams, Diary, August 30, 1874, Adams Papers.

Chapter 4

1. Henry Adams's private library, held at the Massachusetts Historical Society, contains roughly twenty titles related to Buddhist and Hindu studies. Representative titles of non-Western religion include Samuel Johnson's *Oriental Religions and Their*

Relation to Universal Religion, 2 vols. (London: Trübner, 1879); H. H. Wilson, *Essays and Lectures on the Religions of the Hindus*, 2 vols. (London: Trüber & Co., 1861–1862); and Henry Osborn Taylor, *Deliverance: The Freeing of the Spirit in the Ancient World* (New York: Macmillan, 1915).

On the introduction of Eastern thought to nineteenth-century American elites like Henry, see Thomas A. Tweed, *The American Encounter with Buddhism, 1844–1912: Victorian Culture and the Limits of Dissent* (Chapel Hill: University of North Carolina Press, 2000); Christopher E. G. Benfey, *The Great Wave: Gilded Age Misfits, Japanese Eccentrics, and the Opening of Old Japan* (New York: Random House, 2003); and David Weir, *American Orient: Imagining the East from the Colonial Era through the Twentieth Century* (Amherst: University of Massachusetts Press, 2011). For shifting interpretations of what constitutes "American Buddhism" and why scholars struggle to trace its diffusion, see Peter N. Gregory, "Describing the Elephant: Buddhism in America," *Religion and American Culture: A Journal of Interpretation* 11 (2001): 233–263.

2. Henry Adams issued this work, also known as *The History of the United States, during the Administrations of Thomas Jefferson and James Madison*, in nine volumes between 1889 and 1891.

3. Henry Adams to John Hay, June 11, [1886], in *The Letters of Henry Adams*, 6 vols., ed. J. C. Levenson et al. (Cambridge, MA: Belknap Press of Harvard University Press, 1982–1988), 3:11–12. Hereafter cited as Levenson, *Letters of Henry Adams*. John La Farge published his account of the trip in *An Artist's Letters from Japan* (New York: Century Co., 1897). Henry's elder brother, Charles Francis Jr., was president of the Union Pacific Railroad on which they traveled.

4. James Turner, *Without God, without Creed: The Origins of Unbelief in America* (Baltimore: John Hopkins University Press, 1985). Broadly interpreted, the Buddhist concept of nirvana is founded on Four Noble Truths: Suffering exists; suffering has a cause; suffering has an end; there is a cause to the end of suffering, and that path brings enlightenment.

5. Turner, *Without God, without Creed*, 171–202.

6. Charles Taylor, *A Secular Age* (Cambridge, MA: Belknap Press of Harvard University Press, 2007).

7. Henry Adams to John Hay, January 23, 1883, in *The Letters of Henry Adams, 1858–1891*, 2 vols., ed. Worthington Chauncey Ford (Boston: Houghton Mifflin, 1930), 347. Hereafter cited as Ford, *Letters of Henry Adams*.

8. For a reconsideration of categorizing Anglo-American scholars of Henry's era as either religious or secular, see Frank M. Turner, *Contesting Cultural Authority: Essays in Victorian Intellectual Life* (Cambridge: Cambridge University Press, 1993), 3–37.

9. Henry Adams to Charles Milnes Gaskell, [August] 7, [1914]; to Lawrence Mason, April 1, 1915, in Levenson, *Letters of Henry Adams*, 6:657, 692.

10. Mark A. Noll, *The Civil War as a Theological Crisis* (Chapel Hill: University of North Carolina Press, 2006); Anne C. Rose, *Victorian America and the Civil War* (New York: Cambridge University Press, 1992); Mary Farrell Bednarowski, *American Religion: A Cultural Perspective* (Englewood Cliffs, NJ: Prentice-Hall, 1984).

11. Henry Adams, *The Education of Henry Adams* (Cambridge, MA: Riverside Press, 1918), 34, 35.

12. Henry Adams, *Education*, 36.

13. Henry Adams, *Education*, 15.

14. Only five siblings lived to adulthood; Henry's younger brother Arthur (b. 1841) died in 1846.

15. Henry Adams, *Education*, 34, 35.

16. Two modern trilogies serve as the standard reference works on Henry Adams: Ernest Samuels, *Henry Adams: The Young Henry Adams; The Middle Years; The Major Phase* (Cambridge, MA: Harvard University Press, 1966); and Edward Chalfant, *Both Sides of the Ocean: A Biography of Henry Adams, His First Life, 1838–1862; Better in Darkness: A Biography of Henry Adams, His Second Life, 1862–1891; Improvement of the World: A Biography of Henry Adams, His Last Life, 1891–1918* (Hamden, CT: Archon Books, 1982–2001). Significant, well-focused anthologies include David R. Contosta and Robert Muccigrosso, eds., *Henry Adams and His World* (Philadelphia: American Philosophical Society, 1993); and William Merrill Decker and Earl N. Harbert, eds., *Henry Adams and the Need to Know* (Charlottesville: University Press of Virginia, 2005).

    Confronted by the eponymous *Education*, most scholars have employed one of three methods to profile Henry: by using psychobiography, by isolating a single strand of his output for manageable analysis, or by grouping him with like-minded cosmopolitan thinkers. See, for example, Max I. Baym, *The French Education of Henry Adams* (New York: Columbia University Press, 1951); Robert A. Hume, *Runaway Star: An Appreciation of Henry Adams* (Ithaca, NY: Cornell University Press, 1951); J. C. Levenson, *The Mind and Art of Henry Adams* (Boston: Houghton Mifflin, 1957); Melvin E. Lyon, *Symbol and Idea in Henry Adams* (Lincoln: University of Nebraska Press, 1970); William Dusinberre, *Henry Adams: The Myth of Failure* (Charlottesville: University Press of Virginia, 1980); T. J. Jackson Lears, *No Place of Grace: Antimodernism and the Transformation of American Culture, 1880–1920* (New York: Pantheon Books, 1981); Michael O'Brien, *Henry Adams and the Southern Question* (Athens: University of Georgia Press, 2005); and Gary Wills, *Henry Adams and the Making of America* (Boston: Houghton Mifflin, 2005).

17. Henry opens the *Education* with a Boston venue and an "uncle" minister presiding, on p. 3.

18. Members' Registers, Vol. 3, p. 294, United First Parish Church of Quincy, Massachusetts. I am grateful to Pastor Emeritus Reverend Sheldon Bennett, Pastor Reverend Rebecca Froom, Gary Haynes, and member Bill Westland for

sharing the wealth of baptismal, marriage, and membership records held at the church, now Unitarian Universalist.

19. Aida DiPace Donald and David Donald, eds., *The Diary of Charles Francis Adams*, 8 vols. (Cambridge, MA: Belknap Press of Harvard University Press, 1989), 8:114–115. Lunt preached from Hebrews 12:14 and Mark 7:11–12.

20. Thomas C. Upham, *Ratio Disciplinæ, or the Constitution of the Congregational Churches* (Portland, ME: Shirley and Hyde, 1829), 21–22.

21. Sidney E. Mead, *The Lively Experiment: The Shaping of Christianity in America* (New York: Harper and Row, 1963), 103–133.

22. John Mitchell, *A Guide to the Principles and Practices of the Congregational Churches of New England: With a Brief History of the Denomination* (Northampton, MA: J. H. Butler, 1838), 39.

23. The Reverend Sheldon Bennett, in discussion with the author, January 28, 2014. For the development of First Church, see Charles Francis Adams Jr., *The History of Braintree, Massachusetts (1639–1708): The North Precinct of Braintree (1708–1792) and the Town of Quincy (1792–1889)* (Cambridge, MA: Riverside Press, 1891), 10–57, 144–157.

24. On American Christians' pursuit of (Germanic) philosophical idealism, which predicated a "spiritualizing" God but resisted the idea that the complexity of human progress was reducible to a few universal variables, see F. H. Johnson and H. D. Lloyd, "Immanent God and Creative Man," in *The Paradox of Progressive Thought*, ed. David W. Noble (Minneapolis: University of Minnesota Press, 1958), 125–156; and Paul K. Conkin, *The Uneasy Center: Reformed Christianity in Antebellum America* (Chapel Hill: University of North Carolina Press, 1995), 97, 148.

25. Lears, *No Place of Grace*, 117–118.

26. Catherine L. Albanese, *A Republic of Mind and Spirit: A Cultural History of American Metaphysical Religion* (New Haven, CT: Yale University Press, 2007); Louis Menand, *The Metaphysical Club* (New York: Farrar, Straus and Giroux, 2001); Russell B. Goodman, *American Philosophy before Pragmatism* (New York: Oxford University Press, 2015); and Allen W. Wood and Songsuk Susan Hahn, eds., *The Cambridge History of Philosophy in the Nineteenth-Century, 1790–1870* (Cambridge: Cambridge University Press, 2012).

27. Samuels, *Henry Adams: The Middle Years*, 204.

28. Frances Snow Compton [Henry Adams], *Esther* (New York: Henry Holt, 1884), 8.

29. Albanese, *A Republic of Mind and Spirit*; Menand, *The Metaphysical Club*; Nathan O. Hatch, *The Democratization of American Christianity* (New Haven, CT: Yale University Press, 1989); Leigh Eric Schmidt, *Restless Souls: The Making of American Spirituality* (San Francisco: HarperSanFrancisco, 2005).

30. Sydney E. and David D. Hall, *A Religious History of the American People* (New Haven, CT: Yale University Press, 2004), 129, 842–856.

31. Henry Adams to Charles Milnes Gaskell, March 7, 1870, in *A Cycle of Adams Letters*, 2 vols., ed. Worthington C. Ford (Boston: Houghton Mifflin, 1920), 1:167. Hereafter cited as Ford, *Cycle*.

32. On the Anglo-American "gentleman-scholar" archetype, see Eugene Charlton Black, ed., *Victorian Culture and Society* (New York: Harper and Row, 1973); Daniel Walker Howe, "The Victorian Period in American History," in *The Victorian World*, ed. Martin Hewitt (London: Routledge, 2012), 708–724; and Edmund Richardson, *Classical Victorians: Scholars, Scoundrels and Generals in the Pursuit of Antiquity* (Cambridge: Cambridge University Press, 2013), 58–60.

33. Harvey Levenstein, *Seductive Journey: American Tourists in France from Jefferson to the Jazz Age* (Chicago: University of Chicago Press, 1998), 3–36; Annette G. Aubert, *The German Roots of Nineteenth-Century American Theology* (New York: Oxford University Press, 2013); and Christine Guth, *Longfellow's Tattoos: Tourism, Collecting, and Japan* (Seattle: University of Washington Press, 2004).

34. Linda K. Kerber and Walter John Morris, "Politics and Literature: The Adams Family and the *Port Folio*," *William and Mary Quarterly* 23 (1966): 450–476.

35. Tim Youngs, ed., *Travel Writing in the Nineteenth Century: Filling the Blank Spaces* (London: Anthem Press, 2006), 1–16; William W. Stowe, "Henry Adams, Traveler," *New England Quarterly* 64 (1991): 197–205.

36. Harold F. Smith, *American Travellers Abroad: A Bibliography of Accounts Published before 1900* (Carbondale: Southern Illinois University, 1969), 9–10, 33, 37, 39.

37. Lewis Perry, *Boats against the Current: American Culture between Revolution and Modernity, 1820–1860* (New York: Oxford University Press, 1993), 125–140; John Carlos Rowe, "Nineteenth-Century United States Literary Culture and Transnationality," *PMLA* 118 (2003): 78–89; Tom Lutz, *Cosmopolitan Vistas: American Regionalism and Literary Value* (Ithaca, NY: Cornell University Press, 2004); and Philip Gould, "Catharine Sedgwick's Cosmopolitan Nation," *New England Quarterly* 78 (2005): 232–258.

38. Nicola J. Watson, ed., *Literary Tourism and Nineteenth-Century Culture* (Basingstoke: Palgrave Macmillan), 1–13, 175–210.

39. Henry Adams, *Education*, 16.

40. Henry Adams, *Education*, 70.

41. Guth, *Longfellow's Tattoos*.

42. Mark Rennella, *The Boston Cosmopolitans: International Travel and American Arts and Letters* (New York: Palgrave Macmillan, 2008); Leslie Butler, *Critical Americans: Victorian Intellectuals and Transatlantic Liberal Reform* (Chapel Hill: University of North Carolina Press, 2000); and James T. Kloppenberg, *Uncertain Victory: Social Democracy and Progressivism in European and American Thought, 1870–1920* (New York: Oxford University Press, 1996). On American cosmopolitanism and the evolution of world citizenship as a modern ideal between the eighteenth and twentieth centuries, see David Gavin Kendall, Ian Woodward, and Zlatko Skrbiš, *The Sociology of Cosmopolitanism: Globalization,*

Identity, Culture and Government (New York: Palgrave Macmillan, 2009); and Pauline Kleingeld, *Kant and Cosmopolitanism* (Cambridge: Cambridge University Press, 2012).

43. James M. Volo and Dorothy Denneen Volo, *Family Life in 19th-Century America* (Westport, CT: Greenwood Press, 2007), 344–347.

44. Kay Dian Kriz, "Introduction: The Grand Tour," *Eighteenth-Century Studies* 31 (1997): 87–89.

45. Henry Adams to Charles Francis Adams Jr., April 22, 1859, in Ford, *Letters of Henry Adams*, 1:35.

46. Henry Adams to Charles Francis Adams Jr., December 17–18, 1858, in Ford, *Cycle*, 1:10.

47. Kristin Schwain, *Signs of Grace: Religion and American Art in the Gilded Age* (Ithaca, NY: Cornell University Press, 2008); David Morgan, *Protestants and Pictures: Religion, Visual Culture, and the Age of American Mass Production* (New York: Oxford University Press, 1999).

48. Before Adams's marriage, his letters reveal a general appreciation for sacred art, but he did not manage his own money enough to buy more than a stray engraving or two. Later, Adams took a more active role in shopping for art, much of it religious in nature. Over the previous three generations, plenty of Adamses sat for portraits with an array of Anglo-American artists and photographers. Sponsoring them became a part of family tradition. Henry's investment, then, often began with finding a promising artist to patronize. For example, starting with the Japanese sojourn of 1886, Adams subsidized a great deal of La Farge's work and travels, including their eighteen-month joint odyssey in the South Seas, 1890–1891. With John Hay, Adams commissioned adjoining Romanesque townhouses in Washington, DC, from architect Henry Hobson Richardson. Adams patronized Tiffany and Company for custom-made birthday baubles for his nieces, and Isabella Stewart Gardner sought him to consult on art purchases for her Fenway mansion.

Photographs of Adams's various household interiors, held in the Massachusetts Historical Society, show trays and tables laden with the exotic ornaments that he purchased in consultation with Meiji-era art historian Ernest Fenollosa and William Sturgis Bigelow, later the primary donor to the Asian galleries of the new Museum of Fine Arts, Boston. On Adams as art collector and patron, see Ernst Scheyer, *The Circle of Henry Adams: Art and Artists* (Detroit, MI: Wayne State University Press, 1970); Marc Friedlaender, "Henry Hobson Richardson, Henry Adams, and John Hay," *Journal of the Society of Architectural Historians* 29 (1970): 231–246; and James L. Yarnall, *Recreation and Idleness: The Pacific Travels of John La Farge* (New York: Vance Jordan Fine Art, 1998).

49. Harry S. Stout, *Upon the Altar of the Nation: A Moral History of the American Civil War* (New York: Viking, 2006); Noll, *The Civil War as a Theological Crisis*;

and Alice Fahs, *The Imagined Civil War: Popular Literature of the North and South, 1861–1865* (Chapel Hill: University of North Carolina Press, 2001).

50. Rose, *Victorian America and the Civil War.*

51. Henry Adams to Charles Francis Adams Jr., January 8, 1861, in Ford, *Cycle*, 1:77. The reference is to 2 Kings 8:13.

52. Henry Adams to Charles Francis Adams Jr., December 28, 1861, in Ford, *Cycle*, 1:94.

53. Henry Adams, *Education*, 32.

54. Charles Francis Adams Jr. to Henry Adams, January 1862, in Ford, *Cycle*, 1:102–103.

55. Charles I. Glicksberg, "Henry Adams the Journalist," *New England Quarterly* 21 (1948): 232–236.

56. Henry Adams to Charles Francis Adams Jr., May 1, 1863, in Ford, *Cycle*, 1:281–282.

57. Mark A. Noll, *America's God: From Jonathan Edwards to Abraham Lincoln* (Oxford: Oxford University Press, 1992), 422–438; George N. Frederickson, *The Inner Civil War: Northern Intellectuals and the Crisis of the Union* (Urbana: University of Illinois Press, 1993); Nina Silber, *The Romance of Reunion: Northerners and the South, 1865–1900* (Chapel Hill: University of North Carolina Press, 1993); and Drew Gilpin Faust, *This Republic of Suffering: Death and the American Civil War* (New York: Knopf, 2008).

58. Henry Adams to Charles Francis Adams Sr., May 1 and 11, 1863, in Ford, *Cycle*, 1:281–282; 2:11–12.

59. When Charles Francis Adams Jr. presented his *Autobiography* (Boston: Houghton Mifflin, 1916), he asked that it not be read solely as a "memoir of war reminiscences," but those stories form its core. To compose it, he relied on battle-field diaries (which he then burned) and family letters (which he saved, now part of the Adams Family Papers—All Generations and Charles Francis Adams (Jr.) Papers collections at the Massachusetts Historical Society).

60. Charles Francis Adams Jr. to Henry Adams, April 6, 1862, in Ford, *Cycle*, 1:129.

61. "All is best, though we oft doubt, / What th'unsearchable dispose / Of highest wisdom brings about, / And ever best found in the close. / Oft he seems to hide his face, / But unexpectedly returns / And to his faithful Champion hath in place / Bore witness gloriously . . ." (lines 1745–1750). See also Matthew 25:14–30.

62. Charles Francis Adams Sr. to Charles Francis Adams Jr., June 17, 1864, in Ford, *Cycle*, 2:145–147.

63. Henry Adams to Charles Francis Adams Jr., May 21, 1869, in Ford, *Letters of Henry Adams*, 1:160.

64. Henry Adams to Charles Francis Adams Jr., June 5, 1860, in Levenson, *Letters of Henry Adams*, 1:xv.

65. Henry Adams to Charles Francis Adams Jr., November 16, 1867, in Levenson, *Letters of Henry Adams*, 1:557.

66. Henry Adams to Charles Francis Adams Jr., May 10, 1865, in Levenson, *Letters of Henry Adams*, 1:495–496.

67. Henry Adams to Charles Francis Adams Jr., September 25, 1863, in Ford, *Cycle*, 2:88.

68. Henry Adams to Henry Cabot Lodge, January 2, 1873, in Levenson, *Letters of Henry Adams*, 2:155.

69. Adams began his seminar with the rise of the (Direct) Capetian dynasty in France.

70. For Henry's 1871–1876 editorship, see Edward Chalfant, ed., *Sketches for the North American Review by Henry Adams* (Hamden, CT: Archon Books, 1982); Charles I. Glicksberg, "Henry Adams the Journalist," *New England Quarterly* 21 (1948): 232–236; and Joanne Jacobson, *Authority and Alliance in the Letters of Henry Adams* (Madison: University of Wisconsin Press, 1992).

71. Henry Adams to Charles Milnes Gaskell, March 26, 1872, in Levenson, *Letters of Henry Adams*, 3:133–134.

72. Catherine L. Albanese, "Exchanging Selves, Exchanging Souls," in *Retelling U.S. Religious History*, ed. Thomas A. Tweed (Berkeley: University of California Press, 1997), 200–226; Schmidt, *Restless Souls*; Hatch, *Democratization of American Christianity*.

73. The life and art of Clover Adams have received new attention thanks to the biographer Natalie Dykstra's *Clover: A Gilded and Heartbreaking Life* (Boston: Houghton Mifflin Harcourt, 2012). See also Otto Friedrich, *Clover* (New York: Simon and Schuster, 1979); Eugenia Kaledin, *The Education of Mrs. Henry Adams* (Philadelphia: Temple University Press, 1981); and Patricia O'Toole, *The Five of Hearts: An Intimate Portrait of Henry Adams and His Friends, 1880–1918* (New York: C. N. Potter, 1990).

74. *The Letters of Mrs. Henry Adams*, ed. Ward Thoron (Boston: Little, Brown, and Company, 1936), xiii.

75. Dykstra, *Clover*, 10, 109–115.

76. The newlyweds passed by two other notable Americans cruising the Nile that summer, an elderly Ralph Waldo Emerson and a teenage Theodore Roosevelt, for which see Benfey, *Great Wave*, 138.

77. Henry Adams and Marian Hooper Adams to Robert William Hooper, July 9–19, 1872, in Levenson, *Letters of Henry Adams*, 3:143–145. Clover photographed Henry at work in their stateroom on the *Isis* (Henry Adams and Marian Hooper Adams Photographs Collections, Massachusetts Historical Society).

78. On nineteenth-century American travel in the Middle East, see Lester Irwin Vogel, *To See a Promised Land: Americans and the Holy Land in the Nineteenth Century* (University Park: Pennsylvania State University Press, 1993); Brian Yothers, *The Romance of the Holy Land in American Travel Writing, 1790–1876* (Aldershot: Ashgate, 2007); and Stephanie Stidham Rogers, *Inventing the Holy Land: American Protestant Pilgrimage to Palestine, 1865–1941* (Lanham,

MD: Lexington Books, 2011). Brooks Adams covered some of the same ground in the early twentieth century.

79. Paula Sanders, *Creating Medieval Cairo: Empire, Religion, and Architectural Preservation in Nineteenth-Century Egypt* (Cairo: American University in Cairo Press, 2008).

80. Jeffrey Alan Melton, *Mark Twain, Travel Books, and Tourism: The Tide of a Great Popular Movement* (Tuscaloosa: University of Alabama Press, 2002); Vogel, *To See a Promised Land*; and Rogers, *Inventing the Holy Land*.

81. Rennella, *Boston Cosmopolitans*, 2, 7, 11–12; David A. Hollinger, *Postethnic America: Beyond Multiculturalism* (New York: Basic Books, 2000), 3–5, 84–88; Lutz, *Cosmopolitan Vistas*, 3; and Daniel T. Rogers, *Atlantic Crossings: Social Politics in a Progressive Age* (Cambridge, MA: Belknap Press of Harvard University Press, 1998).

82. Maureen E. Montgomery, "'Natural Distinction': The American Bourgeois Search for Distinctive Signs in Europe," in *The American Bourgeoisie: Distinction and Identity in the Nineteenth Century*, eds. Sven Beckert and Julie B. Rosenbaum (New York: Palgrave Macmillan, 2010), 27–44.

83. Clover Adams to Robert William Hooper, April 21, 1873, in Thoron, *Letters of M. H. Adams*, 99.

84. Clover Adams to Robert William Hooper, February 16, 1873, in Thoron, *Letters of M. H. Adams*, 75–76.

85. Clover Adams to Robert William Hooper, February 16, 1873, in Thoron, *Letters of M. H. Adams*, 75–76. The temple was restored and installed in the Metropolitan Museum of Art in New York City in 1978.

86. Clover Adams to Robert William Hooper, December 5, 1872, in Thoron, *Letters of M. H. Adams*, 60–61. Muslims mark the month of Ramadan with fasting and prayer; nineteenth-century American Christians like the Adamses often interpreted it as a Muslim version of Lent.

87. Clover Adams to Robert William Hooper, January 1, 1873, in Thoron, *Letters of M. H. Adams*, 64–65.

88. Henry Adams to Charles Milnes Gaskell, November 21, 1879, in Ford, *Cycle*, 1:317.

89. Henry Adams refined his theory of the scientific approach to history and its scholarly implications in three key essays: *The Tendency of History* (Washington, DC: Government Printing Office, 1896); "The Rule of Phase, Applied to History," in *The Degradation of Democratic Dogma*, ed. Brooks Adams (New York: Macmillan, 1919), 263–311; and *A Letter to American Teachers of History* (Washington, DC: Press of J. H. Furst Co., 1910).

90. See, for example, Roger Finke and Rodney Starke, "Turning Pews into People: Estimating 19th Century Church Membership," *Journal for the Scientific Study of Religion* 25 (1986): 180–192.

91. Amanda Porterfield and John Corrigan, eds., *Religion in American History* (Chichester: Wiley-Blackwell, 2010), 229–265; Ahlstrom and Hall, *Religious*

History, 763–872; and Andrew Preston, *Sword of the Spirit, Shield of Faith: Religion in American War and Diplomacy* (New York: Knopf, 2012).

92. Clover Adams to Robert William Hooper, May 13, 1883, in Thoron, *Letters of M. H. Adams*, 448.

93. Henry Adams to William James, July 27, 1882, in Levenson, *Letters of Henry Adams*, 3:464.

94. Clover Adams to Robert William Hooper, January 18 and February 5, 1882, in Thoron, *Letters of M. H. Adams*, 328, 329, 344.

95. Henry's authorship was not known until after his death. At times, Clover Adams, John Hay, and Clarence King were misidentified as the author of the wildly successful *Democracy* (New York: Henry Holt, 1908).

96. V. L. Parrington, *Main Currents in American Thought: An Interpretation of American Literature from the Beginnings to 1920*, vol. 3 (1927; repr., Norman: University of Oklahoma Press, 1987); James B. Salazar, *Bodies of Reform: The Rhetoric of Character in Gilded Age America* (New York: New York University Press, 2004); and Brooks D. Simpson, *The Political Education of Henry Adams* (Columbia: University of South Carolina Press, 1996).

97. David Mislin, "'Never Mind the Dead Men': The Damnation of Theron Ware and the Salvation of American Protestantism," *Journal of the Historical Society* 11 (2011): 463–491.

98. John Adams to John Taylor, December 17, 1814, Washburn Autograph Collection, Massachusetts Historical Society.

99. Henry Adams, *Democracy*, 5, 10, 12.

100. Henry Adams, *Democracy*, 22, 122.

101. Henry Adams, *Democracy*, 66, 76, 117.

102. Henry Adams, *Democracy*, 67.

103. Henry Adams, *Democracy*, 17.

104. Henry Adams, *Democracy*, 20.

105. Henry Adams, *Democracy*, 78–79.

106. Henry Adams, *Democracy*, 57.

107. Henry Adams, *Democracy*, 87–88, 91, 171.

108. Henry Adams, *Democracy*, 253.

109. Henry Adams, *Democracy*, 179.

110. Henry Adams, *Democracy*, 370.

111. Warren Adelson, *Sargent's Venice* (New Haven, CT: Yale University Press, 2006).

112. Clover Adams to Robert William Hooper, October 20, 1872; to Ellen Gurney, October 27, 1872, in Thoron, *Letters of M. H. Adams*, 52, 53.

113. Henry Adams to William James, July 27, 1882, in Levenson, *Letters of Henry Adams*, 3:464.

114. Dykstra, *Clover*; Friedrich, *Clover*; Kaledin, *Education of Mrs. Henry Adams*; and O'Toole, *Five of Hearts*.

115. Henry Adams to John Hay, August 23, 1886, in Levenson, *Letters of Henry Adams*, 3:34.

116. R. P. Blackmur, "The Novels of Henry Adams," *Sewanee Review* 51 (1943): 281–304; Edward N. Saveth, "The Heroines of Henry Adams," *American Quarterly* 8 (1956): 231–242; David F. Musto, "'Heart's Blood': Henry Adams's Esther and Wife Clover," *New England Quarterly* 71 (1998): 266–281; and Eric Rauchway, "Regarding Henry: The Feminist Henry Adams," *American Studies* 40 (1999): 53–73.

117. Henry Adams, *Esther*, 7.

118. Johnson and Lloyd, "Immanent God and Creative Man"; Conkin, *Uneasy Center*.

119. Henry Adams, *Mont-Saint-Michel and Chartres* (Cambridge, MA: Riverside Press, 1919), 198.

120. Richard F. Miller, "Henry Adams and the Influence of Woman," *American Literature* 18 (1947): 291–298; John Gatta, *American Madonna: Images of the Divine Woman in Literary Culture* (New York: Oxford University Press, 1997); and Jacobson, *Authority and Alliance*.

121. Key studies of how Gilded Age literature came to guide Progressive politics on issues related to gender, race, and urbanization include Eric J. Sundquist, *To Wake the Nations: Race in the Making of American Literature* (Cambridge, MA: Belknap Press of Harvard University Press, 1993); Judy Arlene Hilkey, *Character Is Capital: Success Manuals and Manhood in Gilded Age America* (Chapel Hill: University of North Carolina Press, 1997); Joel Shrock, *The Gilded Age* (Westport, CT: Greenwood Press, 2004), 39–40, 151–182; and Mark Storey, *Rural Fictions, Urban Realities: A Geography of Gilded Age American Literature* (New York: Oxford University Press, 2013).

122. Parrington, *Main Currents in American Thought*; Maurice S. Lee, *Uncertain Chances: Science, Skepticism, and Belief in Nineteenth-Century American Literature* (New York: Oxford University Press, 2012).

123. Henry Adams, *Esther*, 43–44.

124. James F. O'Gorman, ed., *The Makers of Trinity Church in the City of Boston* (Amherst: University of Massachusetts Press, 2004), 14–21.

125. Henry Adams, *Mont-Saint-Michel*; Miller, "Henry Adams and the Influence of Woman"; Gatta, *American Madonna*.

126. Ann Douglas, *The Feminization of American Culture* (New York: Knopf, 1977).

127. Henry Adams, *Esther*, 78.

128. On the growing acceptability of unbelief in late nineteenth-century America and its literary manifestations, see especially Turner, *Without God, without Creed*; and Lee, *Uncertain Chances*.

129. Henry Adams, *Esther*, 83.

130. Schwain, *Signs of Grace*; Morgan, *Protestants and Pictures*; and Lears, *No Place of Grace*.

131. Dykstra, *Clover*, 158–159.

132. Henry Adams, *Mont-Saint-Michel*, 145.

133. "Death of Mrs. Henry Adams," *Boston Herald*, December 7, 1885.

134. For sketches of the Adams monument and Henry's instructions, see Augustus Saint-Gaudens, *The Reminiscences of Augustus Saint-Gaudens* (New York: Century Co., 1913), 1:356–362; and Thoron, *Letters of M. H. Adams*, 455–459.

135. Sushil Madhava Pathak, *American Missionaries and Hinduism: A Study of Their Contacts from 1813 to 1910* (Delhi, India: Munshiram Manoharlal, 1967); Carl T. Jackson, *The Oriental Religions and American Thought: Nineteenth-Century Explorations* (Westport, CT: 1981); Tweed, *American Encounter with Buddhism*; Sibnarayan Ray, *Bengal Renaissance: The First Phase* (Calcutta, India: Minerva Associates, 2000); and Susan S. Bean, *Yankee India: American Commercial and Cultural Encounters with India in the Age of Sail, 1784–1860* (Salem, MA: Peabody Essex Museum, 2001).

136. William Sturgis Bigelow, *Buddhism and Immortality* (Boston: Houghton Mifflin, 1908), 75.

137. Henry Adams, *Esther*, 40.

138. Edward E. Salisbury, *Memoir on the History of Buddhism* (Boston: S. M. Dickinson, 1844), 7–8.

139. Samuel S. Hill, "Religion and the Results of the American Civil War," in *Religion and the American Civil War*, eds. Randall M. Miller, Harry S. Stout, and Charles Reagan Wilson (New York: Oxford University Press, 1998), 360–384; Tweed, *American Encounter with Buddhism*, 2–11; Rose, *Victorian America and the Civil War*; Susan Curtis, *A Consuming Faith: The Social Gospel and Modern American Culture* (Baltimore: Johns Hopkins University Press, 1991); and John L. Thomas, "Romantic Reform in America, 1815–1865," *American Quarterly* 17 (1965): 656–681.

140. Weir, *American Orient*, 78–79, 110–111, 177.

141. Henry Adams to Anne Palmer Fell, December 5, 1886, Adams Family Papers Additions, Massachusetts Historical Society. The Adams-Fell letters provide new insight into how Henry coped with Clover's death.

142. Henry Adams to Theodore F. Dwight, June 28, [1886], in Levenson, *Letters of Henry Adams*, 3:13. Dwight was Henry's personal secretary.

143. Henry Adams to John Hay, September 9, 1886, in Levenson, *Letters of Henry Adams*, 3:37.

144. Henry's Japanese tour is well documented in the letters he sent to secretary Theodore F. Dwight and others, selected and published in the third volume of Levenson, *Letters of Henry Adams*. See also Pierre Lagayette, "Henry Adams's Aesthetic Ragbag," *Revue française d'études américaines* 7 (1979): 17–30; Henry Adams, "The Mind of Henry Adams," in *John La Farge* (New York: Abbeville Press, 1987); James L. Yarnall, "John La Farge and Henry Adams in Japan," *American Art Journal* 21 (1989): 40–77; and Benfey, *Great Wave*, 105–107, 120, 128–157.

145. Henry Adams, *Education*, 489.

146. Henry Adams and Marian Hooper Adams Photographs Collections, Massachusetts Historical Society.

147. Alfred D. Chandler, *The Visible Hand: The Managerial Revolution in American Business* (Cambridge, MA: Belknap Press, 1977); Alan Trachtenberg, *The Incorporation of America: Culture and Society in the Gilded Age* (New York: Hill and Wang, 1982); T. J. Jackson Lears, "From Salvation to Self-Realization: Advertising and the Therapeutic Roots of the Consumer Culture, 1800–1930," in *The Culture of Consumption: Critical Essays in American History, 1880–1980*, ed. Richard Wightman Fox and T. J. Jackson Lears (New York: Pantheon, 1983), 1–38; Lears, *No Place of Grace*; and Morgan, *Protestants and Pictures*.

148. Henry Adams, "Japan Expenses," Notebook, Adams Papers.

149. Isaac Weiner, *Religion Out Loud: Religious Sound, Public Space, and American Pluralism* (New York: New York University Press, 2014).

150. Gillis J. Harp, *Positivist Republic: Auguste Comte and the Reconstruction of American Liberalism, 1865–1920* (University Park: Pennsylvania State University Press, 1995); D. H. Meyer, "The Victorian Crisis of Faith" in *Victorian America*, ed. Geoffrey Blodgett (Philadelphia: University of Pennsylvania Press, 1976); Jean de Groot, ed., "Homegrown Positivism: Charles Darwin and Chauncey Wright," in *Nature in American Philosophy* (Washington, DC: Catholic University of America Press, 2004), 53–71; Keith Newlin, ed., *The Oxford Handbook of American Literary Naturalism* (New York: Oxford University Press, 2011); Donald Pizer, *Realism and Naturalism in Nineteenth-Century American Literature* (Carbondale: Southern Illinois University Press, 1966); and Henry F. May, *Protestant Churches and Industrial America* (New York: Harper and Row, 1967).

151. Henry Adams to Brooks Adams, August 8, 1899, Adams Papers.

152. Carl T. Jackson, *A Vedanta for the West: The Ramakrishna Movement in the United States* (Bloomington: Indiana University Press, 1994); Timothy Miller, ed., *America's Alternative Religions* (Albany: State University of New York Press, 1995), 173–179; and Richard Hughes Seager, *The World's Parliament of Religions: The East/West Encounter, Chicago, 1893* (Bloomington: Indiana University Press, 1995).

153. Amanda Porterfield, *The Protestant Experience in America* (Westport, CT: Greenwood Press, 2006), 192–194.

154. Henry Adams to Brooks Adams, January 24, 1896, Adams Papers.

155. Henry Adams to Brooks Adams, April 2, 1896, Adams Papers.

156. See, for example, Jonathan D. Sarna, ed., *Minority Faiths and the American Protestant Mainstream* (Urbana: University of Illinois Press, 1998); Naomi W. Cohen, "Antisemitism in the Gilded Age: The Jewish View," *Jewish Social Studies* 41 (1979): 187–210; and John Higham, *Strangers in the Land: Patterns of American Nativism, 1860–1925* (New Brunswick, NJ: Rutgers University Press, 1955).

157. Henry Adams to Charles Milnes Gaskell, October 6, 1895, in Levenson, *Letters of Henry Adams*, 4:333.

158. Henry Adams to Elizabeth Cameron, July 15, 1891, in Ford, *Letters of Henry Adams*, 1:507.

159. On Henry's intense intellectual attraction to Buddhism, see Vern Wagner, "The Lotus of Henry Adams," *New England Quarterly* 27 (1964): 75–94.

160. Henry Adams to Elizabeth Cameron, September 13, 1891, in Ford, *Letters of Henry Adams*, 1:523–527.

161. Henry Adams, "Buddha and Brāhma," *Yale Review* 5 (October 1915): 82–89.

162. Gaston Migeon, *Art et Décoration*, cited in Saint-Gaudens, *Reminiscences*, 1:366.

163. Henry Adams to Brooks Adams, March 4, 1900, Adams Papers.

164. Peter Novick, *That Noble Dream: The "Objectivity Question" and the American Historical Profession* (Cambridge: Cambridge University Press, 1988).

165. Gavin Kendall, ed., "Introduction," in *The Sociology of Cosmopolitanism* (New York: Palgrave Macmillan, 2009), 25–26. Kendall defines cosmopolitans as transcultural actors rooted in first-world privilege, and argues that the philosophy is a route to developing a "moral self" *and* the specialist knowledge needed to form communities of interest/activism. "Cosmopolitanism is an intellectual and political project," Kendall argues, "that makes the promise of a global civil society" (149). To connect this with the post-Enlightenment philosophy that Henry's generation inherited, see Roland Pierik and Wouter Werner, eds., *Cosmopolitanism in Context: Perspectives from International Law and Political Theory* (Cambridge: Cambridge University Press, 2010); and Kleingeld, *Kant and Cosmopolitanism*. For a medieval version of the same theme, centered on exploring sites of exchange for Christian universalists (a practice that often "demonized cultural differences"), and one that Henry likely favored, see John M. Ganim and Shayne Aaron Legassie, eds., *Cosmopolitanism in the Middle Ages* (New York: Palgrave Macmillan, 2013).

166. For Henry Adams's scientific approach to history, see his *Tendency of History*; "The Rule of Phase, Applied to History," 263–311; and *A Letter to American Teachers of History*.

167. Henry Adams to Charles Milnes Gaskell, April 18, 1871, in Levenson, *Letters of Henry Adams*, 2:106–107.

168. Dorothy Ross, *The Origins of American Social Science* (Cambridge: Cambridge University Press, 1991); Novick, *That Noble Dream*; and Thomas L. Haskell, *Objectivity Is Not Neutrality: Explanatory Schemes in History* (Baltimore: Johns Hopkins University Press, 1998).

169. Meyer, "The Victorian Crisis of Faith," 77.

170. Teith R. Burich, "Henry Adams, the Second Law of Thermodynamics, and the Course of History," *Journal of the History of Ideas* 48 (1987): 467–482.

171. Henry tweaked his phrasing of the law when he wrote about it in the context of history writing, and brother Brooks would do the same.

172. See, especially, Ernst Scheyer, "Henry Adams 'Monte-Saint-Michel and Chartres,'" *Journal of the Society of Architectural Historians* 13 (1954): 3–10; and John P. McIntyre, "Henry Adams and the Unity of Chartres," *Twentieth Century Literature* 7 (1962): 159–171.

173. Mark Edwards, "'My God and My Good Mother': The Irony of Horace Bushnell's Gendered Republic," *Religion and American Culture: A Journal of Interpretation* 13 (2003): 111–137.

174. Henry Adams, *Mont-Saint-Michel*, 44.

175. Henry Adams, *Mont-Saint-Michel*, 1.

176. Henry Adams to Brooks Adams, February 18, 1896, Adams Papers. The Roman Catholic archbishop John Joseph Keane was a frequent visitor to Henry's Washington, DC, home.

177. Henry Adams to Mabel Hooper La Farge, April 29, 1902, in Levenson, *Letters of Henry Adams*, 5:381.

178. Henry Adams to Mabel Hooper La Farge, June 17, 1902, in Levenson, *Letters of Henry Adams*, 6:25. Henry leased an 18-horsepower Mercedes at eighty pounds per month during his 1904–1905 tour of French cathedrals. He made frequent mention of "the machine" and its costly repairs in his letters (same, 5:591–607 passim, 654–687 passim, 705, 715; 6:147).

179. Henry Adams to Ward Thoron, July 28, 1914, in Levenson, *Letters of Henry Adams*, 6:654.

Chapter 5

1. Scrapbooks and loose photographs, Henry Adams Photograph Collection, Massachusetts Historical Society.

2. Laurel A. Racine, *Historic Furnishings Report: The Birthplaces of Presidents John Adams and John Quincy Adams*, 10 vols. (Charlestown, MA: Northeast Museum Services Center, National Park Service, 2001), 4:423–426; 5:508–514. I am grateful to Adams National Historical Park deputy superintendent Caroline Keinath and her staff, who shared their expert knowledge of the site on multiple research visits between October 2009 and May 2014.

3. Thornton Anderson, *Brooks Adams: Constructive Conservative* (Ithaca, NY: Cornell University Press, 1951), xiii.

4. Brooks's political thought has drawn attention, but the entirety of his life and work has attracted few full-scale biographies. Mainly, scholars sketch Brooks's religious explorations by placing him within the "Adams tribe" of Protestant presidents and public intellectuals. The key texts are Charles A. Madison, "Brooks Adams, Caustic Cassandra," *American Scholar* 9 (1940): 214–227; Anderson, *Brooks Adams*; Arthur F. Beringause, *Brooks Adams: A Biography* (New York: Knopf, 1955); Timothy Paul Donovan, *Henry Adams and Brooks Adams: The Education of Two American Historians* (Norman: University of Oklahoma Press, 1961); Abigail Adams Homans, *Education by Uncles* (Boston: Houghton Mifflin,

1966); Wilhelmina S. Harris, "The Brooks Adams I Knew," *Proceedings of the Massachusetts Historical Society*, 3d ser., 80 (1968): 94–113; Paul C. Nagel, "Brooks Adams after Half a Century," *Proceedings of the Massachusetts Historical Society*, 3d ser., 90 (1978): 38–57; and Nagel, *Descent from Glory: Four Generations of the John Adams Family* (Cambridge, MA: Harvard University Press, 1999). See also Perry Miller's introduction to the 1962 edition of Brooks Adams, *The Emancipation of Massachusetts* (Boston: Houghton Mifflin), v–xl.

5. Daniel Aaron, "The Unusable Man: An Essay on the Mind of Brooks Adams," *New England Quarterly* 21 (1948): 3–33. This description has been variously attributed to Brooks, to his nieces, and to Theodore Roosevelt. Henry often attacked his brother's writing as "damnably superfluous," as with Brooks's unpublished [ca. 1905–1909] biography of John Quincy Adams, a typescript of which is held in the Adams Papers along with a copy of Henry's many edits.

6. Charles Hirschfeld, "Brooks Adams and American Nationalism," *American Historical Review* 69 (1964): 371–392.

7. Brooks Adams to Henry Cabot Lodge [ca. 1894], Henry Cabot Lodge Papers, Massachusetts Historical Society.

8. James Turner, *Without God, without Creed: The Origins of Unbelief in America* (Baltimore: John Hopkins University Press, 1985); Margaret Bendroth, *The Last Puritans: Mainline Protestants and the Power of the Past* (Chapel Hill: University of North Carolina Press, 2015).

9. Bendroth, *The Last Puritans*, 3.

10. Charles Francis Adams Jr., *Charles Francis Adams, 1835–1915: An Autobiography* (Boston: Houghton Mifflin, 1916), 13–14.

11. Abigail Brooks Adams to Henry Adams, January 30, 1859; Mary Louisa Adams to Henry Adams, August 20, 1860, Adams Papers.

12. Abigail Brooks Adams to Henry Adams, January 4, 1860, Adams Papers.

13. Rennella, *The Boston Cosmopolitans: International Travel and American Arts and Letters* (New York: Palgrave Macmillan, 2008), 18–19; Joel Shrock, *The Gilded Age* (Westport, CT: Greenwood Press, 2004), 122–123; Sean Dennis Cashman, *America in the Gilded Age: From the Death of Lincoln to the Rise of Theodore Roosevelt* (New York: New York University Press, 1993); John F. Kasson, *Amusing the Million: Coney Island at the Turn of the Century* (New York: Hill and Wang, 1978); and Robert W. Rydell, *All the World's a Fair: Visions of Empire at American International Expositions, 1876–1916* (Chicago: University of Chicago Press, 1984).

14. Beringause, *Brooks Adams*, 24–35.

15. Henry Adams to Charles Francis Adams Jr., December 24, 1863, Adams Papers.

16. Henry Adams, *The Education of Henry Adams* (Cambridge, MA: Riverside Press, 1918), 55.

17. Jon H. Roberts and James Turner, *The Sacred and the Secular University* (Princeton, NJ: Princeton University Press, 2000); George M. Marsden, *The Soul of the American University: From Protestant Establishment to Established Nonbelief*

(New York: Oxford University Press, 1994; and James Tunstead Burchtaell, *The Dying of the Light: The Disengagement of Colleges and Universities from Their Christian Churches* (Grand Rapids, MI: Eerdmans, 1998).

18. Marsden, *The Soul of the American University*, 181–195. See also Charles William Norton, "The New Education," *Atlantic Monthly*, February 1869, 203–220; and Hugh Hawkins, "Charles W. Eliot, University Reform, and Religious Faith in America, 1869–1909," *Journal of American History* 51 (1964): 191–213.

19. Beringause, *Brooks Adams*, 39–44.

20. Brooks Adams to Charles Francis Adams Sr., March 24, 1868, Adams Papers.

21. Brooks Adams to Charles Francis Adams Sr., March 24, 1868.

22. Anderson, *Brooks Adams*, 20.

23. Charles Francis Sr., secured a $15.5 million damages settlement in gold from Great Britain to compensate for British-built Confederate cruisers' attacks on Union ships. For the negotiations that resolved the "Alabama Claims," and for Brooks's service as his secretary, see Martin B. Duberman, *Charles Francis Adams, 1807–1886* (Boston: Houghton Mifflin, 1961); Frank Warren Hackett, *Reminiscences of the Geneva Tribunal of Arbitration, 1872, The Alabama Claims* (Boston: Houghton Mifflin, 1911); and Beringause, *Brooks Adams*, 50–53.

24. Many of Brooks's political editorials were unsigned or published with "anonymous" bylines, but two scrapbooks kept at the Adams National Historical Park confirm his authorship.

25. Beringause, *Brooks Adams*, 63–67.

26. Beringause, *Brooks Adams*, 63–67.

27. See, for example, Henry Adams to Brooks Adams, March 3, 1872, in *The Letters of Henry Adams*, 6 vols., ed. J. C. Levenson et al. (Cambridge, MA: Belknap Press of Harvard University Press, 1982–1988), 3:131–132.

28. Brooks Adams to Charles Deane, July 8, 1885, Charles Deane Papers, Massachusetts Historical Society.

29. Also known as the "Schoolroom Poets," Longfellow and William Cullen Bryant, John Greenleaf Whittier, James Russell Lowell, and Oliver Wendell Holmes Sr. all used early American storytelling and popular poetics to "teach" aspects of good moral character. See Thomas Wortham, "Bryant and the Fireside Poets," in *The Columbia Literary History of the United Sates*, ed. Emory Elliott et al. (New York: Columbia University Press, 1988), 278–288.

30. Gretchen A. Adams, *The Specter of Salem: Remembering the Witch Trials in Nineteenth-Century America* (Chicago: University of Chicago Press, 2008); Bendroth, *The Last Puritans*; and Joseph A. Conforti, *Imagining New England: Explorations of Regional Identity from the Pilgrims to the Mid-twentieth Century* (Chapel Hill: University of North Carolina Press, 2001).

31. "THE CONGREGATIONALISTS: The National Council of Orthodox Congregational Churches," *New York Times*, June 18, 1865; "Declaration of Faith," *The Farmer's Cabinet* (Amherst, NH), June 29, 1865.

32. "Orthodoxy and Puritanism," *Boston Investigator*, July 5, 1865.

33. "Sabbath Observance—Evangelicals," *Boston Investigator*, January 21, 1880. The author refers to the Congregationalist Samuel Hopkins (1721–1803), a Calvinist theologian active in John and Abigail Adams's era.

34. "Business in Religion and Religion in Business," *The Farmer's Cabinet* (Amherst, NH), November 12, 1868. See Carroll Smith-Rosenberg, *Religion and the Rise of the American City: The New York City Mission Movement, 1812–1870* (Ithaca, NY: Cornell University Press, 1971); John Tomsich, *A Genteel Endeavor: American Culture and Politics in the Gilded Age* (Stanford, CA: Stanford University Press, 1971); and Frederic Cople Jaher, *The Urban Establishment: Upper Strata in Boston, New York, Charleston, Chicago, and Los Angeles* (Urbana, IL: University of Illinois Press, 1982).

35. "Oration Delivered by Hon. S. L. Spink at Yankton, D. T., July 4th, 1865," *Union and Dakotaian* (Yankton, SD), July 15, 1865.

36. "The City," *Galveston Daily News*, January 2, 1880.

37. "Shall We Give Up Our Puritan Faith?," *Vermont Chronicle* (Burlington, VT), July 1, 1865.

38. Brooks Adams, *Emancipation*, 215–216, 349.

39. Brooks persisted with this theory of history writing throughout his life, most notably in the *Emancipation*, *The Law of Civilization and Decay: An Essay on History* (New York: Vintage Books, 1955 ed.), and *The Theory of Social Revolutions* (New York: Macmillan, 1913). Several comprehensive studies of Brooks's theories appear in Anderson, *Brooks Adams*; Beringause, *Brooks Adams*; Donovan, *Henry Adams and Brooks Adams*; and Robert L. Beisner, "Brooks Adams and Charles Francis Adams Jr.: Historians of Massachusetts," *New England Quarterly* 35 (1962): 48–70.

40. Brooks Adams, *Emancipation*, 213.

41. Brooks Adams to Charles Deane, July 8, 1885, Charles Deane Papers. See also his letters to Deane of January 13 and 26, 1886, and September 14, 1887.

42. Brooks Adams, *Emancipation*, 235–248; David D. Hall, ed., *The Antinomian Controversy, 1636–1638: A Documentary History* (Durham, NC: Duke University Press, 1990), i–xvii; and Timothy D. Hall, "Assurance, Community, and the Puritan Self in the Antinomian Controversy, 1636–38," in *Puritanism and Its Discontents*, ed. Laura Lunger Knoppers (Newark: University of Delaware Press, 2003), 197–209.

43. Brooks Adams, *Emancipation*, 311–348.

44. Brooks Adams, *Emancipation*, 212, 397; Beringause, *Brooks Adams*, 80–94.

45. Brooks Adams, *Emancipation*, 171–213.

46. Brooks Adams, *Emancipation*, 174.

47. Brooks Adams, *Emancipation*, 197.

48. Brooks Adams, *Emancipation*, 209–212, 249–274.

49. Brooks Adams, *Emancipation*, 249.

50. On the Quaker experience in early America, see Thomas. D. Hamm, *The Quakers in America* (New York: Columbia University Press, 2003); Carla Gardina Pestana, *Quakers and Baptists in Colonial Massachusetts* (Cambridge: Cambridge University Press, 1991); and Mary Maples Dunn, "Saints and Sisters: Congregational and Quaker Women in the Early Colonial Period," *American Quarterly* 30 (1978): 582–601.

51. Brooks Adams, *Emancipation*, 298–348.

52. Brooks Adams, *Emancipation*, 319.

53. Brooks Adams, *Emancipation*, 318–319.

54. Brooks Adams, *Emancipation*, 212.

55. Brooks Adams, *Emancipation*, 386–406. The literature on the Salem witchcraft trials and their legacy is immense, but see, for example, Gretchen Adams, *Specter of Salem*; Emerson W. Baker, *A Storm of Witchcraft: The Salem Trials and the American Experience* (New York: Oxford University Press, 2014); Paul S. Boyer and Stephen Nissenbaum, *Salem Possessed: The Social Origins of Witchcraft* (Cambridge, MA: Harvard University Press, 1974); Carol F. Karlsen, *The Devil in the Shape of a Woman: Witchcraft in Colonial New England* (New York: Norton, 1987); Mary Beth Norton, *In the Devil's Snare: The Salem Witchcraft Crisis of 1692* (New York: Knopf, 2002); and Perry Miller, *The New England Mind*, 2 vols. (Boston: Beacon Press, 1961).

56. Brooks Adams, *Emancipation*, 393.

57. Brooks Adams, *Emancipation*, 407–483.

58. Brooks Adams to Charles Deane, January 26, 1886, Charles Deane Papers.

59. Brooks Adams, *Emancipation*, 407–408.

60. Brooks Adams, *Emancipation*, 533–534.

61. Brooks Adams, *Emancipation*, 486.

62. Brooks Adams, *Emancipation*, 205.

63. Brooks Adams to Charles Deane, January 26, 1886, Charles Deane Papers.

64. "Adams's *Emancipation of Massachusetts*," *The Nation* 44 (1887): 189–190. For a wider view of the book's critical reception, see also Perry Miller's "Introduction" to the 1962 edition, xviii–xxvii.

65. Brooks Adams to Henry Adams, March 10, 1887, Henry Adams Papers, Houghton Library, Harvard University.

66. "Adams-Davis," *Boston Daily Globe*, September 9, 1889. It was a three-week courtship.

67. See, for example, "Women Were Interested. Pres Andrews and Hon. Brooks Adams Enlighten Them on 'Honest Money' at the Mystic Valley Club Dinner," *Boston Daily Globe*, May 22, 1895.

68. Brooks Adams to Henry Adams, March 22, 1887, Henry Adams Papers, Houghton Library.

69. Anderson, *Brooks Adams*, 44–100; and Beringause, *Brooks Adams*, 95–210. Brooks's comments on Indian culture and economy appear most in his letters to Henry,

dated December 23, 1895, to April 22, 1896, Henry Adams Papers, Houghton Library.

70. The Adams family suffered serious losses in the financial panic of 1893.

71. Henry Adams to Brooks Adams, June 5, 1905, in Levenson, *Letters of Henry Adams*, 5:668.

72. Brooks Adams to Henry Adams, September 21, 1895, Henry Adams Papers, Houghton Library.

73. Brooks Adams to Charles Deane, January 26, 1886, Charles Deane Papers.

74. Brooks Adams, *Law of Civilization and Decay*, 3–7.

75. Anderson, *Brooks Adams*, 44–72; Beringause, *Brooks Adams*, 104–143; Gary Marotta, "The Economics of American Empire: The View of Brooks Adams and Charles Arthur Conant," *American Economist* 19 (1975): 34–37; and Madison, "Brooks Adams, Caustic Cassandra."

76. Brooks Adams to Henry Adams, May 14, 1895, Henry Adams Papers, Houghton Library.

77. Brooks Adams to Henry Adams, May 14, 1895.

78. Susan Curtis, *A Consuming Faith: The Social Gospel and Modern American Culture* (Baltimore: Johns Hopkins University Press, 1991); Ronald C. White and C. Howard Hopkins, *The Social Gospel: Religion and Reform in Changing America* (Philadelphia: Temple University Press, 1976); and Sydney E. Ahlstrom and David D. Hall, *A Religious History of the American People* (New Haven, CT: Yale University Press, 2004), 785–804.

79. Washington Gladden, *Working People and Their Employers* (London: Funk and Wagnalls, 1894).

80. Rauschenbusch, quoted in White and Hopkins, *Social Gospel*, 36.

81. Wendy J. Deichman Edwards and Carolyn De Swarte Gifford, *Gender and the Social Gospel* (Urbana: University of Illinois Press, 2003); Kathryn Kish Sklar, "Hull House in the 1890s: A Community of Women Reformers," *Signs* 10 (1985): 658–677; Curtis, *A Consuming Faith*; White and Hopkins, *Social Gospel*.

82. Milton Friedman and Anna Jacobson Schwartz, *A Monetary History of the United States, 1867–1960* (Princeton, NJ: Princeton University Press), 108–122; W. Jett Lauck, *The Causes of the Panic of 1893* (Boston: Houghton, Mifflin, 1907).

83. Brooks Adams, *Law of Civilization and Decay*, 3–7; and see also Brooks Adams to William James, April 16, 1887, William James Papers, Houghton Library, Harvard University. On the wide-ranging reaction to and use of English scientist Charles Darwin's theories of natural selection in American thought and culture, see, for example, Jon H. Roberts, *Darwinism and the Divine in America: Protestant Intellectuals and Organic Evolution, 1859–1900* (Madison: University of Wisconsin Press, 1988); and Ronald L. Numbers and John Stenhouse, eds., *Disseminating Darwinism: The Role of Place, Race, Religion, and Gender* (New York: Cambridge University Press, 1999).

84. Brooks Adams, "The Heritage of Henry Adams," in Henry Adams, *The Degradation of the Democratic Dogma* (New York: Macmillan, 1920), 99.

85. Brooks Adams to Henry Adams, June 30, 1895, Henry Adams Papers, Houghton Library.

86. Brooks Adams to William James, April 16, 1887, William James Papers, Houghton Library.

87. Brooks Adams, *Law of Civilization and Decay*, 304.

88. Brooks Adams, *Law of Civilization and Decay*, 285–208; and Vincent J. Cannato, *American Passage: The History of Ellis Island* (New York: Harper, 2009).

89. Oliver Wendell Holmes Sr., to Sir Frederick Pollock, October 21, 1895, in *Holmes-Pollock Letters: The Correspondence of Mr. Justice Holmes and Sir Frederick Pollock, 1874–1932*, 2 vols., ed. Mark A. DeWolfe-Howe (Littleton, CO: F. B. Rothman, 1994), 1:64.

90. See, for example, Brooks Adams's letters to Henry Adams of February 26, August 17, and October 28, 1896, Henry Adams Papers, Houghton Library.

91. Benjamin S. Terry, "Review: *The Law of Civilization and Decay*," *American Journal of Sociology* 2 (1896): 467–472.

92. Henry Adams to Elizabeth Cameron, October 4, 1894, Adams-Cameron Letters, Massachusetts Historical Society.

93. "Mr. Brooks Adams, Gadfly," *Boston Daily Globe*, November 20, 1915.

94. Brooks Adams, "Unity in Modern Education: General View, Historical and Psychological," *Boston University School of Law Bulletins of Year, 1908*, 9–11.

95. Brooks Adams and Melville M. Bigelow, *Centralization and the Law: Scientific Legal Education, An Illustration* (Boston: Little, Brown, 1906).

96. Brooks Adams to Henry Adams, October 13, 1901, Henry Adams Papers, Houghton Library.

97. "Many Evils to Right," *Boston Daily Globe*, November 29, 1907.

98. Brooks Adams, *Address by Brooks Adams at the 275th Anniversary of the First Parish Church, Quincy, 11 October, 1914* (Quincy, MA: s.n., 1914).

99. "Assumes His New Pastorate: Rev. Adelbert L. Hudson Becomes Pastor of First Church," *Quincy Daily Ledger*, March 4, 1912.

100. Records, Registers, and Scrapbooks of United First Parish Church, Quincy, Massachusetts. See also Sheldon W. Bennett, *Freedom, Friendship, and Faith: A Noble Heritage through 350 Years* (Quincy, MA: United First Parish Church [Unitarian], 350th Anniversary Booklet, 1989); and Peggy A. Albee et al., *United First Parish Church (Unitarian) Church of the Presidents Historic Structure Report* (Lowell, MA: Northeast Cultural Resources Center for National Park Service).

101. Brooks Adams, *Address*.

102. Gospel of Mark 9:24.

103. Beringause, *Brooks Adams*, 385–386.

104. Philip Goff and Paul Harvey, eds., *Themes in Religion and American Culture* (Chapel Hill: University of North Carolina Press, 2004); Randall Balmer, *Religion*

in Twentieth Century America (New York: Oxford University Press, 2001); Mark Hulsether, *Religion, Culture and Politics in the Twentieth-Century United States* (New York: Columbia University Press, 2007); Harry S. Stout and D. G. Hart, eds., *New Directions in American Religious History* (New York: Oxford University Press, 1997); Michael J. Lacey, ed., *Religion and Twentieth-Century American Intellectual Life* (New York: Cambridge University Press, 1989); T. J. Jackson Lears, *No Place of Grace: Antimodernism and the Transformation of American Culture, 1880–1920* (New York: Pantheon Books, 1981); Lears, *Rebirth of a Nation: The Making of Modern America, 1877–1920* (New York: HarperCollins, 2009); and Paul A. Carter, *The Spiritual Crisis of the Gilded Age* (DeKalb: Northern Illinois University Press, 1971).

105. Goff and Harvey, *Themes in Religion and American Culture.*

106. "Obituary, Mrs. Brooks Adams," *Boston Daily Globe,* December 15, 1926.

107. For the nature of Brooks's relationship with Bellamy Storer and the friars of Portsmouth Abbey, described here and later, see Leonard Sargent, "An Adams in a Monastery," *Commonweal* 13 (1930): 156–157.

108. Gordon Beattie, *Gregory's Angels: A History of the Abbeys, Priories, Parishes and Schools of the Monks and Nuns Following the Rule of Saint Benedict in Great Britain, Ireland and Their Overseas Foundations* (Leominster: Gracewing, 1997), 149.

109. Sargent, "An Adams in a Monastery"; and Beringause, *Brooks Adams,* 385–386.

110. *Journal of the Constitutional Convention of the Commonwealth of Massachusetts, 1917* (Boston: Wright and Potter, 1917–1919); John Allen Hague, "The Massachusetts Constitutional Convention: 1917–1919: A Study of Dogmatism in an Age of Transition," *New England Quarterly* 27 (1954): 147–167; Augustus Peabody Loring, "A Short Account of the Massachusetts Constitutional Convention 1917–1919," *New England Quarterly* 6 (1933): 1–99; and Hirschfeld, "Brooks Adams and American Nationalism."

111. Brooks Adams, *Emancipation,* 3–168.

112. Brooks Adams, *Emancipation,* 167, 168.

113. Lester I. Vogel, *To See a Promised Land: Americans and the Holy Land in the Nineteenth Century* (University Park: Pennsylvania State University Press, 1993); Stephanie Sidham Rogers, *Inventing the Holy Land: American Protestant Pilgrimage to Palestine, 1865–1941* (Lanham, MD: Lexington Books, 2011); and Hillary Kaell, *Walking Where Jesus Walked: American Christians and Holy Land Pilgrimage* (New York: New York University Press, 2014).

114. Charles Sr.'s set resides at the Adams National Historical Park, just outside Brooks's bedroom.

115. Marc Friedlaender, "Brooks Adams 'en Famille,'" *Proceedings of the Massachusetts Historical Society,* 3d ser., 80 (1968): 77–93; and Wilhelmina S. Harris, *Adams National Historic Site: A Family's Legacy to America* (Washington, DC: US Department of the Interior, National Park Service, 1983).

116. Friedlaender, "Brooks Adams 'en Famille.'"

117. Thomas A. Tweed, *Crossing and Dwelling: A Theory of Religion* (Cambridge, MA: Harvard University Press, 2006).

Epilogue

1. Kariann Yokota, *Unbecoming British: How Revolutionary America Became a Postcolonial Nation* (Oxford: Oxford University Press, 2011).
2. Abigail Adams to John Quincy Adams, July 21, 1786, in *Adams Family Correspondence*, 13 vols., ed. Sara Martin et al. (Cambridge, MA: Belknap Press of Harvard University Press, 1963–), 7:276.
3. Martha Banta, "Being a 'Begonia' in a Man's World," in *New Essays on the Education of Henry Adams*, ed. John Carlos Rowe (Cambridge: Cambridge University Press, 1996), 53.
4. Many important works exist to outline the momentous shifts in religion and culture that the Victorian Adamses experienced and reflected upon, including R. W. B. Lewis, *The American Adam: Innocence, Tragedy and Tradition in the Nineteenth Century* (Chicago: University of Chicago Press, 1955); D. H. Meyer, *The Instructed Conscience: The Shaping of the American National Ethic* (Philadelphia: University of Pennsylvania Press, 1972); Clive Bush, *The Dream of Reason: American Consciousness and Cultural Achievement from Independence to the Civil War* (London: Edward Arnold, 1977); Harold P. Simonson, *Radical Discontinuities: American Romanticism and Christian Consciousness* (Rutherford, NJ: Fairleigh Dickinson University Press, 1983); David Morse, *American Romanticism*, vol. 1, *From Cooper to Hawthorne* (Totowa, NJ: Barnes and Noble Books, 1987); Conrad Edick Wright, ed., *American Unitarianism, 1805–1865* (Boston: Massachusetts Historical Society and Northeastern University Press, 1989); Lewis Perry, *Boats against the Current: American Culture between Revolution and Modernity, 1820–1860* (New York: Oxford University Press, 1993); Anne C. Rose, "Religious Individualism in Nineteenth-Century American Families," in *Perspectives on American Religion and Culture*, ed. Peter W. Williams (Malden, MA: Blackwell, 1999); James E. Block, *A Nation of Agents: The American Path to a Modern Self and Society* (Cambridge, MA: Belknap Press of Harvard University Press, 2002); John Gatta, *Making Nature Sacred: Literature, Religion, and Environment in America from the Puritans to the Present* (New York: Oxford University Press, 2004); Daniel Walker Howe, *What Hath God Wrought: The Transformation of America, 1815–1848* (New York: Oxford University Press, 2007); Paul E. Johnson, *The Early American Republic, 1789–1829* (New York: Oxford University Press, 2007); and Lorman Ratner, Paula T. Kaufman, and Dwight L. Teeter, Jr., *Paradoxes of Prosperity: Wealth-Seeking versus Christian Values in Pre–Civil War America* (Urbana: University of Illinois Press, 2009).
5. On the Puritan roots and the un-Puritan manifestations of civil religion in the early republic, see William De Loss Love, *The Fast and Thanksgiving Days of New England* (Boston: Houghton, Mifflin, 1895), and David Waldstreicher, *In the*

Midst of Perpetual Fetes: The Making of American Nationalism, 1776–1820 (Chapel Hill: University of North Carolina Press, 1997). The comprehensive account of the era's plague remains Charles E. Rosenberg's *The Cholera Years: The United States in 1832, 1849, and 1866* (Chicago: University of Chicago Press, 1962).

6. John Quincy Adams, Diary, December 31, 1812, Adams Papers.

7. Explorations of American Victorianism and the intellectual legacy of the Civil War also round out the story of the Adams family's religious development, including William G. McLoughlin, *The Meaning of Henry Ward Beecher: An Essay on the Shifting Values of Mid-Victorian America, 1840–1870* (New York: Knopf, 1970); Geoffrey Blodgett, ed., *Victorian America* (Philadelphia: University of Pennsylvania Press, 1976); Irving H. Bartlett, *The American Mind in the Mid-nineteenth Century* (Arlington Heights, IL: H. Davidson, 1982); Burton Raffel, *American Victorians: Explorations in Emotional History* (Hamden, CT: Archon Books, 1984); Thomas J. Schlereth, *Victorian America: Transformations in Everyday Life, 1876–1915* (New York: HarperCollins, 1991); Steve Ickingrill, Stephen Mills, and H.C. Allen, *Victorianism in the United States: Its Era and Its Legacy* (Amsterdam: VU University Press, 1992); and Anne C. Rose, *Victorian America and the Civil War* (New York: Cambridge University Press, 1992).

8. E. Brooks Holifield, *Theology in America: Christian Thought from the Age of the Puritans to the Civil War* (New Haven, CT: Yale University Press, 2003).

9. Charles Francis Adams, August 19, 1832, in *The Diary of Charles Francis Adams*, 8 vols., ed. Aida DiPace Donald and David Donald (Cambridge, MA: Belknap Press of Harvard University Press, 1964–), 4:348–349.

10. For this synthesis of American religion, see Mark A. Noll, *America's God: From Jonathan Edwards to Abraham Lincoln* (Oxford: Oxford University Press, 1992).

11. On the parallel paths of Christianity and democracy in America, see Sidney E. Mead, *The Lively Experiment: The Shaping of Christianity in America* (New York: Harper and Row, 1963); Jon Butler, *Awash in a Sea of Faith: Christianizing the American People* (Cambridge, MA: Harvard University Press, 1990); Noll, *America's God*; Mark A. Noll and Luke E. Harlow, eds., *Religion and American Politics: From the Colonial Period to the Present* (Oxford: Oxford University Press, 2007); James H. Hutson, *Church and State in America: The First Two Centuries* (New York: Cambridge University Press, 2008); and Andrew R. Murphy, *Prodigal Nation: Moral Decline and Divine Punishment from New England to 9/11* (Oxford: Oxford University Press, 2009).

12. David W. Mislin, *Saving Faith: Making Religious Pluralism an American Value at the Dawn of the Secular Age* (Ithaca, NY: Cornell University Press, 2015).

13. Thomas A. Tweed, *Crossing and Dwelling: A Theory of Religion* (Cambridge, MA: Harvard University Press, 2006).

14. For Henry's and brother Brooks's roles as prominent Victorian intellectuals, the genesis of cosmopolitan critique, and the cultural complexity of administering meaningful social reform in the Gilded Age, see Paul A. Carter, *The Spiritual*

Crisis of the Gilded Age (DeKalb: Northern Illinois University Press, 1971); William R. Hutchison, *The Modernist Impulse in American Protestantism* (Cambridge, MA: Harvard University Press, 1976); T. J. Jackson Lears, *No Place of Grace: Antimodernism and the Transformation of American Culture, 1880–1920* (New York: Pantheon Books, 1981); Lears, *Rebirth of a Nation: The Making of Modern America, 1877–1920* (New York: HarperCollins, 2009); John N. Ingham, *Assault on Victorianism: The Rise of Popular Culture in America, 1890–1945* (Toronto: Canadian Scholars' Press, 1987); Mark C. Carnes and Clyde Griffen, eds., *Meanings for Manhood: Constructions of Masculinity in Victorian America* (Chicago: University of Chicago Press, 1990); Leslie Butler, *Critical Americans: Victorian Intellectuals and Transatlantic Liberal Reform* (Chapel Hill: University of North Carolina Press, 2000); David A. Hollinger, *Postethnic America: Beyond Multiculturalism* (New York: Basic Books, 2000); David A. Hollinger, *Cosmopolitanism and Solidarity: Studies in Ethnoracial, Religious, and Professional Affiliation in the United States* (Madison: University of Wisconsin Press, 2006); Louis Menand, *The Metaphysical Club* (New York: Farrar, Straus and Giroux, 2001); John Carlos Rowe, "Nineteenth-Century United States Literary Culture and Transnationality," *PMLA* 118 (2003): 78–89; Tom Lutz, *Cosmopolitan Vistas: American Regionalism and Literary Value* (Ithaca, NY: Cornell University Press, 2004); Gerard Delanty, "The Cosmopolitan Imagination," *Revista CIDOB d'Afers Internacionals* 82/83 (2008): 217–230; Mark Rennella, *The Boston Cosmopolitans: International Travel and American Arts and Letters* (New York: Palgrave Macmillan, 2008); and Nicola J. Watson, ed., *Literary Tourism and Nineteenth-Century Culture* (Basingstoke: Palgrave Macmillan, 2009).

15. With *Sword of the Spirit, Shield of Faith: Religion in American War and Diplomacy* (New York: Knopf, 2012), Andrew Preston has analyzed the relationship between American diplomacy and Christian doctrine, but more scholarship is needed on the role of religion in foreign policy formation during the early national era.

16. See, for example, Andrew Delbanco, *The Puritan Ideal* (Cambridge, MA: Harvard University Press, 1989); Robert N. Bellah et al., *Habits of the Heart: Individualism and Commitment in American Life* (Berkeley: University of California Press, 1985); Robert D. Putnam, *Bowling Alone: The Collapse and Revival of American Community* (New York: Simon and Schuster, 2000); Thomas Bender, *Community and Social Change in America* (New Brunswick, NJ: Rutgers University Press, 1978); Christopher Lasch, *The Culture of Narcissism: American Life in an Age of Diminishing Expectations* (New York: Norton, 1978); and David Reisman et al., *The Lonely Crowd: A Study of the Changing American Character* (New Haven, CT: Yale University Press, 1950).

17. Brooks Adams, "The Alternative" and "The Contest," *Boston Daily Advertiser*, December 9 and 11, 1875.

18. Records, Registers, and Scrapbooks of United First Parish Church, Quincy, Massachusetts.

SELECTED BIBLIOGRAPHY

Abzug, Robert H. *Cosmos Crumbling: American Reform and the Religious Imagination*. New York: Oxford University Press, 1994.

Ahlstrom, Sydney E., and David D. Hall. *A Religious History of the American People*. New Haven, CT: Yale University Press, 2004.

Albanese, Catherine L. *A Republic of Mind and Spirit: A Cultural History of American Metaphysical Religion*. New Haven, CT: Yale University Press, 2007.

Allen, David Grayson. *In English Ways: The Movement of Societies and the Transfer of English Local Law and Custom to Massachusetts Bay, 1600–1690*. Chapel Hill: University of North Carolina Press, 1981.

Allgor, Catherine. *Parlor Politics: In Which the Ladies of Washington Help Build a City and a Government*. Charlottesville: University Press of Virginia, 2000.

Anderson, Thornton. *Brooks Adams: Constructive Conservative*. Ithaca, NY: Cornell University Press, 1951.

Anderson, Virginia DeJohn. *New England's Generation: The Great Migration and the Formation of Society and Culture in the Seventeenth Century*. New York: Cambridge University Press, 1991.

Atkins, Annette. *We Grew Up Together: Brothers and Sisters in Nineteenth-Century America*. Urbana: University of Illinois Press, 2001.

Backer, George E. "John Quincy Adams as a Unitarian." *Unitarian Review and Religious Magazine* 16 (1881): 135–153.

Bailyn, Bernard. *The Barbarous Years: The Peopling of British North America: The Conflict of Civilizations, 1600–1675*. New York: Knopf, 2012.

Baker, Emerson W. *A Storm of Witchcraft: The Salem Trials and the American Experience*. New York: Oxford University Press, 2014.

Balmer, Randall. *Religion in Twentieth Century America*. New York: Oxford University Press, 2001.

Barker-Benfield, G. J. *John and Abigail Adams: The Americanization of Sensibility*. Chicago: University of Chicago Press, 2010.

Beckert, Sven. *The Monied Metropolis: New York City and the Consolidation of the American Bourgeoisie, 1850–1896*. New York: Cambridge University Press, 2001.

Beisner, Robert L. "Brooks Adams and Charles Francis Adams, Jr.: Historians of Massachusetts." *New England Quarterly* 35 (1962): 48–70.

Bemis, Samuel Flagg. *John Quincy and the Foundations of American Foreign Policy; John Quincy Adams and the Union*. New York: Knopf, 1949, 1956.

Bender, Thomas. *Community and Social Change in America*. New Brunswick, NJ: Rutgers University Press, 1978.

Bendroth, Margaret. *The Last Puritans: Mainline Protestants and the Power of the Past*. Chapel Hill: University of North Carolina Press, 2015.

Beneke, Chris, and Christopher S. Grenda, eds. *The First Prejudice: Religious Tolerance and Intolerance in Early America*. Philadelphia: University of Pennsylvania Press, 2011.

Benes, Peter. *Meetinghouses of Early New England*. Amherst: University of Massachusetts Press, 2012.

Benfey, Christopher E. G. *The Great Wave: Gilded Age Misfits, Japanese Eccentrics, and the Opening of Old Japan*. New York: Random House, 2003.

Bercovitch, Sacvan. *The Puritan Origins of the American Self*. New Haven, CT: Yale University Press, 1975.

Beringause, Arthur F. *Brooks Adams: A Biography*. New York: Knopf, 1955.

Bingham, Emily. *Mordecai: An Early American Family*. New York: Hill and Wang, 2003.

Block, James E. *A Nation of Agents: The American Path to a Modern Self and Society*. Cambridge, MA: Belknap Press of Harvard University Press, 2002.

Blodgett, Geoffrey, ed. *Victorian America*. Philadelphia: University of Pennsylvania Press, 1976.

Bonomi, Patricia U. *Under the Cope of Heaven: Religion, Society, and Politics in Colonial America*. New York: Oxford University Press, 1986.

Boydston, Jeanne. *Home and Work: Housework, Wages, and the Ideology of Labor in the Early Republic*. New York: Oxford University Press, 1990.

Boyer, Paul S. *Urban Masses and Moral Order in America, 1820–1920*. Cambridge, MA: Harvard University Press, 1978.

Braude, Ann. *Radical Spirits: Spiritualism and Women's Rights in Nineteenth-Century America*. Boston: Beacon Press, 1989.

Bremer, Francis J. *The Puritan Experiment: New England Society from Bradford to Edwards*. Hanover, NH: University Press of New England, 1995.

Brookhiser, Richard. *America's First Dynasty: The Adamses, 1735–1918*. New York: Free Press, 2002.

Bruce, Dickson D., Jr. *Earnestly Contending: Religious Freedom and Pluralism in Antebellum America.* Charlottesville: University Press of Virginia, 2013.

Buell, Lawrence. *New England Literary Culture from Revolution through Renaissance.* New York: Cambridge University Press, 1986.

Bush, Clive. *The Dream of Reason: American Consciousness and Cultural Achievement from Independence to the Civil War.* London: Edward Arnold, 1977.

Bushman, Richard L. *The Refinement of America: Persons, Houses, Cities.* New York: Knopf, 1992.

Butler, Jon. *Awash in a Sea of Faith: Christianizing the American People.* Cambridge, MA: Harvard University Press, 1990.

Butler, Leslie. *Critical Americans: Victorian Intellectuals and Transatlantic Liberal Reform.* Chapel Hill: University of North Carolina Press, 2000.

Carnes, Mark C., and Clyde Griffen, eds. *Meanings for Manhood: Constructions of Masculinity in Victorian America.* Chicago: University of Chicago Press, 1990.

Carter, Paul A. *The Spiritual Crisis of the Gilded Age.* DeKalb: Northern Illinois University Press, 1971.

Chalfant, Edward. *Both Sides of the Ocean: A Biography of Henry Adams, His First Life, 1838–1862; Better in Darkness: A Biography of Henry Adams, His Second Life, 1862–1891; Improvement of the World: A Biography of Henry Adams, His Last Life, 1891–1918.* Hamden, CT: Archon Books, 1982–2001.

Coleman, Marilyn, Lawrence H. Ganong, and Kelly Warzinik. *Family Life in 20th-Century America.* Westport, CT: Greenwood Press, 2007.

Conkin, Paul K. *The Uneasy Center: Reformed Christianity in Antebellum America.* Chapel Hill: University of North Carolina Press, 1995.

Contosta, David R., and Robert Muccigrosso, eds. *Henry Adams and His World.* Philadelphia: American Philosophical Society, 1993.

Cooper, James F., Jr. *Tenacious of Their Liberties: The Congregationalists in Colonial Massachusetts.* New York: Oxford University Press, 1999.

Cott, Nancy F. *The Bonds of Womanhood: "Woman's Sphere" in New England, 1780–1835.* New Haven, CT: Yale University Press, 1997.

Cressy, David. *Coming Over: Migration and Communication between England and New England in the Seventeenth Century.* New York: Cambridge University Press, 1987.

Curtis, Susan. *A Consuming Faith: The Social Gospel and Modern American Culture.* Baltimore: Johns Hopkins University Press, 1991.

Cushing, John D. "Notes on Disestablishment in Massachusetts, 1780–1833." *William and Mary Quarterly* 26 (1869): 169–190.

Dawson, Jan C. *The Unusable Past: America's Puritan Tradition, 1830 to 1930.* Chico, CA: Scholars Press, 1984.

Decker, William Merrill, and Earl N. Harbert, eds. *Henry Adams and the Need to Know.* Charlottesville: University Press of Virginia, 2005.

Delbanco, Andrew. *The Puritan Ordeal.* Cambridge, MA: Harvard University Press, 1989.

Demos, John. *Past, Present, and Personal: The Family and Life Course in America.* New York: Oxford University Press, 1986.

Dorrien, Gary J. *The Making of American Liberal Theology: Imagining Progressive Religion, 1805–1900.* Louisville, KY: Westminster John Knox Press, 2001.

Dreisbach, Daniel L., and Mark David Hall, eds. *Faith and the Founders of the American Republic.* New York: Oxford University Press, 2014.

Duberman, Martin B. *Charles Francis Adams, 1807–1886.* Boston: Houghton Mifflin, 1961.

Dykstra, Natalie. *Clover: A Gilded and Heartbreaking Life.* Boston: Houghton Mifflin Harcourt, 2012.

Ellis, Joseph P. *Passionate Sage: The Character and Legacy of John Adams.* New York: Norton, 1993.

Faust, Drew Gilpin. *This Republic of Suffering: Death and the American Civil War.* New York: Knopf, 2008.

Fischer, David Hackett. *Albion's Seed: British Folkways in America.* New York: Oxford University Press, 1992.

Fluhman, J. Spencer. *"A Peculiar People": Anti-Mormonism and the Making of Religion in Nineteenth-Century America.* Chapel Hill: University of North Carolina Press, 2012.

Foreman, Amanda. *A World on Fire: Britain's Crucial Role in the American Civil War.* New York: Random House, 2010.

Franchot, Jenny. *Roads to Rome: The Antebellum Protestant Encounter with Catholicism.* Berkeley: University of California Press, 1994.

Friedlaender, Marc. "Brooks Adams 'en Famille.'" *Proceedings of the Massachusetts Historical Society,* 3d ser., 80 (1968): 77–93.

Games, Alison. *Migration and the Origins of the English Atlantic World.* Cambridge, MA: Harvard University Press, 1999.

Garrett, Elisabeth Donaghy. *At Home: The American Family, 1750–1870.* New York: Abrams, 1990.

Gatta, John. *Making Nature Sacred: Literature, Religion, and Environment in America from the Puritans to the Present.* New York: Oxford University Press, 2004.

Gaustad, Edwin S. *Faith of Our Fathers: Religion and the New Nation.* San Francisco: Harper and Row, 1987.

Gelles, Edith B. *Portia: The World of Abigail Adams.* Bloomington: Indiana University Press, 1992.

Ginzburg, Carlo, John Tedeschi, and Anne C. Tedeschi. "Microhistory: Two or Three Things That I Know about It." *Critical Inquiry* 20 (1993): 10–35.

Goff, Philip, and Paul Harvey, eds. *Themes in Religion and American Culture.* Chapel Hill: University of North Carolina Press, 2004.

Grant, James. *John Adams: Party of One.* New York: Farrar, Straus and Giroux, 2005.

Gregory, Peter N. "Describing the Elephant: Buddhism in America." *Religion and American Culture: A Journal of Interpretation* 2 (2001): 223–263.

Greven, Philip J. *The Protestant Temperament: Patterns of Child-Rearing, Religious Experience, and the Self in Early America*. New York: Knopf, 1977.

Grossberg, Michael. *Governing the Hearth: Law and the Family in Nineteenth-Century America*. Chapel Hill: University of North Carolina Press, 1985.

Guth, Christine. *Longfellow's Tattoos: Tourism, Collecting, and Japan*. Seattle: University of Washington Press, 2004.

Gutjahr, Paul C. *An American Bible: A History of the Good Book in the United States, 1777–1780*. Stanford, CA: Stanford University Press, 1999.

Guyatt, Nicholas S. *Providence and the Invention of the United States, 1607–1876*. Cambridge: Cambridge University Press, 2007.

Hall, David D., ed. *Lived Religion in America: Toward a History of Practice*. Princeton, NJ: Princeton University Press, 1997.

Hanley, Mark Y. *Beyond a Christian Commonwealth: The Protestant Quarrel with the American Republic, 1830–1860*. Chapel Hill: University of North Carolina Press, 1994.

Haraszti, Zoltán. *John Adams and the Prophets of Progress*. Cambridge, MA: Harvard University Press, 1952.

Harbert, Earl N. "Charles Francis Adams (1807–1886): A Forgotten Family Man of Letters." *Journal of American Studies* 6 (1972): 249–265.

Hareven, Tamara K., and Andrejs Plakans, eds. *Family History at the Crossroads: A Journal of Family History Reader*. Princeton, NJ: Princeton University Press, 1987.

Harris, Wilhelmina S. "The Brooks Adams I Knew." *Proceedings of the Massachusetts Historical Society*, 3d ser., 80 (1968): 94–113.

Hatch, Nathan O. *The Democratization of American Christianity*. New Haven, CT: Yale University Press, 1989.

Hemphill, C. Dallett. *Siblings: Brothers and Sisters in American History*. New York: Oxford University Press, 2011.

Hempton, David. *Evangelical Disenchantment: Nine Portraits of Faith and Doubt*. New Haven, CT: Yale University Press, 2008.

Holifield, E. Brooks. *Theology in America: Christian Thought from the Age of the Puritans to the Civil War*. New Haven, CT: Yale University Press, 2003.

Holland, David F. *Sacred Borders: Continuing Revelation and Canonical Restraint in Early America*. New York: Oxford University Press, 2011.

Hollinger, David A. *Cosmopolitanism and Solidarity: Studies in Ethnoracial, Religious, and Professional Affiliation in the United States*. Madison: University of Wisconsin Press, 2006.

Holton, Woody. *Abigail Adams*. New York: Free Press, 2009.

Homans, Abigail Adams. *Education by Uncles*. Boston: Houghton Mifflin, 1966.

Howe, Daniel Walker. *What Hath God Wrought: The Transformation of America, 1815–1848*. New York: Oxford University Press, 2007.

Hunter, Jean E., and Paul T. Mason, eds. *The American Family: Historical Perspectives*. Pittsburgh: Duquesne University Press, 1991.

Hutchison, William R. *The Modernist Impulse in American Protestantism*. Cambridge, MA: Harvard University Press, 1976.

Hutson, James H. *Church and State in America: The First Two Centuries*. New York: Cambridge University Press, 2008.

Ickingrill, Steve, Stephen Mills, and H. C. Allen. *Victorianism in the United States: Its Era and Its Legacy*. Amsterdam: VU University Press, 1992.

Ingham, John N. *Assault on Victorianism: The Rise of Popular Culture in America, 1890–1945*. Toronto: Canadian Scholars' Press, 1987.

Jacobson, Joanne. *Authority and Alliance in the Letters of Henry Adams*. Madison: University of Wisconsin Press, 1992.

Johnson, Paul E. *The Early American Republic, 1789–1829*. New York: Oxford University Press, 2007.

Jones, James William. *The Shattered Synthesis: New England Puritanism before the Great Awakening*. New Haven, CT: Yale University Press, 1973.

Kaplan, Fred. *John Quincy Adams: American Visionary*. New York: Harper, 2014.

Kerber, Linda K. *Women of the Republic: Intellect and Ideology in Revolutionary America*. New York: Norton, 1986.

Kilbride, Daniel. *Being American in Europe, 1750–1860*. Baltimore: Johns Hopkins University Press, 2013.

Lears, T. J. Jackson. *No Place of Grace: Antimodernism and the Transformation of American Culture, 1880–1920*. New York: Pantheon, 1981.

Lee, Maurice S. *Uncertain Chances: Science, Skepticism, and Belief in Nineteenth-Century American Literature*. New York: Oxford University Press, 2012.

Levenstein, Harvey. *Seductive Journey: American Tourists in France from Jefferson to the Jazz Age*. Chicago: University of Chicago Press, 1998.

Levin, Phyllis Lee. *Abigail Adams: A Biography*. New York: St. Martin's, 1987.

Lewis, R. W. B. *The American Adam: Innocence, Tragedy and Tradition in the Nineteenth Century*. Chicago: University of Chicago Press, 1955.

Lockwood, Allison. *Passionate Pilgrims: The American Traveler in Great Britain, 1800–1914*. New York: Cornwall Books, 1981

Love, William DeLoss. *The Fast and Thanksgiving Days of New England*. Boston: Houghton Mifflin, 1895.

Lutz, Tom. *Cosmopolitan Vistas: American Regionalism and Literary Value*. Ithaca, NY: Cornell University Press, 2004.

Madison, Charles A. "Brooks Adams, Caustic Cassandra." *American Scholar* 9 (1940): 214–227.

Maffly-Kipp, Laurie F., Leigh E. Schmidt, and Mark Valeri, eds. *Practicing Protestants: Histories of Christian Life in America, 1630–1965*. Baltimore: Johns Hopkins University Press, 2006.

Maier, Pauline. "The Pope at Harvard: The Dudleian Lectures, Anti-Catholicism, and the Politics of Protestantism." *Proceedings of the Massachusetts Historical Society*, 3d ser., 97 (1985): 16–41.

May, Henry F. *Protestant Churches and Industrial America*. New York: Harper and Row, 1967.

McCullough, David. *John Adams*. New York: Simon and Schuster, 2001.

McDannell, Colleen. *The Christian Home in Victorian America, 1800–1940*. Bloomington: Indiana University Press, 1994.

McGreevy, Patrick. *Imagining Niagara: The Meaning and Making of Niagara Falls*. Amherst: University of Massachusetts Press, 1994.

McMahon, Lucia. *Mere Equals: The Paradox of Educated Women in the Early American Republic*. Ithaca, NY: Cornell University Press, 2012.

Mead, Sidney E. *The Lively Experiment: The Shaping of Christianity in America*. New York: Harper and Row, 1963.

Miller, Perry. *Errand into the Wilderness*. Cambridge, MA: Belknap Press of Harvard University Press, 1956.

Miller, Randall M., Harry S. Stout, and Charles Reagan Wilson, eds. *Religion and the American Civil War*. New York: Oxford University Press, 1998.

Mislin, David W. *Saving Faith: Making Religious Pluralism an American Value at the Dawn of the Secular Age*. Ithaca, NY: Cornell University Press, 2015.

Modern, John Lardas. *Secularism in Antebellum America*. Chicago: University of Chicago Press, 2011.

Morgan, David. *Protestants and Pictures: Religion, Visual Culture, and the Age of American Mass Production*. New York: Oxford University Press, 1999.

Morison, Samuel Eliot. *Three Centuries of Harvard, 1636–1936*. Cambridge, MA: Belknap Press of Harvard University Press, 1965.

Mulvey, Christopher. *Transatlantic Manners: Social Patterns in Nineteenth-Century Anglo-American Travel Literature*. Cambridge: Cambridge University Press, 1990.

Murphy, Andrew R. *Prodigal Nation: Moral Decline and Divine Punishment from New England to 9/11*. New York: Oxford University Press, 2009.

Nagel, Paul C. *Descent from Glory: Four Generations of the John Adams Family*. New York: Oxford University Press, 1983.

Noll, Mark A. *America's God: From Jonathan Edwards to Abraham Lincoln*. New York: Oxford University Press, 1992.

O'Brien, Michael. *Mrs. Adams in Winter: A Journey in the Last Days of Napoleon*. New York: Farrar, Straus and Giroux, 2010.

O'Connor, Thomas H. *Civil War Boston: Home Front and Battlefield*. Boston: Northeastern University Press, 1997.

O'Toole, James M. *The Faithful: A History of Catholics in America*. Garden City, NY: Doubleday, 1985.

Pardes, Ilana. *Melville's Bibles*. Berkeley: University of California Press, 2008.

Parrington, V. L. *Main Currents in American Thought: An Interpretation of American Literature from the Beginnings to 1920*. 1927. Reprint, Norman: University of Oklahoma Press, 1987.

Perry, Lewis. *Boats against the Current: American Culture between Revolution and Modernity, 1820–1860*. New York: Oxford University Press, 1993.

Porterfield, Amanda. *The Protestant Experience in America*. Westport, CT: Greenwood Press, 2006.

Preston, Andrew. *Sword of the Spirit, Shield of Faith: Religion in American War and Diplomacy*. New York: Knopf, 2012.

Racine, Laurel A. *Historic Furnishings Report: The Birthplaces of Presidents John Adams and John Quincy Adams*. 10 vols. Charlestown, MA: Northeast Museum Services Center, National Park Service, 2001.

Ratner, Lorman, Paula T. Kaufman, and Dwight L. Teeter Jr. *Paradoxes of Prosperity: Wealth-Seeking versus Christian Values in Pre–Civil War America*. Urbana: University of Illinois Press, 2009.

Rauchway, Eric. "Regarding Henry: The Feminist Henry Adams." *American Studies* 40 (1999): 53–73.

Rennella, Mark. *The Boston Cosmopolitans: International Travel and American Arts and Letters*. New York: Palgrave Macmillan, 2008.

Richter, Amy. *At Home in Nineteenth-Century America: A Documentary History*. New York: New York University Press, 2015.

Roberts, Jon H., and James Turner. *The Sacred and the Secular University*. Princeton, NJ: Princeton University Press, 2000.

Rogers, Daniel T. *Atlantic Crossings: Social Politics in a Progressive Age*. Cambridge, MA: Belknap Press of Harvard University Press, 1998.

Rogers, Stephanie Sidham. *Inventing the Holy Land: American Protestant Pilgrimage to Palestine, 1865–1941*. Lanham, MD: Lexington Books, 2011.

Rose, Anne C. *Victorian America and the Civil War*. New York: Cambridge University Press, 1992.

Rosenberg, Charles E. *The Cholera Years: The United States in 1832, 1849, and 1866*. Chicago: University of Chicago Press, 1962.

Ruether, Rosemary Radford. *Christianity and the Making of the Modern Family*. Boston: Beacon Press, 2000.

Sarna, Jonathan D. *American Judaism: A History*. New Haven, CT: Yale University Press, 2004.

Sassi, Jonathan D. *A Republic of Righteousness: The Public Christianity of the Post-Revolutionary New England Clergy*. New York: Oxford University Press, 2001.

Scheyer, Ernst. *The Circle of Henry Adams: Art and Artists*. Detroit, MI: Wayne State University Press, 1970.

Schlereth, Thomas J. *Victorian America: Transformations in Everyday Life, 1876–1915*. New York: HarperCollins, 1991.

Schmidt, Leigh Eric. *Restless Souls: The Making of American Spirituality*. San Francisco: HarperSanFrancisco, 2005.

Schwain, Kristin. *Signs of Grace: Religion and American Art in the Gilded Age*. Ithaca, NY: Cornell University Press, 2008.

Seager, Richard Hughes. *The World's Parliament of Religions: The East/West Encounter, Chicago, 1893*. Bloomington: Indiana University Press, 1995.

Sears, John F. *Sacred Places: American Tourist Attractions in the Nineteenth Century*. New York: Oxford University Press, 1989.

Sellers, Charles. *The Market Revolution: Jacksonian America, 1815–1846*. New York: Oxford University Press, 1991.

Sibley, John Langdon, and Clifford K. Shipton, *Sibley's Harvard Graduates*. 18 vols. Boston: Massachusetts Historical Society, 1873–1999.

Simonson, Harold P. *Radical Discontinuities: American Romanticism and Christian Consciousness*. Rutherford, NJ: Fairleigh Dickinson University Press, 1983.

Sklansky, Jeffrey P. *The Soul's Economy: Market Society and Selfhood in American Thought, 1820–1920*. Chapel Hill: University of North Carolina Press, 2002.

Smith, Margaret Bayard. *The First Forty Years of Washington Society*. New York: C. Scribner's Sons, 1906.

Steig, Margaret. *Laud's Laboratory: The Diocese of Bath and Wells in the Early Seventeenth Century*. Lewisburg, PA: Bucknell University Press, 1982.

Stokes, Melvyn, and Stephen Conway, eds. *The Market Revolution in America: Social, Political, and Religious Expressions, 1800–1880*. Charlottesville: University Press of Virginia, 1996.

Stout, Harry S. *Upon the Altar of the Nation: A Moral History of the American Civil War*. New York: Viking, 2006.

Stout, Harry S., and D. G. Hart, eds. *New Directions in American Religious History*. New York: Oxford University Press, 1997.

Taylor, Charles. *A Secular Age*. Cambridge, MA: Belknap Press of Harvard University Press, 2007.

Thompson, C. Bradley. *John Adams and the Spirit of Liberty*. Lawrence: University Press of Kansas, 1998.

Trachtenberg, Alan. *The Incorporation of America: Culture and Society in the Gilded Age*. New York: Hill and Wang, 1982.

Tucker, Louis Leonard. *The Massachusetts Historical Society: A Bicentennial History, 1791–1991*. Boston: Massachusetts Historical Society and Northeastern University Press, 1995.

Turner, James. *Without God, Without Creed: The Origins of Unbelief in America*. Baltimore: Johns Hopkins University Press, 1985.

Turner, Victor, and Edith Turner. *Image and Pilgrimage in Christian Culture: Anthropological Perspectives*. New York: Columbia University Press, 1978.

Tweed, Thomas A. *Crossing and Dwelling: A Theory of Religion*. Cambridge, MA: Harvard University Press, 2006.

Vogel, Lester Irwin. *To See a Promised Land: Americans and the Holy Land in the Nineteenth Century*. University Park: Pennsylvania State University Press, 1993.

Waldstreicher, David. *In the Midst of Perpetual Fetes: The Making of American Nationalism, 1776–1820*. Chapel Hill: University of North Carolina Press, 1997.

Waters, Ronald G. *American Reformers, 1815–1860*. New York: Hill and Wang, 1997.

Watson, Nicola J., ed. *Literary Tourism and Nineteenth-Century Culture*. New York: Palgrave Macmillan, 2009.

Wearn, Mary McCartin, ed. *Nineteenth-Century American Women Write Religion: Lived Theologies and Literature*. Farnham, UK: Ashgate, 2014.

Westerkamp, Marilyn J. *Women and Religion in Early America, 1600–1850: The Puritan and Evangelical Traditions*. New York: Routledge, 1999.

Willis, Gary. *Henry Adams and the Making of America*. Boston: Houghton Mifflin, 2005.

Wilson, Daniel Munro. *Where American Independence Began: Quincy, Its Famous Group of Patriots; Their Deeds, Homes, and Descendants*. Boston: Houghton, Mifflin, 1902.

Winship, Michael P. *Godly Republicanism: Puritans, Pilgrims, and a City on a Hill*. Cambridge, MA: Harvard University Press, 2002

Winterer, Caroline. *The Mirror of Antiquity: American Women and the Classical Tradition, 1750–1900*. Ithaca, NY: Cornell University Press, 2007.

Wood, Gordon S. *Empire of Liberty: A History of the Early Republic, 1789–1815*. New York: Oxford University Press, 2009.

Wright, Conrad. *A Stream of Light: A Short History of American Unitarianism*. Boston: Skinner House, 1989.

Wright, Conrad Edick, ed. *American Unitarianism, 1805–1865*. Boston: Massachusetts Historical Society and Northeastern University Press, 1989.

Yokota, Kariann. *Unbecoming British: How Revolutionary America Became a Postcolonial Nation*. New York: Oxford University Press, 2011.

Yothers, Brian. *The Romance of the Holy Land in American Travel Writing, 1790–1876*. Aldershot, UK: Ashgate, 2007.

Youngs, Tim, ed. *Travel Writing in the Nineteenth Century: Filling the Blank Spaces*. London: Anthem Press, 2006.

Zagarri, Rosemarie. *Revolutionary Backlash: Women and Politics in the Early American Republic*. Philadelphia: University of Pennsylvania Press, 2007.

INDEX

Adams, Abigail (1744–1818), and
Catholicism, 30; and Christian
patriotism, 29–30; death of, 39;
education of, 24–25, 32, 133–134;
as First Lady, 33; marriage of, 24;
mentioned, 148, 168; portrait of,
29 (illus.); and providentialism,
24, 25–26, 31, 32–33, 34, 40; and
Puritans, 20; relationship with
family, 46, 84; religious practices
and views of, 7–40; and republican
motherhood, 27–30; travels of,
27, 30, 31; and Unitarianism, 49;
and universalism, 30, 31–32; use of
Christianity, 2, 8, 20–21, 27–30; and
worship aesthetics, 30, 31

Adams, Abigail Brown Brooks (1808–
1889), death of, 116, 183; diary
of, 96; health of, 111; marriage
of, 93–97; parenting of, 170; portrait
of (illus.), 95, 110; religious practices
and views of, 96–97, 99; wealth of,
96, 127

Adams, Brooks (1848–1927), and
Anglicanism, 171; and B. Storer, 193;
and Bible, 168, 192; career of,
166, 169, 174, 175, 189, 194; and
Catholicism, 171, 184, 192–194;
education of, 115, 168, 169, 170–
174, 179, 193–195; *Emancipation of
Massachusetts*, 169, 175–183, 194;
and Episcopal Church, 192; and
family history, 1–2; health of, 175;
Law of Civilization and Decay,
169, 183–189; and lay prophecy,
169, 183–189, 195–196; marriage
of, 168, 183, 184; mentioned, 158;
portrait of (illus.), 172; and
Presbyterianism, 171; and
providentialism, 169; relationship
with family, 174, 175; religious
practices and views of, 168–196;
theories of history, 175, 178–189;
Theory of Social Revolutions, 189;
travels of, 115, 169, 170–171, 175,
184–185, 189–190, 190, 194, 195; and
Unitarianism, 171, 190–192; wealth
of, 191; and World War I, 167,
191, 192; and worship aesthetics,
184, 195

and science, 2, 52, 120, 144, 158; in
Spain, 5; and US diplomacy, 5, 9,
35, 56, 57, 64. *See also* Pluralism;
secularism; skepticism
Remington, Frederic, 188
Rock Creek Cemetery (Washington,
DC), 151–152, 154, 162, 177
Romanticism, 67
Roosevelt, Theodore, 169
Rotterdam, Netherlands, 42
Rush, Dr. Benjamin, 21, 36, 37
Russia, 37, 57–60, 62–63, 63, 84
Russian Orthodox Church, 48, 58, 85

Sabbatarianism, 90
sacraments, baptism, 18, 24, 63, 124;
communion, 11, 15, 47–48, 111;
marriage, 24, 44, 46, 63, 116;
reconciliation, 30
Saint-Gaudens, Augustus, 151, 152, 154,
160, 177
saints, Augustine of Hippo, 120;
David, 9; Francis of Assisi, 193;
martyrs, 130; Paul, 62;
Peter, 62
Salem, Massachusetts, 26, 41, 77–78,
179, 181–182
Sargent, Dom Leonard, 193
Sargent, John Singer, 146
Savage, Edward, 59
Schleiermacher, Friedrich, 66
science, 2, 52, 120, 144, 158, 164–165
Scudder, Vita D., 186–187
Second German Baptist Church
(New York City), 186
Second Presbyterian Church
(Washington, DC), 47
secularism, 83, 133, 155, 173, 174,
182–183
Seward, Frances Adline, 74
Shakers, 48
Shakespeare, William, 68, 78
Shaw, Anna Howard, 186–187
Shaw, John, 30
Shaw, Robert Gould, 151
Silvy, C., 172 (illus.)

skepticism, and Adamses, 116, 118,
120, 123–124, 137, 140–142, 146–151,
162, 167; and literature, 143–144;
mentioned, 116, 118
slavery, 46, 69–70, 78, 82, 90, 113
Smith, Abigail Adams, (1765–1813), 37
Smith, Hyrum, 112
Smith, Joseph, 111–113
Smith, Lucy Mack, 113
Smith, William, 24–25
Society of the Cincinnati, 50
Socrates, 1, 4, 151
Somerset, England, 2, 7, 8, 10–12, 14
South Seas, 155
Spain, 5, 9
Spencer, Herbert, 144
spiritualism, 75–78, 115
Spring, Samuel, 55
Squire, William, 10
Sri Lanka, 160
St. John's Episcopal Church
(Washington, DC), 47, 140
St. Mary's Church, 63, 64
St. Michael Bassishaw
(London), 115
St. Paul, Cathedral Church of
(Boston), 193
Sterne, Laurence, 25, 43, 44, 68, 91
Stiles, Joseph Dutton, 77, 77–78
Stone Library, 1, 46, 168
Storer, Bellamy, 193
Story, William Wetmore, 134
Stowe, Harriet Beecher, 90, 159
Stuart, Gilbert, 28, 29
Stuart, Jane, 28, 29
Supreme Court, US, 70, 75
Sweden, 43

taxes, 14, 19
Taylor, Bayard, 128
Taylor, John of Caroline, 71
Tenskwatawa, 38
Terence, 54
Texas, 46
theology. *See* religion
Thibaut de Navarre, 167